The Anointed Son

Princeton Theological Monograph Series

K. C. Hanson, Charles M. Collier, and D. Christopher Spinks, Series Editors

Recent volumes in the series:

Ryan A. Neal
Theology as Hope: On the Ground and Implications of Jürgen Moltmann's Doctrine of Hope

Bernie A. Van De Walle
The Heart of the Gospel: A. B. Simpson, the Fourfold Gospel, and Late Nineteenth-Century Evangelical Theology

Chris Budden
Following Jesus in Invaded Space: Doing Theology on Aboriginal Land

L. Paul Jensen
Subversive Spirituality: Transforming Mission through the Collapse of Space and Time

Elaine A. Heath
Naked Faith: The Mystical Theology of Phoebe Palmer

Jeff B. Pool
God's Wounds: Hermeneutic of the Christian Symbol of Divine Suffering, Volume One: Divine Vulnerability and Creation

Christian T. Collins Winn
"Jesus Is Victor!": The Significance of the Blumhardts for the Theology of Karl Barth

Charles Bellinger
The Trinitarian Self: The Key to the Puzzle of Violence

The Anointed Son
A Trinitarian Spirit Christology

MYK HABETS

☞PICKWICK *Publications* · Eugene, Oregon

THE ANOINTED SON
A Trinitarian Spirit Christology

Princeton Theological Monograph Series 129

Copyright © 2010 Myk Habets. All rights reserved. Except for brief quotations in critical publications or reviews, no part of this book may be reproduced in any manner without prior written permission from the publisher. Write: Permissions, Wipf and Stock Publishers, 199 W. 8th Ave., Suite 3, Eugene, OR 97401.

Pickwick Publications
An Imprint of Wipf and Stock Publishers
199 W. 8th Ave., Suite 3
Eugene, OR 97401

www.wipfandstock.com

ISBN 13: 978-1-60608-458-8

Cataloging-in-Publication data:

Habets, Myk.

    The anointed son : a trinitarian Spirit Christology / Myk Habets.

    x + 330 p. ; 23 cm. Includes bibliographical references and index.

    Princeton Theological Monograph Series 129

    ISBN 13: 978-1-60608-458-8

    1. Holy Spirit. 2. Holy Spirit—Biblical teaching. 3. Trinity—History of doctrines. I. Title. II. Series.

BT121.3 .H33 2010

Manufactured in the U.S.A.

An alternate version of chapter 4 appeared as "Developing a Retroactive Hermeneutic: Johannine Theology and Doctrinal Development," *American Theological Inquiry* 1.2 (2008) 77–89, © Wipf & Stock Publishers, used with permission.

An alternate version of chapter 6 appeared as "Spirit Christology: Seeing in Stereo," *Journal of Pentecostal Theology* 11.2 (2003) 199–235, © Koninklijke Brill N.V, used with permission.

Scripture taken from the NEW AMERICAN STANDARD BIBLE(R), Copyright © 1960, 1962, 1963, 1968, 1971, 1972, 1973, 1975, 1977, 1995 by The Lockman Foundation. Used by permission.

*To Warwick and Marian Rope, for friendship
and encouragement when it was needed.*

Contents

Acknowledgments / ix

1. Spirit Christology: Awaiting the Promise / 1
2. Understanding Jesus: Approaches to Christology / 10
3. Logos and Spirit: God's Two Hands / 53
4. Interpreting the Evidence: Christology in New Testament Scholarship / 89
5. Explaining Jesus: The Testimony of the New Testament Writers / 118
6. And Then There Were Three: Spirit Christology and the Trinity / 188
7. "Justified by the Spirit"? Developing a Third Article Theology / 228
8. Receiving the Promise: Spirit Christology for Ministry and Mission / 258

Bibliography / 281
Scripture Index / 319
Subject Index / 326

Acknowledgments

MY DEBTS TO FAMILY and friends are large ones, never to be repaid. However, let me make an installment payment by acknowledging the encouragement received by so many. While research is an intensely isolated discipline it is also the product of a community. I would like to acknowledge my appreciation for the support of my community. Warwick and Marion Rope encouraged me in difficult times and through their generosity made aspects of this research possible—thank you. Dr. Graham Redding provided generous comments on the design of the study for which I am grateful. Dr. Graham McFarlane and Professor Max Turner of London School of Theology were models of gracious engagement with my project midway through its gestation and were a source of great encouragement. Carey Baptist College and the Laidlaw Carey Graduate School provide a stimulating research climate, my especial thanks to my colleague Dr. George Wieland for his suggestion of the chapter titles.

To the many family and friends who have obligingly sat through oral recitations of my research willingly or otherwise, thank you for your grace and understanding; that includes you mum and dad, and Pete and Fleur. Finally, as ever, my deepest appreciation goes to my wife Odele for her constant encouragement and love, and of course, to my children Sydney and Liam who have no idea what daddy does all day but are glad he doesn't do it all night (. . . often!).

During the course of my research and writing I was conscious of the Spirit's presence in and through the Word. My prayer is that the Spirit of Sonship may breathe through the pages of this book, opening up new possibilities for the future, especially for those engaged in the ministry of Word and Sacrament for whom this work is written.

Myk Habets
Doctor Serviens Ecclesiae
Auckland, New Zealand

1

Spirit Christology

Awaiting the Promise

Setting Christology in a pneumatic framework is a clear and challenging mandate of present-day theology. Barth's own christological achievement, however, serves as a warning that it will be no easy task.

—Philip J. Rosato

If one finally adds that we receive also the Gospel only through the Paraclete, then one could with good reason not merely open the entire dogmatics with pneumatology, but even make the Work of the Spirit the theme of the whole.

—Werner Elert

I personally think that a theology of the Spirit might be all right after AD 2000, but now we are still too close to the eighteenth and nineteenth centuries. It is still too difficult to distinguish between God's Spirit and man's spirit.

—Karl Barth (1963)

Nobody has all the answers—I certainly do not. But one way to make progress is to look at issues in a new way and enter into conversation. Theology does not depend on any single theologian. Truth will yield its secrets to the body of Christ if we will listen to God and to one another humbly, accepting correction.

—Clark H. Pinnock

IN HIS CHAPTER ENTITLED "Concluding Unscientific Postscript on Schleiermacher," Barth reflected on his own Christological programme and made the astounding comment that all his theological investigations could have been pursued via a theology of the third article. In his words:

> What I have already intimated here and there to good friends, would be the possibility of a theology of the third article, in other words, a theology predominantly and decisively of the Holy Spirit. Everything which needs to be said, considered, and believed about God the Father and God the Son in an understanding of the first and second articles might be shown and illuminated in its foundations through God the Holy Spirit, the *vinculum pacis inter Patrem et Filium*.[1]

Barth wrote these words in his Göttingen lectures of 1923/24. The great christocentrist was advocating the possibility of a thorough Spirit Christology that would complement the dominant Logos Christology[2]: a Christological programme pursued from a Trinitarian perspective, highlighting the mutual relations between the Son and the Spirit in the incarnation. Many have directly or indirectly followed Barth's suggestion. Eastern Orthodox, Roman Catholic, and Protestant theologians are taking up the challenge to incorporate Trinitarian doctrine into all of the various *loci* of theology. Within contemporary theology a pneumatically oriented approach to Christology is being advanced across denominational and traditional lines. The present study is one such proposal towards the recovery of Spirit Christology in such a Trinitarian context.

As we enter a new chronological era—the twenty-first century—and all the changes that come with it, we are also entering a new era in theology. At the forefront of this shift has been the doctrine of the Trinity. It is not my intent to trace the development of theological thought in detail, but what theologians affirm today is that Trinitarian studies have revolutionised the content of our theology. Instead of being the superfluous post-script of a systematic theology, the doctrine of the Trinity now holds pride of place at the forefront of most major theological textbooks—a trend which I applaud. But just as other theological innovations resulted in a mature elucidation of Christian faith, so the glut of Trinitarian studies seems to me to be entering into a new, mature phase. That phase may be characterised as the emergence of truly systematic constructive theology in which the doctrines of

---

1. Barth, *Theology of Schleiermacher*, 278.

2. Barth made use of a Spirit Christology at two key points even within his Logos-dominated *CD*. He introduces the insights of a Pneuma-sarx Christology when he explains the miracle of Christmas as one brought about by the Holy Spirit and when Barth is faced with accounting for the distinctiveness of Jesus's humanity. Barth, *CD* III/2, 334. See the commentary of Rosato, *Spirit as Lord*, chapters 5, 6, and 7.

theology proper, Christology and pneumatology, all within a Trinitarian structure, are informing and articulating new models of both the Trinity itself, and of the three constitutive elements.³ This in part is illustrated by Yves Congar, the well respected Roman Catholic theologian of the Holy Spirit who began the introduction to his work *The Word and the Spirit* with the assertion, "If I were to draw but one conclusion from the whole of my work on the Holy Spirit, I would express it in these words: no Christology without pneumatology and no pneumatology without Christology."⁴ This study draws out the implications of this axiom, in an attempt to redefine both Christology and pneumatology, and ultimately our conceptions or models of the Trinity.

The current work is borne out of an abiding conviction that all theology is Trinitarian and, more specifically, that theology ought to maintain the integrity of Jesus and Spirit, not Jesus versus Spirit. One way to advance our understanding of Trinitarian theology is to examine more closely the reciprocal relations between Jesus and Spirit. Christopher Schwöbel makes the comment that Christology is in a crisis at present. In fact he goes so far as to say that "Modern Christology and the description Christology in crisis are almost equivalents."⁵ In order to remedy this crisis we cannot simply return to past orthodox constructions nor can we afford to leave them behind. Rather, the tightrope of theological traditionalism and modernism will have to be walked carefully. One of the best ways to do this is through reclaiming a Trinitarian account of Spirit Christology. I take up the challenge issued by Philip Rosato when he wrote "setting Christology in a pneumatic framework is a clear and challenging mandate of present-day theology."⁶ He also serves a warning that it will be no easy task. What Rosato is calling for is seminal works in what has come to be known as Spirit Christology. This book is my contribution.

---

3. LaCugna and McDonnell, "Returning from 'The Far Country': Theses for a Contemporary Trinitarian Theology," 192, recommend "the dynamics of Trinitarian thinking must permeate the whole theological endeavour . . . we reaffirm the *perichoresis* (mutual inter-dependence) between doctrines, in particular between Christology, pneumatology and Trinitarian doctrine. Each doctrine gains in richness by being developed in concert with each of the others." It is to this end that the current study works.

4. Congar, *Word and the Spirit*, 1.

5. Schwöbel, "Christology and Trinitarian Thought," 113.

6. Rosato, *Spirit as Lord*, 179.

Spirit Christology is not a precisely definable Christological construction. It is interdisciplinary and, as such, complex. For that reason no one monograph will be sufficient to exhaustively present its case. The best that can be achieved is the delineation of its constituent parts and that is why one of the aims of this book is to *recover* a Spirit Christology. Even the title of this doctrine is disputed as it goes by the name: "Spirit-Christology,"[7] "Spirit-oriented Christology,"[8] "pneumatological or pneumatologically oriented Christology,"[9] and "Pneuma-sarx Christology."[10] For the sake of brevity and clarity I employ the title "Spirit Christology."

More germane to the study than the terms employed is the meaning conveyed. In contemporary theology the term Spirit Christology ranges in meaning from the most comprehensive form, which posits Spirit as the divine element in the person of Jesus Christ, to the more narrow sense in which we are using it for the reciprocal relationship between the Spirit and Jesus. In the former case, the displacement of Logos Christology can be seen as a proposal to reach an alternative metaphysical understanding of the operation of divinity in Jesus, one that abandons the Chalcedonian definition of one person in two natures in preference for a Christology of "inspiration." In so doing, the identity between Spirit and Logos works to revise the concept of Logos from a pre-existent divine person, to that of a cosmic principle of reason or order and emphasises a more functional notion of Logos as God's activity in the world. This model of Spirit Christology is considered unorthodox and has been consistently rejected by evangelical theologians. The proposals and reasons for its insufficiency will be examined in chapter 5.

The model of Spirit Christology advocated here is one that seeks to articulate the relationship between the "person" of the Holy Spirit and the "person" of the Son, both in the incarnation and in the work of

---

7. Del Colle, *Christ and the Spirit*. Del Colle has altered his nomenclature from "Spirit-Christology" to "Spirit-christology" in his article "Spirit-Christology: Dogmatic Foundations for Pentecostal—Charismatic Spirituality," 91–112.

8. Wong, *Logos-Symbol in the Christology of Karl Rahner*, 244 n. 109, and "Holy Spirit in the Life of Jesus and of the Christian," 57–95. For Wong "Spirit-Christology" is used to indicate the replacement of Logos Christology while Spirit oriented Christology is not.

9. Rosato, "Spirit-Christology: Ambiguity and Promise," 423–49, uses this along with Spirit-Christology while Walter Kasper frequently labels his position "Christology in a pneumatological perspective," *Jesus the Christ*, 267.

10. Used variously in the early Church in distinction to Logos-sarx.

redemption including the intra-Trinitarian relations. By using the word "person" I presume fidelity with Nicene and Chalcedonian orthodoxy of three persons in one Trinitarian being, and in the case of Christ, two natures in one person. Hence, this model of Spirit Christology attempts to inform Christology with an equally important and central pneumatology, while at the same time enriching the integrity of the doctrine of the Trinity.

Spirit Christology is a Christological construction formulated from a Spirit-oriented direction. It is a Christology which recognises that its dynamism must proceed from a robust pneumatology. Spirit Christology has enjoyed a renaissance in recent theological efforts among both Protestant and Roman Catholic scholars. However, Spirit Christology may proceed in a number of directions. Two of these pathways may be broadly identified as either "Trinitarian" or "post-Trinitarian." The latter option is merely an early heresy reaffirmed in modern times—adoptionism. I shall be arguing for the former, an orthodox Trinitarianism. This accounts for the subtitle of this book, "A Trinitarian Spirit Christology."

Because Spirit and Jesus are intimately related we would do violence to split them apart either in our conceptions or our theology. I propose Spirit Christology as a complementary Christological model, not a substitute for the dominant Logos Christology of traditional or classical Christological construction. It is my belief that a Spirit Christology will enhance the older model, adding a much needed pneumatological element. Spirit Christology focuses theological reflection on the role of the Holy Spirit in Christology proper. It seeks to understand both who Christ is and what Christ has done from the perspective of the Holy Spirit.

> What is new and distinctive in Spirit Christology is that, on the level of theological construction and doctrinal interpretation, it proposes that the relationship between Jesus and God and the role of Christ in redemption cannot be fully understood unless there is an explicitly pneumatological dimension. In other words, the relationship between Jesus and the Spirit is as important to conveying the truth of the christological mystery with its soteriological consequences as that of Jesus and the Word.[11]

Like all theologies a Spirit Christology is extrapolated from just one set of data and fulfils one methodological function. Spirit Christology relativizes the tendency to set up one theology as absolute, *the only* way

---

11. Del Colle, *Christ and the Spirit*, 4.

of understanding, in this case, Christology. It is for that reason that I advocate multiple perspectives in theology, specifically the complementary nature of Spirit Christology with the existing Logos Christology of the classical Western tradition.

Given the complex nature of a doctrine of Spirit Christology it cannot be expected to answer every Christological or Trinitarian question that could be raised. It seeks to inform on a much broader scale than traditional systematic theological constructs. For instance, in traditional theology we have tended to separate the treatments of the identity and mission of Christ. A Spirit Christology argues that this is an artificial distinction and treats of them both together where possible, as in the New Testament. Also the very name "Spirit Christology" implies that both Christology and pneumatology are being treated together, and it will become evident that the Trinity itself comes into the centre of discussion. Spirit Christology must be related to some theory of Trinitarian construction where the unity and distinction of the divine persons has been thoroughly formulated. Spirit Christology is an attempt to account for the identity and mission of Jesus Christ from a pneumatic viewpoint, but not exclusively so. It seeks to build a Trinitarian construction from the pneumatological and Christological reciprocity to the Father. Anything less than a mutual reciprocity between Christology and pneumatology in the articulation of what Christians mean by God, revelation, and redemption, results in a diminution of the full deposit of the faith.[12] McIntyre speaks of the modern church's "betrayal" of the biblical tradition when it does not recognise adequately the relation that existed between Christ and Spirit in the Gospels and indeed the entire New Testament.[13] I am in fundamental agreement.

As Roger Haight stated in his short paper, "the development of any Christological position is extremely complex, and this prohibits a comprehensive development of a position that included thorough argumentation at each stage."[14] I can only concur. The aim is rather to bring the many elements that recommend a Spirit Christology together, in a coherent fashion, echoing the sentiments of Clark Pinnock when he wrote "this [thesis] is an attempt to view old truths from fresh angles

---

12. Ibid., 4.
13. McIntyre, *Shape of Pneumatology*.
14. Haight, "Case for Spirit Christology," 259.

and in new contexts in order to hear a relevant word from the Lord. Its success will depend on whether this is what happens."[15]

The prior definition has been given at this early stage in order to suggest what cannot be accomplished in the following pages. This is not an exhaustive investigation into the history of Christian doctrine relevant to the appearance of Spirit Christology or even into the wide spectrum of Spirit Christology today. Rather, this enquiry seeks to define Spirit Christology within a Trinitarian perspective and to argue for it as a valid and much needed complement to our existing and dominant Logos Christology.

Spirit Christology complements Logos Christology in the same way in which Christ and the Spirit are mutually constitutive. Or at least this should be the case. The history of Christian thought shows that Logos Christology has dominated resulting in both an eclipse of Trinitarian doctrine and a diminution of pneumatology. Recently there have been calls to reclaim a theology of the Third Article in order to present a Trinitarian theology that is faithful to Scripture, the Great Tradition, and one which is existentially viable. While studies examine various aspects of Spirit Christology there has yet to appear a work that introduces the doctrine, examines the various mutually exclusive proposals, and offers a constructive Trinitarian proposal. The present work does this, introducing the constituent features of a Spirit Christology that is Trinitarian, orthodox, and contemporary. I propose a model of Spirit Christology which complements rather than replaces Logos Christology and does so in a robustly Trinitarian framework. Within contemporary theology a pneumatically oriented approach to Christology is being advanced across denominational and traditional lines. Those wanting to navigate their way through the many competing proposals for a Third Article Theology will find a comprehensive map here.

In order to achieve this, the current study is divided into eight chapters. Chapter 1 introduces the scope of the study and provides some initial definitions. Chapter 2 deals with the strictly methodological considerations in Christology in which I propose a way ahead for Christological methodology by uniting within one model that which has been separate, that is, ontology and function, the person and work of Jesus, and the methodological orientations of working from below or above.

---

15. Pinnock, *Flame of Love*, 216.

In chapter 3 I turn our attention to an historical investigation of the post-canonical (Patristic) period to reveal how the earliest Christologies were constructed, especially in relation to *pneuma* and *Logos*. Here we shall witness the place of Logos and Spirit Christology within the early church along with the progressive predominance of Logos over Spirit in Christology—a legacy enshrined in creedal formula at Chalcedon and now dominant in Western Christology especially. Of special mention will be the theologies of Ignatius, Athanasius, and the Cappadocians, all of whom managed to incorporate pneumatology meaningfully into their Christological and Trinitarian constructions.

Moving on from strictly methodological and historical considerations, chapter 4 deals with the hermeneutics of doctrinal formulation and development. This requires a brief survey of the New Testament witness to Jesus and Spirit. A revised hermeneutical tool is required by a Spirit Christology by which the canonical authenticity of the doctrine is established, I suggest a way forward by means of a retroactive hermeneutic.

Having examined the various ways biblical scholarship has approached the question of Jesus's identity and having proposed a doctrine of theological enrichment, allied to a retroactive hermeneutic, chapter 5 surveys the New Testament testimony to Jesus's identity and mission. After a brief examination of the Pauline corpus, six disclosure episodes in the life of Christ which reveal his messianic identity and mission are surveyed.

After surveying the methodological questions, the post-canonical period and the biblical frame, we shall then be in a position to more fully assert in chapter 6 what a Spirit Christology is and why it is felt to be a much needed complement to our existing Christological method. We shall also note the Trinitarian implications and enrichment that a Spirit Christology has to offer by tracing the rise of modern Spirit Christology in two directions, Trinitarian and post-Trinitarian. An argument will be made for the orthodoxy and coherence of the former over the latter.

In chapter 7 the broader context into which a Spirit Christology is established is examined, specifically the rise of what has come to be known as Third Article Theology. Central to such a Third Article Theology is the practice of starting theological reflection with the Spirit and re-examining the *loci* of theology from that vantage point. I offer my own suggestions on why this is a valid way of conducting a twenty-first century theology and what it may look like. Finally, in chapter 8 I conclude with a retrospect and prospect by identifying the distinguishing features of a Trinitarian Spirit Christology and considering the fecundity of this theological contribution to systematic theology, ministry, and mission.

This book represents an introduction to the theology of a Spirit Christology, where the traditional *loci* of pneumatology and Christology, classically treated apart, are now interwoven into a coherent perspective.

The burgeoning literature in the area of Christology, pneumatology, and Trinitarianism necessitates a conscious choice of one's conversation partners. As a result, I have attempted to be as comprehensive as possible in my review of the literature while discussing only those writings which have asserted something significant in relation to Spirit Christology. While I could have limited myself to a single tradition, for instance Protestantism, and focused on contemporary theologians such as Jürgen Moltmann, and D. Lyle Dabney, or conversely, on Roman Catholicism and focused on contemporary theologians such as Ralph Del Colle, David Coffey, and Philip Rosato, I have chosen not to limit myself to any single tradition. This decision was facilitated by two factors; my own theological stance and the orientation of Spirit Christology. First, coming from a Reformed and Evangelical context I wish to take up the challenge of engagement with alternate traditions. Second, I wish to pursue the ecumenical ideal which a theology of the Holy Spirit engenders, and which a Spirit Christology is poised to facilitate.

These pages offer a constructive proposal. This proposal is tentative and not beyond future modification. However, given this rejoinder, it is my conviction, confirmed increasingly throughout my research and as I have taught this material to numbers of students, church groups, and seminars that the model proposed is intensely biblical, in harmony with orthodoxy, and holds out promise for the contemporary church in the world.

2

Understanding Jesus

Approaches to Christology

*The confession of faith in Jesus is not to be separated from Jesus'
significance for us. The soteriological interest cannot, however,
be the principle of Christological doctrine.*

—Wolfhart Pannenberg

The true key to Christ's person is in His work.

—Leon Morris

*In our time at least it must be clear that we have to find our faith
in a living encounter with Jesus the Christ—
an encounter which is of course sustained by the Spirit.*

—Karl Rahner

CHRISTOLOGY CONSTITUTES THE HEART of theology,[1] as it focuses on God's work of salvation in the historical figure of Jesus of Nazareth. To know God we must know Jesus Christ. Therefore Jesus Christ is the express revelation of God. The answer to the question, "Who is God?" is revealed in the person of Jesus Christ. To know the plan of God for humanity is to see this plan worked out in the economy of redemption, that is, in the birth, life, death, burial, resurrection and exaltation of the Son of God, Jesus Christ. As Bloesch reminds us, "Whereas philosophy ponders the nature of God in the abstract, theology reflects on the divine-human encounter in history as we find this in Jesus Christ."[2]

---

1. A helpful discussion of Christ as the "center" is found in Weber, *Foundations of Dogmatics*, vol. 2, 3–8.
2. Bloesch, *Jesus Christ*, 15.

The identity of Jesus is the key issue within historical and contemporary biblical and theological scholarships. While many of the issues relating to the discussion of prolegomena do not concern us here, I shall investigate three key issues related to our study of Spirit Christology. In doing so I shall refer to the now standard dichotomies or the dialectical tensions involved in the identity of Jesus Christ as utilized by New Testament scholarship. These dichotomies, articulated below, are merely the tools of scholarship which I shall employ to highlight the theological progression within both Scripture and the tradition. After consideration of these dichotomies and their intrinsic interrelationship we shall have laid the platform for the real discussion—how to understand the economic and immanent Trinity.

The first of three methodological issues concerns the question over the correct orientation of Christology; is it specifically functional or ontological? After a brief examination I argue for a *via medians* better suited to both the biblical record and our modern culture. The second issue concerns the question over priority concerning the person and work of Jesus Christ, specifically within systematic theology. The final issue this chapter examines is the proper starting place in Christological reflection; is it from above or from below? I ask if these must be understood as mutually exclusive methodologies or should they be seen as complementary? If my argument for the complementarity of these approaches is accepted then I hope to have established the coherence between an inspirational and incarnational Christology, through a synthetic unity of the two in what can be described as an inspirational-incarnational Christology.[3] The language is not elegant and there may be a much bet-

---

3. Haight, *Jesus Symbol of God*, 455, prefers "empowerment" over "inspiration." Empowerment as a metaphor retains the complete personality of Jesus of Nazareth while at the same time presenting the active and empowering presence of God himself with Jesus. In this way God's presence and empowerment does not overpower Jesus but activates human freedom so that it is enhanced and not taken over. Jesus's human existence is fulfilled and not replaced. Hick in *Myth of God Incarnate*, uses "inspiration" but this is considered too thin for the Christology envisaged here. Lampe, *God as Spirit*, and Tillich, *Systematic Theology*, use the metaphor of "possession." Jürgen Moltmann speaks of "incarnation," *Way of Jesus Christ*. At least Moltmann has the benefit of capturing that in which a Logos and Spirit Christology agree, but it fails to differentiate the two adequately. For Haight, both Logos and Spirit are merely symbols. See the critique of Haight's Spirit Christology by Wright, "Roger Haight's Spirit Christology," 729–35, Imbelli, "New Adam and Life-giving Spirit," 233–52, and Weinandy, "Case for Spirit Christology," 173–88.

ter way of saying it, but that is in essence what I am espousing. Along these lines, it may be said that an orthodox[4] Spirit Christology is, in reality, a pneumatic Logos Christology, or alternatively, an incarnational Christology from a pneumatological perspective. After examining these methodological issues we will be better placed to evaluate and discuss the implications and usefulness of a Spirit Christology alongside, informing, and complementing the classical Christological paradigm.[5]

MUST FUNCTION ECLIPSE ONTOLOGY?

The Relevance of this Discussion

In this section, the relation of the mission of Christ to the identity of Christ will be investigated. At the heart of this discussion are the questions, "How do we talk about Jesus Christ?" and, "How is his unity with God to be expressed?" Is it merely a unity of works—Jesus *does* what God does? Or is it a unity of being—Jesus is (to use the language of Nicaea), "very God of very God"? I contend that the biblical witness, and that of the Patristic era, holds together both the person and work of Christ and as such moves comfortably from function to ontology. The Patristic writers subordinate the atonement to the incarnation, whereas classical Christology tends to reverse this in emphasizing atonement over incarnation. This is especially evident within streams of Reformed Protestantism. A Spirit Christology seeks to hold the two together, as does the biblical witness. In this way, the mission of Christ reveals his identity and the person of Christ further clarifies the work of atonement. The person of Christ, who works for us, confronts us within the construct of a Spirit Christology. Therefore, Christ's work informs his person.

---

4. Throughout this study I use the term "orthodox" in its historic sense to refer to *orthos* "right," and *doxa* "opinion," meaning right belief as opposed to heresy on the one hand, or "Eastern Orthodoxy" on the other. See the definitions and development given in McGrath, *Christian Theology*, 145–49, Wells, *Person of Christ*, 86–91 and Turner, *Pattern of Christian Truth*, 95–148.

5. By "classical" I refer to statements that embody the revealed truth content of Christianity and are therefore normative for the universal church, such as are found in the Ecumenical creeds of Christendom, especially Nicaea and the Definition of Chalcedon. Synonyms for "classical" include apostolic or catholic. See Packer, "Orthodoxy," in *EDT*, 808.

A Spirit Christology affirms that the incarnation is atoning; as atonement involves the active and passive obedience of Christ. Classical theology is so consistently crucicentric to the point that atonement has been all but reduced to the passive obedience of Christ. The result of this is that Christ's active obedience is relegated to some Christological novelty reserved for nativity plays at Christmas.[6] Indeed the life of Jesus: his temptations, prayer life, compassion, and general daily historical existence, is seldom meditated upon or presented as a model for us to follow.[7] In the modern church Christ's miracles and supernatural ministry are highlighted to the relative neglect of his sense of justice, peace, and single-minded devotion to the Father's will. This is true despite the now *passé* WWJD? ("What Would Jesus Do?") phenomenon, which, despite its intent to retrieve a robust *imitatio Christi,* ended up throwing youth back upon themselves due to an almost complete ignorance of the actual life of Christ. In its almost total concentration on the cross, classical Christology has lost sight of the true humanity of Christ, lived out through his relationship with the Father in the empowering presence of the Spirit.[8] It is here that a Spirit Christology speaks loudly.

Perhaps this is the reason why classical Christology has been so reluctant to adopt a Christology from below. It appears to be totally irrelevant to our concept of atonement (that is, the cross), the "real" activity of the incarnation. Without wishing to be misunderstood, the incarnation and the atonement are inseparable; the atonement gives us

---

6. Gunton, *Promise of Trinitarian Theology*, 2nd ed., 48, argues that Augustine initiated this trend.

7. This position would appear to be shared by Wright, *Jesus and the Victory of God*. Wright traces this situation back beyond the so-called first quest to the sixteenth century reformers. He affirms that "it would not, then, be much of a caricature to say that orthodoxy, as represented by much popular preaching and writing, has had no clear idea of the purpose of Jesus's ministry," ibid., 14. He identifies Melanchthon's phrase as typical of this situation; "This is to know Christ, to know his benefits . . . unless one knows why Christ took upon himself human flesh and was crucified, what advantage would accrue from having learned his life's history?" Philip Melanchthon, *Loci Communes*, 1521, quoted by Wright, 15 n. 27.

8. Torrance, *Theology in Reconstruction*, 134, noted long ago that "For too long in Protestant, as well as in Roman, theology the full place of the Humanity of Christ has been neglected." The work of Thomas and his brother James Torrance has sought to rectify this largely western trend, especially through the stress on the vicarious humanity of Christ.

understanding and appreciation of the incarnation and the incarnation enlightens the atonement.

The Rise of Functional Christology—Yesterday and Today

The history of Christian thought is one of tension, and within Christology this tension has on many occasions reached breaking point. One such tension is that between function and ontology. Millard Erickson defines functional Christology as "an approach to the person of Christ which emphasizes what he did rather than what he is." He then adds that "functional Christology often includes the idea that it is either unnecessary or improper to go beyond them [the biblical writers' concern with functional terms]."[9] William Schutter states that all functional Christologies have one thing in common: the belief that "Jesus is not God; he is God's tool. Jesus is God's agent and representative."[10]

While this is a rather slanted definition of function, functional Christology is the most readily evident interpretation of Jesus's unity with God. Jesus did function in a divine manner. Even from a cursory glance at New Testament passages such as 2 Cor 5:19 and John 4:34, and 9.4 we can see that God was clearly at work within Jesus. A functional unity with God, therefore, is compatible with a volitional unity with God and in Jesus Christ we see a human being perfectly submitting his will to that of the Father. In the will of Jesus we see the will of God in action.

But the question remains, "Does the New Testament stress only what Jesus did?" or "Does it also mention who he was, in a metaphysical sense, as well?" "If both are present, which view is dominant?" And finally, "Does one lead into the other?" The answers to these questions will occupy our attention throughout this chapter. However, it does seem self-evident that function presupposes ontology, and so the one naturally leads to the other. Extreme functionalists, those who only allow the Bible to provide functional statements,[11] argue that Jesus's own self-understanding was that of divine agent, not divine person or metaphysical status. Hence, he can only be afforded functional status and not ontological status. This position accords well with Erickson's definition above. While it is true that Jesus referred more to his activity than to his origin or person, the

---

9. Erickson, *Word Became Flesh*, 216.
10 Schutter, "Continuing Crisis for Incarnational Doctrine," 84.
11. This includes Lampe, *God as Spirit*, and Dunn, *Christology in the Making*.

thesis that Jesus was merely a tool of God must be rejected. We see this most clearly in the synoptic use of the title "Messiah." The function of Messiah is divine by nature.[12]

Many biblical scholars have traced this avoidance of ontological matters within the New Testament to the Hebrew mindset. Extreme functionalists argue that there are no ontological references of any kind in the entire Bible, let alone those concerning Jesus Christ. It has been claimed that the Hebrew people did not ask such questions. Montefiore maintains the Hebrews had no philosophical inquiry, as they were more concerned with dynamic function and personal relationship.[13] However, in his book *The Semantics of Biblical Language*,[14] James Barr brought down the superstructure of the biblical-theology movement by showing that there was no such dichotomy between Hebrew and Greek thinking as maintained by advocates of an extreme view of functionalism. The assumption that the mentality of the Hebrews was non-ontological or non-theoretical has been and must still be called into question.[15]

Extreme functionalists maintain that ontological questions and exploration only happened after the biblical period, when Greek categories became dominant and could be employed by Christians. This shift toward ontology occurred in the Patristic era when Christian theologians began to use Greek philosophical categories as they reflected on the biblical material, and sought to interpret the evidence regarding Jesus Christ. This culminated in the "Definition of Chalcedon" where the authors contemplated who Jesus was rather than what he did. This was a necessary step considering the heresies that they were seeking to combat; heresies regarding the person of Christ that were being formulated in fundamentally ontological categories.[16] However necessary though, ontological claims are foreign to New Testament Christology, it is claimed.

---

12. See Dix, *Jew and Greek*, 79–80.

13. Montefiore, "Towards a Christology for Today," 157.

14. Barr, *Semantics of Biblical Language*.

15. See Ladd, *Theology of the New Testament*, 341. Ladd considers Paul's use of the Aramaic *mar* (Kyrios) to be most instructive. It highlights the fact that this thought was not a product of the Hellenistic community. Also see Henri Blocher, "Immanence and Transcendence in Trinitarian Theology," in *Trinity in a Pluralistic Age*, 104–23.

16. See Cullmann, *Christology of the New Testament*, 4.

Within the early church, Theodotus and the whole Dynamic Monarchian movement stressed the work of Jesus Christ over his person, thus exhibiting early approaches toward a functional Christology. This methodology was developed by Melanchthon as expressed in his famous dictum: "to know Christ is to know his benefits,"[17] through the nineteenth century with Albrecht Ritschl,[18] and into the twentieth century with Emil Brunner,[19] Oscar Cullmann,[20] Hans Küng,[21] and John A. T. Robinson.[22] Oscar Cullmann is perhaps the most persuasive and the most influential of these functional advocates. Grenz claims that he has given us the "most celebrated recent presentation" of a functional Christology.[23] Cullmann states:

> Because the first Christians see God's redemptive revelation in Jesus Christ, for them it is his very nature that he can be known only in his work—fundamentally in the central work accomplished in the flesh. Therefore, considering the New Testament witness, all mere speculation about his natures is an absurdity. Functional Christology is the only kind that exists.[24]

---

17. Melanchthon, *Loci Communes* of 1521, CR 21, 85. The quote goes on to say "for us and not to contemplate, like the schoolmen, his natures and the modes of the Incarnation." In context this was probably a perfectly understandable reaction to the almost perverse theological speculation conducted by the schoolmen.

18 Ritschl, *Christian Doctrine of Justification and Reconciliation*, 385–484. He stressed what Christ does for us instead of who he is.

19 Brunner in his book, *Christian Doctrine of Creation and Redemption*, 322, declares, "The way to the knowledge of Jesus leads from the human Jesus to the Son of God and to the Godhead." Compare that to the starting point of his earlier book, *Mediator*. There the
God be known," 201. In *Christian Doctrine of Justification and Reconciliation*, 271–74, Ritschl taught that the work of Christ is the route of access to the person of Christ. On this point I totally agree.

20. Cullmann, *Christology*. In this work it is a little ambiguous as to whether or not Cullmann believes an ontological Christology is valid even if not found in the biblical witness. In a later writing he makes it clear that he does allow for ontological Christologies. He insists that his stress on the acting of God does not exclude discussion of the being of God at all. See Cullmann, "Reply of Professor Cullmann to Roman Catholic Critics," 40.

21. Küng, *On Being a Christian*. Küng does not opt for a functional Christology devoid of ontological elements. However, he does not see ontological elements within the biblical testimony; as his titular Christology highlights (ibid., 390).

22. Robinson, *Human Face of God*.

23. Grenz, *Theology for the Community of God*, 342.

24. Cullmann, *Christology*, 326.

While "the Chalcedonian formula expressed the doctrine of the incarnation in Greek metaphysical categories, 'person,' and 'nature,' is it possible to express this doctrine in ways more suited to today?"[25] Functional Christology is one such attempt to do so. Functional Christology, however, has not been without its detractors. It has elicited much debate in theology over time and has often been dispensed with. Gerald O'Collins represents those who dismiss a functional approach in his work, *What Are They Saying About Jesus?*[26] However, he only dismisses attempts embracing a *purely* functional Christology, an approach that Spirit Christology also dismisses. Evangelicals are especially adverse to any sort of functional Christology as they consider it to play loose with evangelical orthodoxy.[27] Such is not necessarily the case if we can avoid the either/or dichotomy of function versus ontology.

A purely functional Christology cannot help but end up in some form of adoptionism, a doctrine not taught in the New Testament and certainly not an *a priori* condition for a Spirit Christology. I wholeheartedly accept Rahner's statement that "every concept of the incarnation which views Jesus' humanity, either overtly or implicitly, merely as the guise God takes upon himself in order to signalise his speaking presence, is and remains a heresy."[28] But what about starting with function and then moving to ontology? My contention is that a functional Christology is a valid starting point for a contemporary Christology so long as function leads into ontology. It is this complementary approach that characterizes a Spirit Christology.

A *purely* functional Christology is a modern view dominated by the propositions of the *Myth of God Incarnate* movement influenced in turn by the 1950s liberal school. However, a functional Christology proper does not *necessarily* include a lack of belief in the deity of Christ. The earliest Christologies were functional and they quite readily embraced the deity of Jesus Christ. In the next chapter we shall survey the biblical evidence for this statement.

---

25 Erickson, *Flesh*, 215.

26. O'Collins, *What Are They Saying About Jesus?*

27. Runia suggests that "nearly all alternative Christologies opt for a functional Christology over against an ontological Christology," *Present-Day Christological Debate*, 95.

28. Rahner, *Jesus, Man and the Church*, 38.

For Cullmann, a functional Christology is not averse to later reflection in ontological terms. He points out that the Christological controversies of the fourth and fifth centuries centered on the person of Christ, the relationship between Christ and the Father, and the relationship between the two natures of Jesus. His point is that these specific issues are not the explicit concern of the New Testament authors. Cullmann thus accepts the Definition of Chalcedon as being consistent with New Testament Christology when he maintains that the Bible never speaks of the being of Christ in isolation from his function.[29] However, he feels it necessary to disregard these later considerations from all discussion and investigation of New Testament Christology. That does not mean that the church cannot or should not ask and seek to answer ontological questions. But the fourth and fifth century church was wrestling with problems from "the Hellenising of the Christian faith, the rise of Gnostic doctrines, and the views advocated by Arius, Nestorius, Eutyches and others."[30] The New Testament simply did not set out to answer such questions. That, at least, is a brief history of the rise of functional Christologies.

The Contemporary Context

A consciously functional, as opposed to an ontological Christology, increasingly dominates contemporary theology,[31] the argument being that the Greek ontological thinking underlying Chalcedon is obsolete and untenable today.[32] Modern functional Christology emphasizes the point that it is not important for Jesus Christ to be a divine figure. These scholars argue that the Bible never presents him in such terms. Rather, Jesus is always presented as the functioning agent of God; the instrument of God's decisive work. In short he merely functions as God.[33] Jesus acts on behalf of God and that is what constitutes his deity, not some metaphysical nature. Inherent in this is a redefinition of the term "divine."[34]

29. Cullmann, "Reply of Professor Cullmann," 40–41.
30. Cullmann, *Christology*, 3.
31. Erickson, *Flesh*, 225–26.
32. This trend was already underway when Montefiore wrote "Towards a Christology for Today," 156.
33. Robinson, *Human Face of God*, 183–84.
34. Gunton, *Yesterday and Today*, 16, argues that this approach appears to presuppose that to be divine "is the same thing as to be successfully human." He goes on to highlight the philosophical presuppositions behind this view.

Several factors are behind the push towards a functional Christology; first, the belief that it is the biblical approach and second, the belief that the current environment is open to a functional approach, and not to a more speculative or intellectualist view.[35] At the forefront of functional Christology today are those theologians who advocate an adoptionist Christology.[36] An increasing number of theologians see this as the only logical result of functional categories. I believe that this position is one of extreme or purely functional Christology. Its advocates are united in their reaction against Chalcedon and all traces of ontology. Amongst their many arguments against Chalcedon three are important to note. First, they reject Chalcedon's supposed over-dependence upon Greek philosophy which they believe is given more nuance and extra-biblical authority than it deserves.[37] Second, Chalcedon is accused of presenting a predominately ontological Christology as opposed to the predominately functional Christology of the New Testament.[38] Finally, Chalcedon (and all ontological speculation) is said to tend towards a dualism in Jesus Christ and a drive toward Docetism.[39]

Spirit Christology—From Function to Ontology

Considering the two opposing methodologies, functional and ontological, are we to conclude that they are mutually exclusive, or is there a certain complementarity between the two? Given that a functional Christology is a plausible place to begin the search into an understanding

---

35. Erickson, *Flesh*, 228–29, correctly identifies the philosophy of pragmatism as one source of the functionalist approach.

36. Some of the main exponents today being Lampe, *God as Spirit*, Newman, *Spirit Christology*, Lodahl, *Shekinah/Spirit*, Mackey, *Christian Experience of God as Trinity*, and Haight, "Case for Spirit Christology," 257–87.

37. Rosato, "Spirit-Christology: Ambiguity and Promise," 423–49.

38. This argument has been the most persistent amongst more liberal scholars. Many suggest that there is no ontological Christology in Scripture, and that John's Gospel is historically unreliable and so inadmissible. See Robinson, *Honest to God*, 74, and Hick, *Myth of God Incarnate*, for the classic treatment of this theme. More conservative scholars merely claim that Chalcedon is excessively ontological *if it is our only standard of Christological method*. What I am suggesting is a complementary emphasis on functional Christology alongside that of our dominant ontological Christology. Obviously, there can be *no* functional Christology without a corresponding ontological one anyway.

39. See the survey by Lane, "Christology Beyond Chalcedon," 257–81, along with an article defending Chalcedon outright by Bray, "Can we Dispense with Chalcedon," 2–9.

of Jesus's unity with God; can we affirm an ontological identity of Jesus alongside his functional one? As we have already noted many moderns would disagree. However, theirs is surely not the last, complete, or accurate word—only a *purely* functional Christology leads to adoptionism. If we construct our Christology firstly at the functional level and then onto the ontological level we end up with a Spirit Christology that is at once biblical, orthodox, and tantalizingly creative. The result is a new paradigm for systematic theology.

Reginald Fuller concurs that much of the New Testament presentation of Christ is purely functional, especially the Jewish phases. However, in the mission to the Gentiles, the church advanced beyond purely functional statements to make "ontic" statements.[40] Fuller rightly points to passages such as Phil 2:6–11 along with Col 1:18; 2:9, and Heb 1:3,[41] contending that a more than functional deity is in view even if a fully developed doctrine of two natures is not explained.[42] Despite his earlier comment, Cullmann is in full agreement when he writes that Jesus Christ is the "Revealer" and as such this speaks not only of his work but also of his person.[43] The point that Cullmann stresses is that the New Testament always speaks of the person of Jesus in connection with his works, never apart from them.

> If at the peak of New Testament Christological thought Jesus Christ is God in his self-revelation, then we can neither simply speak of the person apart from the work or of the work apart

---

40. Fuller, *Foundations of New Testament Christology*, 248. Fuller considers "ontic" statements to be just short of "ontological" ones. Metaphysics carries two meanings that roughly correspond to what Fuller distinguishes as "ontic" and "ontological." In one sense, metaphysics encompasses any statement about the nature of reality, the technical elaboration and probing of such statements is the other sense of metaphysics. To believe in a transcendent God is to have a metaphysic. To then investigate this transcendent God and his relation to the world, himself, to give the general belief some specific content and interpretation, this is what constitutes scientific theistic metaphysics. It is this later sense that the drafters of Nicaea and Chalcedon were engaged in. They sought to explain or expound in Greek metaphysical terms the doctrine of the incarnation of the divine-human person. They took the ontic language of the New Testament, such as *theos, patēr, monogenēs, huios, sarx, anthrōpos*, and explained them in ontological language of Greek philosophy (*ousia, homoousios, phusis*, and *hypostasis*) or Latin (*substantia, consubtantialis, natura*, and *persona*) (ibid., 249).

41. Erickson, *Flesh*, 230, gives a brief history of development from Semitic functional interpretation of Lohmeyer to Hellenistic thought.

42. Fuller, *Foundations*, 208.

43. Cullmann, *Christology*, 325–26.

from the person. From the very beginning all Christology shows both aspects—even when the ultimate logical conclusions have not yet been drawn.[44]

Functional Christology inevitably raises ontological problems.[45] This is particularly evident when the early church reached the point of affirming that what was incarnated in Jesus was an aspect of the being of God himself, an aspect that was at the same time one with God and yet distinct. As the prologue to the gospel of John suggests, this new aspect of God was united in the person of Jesus Christ in a truly human life. As Fuller summarizes, "functional Christology led inevitably in the New Testament to ontic statements, which in turn posed ontological problems."[46]

What is clear is that even if we wanted to we cannot set the clock back and return to a purely functional Christology. Ontological concerns were not raised for purely speculative reasons but rather to understand, live out, and proclaim the Gospel of God's act of salvation in Jesus of Nazareth. While we cannot return to some kind of purely functional understanding, to be constrained by the ontology of Nicaea or Chalcedon *alone* is also incorrect. Not that these are erroneous ontological propositions (I personally follow and endorse them), but they are culturally conditioned so as to speak to their time. We have to find an ontological language that will communicate in our day that which the Definition of Chalcedon communicated in its day. Currently, there is no universally accepted ontology to speak of, unlike the post-Constantinian period. The solution is not to revert to a pure Biblicism, the stance adopted by the Eastern Orthodox and Fundamentalists, but to search for a meaningful way to present today what the church fathers were seeking to answer in their day.[47] One of the tasks of theology is to clearly articulate the message of faith in *culturally relevant* ways while at the same time bringing this culture under the critique of divine revelation; to contextualize the Gospel without distorting it.[48] This has always been a core concern of

---

44. Ibid., 325–26.
45. Rahner, *Jesus, Man and the Church*, 36.
46. Fuller and Perkins, *Who is This Christ?* 10.
47. Ibid.
48. This echoes the intent of Thielicke when we wrote: "The Gospel must be continuously forwarded to a new address because the recipient is repeatedly changing his place of residence," quoted in Corney, "Seeking Hope in the Ruins of Modernity," 3.

systematic theology. "Theology must be as contextual as it is metaphysical, and it must be as visual as it is cerebral," writes Ray Anderson. He continues, thus, "theological reflection must be done in the context of the Spirit's ministry in the world. Theological reflection must be a 'way of seeing' as well as a way of thinking."[49]

While some extreme functionalists are willing to allow for "incarnational elements" in the New Testament this is not enough.[50] Howard Marshall reminds us that the doctrine of incarnation is not found on the fringe of the New Testament but throughout.[51] Runia correctly claims it to be the organizing principle of the biblical writer's Christology.[52] It is not a matter of being functional only, but it has its roots in Jesus's unique preexistent relationship.

Thankfully, a number of theologians are now making the point that the function of Jesus cannot be separated from his nature. Walter Kasper dismisses the dilemma of an ontological versus a functional Christology as "illusory and a position into which theology should not allow itself to be maneuvered."[53] Gerald O'Collins agrees, "[Jesus's] work indicates *who* he was and is—both in himself and in his relationship to the Father. There can be no satisfactory account of what Jesus does if we dismiss as unimportant the question of who he is. Every soteriological statement has Christological implications."[54] These theologians are saying that action implies prior being, even if that being is only apprehended in action,[55] according to the classical axiom *"agere sequiter esse,"* ("action follows being").[56] Gary Burge perceptively writes, "Jesus functions

---

See Migliore, *Faith Seeking Understanding*, 12 (1–18), where he discusses the various tasks of Christian theology and notes that "the Christian message must be interpreted again and again in new situations and in concepts and images that are understandable to people in those situations. Who is Christ for us *today*? asked Bonhoffer." See also Weinandy, "Theology—Problems and Mysteries," in *Does God Suffer?* 27–39.

49. Anderson, *Soul of Ministry*, 118.
50. Runia, *Christological Debate*, 289.
51. Marshall, "Incarnational Christology in the New Testament," 13.
52. Runia, *Christological Debate*, 95.
53. Kasper, *Jesus the Christ*, 24.
54. O'Collins, *What Are They Saying*, 27, and *Christology*, 17.
55. See Fuller, *Foundations*, 248.
56. "Even if we grant that the early Christian church was more concerned with what Jesus had done than with what kind of person he is, we cannot leave our Christology there. Whenever we ask how something functions, we are also asking about the presup-

uniquely because of his unique status . . . and his being is defined by what he does . . . therefore these two concepts intermingle and the Spirit is one of the threads which weaves them together."[57]

Our current context is suspicious of, and even hostile to metaphysical reflection. This can be traced through several influential philosophies. Logical positivism affirms a synthetic statement is meaningful if there is a set of sense data to verify or falsify it. Existentialism minimizes the objective approach in favor of the subjective approach that focuses on the direct effect of the entity upon the individual who perceives it. And pragmatism insists that the meaning (even the truth) of a proposition is equal to its practical effects.[58] Erickson helpfully notes that fields of scientific inquiry, psychology (particularly behaviorism), philosophical functionalism, and contemporary thought generally, has a stronger interest in precise definition than is displayed by extreme functionalists.[59] In all spheres of investigation, there is a concern to find the entity behind the functions. "An equivalent concern on the part of functional Christologists would lead them both to ask what sort of being Jesus must have been in order to perform the functions which he did, and to specify those functions much more closely."[60]

I trust it is now evident that while functional approaches to Christology provide space for what Jesus did in becoming man to achieve salvation, there are a number of drawbacks to a *purely* functional approach. First, functional Christology is not comprehensive enough to account for the full sweep of the biblical data, as Cullmann admits. Second, most of its modern exponents have espoused a limited twentieth-century view of meaning and truth thus adding to its insufficiency. This is partly due to the fact that they take a "presupposition of anti-supernaturalism" with them into the text. The Bible does not set forth one metaphysical scheme of things, therefore, the extreme functionalist's Christology is

---

positions of the function, for functions do not happen in abstraction. Function assumes some sort of form . . . Setting aside for the moment the question of whether the early Christians asked ontological questions about Jesus, we cannot afford not to, if we wish to be responsible and contemporary . . . Any Christology to be fully adequate must address and integrate ontological and functional matters," Erickson, *Christian Theology*, 702–3.

57. Burge, *Anointed Community*, 72.
58. Erickson, *Flesh*, 236.
59. Ibid., 237.
60. Ibid., 237–38.

incorrect. That is not to say those who are merely concerned with ontology have the day. The extreme ontological practitioners must also realize that most of the biblical material is expressed in functional terms and that this is a valid path into Christology.

In the question over function *or* ontology we must not be shackled into an either/or dilemma. Believing that these two approaches (from below and functional, and from above and ontological) are antithetical will be, and has been to date, an impediment to the sound development of theology. Each has its place and role. However, it is my conviction that the priority of "from below and functional" must be maintained, and a Christology "from above and ontological" must never lose sight of the fact that it is a subsequent reflection on the problems imposed by the former, or else theology will become abstracted and divorced from the reality and experience to which it is a response.

Drawing these two approaches together into a Christology that moves from the functional testimony to ontological implications is what is required; one that relates the identity and mission of Christ together more closely than that of classical Christology. This is an approach that is in total accord with Scripture[61] and dovetails well with classical orthodoxy; and it is a key ingredient in a Spirit Christology. This approach stresses the humanity of Jesus Christ and his function to a much greater extent than does classical Christology, without abrogating his divinity, the ontological reality of Christ.[62]

WHAT CAME FIRST, THE PERSON OR THE WORK?

Having established the necessary relationship between functional and ontological approaches to Christology, the question of the relationship between the identity and mission of Jesus Christ now comes to the fore. Within systematic theology can the person of Christ realistically be separated from his work without distorting one or the other? Which should come first? Should we begin with the person of Christ and then

---

61. One example includes Luke 7:20–22. The answer to the Baptist's question was to look what Jesus was *doing* in order to discern *who* he is. This is a functional approach informing the ontological construction. We are called to do the same.

62. Fully cognizant of this dilemma Bauckham, *God Crucified*, viii, 40, who proposes "a Christology of divine identity . . . as a way to move beyond the standard distinction between 'functional' and 'ontic' Christology." In this way he is embarking on a Christological methodology fully supported in this study. Bauckham develops this further in his *Jesus and the God of Israel*.

derive from that study an understanding of his work or should we begin with his work and from that derive an understanding of his person?[63] Once again we find that the person *versus* work dichotomy is a false one.[64] Within the early church these two *foci* were held firmly together.[65] This approach changed during the medieval period when the scholastic theologians separated the person of Christ (his divinity, humanity, and the unity of the two) from the offices and work of Christ.[66] In so doing they made Christology virtually irrelevant to most believers by eclipsing the soteriological significance of Jesus Christ with metaphysical speculations as to his person.[67]

In the nineteenth and twentieth centuries the opposite tendency developed, building on the Lutheran[68] emphasis of the activity of Christ for us.[69] In his work *The Christian Faith*, Friedrich Schleiermacher took this emphasis on the work of Christ to its limit by beginning and substantiating each doctrinal discussion with Christian experience.[70] He did admit, however, that in theory the person of Christ and his work are inseparable and that Christology can be approached from either direction. In modern theology this approach has been advocated by Paul Tillich who argues that "Christology is a function of soteriology. The problem of soteriology creates the christological question and gives direction to the christological answer."[71]

---

63. Schwöbel, "Christology and Trinitarian Thought," in *Trinitarian Theology Today*, 118.

64. Anderson, *Soul of Ministry*, 97–105.

65. See Hendry, "Christology," in *Dictionary of Christian Theology*, 51–64.

66. Ott, *Fundamentals of Catholic Dogma*, is representative of the scholastic tradition derived from Aquinas.

67. Importantly for our thesis it is also true that "traditionally the work of Christ has been regarded as a topic separate from the application of salvation by the Holy Spirit. As a result, the affinity between justification and the atonement has often been missed," Letham, *Work of Christ*, 177.

68. See *What Luther Says*, vol. 1, 98. Also Melanchthon's now famous phrase, "to know Christ is to know his benefits," *Melanchthon and Bucer*, Library of Christian Classics, 19.21–22.

69. Erickson, *Christian Theology*, 675.

70. Schleiermacher, *Christian Faith*, vol. 2, 355–75.

71. Tillich, *Systematic Theology*, vol. 2, 174.

Traditionally, the person of Christ has been treated separately from his work and this has created a number of problems.[72] First, viewing the "work" as paramount risks reducing the person of Christ to a mere symbol of reconciliation.[73] Second, this relegates the view of "person" to abstraction. That is not to say the concept of "person" is unambiguous.[74] "Person" originally meant "being" (*ousia*) and then more frequently designated the mode of being, or subsistence (*hypostasis*), leading to a view of Christ which is only partly correct. To view the person of Christ as a being existing in and of itself, or of its manifestation, is correct in that there is a prevenience, a priority, of divine being regarding our history, however, we experience this prevenience solely in the confrontation with the Lord Jesus Christ. As Otto Weber wrote;

> We must bear in mind that such "titles of honor" in the New Testament as "the Lord," or "the Christ," or "the Son," do not designate a being in and of itself, which could also be conceived of as ineffective and inactive, but rather, in speaking of a person, they mean this person as the One who encounters us, who carries out his work upon us.[75]

This is an insight that the early church appreciated as they held together the doctrines of Christology and soteriology. The person and work of Christ were held together.[76]

Viewing the work of Christ as the entry into a discussion of his person, and then his person as the right platform from which to talk about his work is therefore understandable. In this sense we retain the early church's commitment to "Christology being a function of soteriology."[77]

---

72. Studer, *Trinity and Incarnation*, xi. Studer also notes the cleavage between Christology and trinitarianism. A problem we shall address later.

73. A doctrine of the person of Christ separate from his work would lead eventually to the question whether this work could not have been accomplished by another agent. See Barth, *CD* IV/1, 127. The other agent in question has become the Church which distributes the "grace" it has received from Christ.

74. See for instance Zizioulas, *Being as Communion*.

75. Weber, *Foundations*, vol. 2, 11.

76. The broadly evangelical traditional includes the "application" of the benefits of Christ's death with Christology. In Hodge, *Systematic Theology*, vol. 1, 313–732; vol. 3, 3–709, where soteriology is the major locus that includes Christology. Cf. Strong, *Systematic Theology*, 665–888.

77. "There would be no Christology if there were no soteriology because it is what Christians claim about Jesus as the bringer or effecter of salvation that generates the

The problem of soteriology creates the Christological question and gives direction to the Christological answer.[78] While there is an implicit danger of subjectivity creating our Christological agenda,[79] this method is thought to be the best approach for two reasons: first, to maintain a greater coherence between soteriology and Christology as the New Testament and the Patristics did; and second, to demonstrate the relevance of the person of Christ so that people can see how this discussion and its conclusions affect them.[80]

Today the older nomenclatures, "person" and "work" are being replaced with the designations "identity" and "mission," as these lie closer to the Hebrew way of thinking that pervades the Bible.[81] Stanley Grenz acknowledges fluidity between the identity and mission of Jesus. He writes: "We cannot understand the identity of our Lord in isolation from his mission in the world. Nor does his action on our behalf make sense apart from understanding who he is."[82] Thus, the mission of Jesus is only understandable as the final statement about his identity.

Systematic theology has normally dealt with the "person" of Christ before going on to the "work" of Christ (soteriology).[83] It was logical to

---

question of his identity. To oversimplify: soteriology makes Christology necessary; Christology makes soteriology possible . . . At the same time, Christology is not reducible to soteriology because, at least in the classical Christian tradition, Christ is always more than Saviour," Keck, "Toward the Renewal of New Testament Christology," 363.

78. This is the position of Tillich, *Systematic Theology*, vol. 2, 150.

79. This caution is to be taken seriously. We are not advocating the view characterized by Rudolf Bultmann that the experience of the *Christus praesens* exhausts the significance of Jesus Christ. Pannenberg, *Jesus—God and Man*, 38–49, surveys a number of these soteriological models to highlight the danger of allowing our subjective views of soteriology to dictate our Christology. Also note the dangers pointed out in Keck, "Toward the Renewal of New Testament Christology," 363–65.

80. "While it must not be allowed to set the agenda, it can be used as the point of contact for more elaborate discussions of his nature," Erickson, *Christian Theology*, 677. See the discussion of worship in this context by France, "Worship of Jesus," 50–70 and James B. Torrance, "Vicarious Humanity of Christ," in *Incarnation*, 127–30.

81. For a modern example see Grenz, *Theology for the Community*, 425. On the term "identity" see the definition given by Vanhoozer, "Does the Trinity Belong in a Theology of Religions? On Angling in the Rubicon and the 'Identity' of God," in *Trinity in a Pluralistic Age*, 41–71, and Frei, *Identity of Jesus Christ*.

82. Grenz, *Theology for the Community*, 425.

83. Karl Barth and Rudolf Bultmann entertained a vigorous argument over the proper order. See Barth, "Rudolf Bultmann: An Attempt to Understand Him," in *Kerygma and Myth*, vol. 2, 96. While admitting that soteriology is an integral part of Christology, he prefers to precede his Christology with a discussion of soteriology.

deal with who Jesus was, before dealing with what he did. Yet the word "Christology" reminds us that *Christos* is prior to *logia*, the phenomenon prior to reflection.[84] Any estimate or interpretation of Jesus is, by its very nature, a response. Pre-Easter Christology must have been highly rudimentary and always inadequate. In formulating their response, Jesus' contemporaries drew upon the language of their cultural traditions; however, this does not mean that in interpreting Jesus they were forcing him into the mould of their previous experience. When a title such as "Son of Man" was conferred on Jesus, particularly after Easter, it was shattered and remolded by what he was and by what he had achieved. We cannot understand who Jesus Christ is therefore, by simply studying the pre-Christian meanings of his various titles because they have to be understood in light of the impact that Jesus' life has had upon them.

On the issue of which comes first, I maintain that soteriology precedes Christology. Eventually, however, we are led to speak, in the same way that systematic theology has done, of Christology before soteriology, but a Christology within a soteriological framework.[85] As Fackre put it, "While soteriology is the framework for the doctrine of Christ, it is necessary to establish *who* is able to do the work of reconciliation before investigating *what* that work is."[86] Put in simple eloquence, "perhaps it is really a question of which comes first, the chicken or the egg."[87] The important point of this discussion is this, the two must be held together and the link between the two must always be in view. To treat the Person of Christ without reference to his work is to entertain a spurious speculative Christology; and to elevate the work of Christ over his person is to distort the Christian Gospel. Those writers, theologians, and preachers who can hold the work and person of Christ together while clearly developing the organic unity of the two will be standing on solid biblical and historical ground.[88] A Spirit Christology is not presented to

---

84. Fuller and Perkins, *Who is This Christ?* 2.

85. It is at this point that we could add that "An even wider circle needs to be drawn to encompass ... Christology," Fackre, "Jesus Christ in Bloesch's Theology," in *Evangelical Theology in Transition*, 99. While Fackre is speaking specifically of Bloesch his comments can be taken as a more general application as well. This wider circle would include anthropology as integral to the development of the doctrine of Christ, along with ethics, election and eschatology, not to mention pneumatology. See Bloesch, *Jesus Christ*.

86. Ibid., 102–3.

87. Fuller and Perkins, *Who is This Christ?* 5.

88. Rahner, *Jesus, Man and the Church*, 28–31.

satisfy the metaphysical curiosities of the theologically minded. Rather, it seeks to aid the faithful interpreter of the Word of God in discovering the unique identity and mission of Jesus Christ; a potentially life saving encounter with the God-man of the Scriptures.

WHAT COMES DOWN MUST GO UP

As we have seen, Christological reflection must be centered on the person of Christ but this does not exclude his work. His work is an integral part of his identity and we cannot come to know Christ in any way other than through his works. We have identified the false dichotomy between functional and ontological approaches and have come to see that they complement each other; no functionality can exist without some prior ontology. The risen and exalted Christ confronts us through his Holy Spirit and draws us into a relationship with the blessed Trinity. This relationship comes about through reflection on and acceptance of Christ's incarnation and atonement.

Christology says two things about Jesus Christ in one statement. Although we seek to keep the person and work of Christ together in all our statements, we ascribe to the man Jesus Christ something that is not ascribed to other humans. Thus all our Christological statements contain an innate duality, whether we speak of the two natures of Christ as at Chalcedon or of the God-man Jesus Christ in his life, death, and resurrection.[89] Without this duality there would no longer be a Christology, but only a study of primitive Christianity in terms of the history of religions.

Therefore, if Christology, in speaking of the one Jesus Christ, always makes statements which are twofold in nature or which consist of two aspects, then the unavoidable question for systematic theology is, "'What is the appropriate order for Christology?" Do we affirm a Christology from "above," beginning with a supernatural Christ before history, or a Christology from "below," beginning with a historical analysis of Jesus as presented in the New Testament? This discussion brings us to the heart of modern Christological methodology. In a recent work Donald Bloesch listed methodology as one of the pivotal issues in Christological

---

89. See the discussion concerning duality and dualism in Gunton, *Yesterday and Today*, 86–102.

discussion today. Amongst these pivotal issues were the contrasting methodologies of above and below.[90]

If Jesus Christ is true man and true God in one person, then it would seem to be obvious that, in terms of method, we can legitimately begin with either approach. Furthermore, these two epistemological approaches have been adopted during the history of doctrine, and both are capable of affirming an orthodox understanding of the God-man.[91] However, on closer examination we shall see that both approaches have inherent strengths and weaknesses. By adopting the traditional terms of "above" and "below" I am conscious of the fact that these are highly metaphorical in character. As such, they are potentially open to a range of divergent definitions. Reference to "above" and "below" does not mean the "divinity" and "humanity" of Jesus Christ respectively. Nor does it mean a "high Christology" which affirms Jesus' deity (often to the exclusion of his humanity) and a "low Christology" which affirms Jesus' humanity (often to the neglect of his divinity) respectively.

Karl Rahner overcame the difficulty of describing these two approaches by presenting a Christology from "above" as the *metaphysical type*, a descending Christology, and from "below" as the *saving type*, an ascending Christology.[92] Like Rahner I prefer the terms "descending" and "ascending" as they retain the continuity of the person of Jesus Christ and are not as likely to create a wedge between his humanity and divinity. However, as theological discussion is entrenched in the terms "above" and "below" I have retained these designations for the sake of clarity and have sought to define them accurately.[93]

Logos Christology and the Method from Above

Classical Christology has been dominated by the method from "above."[94] This classical method has become identified with Logos Christology, picking up the Logos concept from the prologue of John's Gospel.

---

90. Bloesch, *Jesus Christ*, 17. Gunton, *Yesterday and Today* echoes a similar thought.

91. This point is affirmed by Pannenberg when he wrote, "One cannot claim that the incarnational Christology which has ruled the history of the development of the Christological doctrine was simply a mistake," *Jesus*, 35. It can also be said that both approaches have been expressed in a heterodox way.

92. Rahner, *Theology, Anthropology, Christology*, 213–23.

93. Gunton, *Yesterday and Today*, 33.

94. By my use of "classical" see n. 5 of this chapter.

Ancient Christology was formulated on a Christology from above to below.[95] This methodology proceeds by presupposing the eternal deity of the Son and then speaking of his incarnation and humanity, thus it is an *a priori* approach to Christological reflection. This was a direct consequence of working out an abstract and largely philosophically driven formulation of the Trinity and then reading these Trinitarian presuppositions back into Christology. Therefore, the main issue dominating ancient Christology was the relationship between the Trinity and Christology. The doctrine of the Trinity dealt with the essential issue: whether in Jesus Christ, God himself was present. Christological discussion then moved on to the debates over the relationship between his two natures in the one person.[96]

The solution produced in the fourth and fifth centuries implied the precedence of the deity of Jesus over his humanity both structurally and methodologically.[97] Classical Christology therefore, consistently works from above to below and is referred to as the classical epistemological approach, the traditional *modus operandi*; an almost unanimous phenomenon.[98] From the closing of the fourth century the major Christological question has not focused on the deity of the Son, but rather on how to perceive the eternal Son's taking on the form of man and uniting himself with it. Classical Christology and its stress on the above dimension of Christology was carried into the medieval and Reformation eras of the

---

95. Pannenberg, *Jesus*, 33, makes the point that Christology from above began with Ignatius of Antioch and the second-century Apologists. It became determinative for the further history of Christology in the form of Alexandrian Christology of Athanasius in the fourth century and Cyril in the fifth century.

96. Gunton, *Yesterday and Today*, 33–34, highlights two ways the metaphor of above has been used. The first is that of Pannenberg who uses it as the structure of concepts, the descent of the Son from the world above. Gunton rightly points out that this is not strictly a methodological prescription. The second way, the way in which I am employing the term, is that of Ritschl who understands above to be a strictly methodological concept. This would mean a "Christology from above" begins with a concept of God and his relations to the world and then fits into it the human and historical elements provided by the New Testament. To illustrate this last point Gunton uses Origen and Hegel.

97. For the influence of Augustine on the tradition see Portalie, *Guide to the Thought of St. Augustine*; Gunton, *Promise of Trinitarian Theology*; Bloesch, *God The Almighty*, 165–204; and LaCugna, *God With Us*, 80, 91, 97, 101–2, 104.

98. It has only been in recent scholarship that approaches from below have been considered by theologians who also wish to remain within the bounds of orthodoxy.

church[99] and although the emphasis changed, the fundamental structure did not.[100]

Tracing through the Christological controversies of the post-canonical period in his systematic theology, Stanley Grenz considers the rise of classical Christology.[101] Adoptionism[102] (such as the Ebionites)[103] and Docetism[104] (such as the Gnostic threat), first challenged the church's understanding of the identity of Jesus. In reaction to the docetic heresies, church theologians attempted to clarify the Christian affirmation of Jesus as the Divine One. A key strategy in this defense was the Logos Christology employed by the second-century Apologists. Their proposal brought together ideas from Philo, Stoicism, and the Johannine prologue. While using the *logos* concept to resolve the Christological problem concerning the relationship of Jesus to God was a stroke of genius and a novel idea, it did not prevent the possibility of conceiving the link between the Logos and the human Jesus in either an adoptionist or a docetic manner.[105] Grenz concludes that, "the second century ended without the ascendancy of one dominant Christology."[106] The lack of a consistent Christology plunged the next two hundred and fifty years into Christological conflict which would be fought out by representatives of two major "schools"—Antioch and Alexandria. Antiochene Christology

---

99. For references to the Christology of Luther and Calvin see Weber, *Foundations*, vol. 2, 14 n. 46.

100. "Christ's emptying of himself, the form which he took upon himself, the ambiguity with which he encounters us, the inauthenticity which he assumed—all of this can only be understood in terms of classical Christology on the basis of the deific authenticity of the Son," Weber, *Foundations*, vol. 2, 14.

101. Grenz, *Theology for the Community*, 323.

102. Adoptionism is the view that Jesus was a mere man adopted by the Father through the Holy Spirit at some point in his life, most typically his baptism or ascension. See a brief summary in Prestige, *God in Patristic Thought*, 114, and Kelly, *Early Christian Doctrines*, 5th ed., 115–19, 316.

103. See Daniélou, *History of Early Christian Doctrine Before the Council of Nicaea*, vol. 1, *History of Jewish Christianity*, 64.

104. Docetism is the view that the flesh or proper humanity of Jesus was merely an appearance; hence Jesus was the divine Son masquerading in human flesh. See a brief summary in Gonzalez, *History of Christian Thought*, vol. 1, 74, 91, 130, 141; and Kelly, *Early Christian Doctrines*, 141.

105. The various Monarchian groups picked up on this weakness, accusing the proponents of the Logos Christology of bitheism.

106. Grenz, *Theology for the Community*, 323.

was generally characterized by the Jewish mindset and stressed the humanity of Jesus, while Alexandrine Christology was dominated by the Greek mindset and stressed the deity of Jesus Christ.[107]

In response to an over-realized Antiochene Christology, namely Arianism, the Council of Nicaea in AD 325 consolidated the deity of Christ in Christian confession. As Grenz states, the deity of Christ is "the first tenet of orthodoxy."[108] The deity of Christ, however, was expressed in Greek philosophical categories of ontology. Grenz goes on to ask whether there is a historical foundation—a basis in Jesus's life to which we can appeal—or is the deity of Christ a faith construct without any historical foundation?[109] This is the crux of the question. While a Christology from below starts with and takes seriously the historical dimensions of the life of Jesus Christ, a Christology from above is less inclined to deal with the historical details of Jesus life.[110] Rahner notes that the decisive factor in a Christology from above is that Jesus is divine *in a certain way*. "This is self-evident and does not need any further recourse to the experience of Jesus in saving history, from a doctrine of the Trinity, the Logos, and a pre-existing Son of God."[111] And it is this *a priori* approach to Christology which is problematic.

The modern Christological debate over the above and below approaches to Christology can be traced back to Martin Kähler's 1892 es-

---

107. While we must not overdo the differences between these two "schools" there certainly is merit in differentiating between two general theologies. See Grillmeier, *Christ in Christian Tradition*. vol. 1, *From the Apostolic Age to Chalcedon (451)*, and the review by McGrath, *Christian Theology*, 287–91. To avoid the oversimplification of the "two school's" approach, an historically questionable third approach is suggested, a pro-Nicene, Pro-Chalcedonian approach. See Torrance, "Place of the Humanity of Christ in the Sacramental Life of the Church," 3–10. Athanasius is considered representative of this "third School."

108. Grenz, *Theology for the Community*, 324.

109. Ibid., 324–25.

110. Anselm's *Cur Deus Homo?* is an example of this kind of methodology. Throughout this work, in which Anselm seeks to present the logic of the incarnation, he argues from certain givens that he believed exhibited the inner necessity of why God became man, but he did so without actually examining the life and teaching of Jesus! See Brown, "Christology and the Quest of the Historical Jesus," in *Doing Theology for the People of God*, 68–70. Gunton uses Origen as his example, *Yesterday and Today*, 35–39. The same is true of Origen's work earlier in his *De Principiis*, see Gunton, *Yesterday and Today*, 35–39.

111. Rahner, *Theology, Anthropology, Christology*, 218.

say in which he distinguished between *historisch* and *geschichtlich*.[112] The former is the mere facticity of what has occurred, the latter is significant history—the actual effect upon believers of the events of history. The former is found in the chronicled history, the latter is the faith of the apostles as witnessed to in their preaching.[113] This led to the two types of Christological methodology—the modern methods of Christology from above and from below.

In modern Christology the above view is actually a reaction against the "search for the historical Jesus," of the nineteenth century. Having found that no objective reconstruction of the earthly Jesus could be made, this search was eventually abandoned. Barth, Brunner, and Bultmann reacted to these schemes with great force.[114] In addition, this approach had an explicit presupposition that denied the deity of Jesus Christ. Finally, the rise of form criticism ended this quest. Christology from above was the basic strategy and orientation of the earliest centuries of the church, it was also dominant during the pre-critical period of the church, and is today the dominant methodology within Christology.

Brunner's Christology works from above and is a good model to highlight the main features of this methodology.[115] His main points include: the basis of the understanding of Jesus is not to be found in the historical Jesus but in the *kerygma*; there is a marked preference for Pauline material and John rather than the synoptic Gospels; and faith in Jesus does not take its basis and legitimization from rational proof.[116] It is not hard to see how a Christology from above tended towards a speculative Christology. Thus, the method from above prefers to take its

---

112. Kähler, *So-Called Historical Jesus and the Historic, Biblical Christ*. This work first appeared in 1892 and although a mere 45 pages in length its influence was enormous.

113. The terms *historisch* and *geschichtlich* are difficult to translate into English. McGrath, *Making of Modern German Christology*, 2nd ed., 111, provides several English equivalents that include "objective-historical," and "existential-historical."

114. Ibid., and Brown, *Jesus in European Protestant Thought*.

115. Brunner, *Mediator*. Although of a different sort, Barth is also an example in his CD.

116. According to Erickson, "Christology from Above and Christology from Below: A Study of Contrasting Methodologies," in *Perspectives on Evangelical Theology*, 47, Christology from above reached its zenith with Rudolf Bultmann's *Jesus and the Word*. Gunton, *Yesterday and Today*, 40–43, holds up as the ideal representative Georg W. F. Hegel due to his philosophical presuppositions.

content from *a priori* philosophical or theological considerations rather than from the particularities of the biblical story.

Weber notes that the rise of speculative Christology is not the product of historical skepticism as such, but is its correlative. Speculative Christology transforms Jesus Christ into an "idea" as it moves from abstraction to concrete reality. He traces this movement to the view that only the spiritual has the character of valid authority. If Christ is valid, then he cannot be so as an earthly figure or as a person, but only in the spiritual sense. Docetists of the early church propounded this view and it has never quite died out. It surfaced again with the Spiritualists of the Reformation period (however they did not go so far as to deny the historical Jesus). Fichte may be held up as one of the movement's modern architects, when, for instance, he writes, "The metaphysical only, and not the historical, can give us blessedness; the latter can only give us understanding."[117] We may also mention here such figures as Schelling and Kant (who equated "Son of God" with the "idea" of a humanity well pleasing to God), Hegel,[118] and David F. Strauss[119] in whose works the historic and personal is completely devalued. Along with the seminal essay of Kähler,[120] Søren Kierkegaard expounded the roots of this proposal in his book *Philosophical Fragments* (1844).[121] Barth, Brunner, and Bultmann were all heavily influenced by these thinkers as well.[122]

Until the modern period knowledge of Christ from above was thought to be mediated by philosophical or theological speculation. In reaction to modernism and now entrenched within so-called post-mod-

---

117. Fichte, *Way Towards the Blessed Life*, 107.

118. As does Gunton, *Yesterday and Today*, 40–43. He also notes the aspects of below that Hegel advances. In so doing Gunton reminds us that these categories are not as diametrically opposed as scholarship at times indicates.

119. For a survey of these theologians influence and thought see McGrath, *Modern German Christology* along with Brown, *Jesus in European Protestant Thought*.

120. Kähler, *So-Called Historical Jesus*. Grenz, *Theology for the Community*, 325, also mentions the influence the Pietistic movement had with its emphasis on the heart validation of head knowledge.

121. Kierkegaard, *Philosophical Fragments*.

122. Barth inaugurated the "New quest for the historical Jesus," but it was a short lived quest (c. 1906–1914). This movement stressed revelation and spawned the biblical theology movement. The new quest sought to base its construction on the Bultmannian analysis of the early church's proclamation of Jesus's death and resurrection. See Robinson, *New Quest of the Historical Jesus*; and Brown, *Jesus in European Protestant Thought*.

ernism, knowledge of Christ from above is mediated by direct existentialism. Christology from above suggests that our confession of Jesus's deity arises from our current experience of the Christ who confronts us in the present. This has become the dominant method within Protestant theology, especially when Evangelicals and Pentecostals claim to know that Jesus is divine on the basis of an experience of the Lord's presence among them.[123] While the *testimonium internum Spiritus Sancti* ("internal testimony of the Holy Spirit") is certainly biblical, Grenz correctly notes that, "We must demur whenever anyone suggests that our search for the foundation of our affirmation of Jesus's deity simply ends here. We simply cannot agree with the implication that Christology can bypass the history of Jesus of Nazareth."[124] This is one of the drawbacks of a Christology from above: it fails to create sufficient space for the humanity and historic life of Christ. One example of this is the way the Apostles and Nicene Creeds move directly from affirming the incarnation of Jesus from the Virgin Mary to the affirmation of his crucifixion, death, and resurrection with no mention of his sinless life!

Classical Christology is based on the One who discloses himself to us in Christ. This approach seeks to affirm that what we are dealing with in Jesus Christ is not merely the summit of what we essentially are although imperfectly, rather, it is outlining astonishment at the divine condescension of Jesus Christ assuming human flesh, something which accords well with the doctrinal development of the early church. Classical Christology affirms that none other than God reveals himself to us in the incarnation, as the Nicene Creed so clearly states of Christ: "God of God, Light of Light, very God of very God." As classical Christology is rooted in the history of Trinitarian theology which was Christological from the outset, we do not meet in Jesus Christ a *person* who has come into existence; we meet the Father's eternal Son.

Logos Christology has become synonymous with incarnational Christology, a Christology oriented from above and concerned with the descent of the eternal Son. Immediately, questions arise as to the essential

---

123. This valid Reformed emphasis on the *testimonium internum Spiritus Sancti* has been grossly over emphasized by the Pentecostal tradition. Pentecostalism evidences a very high Christology in the sense of a methodology from above to the point that there is little interest in the historical life and person of Christ. All that really seems to matter is how Christ confronts believers today in an existential encounter. In this sense Pentecostals are the true heirs to Schleiermacher's program.

124. Grenz, *Theology for the Community*, 327.

nature of this incarnate person. Theological speculation engages in finding the answer to these and other questions relating to the coexistence of two complete natures in one person, the doctrine of impeccability, the authenticity of his temptations, his seeming lack of omniscience, and the issue of the Son's death; was it God who died on the cross or was it a human being? All of these questions are legitimate and inevitable in our Christology and they have come to govern the discussion.

Criticism of the Methodology from Above

The approach of classical Christology, with the doctrine of the Trinity so closely attached to it, has certain vital truths that we cannot let go of. However, the approach has its difficulties.[125] In the salvation event Jesus himself is God. He is from above. But the fact that he is from above is recognized only through what he has revealed below. We recognize God's being in and of itself only in his being for us and that means, in Jesus Christ (*Christus pro nobis*). We are not sitting in the vantage point from above. We do not have the perspective of God, not even in faith, for faith consists of our accepting God's self-revelation in Jesus Christ.[126] "If Christology is our thinking in faith about the One in whom we believe, then it cannot begin at some point 'above,' since we recognise this 'above' solely in its turning toward us, even though it is shown to be 'above' in that event."[127]

Classical Christology tends towards abstraction in that it speaks of God first in and of himself, separately from his self-revelation. That is, it begins with speculative theology; it starts with a concrete Trinitarian conception and then imposes that upon its Christology, rather than letting God's self-revelation in Jesus Christ inform us of Trinitarian content.[128] Christology is not merely the application of the doctrine of the Trinity. It must rigidly keep to its own questions, which means

---

125. See the criticisms of this method raised by Gunton, *Yesterday and Today*, 7–9, who recognizes the abiding importance of classical Christology but wishes to "take it further," 8.

126. Hansen, "Spirit Christology," 174.

127. Weber, *Foundations*, vol. 2, 21.

128. This practice has been the standard *modus operandi* for both Protestant and Catholic traditions. A cursory glance at any of the major theological textbooks will support this conclusion. As a basic representation see the standard Catholic textbook by Ott, *Fundamentals of Catholic Dogma*, and the enduring Protestant textbook of Berkhof, *Systematic Theology*.

that, methodologically, the doctrine of the Trinity is being controlled by our Christology, and not the other way round: Christology informs Trinitarian theology rather than being conformed to it in some philosophically abstract way.[129]

According to a Christology from above the Trinity is a concrete idea that is reflected onto Christology. Jesus must be *this* sort of person and act in *this* sort of way to be consistent with our trinitarianism. But the reverse is actually the case. A Christology from below presents us with the New Testament revelation of the person of Christ and says that *God* must be like this, and do this sort of activity, because that is what *Christ* did and who Christ was and is. Jesus is God's revelation, and that revelation is a Trinitarian event. The real issue therefore is the movement from the economic to the immanent Trinity.[130]

Christology from above, which begins with an abstract concept of God which it then attempts to relate to Jesus's humanity, cannot avoid becoming a variant of Docetism when taken to its logical conclusion.[131] We end either with the materialization of divinity or with the humanization of an idea. A docetic Christology has affinities with modalism, monophysitism and Apollinarianism. The Word becomes a timeless truth rather than a living address.

Chalcedon espoused a Logos Christology with its emphasis on the condescension and humiliation of the divine Logos, the Son, in taking to himself human nature. After the fifth century the incarnation assumed central importance for theologizing, especially in Protestant theology, as thinkers delved into the actual dynamics of the incarnate life. However, this Logos Christology had inherent weaknesses. It espoused a Greek philosophy in terms of a fixed ontology, one that the New Testament does not unequivocally present. In addition, it tends towards implicit or popular Docetism, whilst not included in our creedal formulas, in practice, a denial of the full humanity of Jesus Christ can result.[132] Although

---

129. See Barth, *CD* IV/1, 52.

130. This is developed further in Chapter Six.

131. See the discussion in Weinandy, *In the Likeness of Sinful Flesh*, 3–7.

132. Rahner, *Theology, Anthropology, Christology*, 106, refers to this phenomenon as people believing the catechism in their heads versus the printed catechism. On the docetic tendency in Christology, Otto Weber, writing in 1962, stated that "today speculative Christology belongs to the past, and there is no one who would be willing to speak in favor of the Docetic view. In spite of that, there is a tendency again today (and it is by no means new) in that direction." Weber, *Foundations*, vol. 2, 5.

proponents of incarnational Christologies from above do not wish to deny Jesus's full humanity, in practice they often picture the incarnate life in terms of the eternal Son "hidden" in a human body. Finally, a Logos Christology exhibits a faulty methodology.[133] It is this last point that I shall discuss more fully.

Like the Pauline and Johannine corpus we also must start from below and take our position with the eyewitnesses, searching for the identity of Jesus by looking at his historical life.[134] "Rather than being the presupposition of Christology, the confession of the incarnation—the Word became flesh—can only be the conclusion of our reflections on Jesus's person,"[135] Grenz concludes. Therefore, we see in Jesus who God is (and what we are to become). We see true Deity and true humanity in the one person of Jesus Christ. "Rather than a description of some purported activity of the eternal Logos, incarnation is a Christological confession."[136]

Clearly, the main criticism of the classical Christological method from above is that it has the disadvantage of tending toward Docetism, Apollinarianism, or monophysitism in that it tends to compromise Jesus's humanity in order to preserve his deity, seemingly at all costs. It has all the answers about Jesus's history before the questions are even asked. A Christology from above can, and has tended to, distort the "history" of Jesus. Fuller and Perkins go so far as to say "in the final analysis it is unorthodox."[137] While this is an overstatement, there are certain weaknesses within this method that must be squarely faced and addressed.

The strength of Christology conducted from above lies in the recognition that the real value and aim of the incarnation was the effect

---

133. Grenz, *Theology for the Community*, 402–3.

134. For surveys of the Pauline corpus see: Fee, "Christology and Pneumatology," 312–31; *Paul, the Spirit, and the People of God*; *Gods Empowering Presence*; Turner, "Significance of Spirit Endowment for Paul," 56–69; Dunn, *Theology of Paul the Apostle*; Martin and Dodd, *Where Christology Began*; and Martin, *Carmen Christi*.

135. Grenz, *Theology for the Community*, 405.

136. Ibid.

137. Fuller and Perkins, *Who is This Christ?* 6. They claim a Christology from above is unorthodox because "it is purchased at the cost of diminishing his full humanity." Fuller and Perkins are obviously overstating their case to make a point. I take the point but not the case. The orthodoxy of a Christological position is not determined upon its relative starting point. A Christology from above is not inherently unorthodox any more than a Christology from below is inherently orthodox.

which the life of Jesus had upon those who believed in him. Thus, the testimony comes from those who most intimately knew him. This approach is also committed to a genuine supernaturalism, something not always the case with Christologies from below. The question to be asked of a Christology from above centers around the substantiality of the belief: is the Christ of faith really the same person as the historic Jesus? Is the *kerygmatic* Christ the real or the true Christ or is he (it?) a figment of the early church? "The problem of subjectivity in one form or another always plagues this type of Christology,"[138] Erickson claims. Another problem with this approach lies in the content of faith. While faith does in the end rest on more than empirical facts, can it exist in the absence of *any* facts? Surely not! We must know what it is we are taking by faith, or (more importantly), we must know *who* it is we are taking by faith. Without the empirical referent, the Christ of faith is reduced to "pictures painted on water or air."[139]

The Rise of the Methodology from Below

An alternative to Christology from above is the methodology of a Christology from below. What follows is a summary of the principal stages in the development of the method of Christology from below. Under the influence of the Enlightenment, classical Christology (from above) was seriously challenged, and its approach was reversed. The exact nature of humanity's relationship to God has always been a problem for classical Christology. For Enlightenment thinkers, *God* is the problem. His existence must first be proven, and the only acceptable way to do that is in terms of what reason can directly assert on the basis of empirical evidence (thanks largely to Cartesian and Kantian philosophies). From this viewpoint a historical personage may merely have the significance of being *primus inter pares* ("first among equals"), someone who is more advanced than the rest in his rational insights into and existential intimacy with the being and nature of God. It was in this sense that Enlightenment theology spoke of Jesus as the "divine" founder of Christianity.

Modern liberal Christology adopted this method also, although it is not to be viewed as the direct continuation of these Enlightenment

---

138. Erickson, "Contrasting Methodologies," 52. See Schwöbel, "Christology and Trinitarian Thought," 117.

139. Brown, "Quest of the Historical Jesus," 70.

attempts. Both Enlightenment and modern liberal Christologies from below are agreed in opposing the classical Christology, but modern liberal Christology from below is directly and more sharply opposed to speculative Christology. We can trace a shift more towards the middle in the works of Aloys E. Biedermann, and the "Hegelian Right" of Philip Marheineke and Karl Daub, who endeavored to unite Idea and History with the help of the concept of Jesus as the "universal man."[140] A further development or "new tack" has progressively shifted the "historicity" of Jesus to the centre.[141] Kähler and Wilhelm Herrmann are representatives of this.[142]

The so-called Quest for the Historical Jesus represents a neo-liberal Christology from below.[143] The modern picture of Jesus is the result of a process of reduction based on the conviction that Jesus could not possibly have been what the Evangelists describe and what the Epistles attest. This view is an *a priori* postulate applied to the sources. Jesus can not have been something other than an exemplary, extraordinary figure or preacher with ethical demands.[144] Under this line of thought Jesus can only be an extremely intensified version of the values or ideals which his modern biographers espouse. Thus their Quest for the Historical Jesus sets out to find an historical figure of their own construction; a person about whom it already knows from the outset, about who and what he can, and cannot have been, in opposition to the early Christian witness.

Christology from below has undergone a series of developments to reach its present form. These developments are rooted in the disciples's first contact with the historical Jesus. Initially, this was a Christology from below which subsequently moved to one from above, following the Pentecost event. Enlightenment Christology accepted a methodology from below based on rational proofs from empirical history; reason causing faith. In the next phase, modern liberal (or neo-liberalism) Christology reacted to speculative Christology but also advocated a

---

140. See references in Weber, *Foundations*, vol. 2, 5.

141. Ibid.

142. See the discussion of these two influences in Pannenberg, *Jesus*, 21–30. When Hermann speaks of "revelation" he does so in a thoroughly Ritschilian manner. Revelation is not limited to a past historical event, but rather it refers to a religious experience in the transcendent dimension of an individual's life in the present. An aspect of the past becomes revelation only if the person allows it to have this function.

143. See the helpful summary in Brown, "Quest of the Historical Jesus," 70–74.

144. For contemporary evaluations of Jesus Christ see Bloesch, *Jesus Christ*, 19–24.

Christology from below: one that was transparent so that through it, the view from above could be seen. The story of Jesus, as in usual history, is such that faith can arise. This position is represented by the Myth of God School and the Quest for the Historical Jesus.[145] Finally, contemporary Christology is again moving towards this position but making the link between the methodologies and results of a Christology from below and a Christology from above more concrete. The net result is that these methodologies are now considered a starting place, not a single orientation.[146] In Colin Gunton's words:

> Christology from below aims to ground what it has to say primarily in the anthropological or, more generally, in that which has to do with time rather than eternity. But it is . . . a *ground*: there is every intention and indeed expectation to leave the ground, to speak theologically as well as anthropologically, and not to remain stranded on the earth.[147]

Therefore, a contemporary Christology from below is clearly different from the many attempts that have preceded it. When I endorse a Christology from below as the basis for a Spirit Christology it is in this Guntonesque sense.

This contemporary Christology from below is clearly against the rise of Christology from above (a Christology that expressly distanced itself from any historical facts concerning Jesus Christ) emerging as a critique and positive methodology against this view. The most significant of the initial contemporary Christologies from below was that of Ernst Käsemann, the founder of a "new quest of the historical Jesus."[148] He affirmed the necessity of building a belief in Jesus based upon a historical search for who Christ was and what he did. In some of these Christologies from below a genuine advance was made beyond the older quest for the historical Jesus. In a Christology from below the old presupposition of denying the deity of Jesus Christ was removed and for many, an authentic Christology could be developed; one that affirmed the genuine and complete deity of Jesus Christ at the end, not the begin-

---

145. It may be fair to say that this approach stresses the idea of the existential *Christus praesens* and reads current experience back into the very being and alleged historicity of Jesus Christ.

146. Turner, *Jesus the Christ*, 86–107.

147. Gunton, *Yesterday and Today*, 11.

148. Käsemann, "Problem of the Historical Jesus," 15–47.

ning, of the historical investigation. For Käsemann there is no possibility of reconstructing any other historical Jesus than that which is presented to us by the *kerygma*. The historical Jesus meets us in the New Testament not as he was in himself, nor as an isolated "individual," but as the Lord of the community which believes in him. A return to history is theologically legitimate, because of the continuity between the historical Jesus and the Christ of faith. The history of Jesus was constitutive for faith, because the earthly and the exalted Lord are one and the same.

The most comprehensive example of a contemporary Christology from below is provided by Wolfhart Pannenberg.[149] While his distinction between a Christology from above versus one from below has been shown to be a "gross oversimplification" his basic thesis is correct.[150] Pannenberg rejects a Christology from above for three reasons, all of which I share. First, it presupposes the divinity of Jesus.[151] The task of Christology is to offer rational support for such a confession, therefore the confession should rise out of Christology, not Christology out of a pre-formed Trinitarianism. In the second place, by taking the divinity of the Logos as its starting point, it tends to neglect the real significance inherent in the distinctive features of Jesus of Nazareth as a real historical man.[152] Finally, strictly speaking, a Christology from above is only possible from the position of God himself. We are limited creatures and must begin and conduct inquiry from this perspective.[153]

Pannenberg wishes to start below in order to affirm the deity of Jesus Christ. It is important to note that his method consciously differs from the older approach exemplified by Brunner[154] in that his is an approach from below *to* above,[155] not from below with the possibility of remaining there.[156] This is a crucial insight to take note of.

149. Pannenberg, *Jesus*, and ibid., *Systematic Theology*, vol. 2, 277–97.

150. This is the conclusion of Gunton, *Yesterday and Today*, 50–51.

151. Pannenberg, *Jesus*, 34.

152. Ibid., 34–35.

153. Ibid., 35. Gunton, *Yesterday and Today*, 19, considers this the weakest of his arguments and entertains a critique of his position.

154. See McGrath, *Modern German Christology*, and Brown, *Jesus in European Protestant Thought*.

155. Pannenberg, *Systematic Theology*, vol. 2, 277. In his approach from below to above he is following Ritschl but in a much modified sense.

156. For a discussion of various proposals of a Christology from below see ibid., 286–97.

Historical inquiry behind the New Testament is both possible and theologically necessary, because it places greater stress on the Gospel records, revealing in them a much greater historicity and clearer picture of Jesus than the older method was willing to allow.[157] The history of the Christ cannot be separated or isolated from world history. The same historical method used for knowing ordinary history applies to the history of the Christ. Furthermore, a Christology from below can present a fully human Jesus in a way that is not so easily achieved by the existing Logos Christology that advances the method from above.[158]

The question is can a Christology oriented from below establish the full deity of Jesus? The majority of contemporary advocates of a Christological methodology from below answer "yes" and point to any number of reasons for this. While most find this basis in Jesus's claim to authority in Christ's proclamation and work,[159] Pannenberg rejects this as all such attempts, in his opinion, fail to prove any such thing as Jesus's divinity. The reason for this is that Jesus's pre-Easter claim to authority is related to the future verification of his message, which will take place through the future judgment. Pannenberg correctly believes that "everything depends upon the connection between Jesus's claim and its confirmation by God."[160]

Such confirmation is found only in the resurrection of Jesus. Pannenberg thus takes the resurrection to be an historical event and uses 1 Corinthians 15:1–11 as his key text.[161] Pannenberg considers the whole of Jesus's ministry to have a "proleptic" character. Like the prophetic utterances of the apocalyptic background, Jesus's claims required future confirmation and vindication. This is why Christ did not respond to the

---

157. It is partly in response to this conclusion that I have decided to focus on the Gospels and not the much traversed Pauline corpus. It is not that the two are in any way in opposition or contradictory, but only that the Gospels have suffered neglect in this area.

158. Hansen, "Spirit Christology," 174–75, has noted that this in itself is not without difficulties as in our own day the notion of "person" is debated. Hansen asks whether Jesus as "man" means perfect man, inclusive man, essential man or integrated man, for instance.

159. Pannenberg, *Jesus*, 257.

160. Ibid., 66.

161. Ibid., 61, 98–106. He also points to the empty tomb as historical evidence. See ibid., 105. See O"Neill, "On the Resurrection as an Historical Question," in *Christ, Faith and History*, 205–19.

Pharisees with an immediate "Sign from heaven." Pannenberg's interpretation rests on his understanding of history.[162] History is revelatory only when it has fully run its course, because only then can we see its direction. It would seem that history has no value for us now. But resurrection, because it is the end of history, having taken place proleptically, is a core means of Divine self-revelation, even within time.[163]

Pannenberg holds that the resurrection must be understood from the viewpoint of the historical traditions to which it belongs. Whereas it has become commonplace to regard an event as a constant and its interpretation as a variable, changing with time, he unites the two. The meaning of an event is the meaning attached to it by the persons into whose history it occurs. Pannenberg points out what the fact of Jesus's resurrection would have meant to his Jewish contemporaries,[164] utilizing six theses to support his argument.[165]

According to Pannenberg the Christology of the New Testament developed backwards, from end to beginning. Early Christians placed their highest Christological emphasis on the return of Jesus at the end time. The next step saw Jesus already exalted to a high Christological status at the resurrection. This high Christology was gradually moved back by the gospels into the lifetime of Jesus so that he was the Messiah, the Son of Man and the Son of God. A further step was to push the question back beyond Christ's earthly ministry to the virgin birth, and then into a doctrine of personal pre-existence.

Patristic thinkers developed this further into the classical Logos Christology where the pre-existence was made to fit the accounts of virginal conception. Here an incarnational Christology (from above) was adapted to fit an inspirational one (from below). Hence, in liberal theology the Gospels are said to witness to two Christologies (or more), as the writers were not aware of each others (often mutually exclusive) perspectives.[166] But for a Christology from below, there are not two rival

---

162. See the comments in McGrath, *Modern German Christology*, 188–92.

163. Pannenberg, "Dogmatic Theses on the Doctrine of Revelation," 134. See Moltmann's reservations over Pannenberg's thesis of prolepsis in *Crucified God*, 176–77.

164. Pannenberg, *Jesus*, 67–69.

165. Ibid., 67–72. Pannenberg's six theses need not be repeated here.

166. Piper, "Virgin Birth," 132, answers well that, if the virginal conception was once a rival to the Pauline and Johannine thesis of pre-existence, for the church fathers the virginal conception confirms pre-existence.

Christologies (or more) in the New Testament, instead there are various complementary Christologies witnessed to by different writers at different times with different emphases, around a unifying centre.

Following Pannenberg, Stanley Grenz represents the most consistent Evangelical representative of a Christology from below.[167] In reaction to a Christology from above that argues for a faith alone construct devoid of historical confirmation, Grenz argues for a Christology from below to above, one that is rooted in the life of Jesus Christ. Grenz acknowledges that there must be some historical foundation for the Christian assertion that Jesus is divine.[168] Yet what aspect of Jesus's life forms this foundation? Surveying the possibilities,[169] Grenz mentions approaches based on the sinlessness of Jesus; his proclamation; and his death. But all of these require, Grenz argues, a prior faith commitment.[170] He then reviews approaches based on Jesus's own claims concerning his person (authority). Grenz considers this a main line of historical foundation, yet "his claim cannot form the definitive historical foundation for the declaration that Jesus is divine,"[171] because other figures had also claimed divine relationship. Jesus's claim forces us to consider who he said and believed he was.[172] Finally, Grenz agrees with his mentor Pannenberg and settles on the resurrection as the fundamental historical revelation of the identity of Jesus the Christ. "What is noteworthy about Jesus, however, is that his claim looked for, and even demanded a future vindication."[173] That vindication Grenz and Pannenberg find in his historical resurrection from the dead.

---

167. Grenz, *Theology for the Community*.

168. In this way Grenz is following his mentor when Pannenberg, *Systematic Theology*, vol. 2, 282, wrote, "For us humans; knowledge of preexistence and the Trinity does not come before knowledge of the man Jesus but rests upon it."

169. Grenz, *Theology for the Community*, 328–39. See Weber, *Foundations*, vol. 2, 37–39, who calls these appeals to biblical history as "blind alleys." He mentions miracles, sinlessness, discourse and resurrection. Weber discounts the resurrection as a historical foundation as it is not a proof which is accessible to all.

170. Grenz, *Theology for the Community*, 328–31.

171. Ibid., 334.

172. See the conclusion offered by Lewis, *Mere Christianity*, 52, and the Christological trilemma offered by Duncan, *Colloquia Peripatetica*, 109.

173. Grenz, *Theology for the Community*, 334 (see 338). Grenz discusses the question as to how the resurrection can be said to be a historical event and clearly restates the thesis of Pannenberg.

While the outline of Grenz, Pannenberg and others who follow them is essentially correct, I do think they have formed a premature conclusion in perceiving the resurrection event as the foundation of a Christology from below. Rather, the *exaltation* event that was *inaugurated* by the cross and resurrection, completed by the ascension and confirmed at Pentecost, should be seen as the historical foundation. Others had been raised from the dead and they were not divine (Lazarus, Jairus's daughter, and others for instance). It was not until the Pentecostal outpouring that the disciples really understood, and believed. Pentecost formed the foundation for the early Christian understanding of the identity of Jesus; an identity informed by the Holy Spirit. The New Testament indicates that the early believers viewed Pentecost as God's confirmation and vindication of Jesus's claims about himself and his mission. Through this act of exaltation/coronation, God himself confirmed Jesus's claim concerning his own uniqueness.

The most convincing support for this position is the soteriological corollary. "Our Christological assertion requires this specific historical basis because the encounter that mediates salvation to us is the encounter with Jesus the Savior,"[174] states Grenz. But we can and must go further. The Holy Spirit can only testify now (Rom 8:16) as he was historically sent by Christ at Pentecost—an event that could only happen in fulfillment of Old Testament prophecy and the proclamation of Jesus Christ himself—"until I go he cannot come" (John 16:7). Pentecost confirmed his exaltation historically, and today it still remains, that each coming of the Spirit upon believers confirms that historical event—the exaltation/coronation of the Son of God to the right hand of the Father. In these pentecostal outpourings the link is made between the cosmic Christ and the personal Lord. They are one and the same person.

The move from below to above is complete. Jesus is one with God. The *kerygmatic* portions of the New Testament are not simply the product of the theologizing of the church, for its foundations lie in the history of Jesus himself. To assert that Jesus is divine is to assert that God has initiated his eschatological reign in the person of Jesus Christ. Because the inaugurator of the kingdom must be the King himself, Jesus's claim as confirmed through the resurrection/exaltation indicates that he is one with God. We have already considered how this unity is to be understood—not just functionally (although that is the start of it)—but also

---

174. Grenz, *Theology for the Community*, 340.

ontologically. Jesus is God because he does what God can do and was confirmed as God's only Son; our knowledge of this today is based on the receiving of his Holy Spirit which authenticates Jesus's proclamation and witnesses to his exaltation.

Spirit Christology—Beyond the Impasse

Is it possible to unite the seemingly mutually exclusive positions of a Christology from below and a Christology from above preserving the best elements of both? Can the two histories, the *kerygmatic* Christ and the historical Jesus, faith and reason, be held together?[175] A Spirit Christology answers in the affirmative.[176] This stems from an orthodox understanding of history[177] wherein revelation is both the historical events and their interpretation;[178] two complementary and harmonious means by which God manifests himself. Both are sources of knowledge of God.[179] The Jesus of history is approached through historical reason and the *kerygmatic* Christ is seized by faith, so we are dealing here with the classic faith-reason dichotomy. The traditional form of this dichotomy was between faith and philosophical reason;[180] here it is between faith and historical reason. In each case the question is the utility and value of reason for grounding faith. As in the historical debate, so here, three positions can be articulated, those of fideism, Thomism, and Augustinianism.

---

175. Weber, *Foundations*, vol. 2, 26–37 and Bloesch, *Jesus Christ*, 143, attempt to bypass talk of above and below by advocating, in their distinctive ways, a "centrist" approach. However, their centrism is little more than a Christology from above with more space allocated to the historical reality of Jesus Christ. See Pannenberg's critique of Weber in *Jesus*, 33 n. 42.

176. As does Lewis and Demarest, *Integrative Theology*, vol. 2, 333, who call their position a "verificational approach." I would prefer to fashion it a properly scientific theology constructed *a posteriori* and if asked to articulate an epistemology would advocate critical realism the most appropriate to the task of orthodox constructive theology.

177. See Pannenberg, *Systematic Theology*, vol. 2, 344, especially n. 57.

178. See Fuller, *Easter Faith and History*, for a good discussion of the relationship between faith and history as well as a critique of various New Testament theologians's approaches to faith and history, including Pannenberg's.

179. See the important work by Barnett, *Jesus and the Logic of History*.

180. See the helpful survey and comment in Bloesch, *Theology of Word & Spirit*, 34–66.

A Christology from above is characterized by a fideism and has its philosophical roots in the works of Kierkegaard[181] and the existentialist school, particularly that of Brunner.[182] Knowledge of the deity is grounded in faith based upon the apostle's enunciation of the *kerygma*, not in historically provable knowledge of the earthly Christ.[183] In contradistinction, a Christology from below shares much with Thomism[184] in its attempt to demonstrate the supernatural character of Christ from historical evidences. Hence, the divine aspect of Christ need not be presupposed as it is the conclusion of the process, not the starting point. The appeal is to historical reason, not to faith or authority on its own. Thus reason plays an important part. The third position is the one represented by the Anselmian dictum *fides quaerens intellectum* ("faith seeking understanding"). It is this last approach which is the most applicable to a Spirit Christology. Here faith precedes reason but does not remain independent of reason as reason is part of the vehicle for faith. Faith provides the prospective or starting point from which reason may function enabling one to understand what they otherwise could not. As Erickson perceptively summarizes: "This would mean following neither faith alone nor historical reason alone, but both together, in an intertwined, mutually dependant, simultaneously progressing fashion."[185]

One pole of this dialectic of faith and reason is evident when a believer comes to a correct perception of Jesus; a perception based on something more than natural understanding (see Matt 16:16 and Peter's confession in Mark 8:28–30 as but two examples). John the Baptist is a good example of the other pole of the dialectic. When asking about the reality of the *kerygmatic* Christ John asks "are you the one who is to come, or shall we look to another?" (Luke 7:19). Jesus's response was to point to his concrete historical deeds. The historical Christ was the confirmation of the Christ of faith.

---

181. Amongst his many works see especially Kierkegaard, *Concluding Unscientific Postscript*; and *Fear and Trembling*.

182. Brunner, *Christian Doctrine of God*.

183. This point is affirmed by a committed adherent to a Christology from above, Erickson, *Flesh*, 626.

184. For an introduction and positive appraisal of Thomism regarding faith and reason see Geisler, *Thomas Aquinas*, 57–69.

185. Erickson, "Contrasting Methodologies," 54. Despite this Erickson still concludes that a Christology from above is his preferred epistemology.

The post-resurrection community of faith came to see, through the historic resurrection, the authentication and vindication of the Son at his enthronement, as authenticated in the event of Pentecost. The giving of the Spirit was to aid them in "remembering" the historical facts and the words of Christ which they did by reflecting on their faith, the product of which was the Gospels. The Gospels start with the presupposition of divinity (based on the end-time events of resurrection and Pentecost) and seek to highlight, authenticate, and strengthen the presupposition with the accounts of the man, Jesus Christ. In the next chapter we shall see more closely some of the ways they did this. Hence, the Epistles and the Gospels are two parts of the same story, in total continuity with each other. One stresses the below to inform the above (the Synoptics), the other contains elements of the above to complement the below (Paul and John). One is a retroactive reading of the historicity of Jesus Christ (Gospels), the other is a further development/enrichment of the *kerygmatic* Christ and the historical Jesus in the life of the church in and through his Spirit (Epistles).

As previously stated, the New Testament presents us with a Christological movement from below to above. Problems arise when we adopt a static epistemology of a Christology *exclusively* from below or *exclusively* from above. A Christology *from below to above* is required; one which is rooted in the historical life of Jesus of Nazareth and concludes with the affirmation of his deity, pre-existence, and Lordship as the cosmic Christ; a development that is already present in the New Testament.[186] And so with Gunton I affirm that "*Methodologically* there is a double movement, corresponding to the human and divine *content* of christological language. Christology is both from above *and* from below."[187]

While it is not improper to construct a Christology from above to below,[188] (as classical Christology has done) it is preferable to proceed

---

186. Torrance, *Theology in Reconstruction*, 38–39, while not explicitly advocating this approach, does make statements compatible with it in when he uses the concept of *prokope*. Jesus life provides for a "way" whereby we are called up to knowledge of God the Father. See his comments based on St. Basil's *De Spiritu Sancto* 16.39 in ibid., 39.

187. Gunton, *Yesterday and Today*, 13. Gunton is not comfortable with Christologies from below. He argues that a Christology from below "is hard put to avoid being a Christology of a divinized man," ibid., 18. While this criticism must be taken seriously I will attempt to show how a Christology from below is not *necessarily* adoptionistic.

188. Pannenberg, *Systematic Theology*, vol. 2., 289, "Only methodologically do we give precedence to arguing from below."

from below to above.[189] What we must keep in mind when constructing a Christology is that the biblical authors encountered Jesus first, and then reflected on his being. They started with his actions, his words, his life, and then pondered as to his essential being. They "followed" him with their feet before they learnt to follow him with their minds (philosophical, theological reflection). Here we must make an often overlooked distinction in contemporary Christology. "Christology from below always pertains to a 'coming to know.' It is epistemological or gnoseological in nature."[190] We only come to know Jesus and what he did, from below. Thus, Christology from below is not concerned with ontology as if Jesus *became* divine from below, that is, that the man Jesus became increasingly divine as he grew in knowledge and intimacy with God.[191] Ontologically, we affirm that the Incarnation is always from above as an orthodox Logos Christology maintains. Only because the Word became flesh from above can we come to know the Son of God from below.[192]

When we start from below we are confronted with Jesus Christ, the God-man.[193] We allow him to speak and act and "reveal" his essential being to us. As the New Testament will witness, Jesus is none other than God himself; God in the flesh and that will be the doxological culmination of any orthodox Christology.

In the awkward language of theological precision the model of Spirit Christology presented here is an inspirational-incarnational Christology, a Christology that proceeds *from below to above*. Not in a sequential linear movement as Pannenberg advocates, for this concedes too much to reason. Nor in a double movement which lays great stress on

---

189. See the comments by Rahner, *Theology, Anthropology, Christology*, 213–23. Rahner concludes that "These two basic types [of Christology] and their mutual interrelationship surely enable us to understand that in present-day Christian theology too there is room for a pluralism of christologies," ibid., 222.

190. Weinandy, *In the Likeness of Sinful Flesh*, 15.

191. What Gunton labels a "degree Christology," in *Yesterday and Today*, 18.

192. This is the point made by Krasevac, "Christology from Above and Christology from Below," 299–306, as cited by Weinandy, *In the Likeness of Sinful Flesh*, 16 n.19: "If a "Christology from below" stops, as it were, with the "low" Christology of an early New Testament tradition (a Christology that does not fully recognize the perfect divinity of Christ), it is to be faulted for failing to carry through consistently its own method to its full historical term. The primary purpose, again, of a "Christology from below" is to *understand* the "high" Christology of the mature Christian confession of faith in terms of its historical development."

193. Weinandy, *In the Likeness of Sinful Flesh*, 14–16.

a transcendent anthropology as Rahner proposes, for this tends towards an adoptionistic conclusion. By contrast, I propose a Christological methodology that seeks to bridge the gulf between Jesus's humanity and divinity (the two nature Achilles heel of classical Christology) by means of the Holy Spirit. This movement lays equal stress on faith and understanding, on Spirit and reason, and on transcendence and immanence. Spirit Christology is a method that holds out the great promise of returning Christian discipleship to its roots; the simple faith and practice of seeking to be like Jesus. At the same time, a Spirit Christology when applied to theology proper, is able to lead us up from Christology (and anthropology), into Trinitarian theology, from the economic Trinity to the ontological Trinity, and from the economy to God's eternity.[194]

What I am yet to provide is the biblical basis for such a Christology (chapter 5) and the theological coherence of this Christology with an orthodox Trinitarianism (chapter 6). However, before traversing this ground it will pay to first be reminded of the historical contexts into which these issues fit (chapter 3 and 4).

---

194. "A total presentation of Christian doctrine must try to integrate Christology from below into the context of its overarching themes, i.e., into the context of the doctrine of God and the economy of his work in and with the world," Pannenberg, *Systematic Theology*, vol. 2, 289.

3

Logos and Spirit

God's Two Hands

*But now the swarm of testimonies shall burst upon you from
which the Deity of the Holy Ghost shall be shown to all . . .
Look at the facts:*

*Christ is born; the Spirit is His Forerunner.
He is baptized; the Spirit bears witness.
He is tempted; the Spirit leads Him up.
He works miracles; the Spirit accompanies Him.
He ascends; the Spirit takes his place.*

—Gregory of Nazianzen

*Certainly the history of Christian doctrine makes it clear that
wherever the Church has allowed the reality of the historical Jesus
Christ to be depreciated there it has also lost a doctrine of the
Holy Spirit . . . The doctrine of the Spirit . . . stands or falls with the
acknowledgement of the active coming and activity of the being of
God himself within our space and time in Jesus Christ.*

—Thomas F. Torrance

*How a historical person can be both a human being and a divine
Person has always been a puzzle which calls for godly bewilder-
ment from the believer and intellectual humility
from the theologian.*

—Adrian Thatcher

AN UNEASY ALLIANCE

CHRISTOLOGICAL REFLECTION THROUGH THE ages has resulted in a number of models or paradigms that seek to explain or illustrate the identity and mission of Jesus the Christ. The present chapter examines the important witness of the Patristic era (c. 100–451 AD) in order to ascertain the "what" and the "how" of Christological development. Special notice shall be paid to the fact that in the earliest witnesses outside of the New Testament, the church held to both paradigms of Logos and Spirit Christology. However, by the fourth century Logos Christology dominated the minds of the great theologians while Spirit Christology was relegated to the heterodox fringe of the tradition. Particular notice will be taken of the Christology of the Cappadocians whose theology acts as a conceptual bridge between East and West, and between a Logos and Spirit Christology.[1]

Historically, what should have been two complementary streams of theology, namely, pneumatology and Christology have experienced what may be called an "uneasy alliance." This is at first surprising, since the New Testament is replete with the intimate and reciprocal relations first between Christ and Spirit in the Gospels in the first place, and then that of pneumatology and Christology as developed in the Epistles.[2] There is no intrinsic reason for an antithesis between incarnation and inspiration, between Word and Spirit.

Looking back at the history of theological thought we can see that while the New Testament itself employs various ways to describe Jesus and his uniqueness the most immediate way is found in the words of John 1:14: "The Word, the Logos became flesh." Taking its vocabulary and impulse from John's Gospel, a Logos Christology starts from a different point than a Spirit Christology. It starts from above with the definition of Jesus as the second Person of the Trinity, who then assumes human nature in the incarnation and then, at the ascension, raises back to his position of glory with the Father (and the Spirit). Notwithstanding the sonship of Jesus or the intention of John's statement, we have to acknowledge that this is not the only way that the New Testament or John's gospel presents the identity of Jesus. An equally legitimate approach is the one elaborated here—that Jesus is unique, largely due to his relationship to the Father in or by the Holy Spirit of God (Spirit Christology).

---

1. Unfortunately it is beyond the scope of this study to consider any of these theologians in depth. The best we can offer is a survey that pinpoints the key areas of development and witness to both Logos and Spirit Christology.

2. See for instance amongst the vast literature the classic overview of Swete, *Holy Spirit in the New Testament*; and for the most comprehensive treatment of Pauline pneumatology, Fee, *Gods Empowering Presence*; along with the works of Dunn, *Christ and the Spirit*, and *Jesus and the Spirit*.

While the two approaches of Logos and Spirit Christology are biblical and ultimately complementary, subsequent theological thought has tended to treat them as rivals and so it is possible to read the history of theological thought as one of oscillation between a Spirit Christology and a Logos Christology. This is acknowledged by Roger Haight:

> . . . Spirit Christology seeks to present a consistent interpretation of Jesus in a way analogous to the Logos Christology that has ruled Christian consciousness since the second century. But unlike the Logos Christology, which tended to place other christologies in a shadow, a Spirit Christology can be understood as a basis for considering, interpreting, and appropriating other New Testament christologies. Spirit Christology should be understood as functioning not in an exclusive but in an inclusive way.[3]

History confirms that in post-biblical theology, Logos Christology has held sway since the fourth century while Spirit Christology has been relegated to the periphery of orthodox Christology. After a brief survey of this we will pay attention to criticisms of the Logos Christology in an attempt to reunite these "two hands" of God, thus achieving a thorough biblical perspective on Christology and its immediate corollaries—pneumatology and the doctrine of the Trinity.

Behind the turbulent debates of the early church (c. 100–451) there are at least three forces that have shaped the formation and formulation of orthodox doctrine. These three forces are the syncretism of the time known as Gnosticism; early Jewish monotheism; and Greek philosophy. Against these three we can see how and why the church developed its Christology. Today in the absence of these specific forces, the questions being asked are: Must our Christology be redefined? And: Should the biblical material again be submitted to open and honest review to regain a once lost dimension that was obscured by these three forces? According to my analysis what came to be known as Logos Christology arose from a combination of these three factors. However, a Spirit Christology suitable for today must be incorporated into this picture if a more complete biblical Christology is to be constructed, a Christology that can immediately speak to contemporary culture.

Throughout the twentieth century Christology has come under considerable theological debate with many dissonant voices calling for a reappraisal of our long standing Christology. Although the voices

---

3. Haight, "Case for Spirit Christology," 271.

are many and varied one unifying theme is the common attack on the Definition of Faith of the Council of Chalcedon (AD 451).[4] Germane to our investigation are the reasons behind the calls for reappraisal and an evaluation of their validity or otherwise, for it is from these attempts at reappraisal that modern Spirit Christologies have emerged. While it is impossible to trace the entire history of the doctrine of Christology, I will briefly state and critically assess the received tradition of the West and East, founded as it is upon the Christology of the Patristic era. Thus, I shall only look at the main architects of Logos Christology and the dissenting voices who advocated some form of Spirit Christology.

The Apostolic Fathers

When Christian thinkers turn their attention to Christology they are faced with what Chesterton described as "a matter more dark and awful than it is easy to discuss."[5] This is as true today as it was then. Jesus Christ is unique and therefore Christology involves a myriad of complexities that must be faced. Within that body of writings known to church history as the Apostolic Fathers we witness an implicit form of Spirit Christology although it is far from developed.[6]

Within the *Shepherd of Hermas,* an important witness to the state of Christianity in Rome in the mid-second century, Spirit Christology is found to reside within a clear adoptionist Christology.[7] Even though Christ is not named it is surely he who is in view throughout this text.[8] One sees this for example when the 'Shepherd' ascribes the incarnation to the Holy Spirit who is also the Son.[9] So *Hermas* reflects a Logos Christology, a Spirit Christology, and even an angel Christology.[10] The 'Shepherd' appears to identify Son with Spirit without any adequate explanation. In some way it is the Spirit that is incarnated in Christ.

---

4. Studer, *Trinity and Incarnation,* 4.
5. Chesterton, *Orthodoxy,* 205.
6. Bobrinskoy, "Indwelling of the Spirit in Christ," 51.
7. For the text of Hermas see *Apostolic Fathers,* 194–290. Parable V, para. 2, ibid., 241–42.
8. For comments on the Christology and trinitarianism in *Hermas* see Grillmeier, *Christ in Christian Tradition* vol. 1, 54 n. 76.
9. *Hermas,* Parable V, para. 6, in *Apostolic Fathers,* 245–46.
10. Grillmeier, *Christ in Christian Tradition,* vol. 1, 57.

Early Spirit Christologies can also be found in Ignatius who names Christ according to his divine nature, *pneumatokos*.[11] At times Ignatius appears to espouse what would go on to become adoptionism. Likewise, Second Clement speaks of Christ "who, being first Spirit, became flesh."[12] This practice appears sporadically in other thinkers such as Lactantius[13] where the word "Spirit" is thought to designate the divinity of Jesus Christ. The same phenomenon can be found in Tertullian to a lesser degree, and Hippolytus and Cyprian.[14] The Father's *monarchia* was strictly adhered to by these Jewish monotheists.[15] What resulted was an adoption of Jesus by the Spirit, hence a confusion over the nature of his preexistence. For some this theme was developed to the point where the Ebionites presented a form of dynamic monarchianism.

In the main, these theologies gave way to the more dominant *logos*/Son Christologies of the Apologists in order to counter threats of Christological heresy, not least of which was the adoptionism and Docetism aroused by these early Spirit Christologies. It is important to note that central to these early attempts to formulate a Christology is the concept of Spirit. The earliest Christian thinkers could not conceive of a Christology devoid of a pneumatic element and hence they developed initial attempts at a Spirit Christology.[16] While far from the orthodoxy of today's standards these early attempts must not be omitted from modern discussion. The fact that throughout the history of Christian thought elements of these initial Spirit Christologies were elaborated (often in the form of what would be called adoptionism) should not put us off

11. Ignatius, *Epistle to the Ephesians* 7, 2 in *Apostolic Fathers*, 86–92.

12. 2 Clement, *Ancient Christian Sermon*, in *Apostolic Fathers*, 65–78. Weinandy, *Does God Change?* xxiii, finds docetic tendencies within Clement's theology due to his stoic notion of *apathia* by which he is able to downplay the sufferings and human experiences of Christ.

13. Grillmeier discusses Lactantius's Spirit Christology and possible binitarianism in *Christ in Christian Tradition*, vol. 1, 190–206. Also see McGuckin, "Spirit Christology: Lactantius and His Sources," 141–48.

14. See Tertullian *Carn.* 18; *Prax.* 26; Cyprian *idol.* II. We may also note the elements of a Spirit Christology in Tatianus's "Speech Against the Greeks" (c. AD 165), which mentions "the heavenly word, born as Spirit from the Father and as Word out of his rational power." Quoted in Berkhof, *Doctrine of the Holy Spirit*, 20 n. 8.

15. Weinandy, *Does God Change?* xxvi.

16. But by no means were they espousing the Spirit Christology recommended in the present study. What they highlight is an initial movement in this direction from the start.

pursuing Spirit Christology as a valid paradigm today, albeit purged of its adoptionistic tendencies.

The Ebionites were Jewish-Christians who formed not a distinct grouping but rather a general banner under which to put various Christological proposals. One thing that they had in common was a denial of the early history of Jesus such as his virgin birth and preexistence. At the baptism they saw the Holy Spirit enter Jesus and in a Gnostic-like fashion considered this to be the union of a heavenly being with the man Jesus, resulting in the Christ—the Son of God.[17]

Alongside Ebionite Christology were the first semblances of an adoptionist Christology proper. Perhaps Theodotus the Elder was the earliest, followed by Theodotus the Younger and his disciples the Melchisedekians.[18] These groups claimed Jesus to be no more than a mediator between God and humanity, a mere man especially graced by God. The Spirit is thus seen as a divine power and not a person, so that Jesus the man is indwelt by the divine power of God. In this manner he was adopted, either at the baptism or after the resurrection (different groups postulated different times). Adoptionists appealed to Christologies of indwelling and merit.[19] As Grillmeier wrote, "these words were later used as labels to denote heresy, although some of their basic concepts would have maintained their significance in the context of the whole of the church's picture of Christ and within the framework of belief in Christ as the true Son of God."[20]

Adoptionism first arose it seems, out of a strictly closed Judaistic monotheism. Under this conception the divine cannot take on human flesh thus the Logos must be an intermediary between God and humanity. At this point the church was forced to develop Trinitarian and Christological dogma side by side if it was to maintain the divine Sonship of Christ alongside his real humanity. This was first attempted in the third century when philosophical influences also worked their way into theological reflection. We see this most clearly in the so called Apologists.

---

17. Grillmeier, *Christ in Christian Tradition*, vol. 1, 76.
18. Grant, *Jesus after the Gospels*, 10–11; 68–82; and 99–105.
19. Del Colle, "Spirit-Christology," 97.
20. Grillmeier, *Christ in Christian Tradition*, 78.

The Apologists and their Successors

An enduring difficulty in all Christological discussion since the incarnation, is the concept that Jesus is uniquely the God-man—he is both human and divine and yet one person. While attempting to understand this point, theological thought has evidenced a consistent pattern; a tendency to overstate the humanity of Christ over his divinity or his divinity over his humanity. Holding these two in biblical tension has been more difficult than New Testament writers could have imagined. How is the unity of Jesus the Christ conceived? While this is not the only question a Christology seeks to answer it is one of the crucial ones and was addressed initially by the Apologists.[21] They set in motion a Christological wave whose ripples still account for the broad contours of Christology today. In relation to Christological methodology, an ontological orientation took precedence over a functional one so that Christology became dominated by a description of the incarnation of the Logos without adequate discussion on the role of the Son's relation to the Father in or by the Holy Spirit (and vice-versa).

When speaking of Christology it is not an overstatement to say with Piet Schoonenberg that "Today in all Christian churches where Christology is seen as important, it is the Logos Christology which stands at the center, whereas Spirit Christology is marginal."[22] This trend is directly traceable to the Apologists. With the emergence of the Apologists, Logos Christology became the dominant and eventually the only Christology of the catholic church.[23] "By the fourth century it had become evident that of all the various titles of majesty for Christ adapted and adopted during the first generations after Jesus, none was to have more momentous consequences than the title Logos."[24] Three sources contributed to the rise of Logos Christology by the Apologists: Christian tradition such as John's prologue, wisdom literature, and Hellenistic phi-

---

21. Schaff, *History of the Christian Church*, vol. 8, 135, rightly points out that there are four elements that enter into the orthodox doctrine concerning Christ: 1) he is true God; 2) he is true man; 3) he is one person; 4) the divine and human in him, with all the personal union and harmony, remain distinct.

22. Schoonenberg, "Spirit Christology and Logos Christology," 353.

23. The Patristic period cemented the dominance of Logos Christology over Spirit Christology. For our purposes the Patristic period covers AD 100–451. For a succinct overview of the period see. McGrath, *Christian Theology*, 5–25.

24. Pelikan, *Jesus Through the Centuries*, 58.

losophy.²⁵ "The Apologists already made something special out of the Logos doctrine and gave it a key position in Christian theology."²⁶

Justin Martyr

Most prominent in constructing an early Logos Christology is Justin Martyr (c. 100–165). In order to answer the question, "what is the nature and identity of the heavenly 'power' that became incarnate in Jesus?" Justin used the current Stoic/Platonic idea of *logos*/reason. In so doing he formulated the first attempt at a systematic Christology, and he may in fact be credited as the Father of Logos Christology. Like the Apostolic Fathers, in his *Apology*, Justin reflects the somewhat confused state of Christology of the time. He appealed to the use of John 1:14 and the use of Logos for Jesus along with 1 Corinthians and Proverbs's use of Wisdom.²⁷ He appears to confuse the use of "Spirit" to express the pre-existent nature of Christ with its use as the name of the third Person of the Godhead. However, unlike the Apostolic Fathers, the Word and not the Spirit now assumes the principle of incarnation for the Apologists. Although the title "Christ" originally signified the anointing of Jesus with the Spirit, this tended to be ignored and "Christ" became either a proper name or a way of emphasizing that in the incarnation human nature was "anointed" with deity. In accord with the prevailing philosophy of the time, namely Middle and Neo-Platonic emanationism, the Apologists thought of Jesus as S/spirit²⁸ since they conceived of S/spirit as the ve-

---

25. Grillmeier, *Christ in Christian Tradition*, vol. 1, 108.

26. Ibid., 109. Grillmeier lists five ways the Apologists used the Logos doctrine: 1) in its cosmological aspect as creative Word, 2) in its noetic aspect as the basis of knowledge and truth, 3) in its moral aspect as the basis and embodiment of the moral law, 4) in its psychological aspect as the original form of thought, and 5) in its saving-historical aspect as Word of revelation and mediator of salvation. See further in Lampe, "Holy Spirit and the Person of Christ," 114.

27. In his "First Apology of Justin the Martyr," in *Early Christian Fathers*, 1.11.1, he does not use *Sophia* but rather *Logos* in a philosophical way. In 1.21.1 he refers to Proverbs 33:6 and speaks of the Logos as the "First thing generated by God." he develops this more in his *Dialogue* where he uses Proverbs 8:22–36 to say the *Logos* (not *Sophia*) is God's generated rational power (*logikē*). Also see *Apology* 1.32.8–10.

28. The convention of "S/spirit" is used to maintain the ambiguity of whether or not it is the Holy Spirit who is in view, a personal being, or the more general concept of spirit.

Logos and Spirit

hicle of deity, God's active presence.[29] Justin called the Logos the first of God's creatures[30] that originated by the will of the Father.[31]

Adolf von Harnack sums up Justin's Christology in the classical formula "Christ is the Logos and Nomos."[32] Due to his reliance upon middle Platonism, by calling the Logos the "servant," "apostle," and "angel" of the absolutely transcendent Father,[33] Justin gives Christ a diminished transcendence that makes him all but a subordinate creature. The Logos is compared to Hermes, the logos-interpreter of Zeus.[34] Thus an implicit subordinationism is introduced into the essential Christology of the church. This would later be developed by Tatian, his disciple, into a firm rejection of the real preexistence of the Logos in a distinct sense. Hippolytus takes this Logos Christology further;[35] Logos and Spirit are in God as *ratio* and *sapientia*, as *dynamis* and decision. In creation, however, the Logos manifests a distinct existence from the Father finally climaxing at the incarnation. Thus Justin and his kin tended to blur the distinction between Son and Spirit making the Spirit the impersonal nature of deity. Christology was understood to be the incarnation of the Logos who was the Spirit as much as the Father is Spirit. In this way it was inevitable that Spirit Christology would be marginalized in orthodox thought. While the Apostles Creed emphasizes the humanity of Jesus, it is noteworthy that Nicaea emphasizes his divinity. The reason for this is due in no small part to Justin's fundamental statements regarding the Logos of God. Already a cleavage had started to work its way between the biblical presentation of the unity of Jesus Christ and the more philosophical "portrait" of Christ by the Apologists.

---

29. See the discussion in Prestige, *God in Patristic Thought*, 17–21, where he cites instances where the use of the term "spirit" is the same as that of the Nicene use of *homoousios* and also how the term was used to designate not the divine nature but the personally divine character of the divine Son. Wolfson, *Philosophy of the Church Fathers*, 183–91 goes further to assert that the early church identified the Spirit with the preexistent Christ.

30. *Apology* I, 21, 1.

31. *Dial.* 61, 1f; Tatian *Or.* 5, 1.

32. Quoted in Grillmeier, *Christ in Christian Tradition*, vol. 1, 90.

33. *Apology* 6.1.3; 62.4; 100.4; 126.1.

34. Ibid., I.21.2; 22.2.

35. Refer to Gonzalez, *History of Christian Thought*, vol. 1, 228–35.

Theophilus of Antioch

Following Justin's lead Logos Christology was further established in the early church. Theophilus of Antioch (late second century), in his *Apostolic Constitutions,* advocated the extreme transcendence of God and again made it hard to speak of any real incarnation. He spoke of the Logos and Sophia, sometimes as separate beings, but often as the two hands of God in the sense of equivalence.[36] The Logos is the Spirit, wisdom, and power of the most high God.[37] In his writings, both are generated by God and both share the same functions of creation and inspiration.[38] However, he never speaks of the Father, Son, and Spirit thus causing a confusion that Irenaeus would attempt to clarify. Perhaps the greatest elaboration on Justin's Logos Christology was the introduction of the Stoic/Middle Platonic distinction between the logos *endiathetos* in the bowels (*splanchna*) of God and the logos *prophorikos* that is spewed forth as Sophia. This spewing forth is equated with the generation of the Logos.[39] Theophilus defined the relationship between Sophia and Logos as follows: Sophia is *in* God (*endiathetos*) while the Logos is *with* God (*prophorikos*). As the voice of God, Theophilus follows Justin's lead in identifying the Logos as the messenger of God.[40] What Justin and in turn Theophilus were attempting to do was present the Gospel in the idiom of contemporary Hellenistic categories, a worthy attempt in its own right. Thought starts in the heart, goes to the head and is emitted by speech. This was the early conception of the Trinity; a conception that strays considerably further from biblical revelation than is commonly admitted.

This transition from an implicit Spirit Christology to an explicit and monopolizing Logos Christology was aided by at least five factors.[41] First, there was the reaction against any form of adoptionism whereby Jesus Christ was "merely an inspired man." Orthodox belief has always been deeply suspicious of any theory that might seem to imply that Jesus was only a man, and a possession or Spirit Christology certainly

---

36. *Apostolic Constitution* 2.18; 2.10.22.
37. Ibid., 2.10; 2.22.
38. Ibid., 1.7; 2.10, 22.
39. See Grant, *Jesus after the Gospels,* 73, who considers this to be a parallel of Athena's birth out of Zeus and Metis.
40. *Apostolic Constitution* 2.22; see Justin *Dialogue* 128.3.
41. Lampe, *God as Spirit,* 120, provides three factors.

appears to teach this in some form in the early church. After the work of Athanasius who strongly argued for the divinity of Christ based on the soteriological argument; any inspirational Christology, or Christology that recognizes the divine element in Jesus as Spirit (either in place of, or alongside Logos), seemed to lessen the fact that Jesus was the Word of God incarnate. The Adoptionists often focused their attention on the baptism of Christ, making that the point of adoption of the man Jesus by the Spirit, thus making him the Christ. In reaction, it was natural for orthodox theologians to stress the realism of the incarnation and the fact that Jesus was fully divine, even before his baptism.

Second, the translation of the Christian faith by the Apologists into the Hellenistic context of the day meant that ontological questions came to the fore. "Thus, if the New Testament spoke of Jesus as being both the ontological Person of the Word made flesh and the bearer of God's Spirit, the latter point gradually disappeared as a theme for theological reflection."[42] We see this trend solidified throughout the scholastic period. Spirit gives way to Word, Spirit Christology gives way to Logos Christology. Logos Christology has a weakness, especially among the Apologists, as Christ is thought to be a mediatorial being between God and humanity. Logos Christology had retained a similar structure from Philo's hierarchical cosmology; the structure of a subordination of the Logos under the Father in the sense that the Logos is a being less than the Father's being and essence. Philo said the Logos is the world reason, and inferior to God because the Logos is not without beginning, but has gone forth out of God.[43]

Third, Spirit Christology was eclipsed by Logos Christology due to the fear of patripassianism. Logos Christology clearly distinguished between God-in-Christ and God-in-himself. It enabled Christian faith to be harmonized with the fundamental principles of Greek philosophy—that God is immutable, impassable, and unchangeable. Hence the long tradition of reading *a priori* philosophically informed Trinitarian doctrine into Christology was engaged; a tradition that is being challenged today.[44]

Fourth, to give a theological account of the differences between the Spirit in Christ and the Spirit in Christians a Logos Christology was

---

42. O'Donnell, "In Him and Over Him," 26.
43. Philo *De. Som.* 7: II, 188; III, 289, 6.
44. See the review by Weinandy, *Does God Suffer?*

advanced by which the Word incarnate became prior to the Spirit of God. This had the net effect of reducing the Spirit to an addendum of Christology. While the New Testament holds Word and Spirit together, later theological thought did not. It took the Reformation to begin to address this situation and today we are witnessing a concerted effort to construct an orthodox Spirit Christology that once again does justice to both Word and Spirit in mutually reciprocal fashion.

Finally, Logos Christology was employed to convince the Gentiles of the truth of the Christian gospel. Middle Platonism offered the Apologists a model for presenting an overall understanding of reality. The Logos is the principle of the cosmos, the knowledge of truth and morality. In favor of this monumental development is the fact that theological reflection had begun. By not simply confining themselves to the *ipssisma verba* of Scripture, the Apologists were able to engage their culture and evangelize the educated. However, a monumental risk was also entertained and it is not certain that the Apologists were entirely successful at avoiding this risk. By utilizing current philosophy they introduced foreign elements into Christian discussion that would work themselves out in numerous ways. The Arian struggles were a direct consequence of a dominant Logos Christology. The Stoic idea of Logos was essentially monistic and Middle Platonism was excessively transcendent. So the account of Jesus Christ bound him to the role of a subordinate mediator, or to a docetic Christology as a result. In commending the gospel to the educated and defending it against pagan and Jewish attacks the Apologists overstated their case and relied too heavily on philosophical paradigms of the day. When the philosophical paradigms shifted, the intellectual validity of the Gospel became obsolete. In the concise words of Ronald Wallace:

> Their conception of the place of Christ was determined, however, rather by current philosophical ideas of the *logos* than by the historic revelation given in the gospel, and for them Christianity tends to become a new law or philosophy and Christ another God inferior to the highest God.[45]

And so while they warded off adoptionism for the time being "The Logos Christology however, just because of its philosophical connota-

---

45. Wallace "Christology," *EDT*, 224.

tions, caused a distortion in the presentation of the gospel."[46] The transition from a pneumatic Christology to Logos Christology was almost complete.

IRENAEUS

Following the Apologists Irenaeus (fl. 175-195) built on the Logos Christology he received but advanced beyond Justin and Theophilus's mediator Christology. He posited Christ as the link between God and humanity. Given the strong transcendence of God that he inherited he adopted Theophilus's teaching about the two powers of God—Logos and Sophia and turned them into the "two hands of God"—Son and Spirit. Irenaeus made the explicit identification of Logos with Son and Sophia with Spirit;[47] the two being the hands of God in the world.[48] In so doing, Irenaeus presented the divine triad as Father, Son and Spirit more adequately than the previously held triad of Father, Logos, and Sophia; he turned back from the overstatements of the Apologists to Scriptural affirmations. In addition, he rejected the distinction between the Logos *endiathetos* and the Logos *prophorikos* of Justin and Theophilus. The incarnation of the one Logos functions as the key to his entire system. Irenaeus asserts that God became man (3.21.1), that God's Logos is Jesus Christ (4.20.4) and that following John's lead, the Logos is the only begotten, that is—Jesus Christ (3.16.2).

In presenting such a strong Logos Christology Irenaeus did not merely reiterate Justin's more Hellenistic presentation; he developed his doctrine of recapitulation where the invisible becomes visible, that unable to suffer—suffers, and insists on both the divinity and humanity of Jesus Christ. Thus, Irenaeus clearly asserts that Jesus was made a man and subject to passions (3.18.1), and in so doing he goes beyond a strict Logos Christology in speaking of the humanity of Jesus in terms of a Last-Adam Christology. Although he was a supporter of the Logos Christology that he had received he also wished to reassert the Church's possession of the Spirit. He thus used language reminiscent of the Apostle Paul's Spirit Christology (5.2.3). He mentions the birth of Jesus by the Holy Spirit (3.21.5), the fact that Jesus is truly flesh and blood (5.14.11), and that his flesh was subject to the limitations of humanity

---

46. Berkhof, *Doctrine of the Holy Spirit*, 21.
47. *Heresies* 2.30.9; 4.7.4; 4.20.3.
48. Ibid., 5.6.1; 5.28.4; 5.1.3; 4.7.4; 4.20.1.

(3.22.2; 5.21.2).⁴⁹ Irenaeus received this Christology from Theophilus but not without criticism at points; for Theophilus, Christ's work is exemplary, for Irenaeus it is efficacious (3.18.7; 3.21.10).

The end of the second century witnessed the rise of Logos Christology but not, however, without some form of corrective in an implicit and undeveloped Spirit Christology. This is especially evidenced within Irenaeus's remarkably creative theology. Irenaeus opposed Gnostic and Apologetic excesses by returning to Scripture while still introducing his own novelties into his Christology. Norris concludes, "There results a portrayal of Jesus as having a dual character—as embodying in himself the unity of two ways of being, spiritual and fleshly, divine and human. This picture establishes the starting point, provides the essential paradigm, and, above all, dictates an agenda for later patristic Christology."⁵⁰ In the years between the end of the second century and the Definition of Chalcedon this trend continued. Logos Christology became more and more the entrenched position of the church and Spirit Christology was increasingly marginalized. The divine elements of Jesus's being were emphasized over the human.

Paul of Samosata & Lactantius

Despite this trend, there is evidence of a recurring theme of Spirit Christology in the pre-Nicene period. Paul of Samosata (fl. 260–272) and Lactantius (c. 250–c. 320) represent a group of early thinkers who were not entirely convinced by the monopolizing of the Logos Christology. Both were Antiochene in their Christology and are regarded as early Adoptionists.⁵¹ What Paul and Lactantius were attempting, however unsuccessfully, was to account for the divine in Christ while maintaining his complete humanity. To do this they identified Christ/Logos with S/spirit hence they can be classed as pre-Nicene binitarians.⁵² Paul of Samosata emphasized the impersonal essence of the S/spirit of God, which had

---

49. "Here something other than the total sufficiency of the words of the Word is implied, and it is significant that from this time the explicit epiclesis of the Spirit makes its appearance in the liturgy," Clark, "Spirit Christology in the Light of Eucharistic Theology," 273.

50. Norris, *Christological Controversy*, 5.

51. Grillmeier, *Christ in Christian Tradition*, vol. 1, 190–206; McGuckin, "Spirit Christology," 141–48.

52. See Grillmeier, *Christ in Christian Tradition*, vol. 1, 198, for a definition of Spirit Christology in the Patristic era along with references in the major writers.

been breathed into Jesus at his baptism; as a bearer of the S/spirit Jesus was different from Moses and the prophets only by degree.[53] In the following centuries the doctrine that Jesus was not a divine person but only a man filled with the Spirit of God, could no longer be advocated as long as a Trinitarian dogma remained in force. However, Paul of Samosata had an influence on subsequent Antiochene Christology, which understood the process of the *homoiōsis theōs* as the path of the unification of Jesus with the Logos.[54] It was only when the authority of the Trinitarian doctrine disappeared in the modern period that adoptionism has again been seriously advocated.[55]

While this Christology was no longer tolerated after Chalcedon (100 years later!) it was by no means an aberrant Christology in its own day. Both Paul and Lactantius were following a well received tradition.[56] McGuckin summed it up, "the obscurity of the Spirit Christology which he preserves, far from isolating Lactantius from the mainstream of Christian tradition, witnesses that he has remained faithful to the most primitive and archaic tradition, one reflecting the very obscurities of the New Testament experience itself."[57] This Spirit Christology would remain a neglected factor in much subsequent Christology, especially after Chalcedon.

Origen

Origen (c. 185–c. 254), the last theologian we shall mention from this era, continued to affirm a Logos Christology. He asserted that the Logos was eternally begotten and he identified Logos with divine wisdom.[58] However, wisdom is not God himself, but a "second God," subordinate to the ultimate Father of all. Origen conceived of the Logos as the first of

---

53. Weinandy, *Does God Change?* xxiv; xxviii; xxxi; 8, 25; 82.

54. Antiochene Christology wavers towards modalism—the Spirit is God's mode of operation within the person of Jesus. See ibid., xxiv.

55. Concepts very similar to Patristic adoptionism have appeared in the works of Kant, Schleiermacher, Ritschle, Adolf van Harnack and others. However, none of these writers made the Spirit the decisive Christological concept as did the Patristic theologians. The precursors to this are said to be the Italian heretics of the late Renaissance in the sixteenth century. Pannenberg, *Jesus*, 121.

56. "It represents a long-standing western tradition, more widespread than has often been imagined," McGuckin, "Spirit Christology," 142.

57. Ibid., 148.

58. *De Princ* 1.2.9.

God's creatures.[59] He spoke expressly of a middle position of the Logos between the one and the many, between the God who transcends all becoming, and created things.[60] Thus, Origen made explicit what was only an implicit subordinationism in Justin which tended to dominate Christology due to the monarchical nature of Jewish monotheism. When Jewish monotheism encountered the philosophy of the day a Platonic emanationism further confirmed this trend.[61] It was taught that the Father had precedence over the Son and the Son over the Spirit.[62] Hence, Christ was subordinated to the Father and the Spirit to both Father and Son.[63] According to Bobrinskoy, "Origen places a notoriously one-sided emphasis on the diverse functions of the Logos ('Enlightener,' 'Pedagogue,' etc.,) to the detriment of the role of the Spirit, which he limits to the work of sanctification within the Church and to inspiration of the Holy Scriptures."[64]

Arianism took mediator Christology to its logical extreme, developing Origen's ideas in a one-sided way by abandoning his idea of the eternal generation of the Son. Arianism was rejected outright and it took all the forces of the early church to formally eradicate this pernicious theology at the council of Nicaea (AD 325). A key to the triumph of orthodoxy was the use of the term *homoousios*. The chief monument of the fourth-century consideration of Jesus as the Logos was the teaching of the Trinity as enshrined in the Nicene Creed. Subsequent Christian thinkers went further; by applying the title of Logos to Jesus Christ,

---

59. Ibid., IV, 4, 1; *Contra Celsum* 5, 39; 8, 12.

60. *Contra Celsum* 3, 34.

61. Weinandy, *Does God Change?* xxvii. Origen's conception of God was determined by his Platonism. For Origen, God is the one, unoriginated transcendent Monad of God the Father. This, by necessity for Origen, meant the Son had to be a secondary God, a *Deuteros Theos*.

62. Torrance, *Theology in Reconstruction*, 212, highlights the fact that this theology makes the Son and the Spirit co-existent with the *kosmos*. This was overcome by the twofold affirmation of a) the doctrine of the Creator Spirit, hence he could not be a creature, and b), the doctrine of the economy of God. Supporting both affirmations is the *homoousios* doctrine applied to both Christ and Spirit by Athanasius and the Cappadocians.

63. *De Princ.* I.2.4; ii.6.3.f. This implicit subordinationism is still with us today as when some speak of the first, second, and third Persons of the Trinity in a hierarchical fashion.

64. Bobrinskoy, "Indwelling of the Spirit in Christ," 52. This is a common fault even today.

theologians and philosophers of the fourth and fifth centuries were trying to give an account of who he was and what he had done. This allowed them to interpret him as the divine clue to the structure of reality (metaphysics) and within metaphysics, to the riddle of being (ontology)—in a word, as the Cosmic Christ.[65]

Early Christian thinkers brought to their interpretation of the biblical account of creation an understanding of the origins of the universe that had been profoundly shaped by the *Timaeus* of Plato (of whom many patristic writers thought had read Genesis!). So from its beginning the Christian view of creation was a mix of divine revelation and philosophical reason. The Logos concept brought these two streams together. "For most of these fourth-century fathers, what bound together the religious-theological cosmogony of the Nicene Creed . . . and the philosophical-scientific cosmology of Plato and of Platonism . . . was the further affirmation of the content of the Logos doctrine (though the term Logos itself did not appear in the Nicene Creed) when it declared that 'through the one Lord Jesus Christ, the Son of God, all things were made.'"[66] But "Logos of God" meant far more when applied to Jesus Christ than the biblical terminology "Word of God." In addition, employing the specific name *Logos* implied that what had come in Jesus Christ was also the Reason and Mind of the cosmos conceived philosophically.[67]

ATHANASIUS

Following Nicaea and preceding Chalcedon, several Christian thinkers will occupy our attention. Like Irenaeus, both Athanasius (c. 296–373) and the Cappadocians were able to stand firmly within the received tradition and develop Logos Christology further, while still retaining a very real place for the Holy Spirit and indeed a very crucial counterbalance to the excesses of mediatorial Logos Christology, by using an implicit Spirit

---

65. Pelikan, *Jesus through the Centuries*, 58.

66. Ibid., 61.

67. This recognition is shared by the majority of historians and theologians today. See the comments of Küng, *Menshwerding Gottes*, 536, and the thesis of Weinandy, *Does God Change?* Along with the standard philosophical surveys such as Popkin, *Pimlico History of Western Philosophy*, 118–39; Chadwick, *Early Christian Thought and the Classical Tradition*; Osbourne, *Emergence of Christian Theology*; Pelikan, *Christianity and Classical Culture*; Stead, *Philosophy in Christian Antiquity*; and Wolfson, *Philosophy of the Church Fathers*.

Christology.⁶⁸ Their stand provides a model for Christological reflection today.

Due to the Arian controversy in the fourth century a radical dissociation between reflection on the divinity of the Word of God and the divinity of the Spirit occurred. Initially, the question of the Holy Spirit was all but ignored. Only in the final stage of his defense of orthodoxy did Athanasius broaden the debate to include the question of the divinity of the Spirit which he was compelled to do because of another heresy—that of the Pneumatomachi.⁶⁹ "His *apologia* of the term '*homoousios*' or 'consubstantial,' however, did not yet furnish him with the conceptual resources needed to define the relation of the Holy Spirit to the Son, other than by an analogy with the relation of the Son to the Father: 'The Spirit,' he affirmed, 'is the image of the Son, just as the Son is the image of the Father.'"⁷⁰ Athanasius argued for the divinity of Christ along soteriological grounds. The Logos accomplishes our restoration by his death on the cross—thus discharging the debt of physical death against us, and through his continued presence enables believers to share in the divine life. This meant that redemption could only be accomplished through God's active presence with humanity. The corollary was that in the incarnation Jesus had to be fully God. Thus, Athanasius repudiated the Arian error on the grounds that if the Logos was merely a mediator between the divine and humanity then salvation had not occurred. Throughout his discussion, Athanasius consistently spoke of the Spirit's relation to Christ as co-equal and *homoousios*.⁷¹

Athanasius's soteriological argument dealt a death blow to Arianism, but his argument also contained an implicit criticism of the received Logos Christology; Logos Christology tends towards subordinationism

---

68. Torrance, *Theology in Reconstruction*, 48, detects in Athanasius's theology a distinct move away from the philosophically driven Logos Christology of Origen and Arianism.

69. Also called "Macedonians." Gonzalez, *History of Christian Thought*, vol. 1, 284–87.

70. *First Letter to Serapion*, 24. See Bobrinskoy, "Indwelling of the Spirit in Christ," 52.

71. It is perfectly true that the eastern tradition has consistently upheld the doctrine of the Spirit as propounded by Athanasius, "from the Father, through the Son, in the Spirit," and continued to maintain and develop a doctrine of the Spirit in the closest association with the doctrine of the Son. See Torrance, *Theology in Reconstruction*, 229. Athanasius's insights were built upon by the Cappadocians and are only today being reintroduced on a wide scale to the Western Tradition. A Spirit Christology is an attempt to combine the best insights from East and West into one coherent framework.

or Docetism, both of which Athanasius rules out as incapable of securing our salvation and inconsistent with the full testimony of Scripture. With Irenaeus he posited a real and direct union of God with humanity in the person of Christ.[72] By harnessing and adopting the significant contribution of Nicaea's *homoousios* doctrine, Athanasius was able to purge Christianity of the Platonic conception of the One, with all its distorting implications.[73] So on the Trinitarian level Athanasius had proved the point convincingly, but the Christological matter was still unresolved.

On the Christological level this created another problem: the gospel portrait of Christ does not fit if the Logos is truly God. This was the Arian counter-claim.[74] The Gospel witness is that Christ hungered, thirsted, experienced human emotions, and showed intellectual ignorance. These are not traits of God but of a creature. This criticism itself, however, evidences the state of the doctrine of God in the Patristic period. The Arians (and much of the early church) assumed that the Logos was the sole real subject in Jesus. Or alternatively, that Jesus was simply the Logos with a body.[75] The second working assumption is that there is an inconsistency between the being of God and the human being. In the absence of Platonism both assumptions are challenged today.

In *Orations Against the Arians,* book three, Athanasius attempts to answer the charges. He posits a difference between the "Logos in himself" and the "Logos in the incarnate state" and in doing so he came very

---

72. And so rejected Origen's emanationism. Weinandy, *Does God Change?* 14–46.

73. This view is advocated strongly by Torrance, *Theology in Reconciliation,* 209–28. He believes Athanasius to have thrown off all traces of Hellenistic rationalism. "Athanasius entirely rejected the cosmological and epistemological dualism of Hellenism, Gnosticism and Origenism . . . he set aside the philosophical notion of the Logos as an impersonal cosmological principle . . . Above all, perhaps, he rejected the Platonic doctrine of God as 'beyond knowledge and being,'" (ibid., 217). We cannot develop here a comprehensive argument for or against this thesis. However, Torrance advocates a minority view that has not been developed significantly since. From my reading of Athanasius he appears to be able to challenge the philosophical constructs of his day at significant points while at others he adopts it without criticism. In terms of the present argument we may say Athanasius, while working within a Logos Christology, can meaningfully incorporate elements of a Spirit Christology.

74. Athanasius *Contra Arianos* 3.27. The Arians asked "How could he (Logos), being God, become man?"

75. This is an extreme form of Logos-sarx Christology. The Logos takes the place of the soul and is united to the flesh in such a way that it becomes the principle of Jesus's existence. This is a thoroughly consistent Logos Christology. We shall see this more clearly in Apollinarianism.

close to the earlier conceptions of Justin and Theophilus. Athanasius allowed for the humanity of Jesus as evidenced in the Gospels,[76] evidently sharing the Arian view of the person of Jesus although not their view of the Logos.[77] However, when it came to accounting for the humanity of Jesus the Christ in the gospels, he had problems. Athanasius did not dismiss the humanity of Christ, on the contrary, he includes passage after passage where he takes it seriously,[78] however, he has no conceptual basis by which to fully justify the humanity of Christ. While not a Docetist his adherence to a Logos Christology meant that he could not *adequately* account for the humanity of Jesus Christ.[79]

Even in the hands of the great Athanasius, Logos Christology brought forth its familiar problems—a Docetic or subordinationist Christology.[80] Weinandy observed that "the real problem resides in Athanasius' inability to state in one consistent conceptual framework both the ontological nature of the union and the distinction that must necessarily be made in order to ensure the integrity of the Logos, and of the humanity."[81] The crux of the problem, as Kelly rightly highlights, is whether Athanasius

---

76. He also spoke of the role of the Spirit as the power of God, the *energeia* of the Son, through whom God realizes his works. *Ad Ser.* 1.20, 30f; *Contra Arianos* 3.5. Because of the space Athanasius allocates to the Spirit in the economy he stands out, along with the Cappadocians, as of immense importance in modern constructions of a Trinitarian Spirit Christology along the lines of which I am presenting here. Because of his Trinitarian Christology Torrance, *Theology in Reconstruction*, 209–28, considers him one of, if not the most important, expounder of the *homoousios* doctrine. I tend to agree with him.

77. Weinandy, *Does God Change?* 20–25.

78. *Contra Arianos* 1.46ff; 2.10ff; etc. Torrance, *Theology in Reconciliation*, 151–56, includes many quotations and a discussion of Athanasius's high view of Christ's real humanity. Torrance acknowledges that his view of Athanasius's Christology is at odds with what he calls the "familiar text books." While I concede the fact that Athanasius did make space for the humanity of Jesus as *homoousios* with us I still come to the conclusion that due to the Logos Christology of the time he was unable to *adequately* account for the two natures in the one person. He did not deny the two natures, but he was unable to account for them under his Christological construct.

79. Because Athanasius held that the Logos indeed was incarnated he insists against the Arians that all the human attributes must be predicated of him. The fact that Athanasius held unswervingly to the true humanity and true divinity of Jesus is not in question. His ability to appropriately speak of these two is seriously questioned. Athanasius *Contra Arianos* 3.32, 3.34.

80. Bloesch, *God The Almighty*, 174, concurs with this view when he writes: "Subordinationism and orthodoxy . . . coexisted in Athanasius."

81. Weinandy, *Does God Change?* 22.

holds that Christ's humanity includes a human rational soul, or whether he regards the Logos as taking the place of one.[82] Despite Athanasius's best attempts at a *communicatio idiomatum*, and the fact that nowhere does he explicitly refuse a human soul to Christ, he never brings out its theological significance.[83] Because of his failure to give adequate space to the human soul of Christ, Athanasius appears incapable of accounting for the ignorance, emotions, agony, and suffering of Jesus, even utilizing his argument about the difference between the Logos in himself, and as incarnate.[84] As with Arius and Apollinaris, his fundamental problem was the Logos-sarx model he was working with.[85] Logos Christology is not a sufficiently comprehensive model for accounting adequately for the full divinity and full humanity of Jesus Christ. The *homoousios* doctrine requires a Trinitarian framework that must incorporate the essential aspects of a Spirit Christology complementing the Logos Christology.

Apollinaris of Laodicea

Following Athanasius was his contemporary and disciple Apollinaris (AD 310–380) who sought to take the discussion further when he advocated that the Logos takes the human form in Jesus, thus Jesus lacked a human intellect or rational soul.[86] In this way, Apollinaris seems to be making explicit what had remained implicit in Athanasius's argument.[87] Apollinaris presented a rudimentary form of a *communicatio idiomatum* where the divine and human natures co-mingle in the one person.[88]

---

82. Kelly, *Early Christian Doctrines*, 286–87. It is not that Athanasius refused Christ a human soul. He clearly states with reference to John 1:14 that the Logos became man and did not just enter man (*Contra Arianos*, 3.30). The issue is his inability due to the Logos Christology to develop this insight meaningfully and in harmony with his Logos Christology.

83. See for instance Athanasius *Contra Arianos* 3.31, 35, 57.

84. Grillmeier, *Christ in Christian Tradition*, vol. 1, 308–26, who comes to the same conclusion. However, Grillmeier is quick to state that this does not make Athanasius an Arian or an Apollinarian. While all three work from a Logos/sarx model only Athanasius keeps his model "open for an explicit doctrine of the soul of Christ. That of Apollinarius is closed," (ibid., 25). We could add Arius to the list. Reaching the same conclusions is Weinandy, *Does God Change?* 24–25.

85. This view is shared explicitly by Weinandy, *Does God Change?* 30.

86. This being the heresy of Apollinarianism. See Walter, "Apollinarianism," 67–68 and Norris, *Christological Controversy*, 103–11.

87. See the discussion in Torrance, *Theology in Reconciliation*, 139–214.

88. Weinandy, *Does God Change?* 27–28. He clarifies Apollinaris's Christology by saying it was a vitalistic and organic unity.

Jesus Christ is the Logos enfleshed, hence, Jesus does not have any human centre of life and consciousness but rather one composite nature.[89] Thus, Apollinaris exhibited his understanding of the logic of the Logos Christology he had received.[90]

Although Apollinaris sought to maintain the unity of Christ his views were condemned as heretical at Rome in AD 377, Constantinople in AD 381, and again at Rome in AD 382. "What is not assumed is not healed" was the theological axe that felled his Christology.[91] By these means Apollinaris moved away from his mentor Athanasius. If the Logos takes the place of the soul it not only becomes the principle of life but also the centre of all human experience, be it hunger, ignorance or agony.[92] That means it is no longer the Word, or Jesus as man, who experiences these things, as Athanasius maintained, but the Godhead of the Logos, for in reality there is no real man, Jesus of Nazareth.[93]

THEODORE OF MOPSUESTIA

In contradistinction to Apollinaris was the teaching of Theodore of Mopsuestia (AD 350–428).[94] Theodore was an Antiochene and a theological descendant of Paul of Samosata.[95] He advocated a Logos-man model. For Theodore, Jesus had two distinct natures; those of the Logos and of the man Jesus.[96] In this way he sought to emphasize the real

---

89. Apollinaris, *Fragments* 45; 74; 76; in Norris, *Christological Controversy*, 107–11.

90. And it may not be an overstatement to say that many in the contemporary church have more in common with Apollinaris than with Chalcedon; in practice if not in creed.

91. The term comes from Gregory Nazianzen, *To Cledonius the Preist against Apollinarius*, ep. CI, *NPNF*, second series, vol. 3, 440. It literally reads, "For that which He has not assumed He has not healed; but that which is united to his Godhead is also saved."

92. It has been pointed out that Apollinaris's concept of the incarnate Logos was not intended in a Monophysite sense. His intention was to safeguard the unity of Christ. Unfortunately he maintained the divinity of Christ by replacing the real humanity. Torrance, *Theology in Reconciliation*, 144–45.

93. See the critique of his position by Gregory Nazianzen in *Ad Cled.* Ep. 101; 102, in *LCC*, vol. 3.

94. Norris, *Christological Controversy*, 113–22.

95. His opponents regarded him as a *Paulus redivivus* teaching an adoptionist Christology after Paul of Samosata. Clark, "Spirit Christology in the Light of Eucharistic Theology," 277.

96. This was the result of his adherence to Nicene orthodoxy and his philosophical presuppositions. However, while Theodore spoke of the one person in two natures he

humanity of Jesus. How was the divine conceived? Was it through the now familiar model of indwelling or inspiration?[97] What separated Jesus from the prophets was the distinctive indwelling of the Logos and Spirit within Jesus.[98] In Jesus, God dwells "as in a Son." From conception, the Logos was said to unite himself to Jesus and, at resurrection, Jesus the human being was shown to have always been one functional identity, one *prosopon* or person with the Logos. In this sense he taught a "prosopic union." Jesus has two hypostases, two natures; the divine which equals the Logos and the human which equals Jesus the man, whom the Logos joined himself to. Theodore does not speak of Christ's deity as Spirit as the Apostolic fathers had, but he does fall into the problem of not adequately distinguishing God in Christ and God in Christ's people.[99] Clark's conclusion is quite correct: "Theodore was condemned, more than anything, by association with Nestorius, but his teaching assured the position of the Spirit in the liturgy and in the thought of the East; in this respect his excursion towards a Spirit Christology has left a permanent and valuable record in Tradition."[100]

NESTORIUS

A contemporary of Theodore, Nestorius (d. 451) dealt with the same concerns. The question he addressed was whether Jesus was the Logos (Athanasius) or indwelt by the Logos (Theodore). Nestorius sided with Theodore's construction saying that the Logos was residing in, but was

---

was no Chalcedonian precursor. The common *prosopon* has no metaphysical or ontological content. It is not a "who" in itself, but a phenomenal representation brought about by the closeness of the two natures. See the interpretation of his Christology by Weinandy, *Does God Change?* 34–37.

97. Theodore writes in his *Baptismal Homily* 4.10, "For even our Lord's body did not enjoy immortality and the power to confer immortality by its own nature, but by the gift of the Holy Spirit. It was by the resurrection from the dead that this body was united with the divine nature, and so became immortal and the source of immortality for others," English translation in Edward Yarnold, *Awe-inspiring Rites* (Collegeville: Liturgical, 1994), 205.

98. Theodore *Baptismal Homily* 4.11 in Yarnold, *Awe-inspiring Rites*, 206.

99. See further in Sullivan, *Christology of Theodore of Mopsuestia*.

100. Clark, "Spirit Christology in the Light of Eucharistic Theology," 278. Theodore developed the role of the Spirit in the incarnation into the role of the Spirit in sacramental action. See Theodore *Baptismal Homily* 4.10 in Yarnold, *Awe-inspiring Rites*, 205. Augustine was able to develop somewhat of a similar role for the Spirit in the Eucharist as well. See Augustine *Tractate on the Gospel of John* 26.13.

not identical to Jesus. Nestorius's ideas came into prominence due to the use of the term *theotokos* ("mother of God") for Mary; he preferred the title *theodokos* ("bearer of God"). In so doing he was affirming an indwelling Christology. Nestorius sought to follow the tradition of the Antiochene School, teaching that Jesus was fully divine and fully human. However, his theory has not escaped the criticism of the "pantomime horse": while Christ appears to be one, at the deepest level he remains two. His views were condemned in AD 431.

These two broad lines of thought, Theodore-Nestorian (a basic Spirit Christology) and Athanasius-Apollinarian (a basic Logos Christology) came to a head in the second quarter of the fifth century and were to be resolved at Chalcedon.[101]

The Three Cappadocians

Before examining Chalcedon, we must make mention of the contribution of the Cappadocians[102] as they represent a blend of Logos and Spirit Christology.[103] Following Nicaea, the Cappadocians further upheld Nicene orthodoxy in the face of a more stringent Arian attack on the soteriological argument. Jesus Christ had to be both divine and human if he were to be a genuine Saviour. This was ratified at the Council of Constantinople (AD 381). However, they did not only repeat earlier Christological statements but significantly built upon the existing tradition, especially the tradition derived from Athanasius. Thus they held in tension differing Christologies and articulated a way of speaking of the unity of God along with incorporating the place of the Holy Spirit in the redemptive economy of the eternal Son. That is, within their Logos Christology they managed to hold onto the biblical truths of the pneumatic dimensions integral to a complete Christology. It is no accident that even today the East has a robust pneumatology to complement its

---

101. In our survey it is impossible to cover every theologian and council. The contribution of Cyril of Alexandria and the Council of Ephesus (AD 431) called to resolve the dispute between Nestorius and Cyril is one such major event we shall have to bypass. See Weinandy, *Does God Change?* 58–63, for an overview of the issues.

102. Basil the Great, his younger brother Gregory of Nyssa and Basil's long-time friend and codefender of the faith Gregory of Nazianzus.

103. See the insightful survey of Torrance, *Theology in Reconstruction*, 220–28. In similar fashion to Bob Bobrinskoy's analysis Torrance identifies and articulates the blend of Logos and Spirit emphases within these theologians, particularly Basil the Great.

Christological teaching, influenced as it is by the contribution of the three Cappadocians.

Within their Trinitarian reflections the Cappadocians considered the questions: What is the place of the Spirit in the redemptive work of the Incarnate Word? And: What is the place of the Holy Spirit within the eternal being of the Son? "In their 'pneumatic Christology', Christ appears in his eternal divinity, as in his humanity that we share, as the full and perfect Temple of the Spirit, who communicates his own Spirit in a permanent Pentecost for the life of the world,"[104] Bobrinskoy tells us. Basil identifies the place of the Spirit within the life of Christ, highlighting the conception, temptation, miracles, and resurrection.[105] Similarly, Gregory Nazianzen speaks of the birth, baptism, and miracles,[106] but he is reluctant to speak of the operation of the Spirit *in* Jesus; the Spirit dwelt in Christ, not as energizing, but as accompanying him who is his equal. Thus, Gregory Nazianzen is able to stress both divine persons without jeopardizing the now traditional vision of Christ's hypostatic unity. This had important implications for later discussions over the Nestorian heresy that afforded too great a role to the Holy Spirit within the life of Christ and led to an adoptionist Christology. Theodore of Mopsuestia would lead the way by emphasizing the humanity of Christ to the neglect of his true divinity, referred to as "anthropological maximalism" or adoptionism.[107] "For the Cappadocian Fathers as well as for St John Chrysostom, to speak of the presence of the Spirit in Jesus at the various stages of his human life is above all to remember that the very name of 'Christ' is supremely a trinitarian and 'pneumatophoric' name."[108]

In their various writings the Cappadocians used the image of "unction" to describe the relationship between Jesus and the Spirit.[109]

> The flesh of the Lord was anointed with a true unction, by the descent upon it of the Holy Spirit, who is called "an oil of rejoicing." The Lord was anointed "in preference to his companions," that is, more than all persons who participate in the life of Christ. For they only receive a partial communion in the Spirit, whereas

---

104. Bobrinskoy, "Indwelling of the Spirit in Christ," 65.
105. See *De Spiritu Sancto* 16.39; 19.49.
106. *Or.* 31.29; 41.5; 41.11.
107. Bobrinskoy, "Indwelling of the Spirit in Christ," 61.
108. ibid.
109. See Basil *De Spiritu Sancto* 16.39; and *Comm. in Ps.* 44, 8.

the Holy Spirit who descended upon the Son of God, as St John affirms, made his dwelling-place within him. How appropriate that the Spirit should be called "the oil of rejoicing"! For one of the fruits cultivated by the Spirit is joy . . . The prophetic word concerning the (unction of the) Saviour refers both to the divine nature and to the economy of the incarnation.[110]

According to the general teaching of Basil, believers receive a partial communion in the Spirit, Jesus receives total communion and this makes him unique. Gregory Nazianzen also speaks of this but it is now commonly recognized that he tends to minimize the aspect of energy or active operation of the Spirit in Jesus.[111] The Spirit sanctifies Christ not by his action (*energeia*) but by the full presence (*parousia*) of the Anointing One (the Spirit). *Unction* then, is a symbol to express the intimate relationship between Christ and the Spirit.[112]

This reciprocal relationship between Jesus and the Spirit extends beyond the economy and corresponds to the mystery of the unity and the ineffable communion that exists between the Spirit and the Son from all eternity, thus raising the discussion from the economic to the immanent level. Again from Basil, "The [Psalmists] prophetic word concerning the unction of the Saviour refers both to the divine nature and to the economy of the Incarnation."[113]

The precise nature of the divinity of Jesus Christ was still left unanswered. Theologians of the third and fourth centuries developed various proposals in this regard. As we have already seen, there were basically two schools of thought that emerged, although it is unwise to take the respective caricatures of either school too far.[114] On the one hand is the Antiochene school with its so-called "Word-man" Christology. In the extreme form this resulted in Nestorianism—that Jesus Christ is actually two beings residing in one. The other school was the Alexandrian and its

---

110. Quoted in Bobrinskoy, "Indwelling of the Spirit in Christ," 62. See *Comm. in Ps.* 44.8.

111. See his *Or.* 30.21.

112. Gregory Nyssa also applies this thinking in his *C. Eunom.* II.2, and the term appears again in *C. Eunom* 1.1.22.

113. *Comm. in Ps* 44.8.

114. See Wells, *Person of Christ*, 98–109; Clark, "Spirit Christology in the Light of Eucharistic Theology," 273–76; Schaff, *History of the Christian Church*, vol. 4, 3; §13–140, Kelly, *Early Christian Doctrines*, 153–58, 301–2; Sellers, *Two Ancient Christologies*; and Need, *Truly Divine and Truly Human*, 17–39.

so-called "Word-flesh" Christology.[115] In its extreme form this resulted in both Apollinarianism and Eutychianism. As we have seen, Apollinaris and his followers claimed that the soul of Jesus was replaced by the Logos but this was squarely refuted by the Nicene Creed. Eutychianism said that Christ had only one nature and hence became docetic, that is, that Jesus Christ has only the appearance of humanity. This, the Chalcedonian Definition clearly rejected.

The Council of Chalcedon—AD 451

With the Definition of Chalcedon (AD 451) the final touches were set in place for a full-orbed Logos Christology.[116] The Definition meant that quite plainly Jesus Christ was not merely a man indwelt by the Holy Spirit and thus adopted, but was "very God of very God." Moving beyond the Nicene Creed, the Council of Chalcedon further clarified in terms of a two nature Christology, the uniqueness of Jesus and solidified in creedal form a Logos Christology. While this in itself was a masterful move and one that cut the legs off many heresies threatening the church of the day, the Definition does have some deficiencies when viewed from our contemporary perspective. One of the main deficiencies of the Definition is, as I see it, that it does not leave sufficient space for the equally important Spirit Christology of the Bible and the early church. By the end of the fifth century the orthodox expression of Christological belief was contained wholly within that of a Logos Christology. As I have shown, this was due to the various threats of the time (including adoptionism, syncretism, Jewish and Greek factors), and the advantageous use of the Logos concept by the Apologists. Once Christology found creedal expression it had the effect of safeguarding sound doctrine. It also, however, tended to hinder new and significant theological reflection on the central themes of the faith. This condition prevailed throughout the middle-ages (scho-

---

115. Behind the Word-man and Word-flesh differences lie the philosophical underpinnings of each school. Broadly speaking but still useful we can identify the Alexandrian school as Platonic and the Antiochene as Aristotelian. This divergence goes a long way in accounting for their different constructions of Christology. This distinction has been identified and articulated by Weinandy, *Does God Change?* 32–33; and Need, *Truly Divine and Truly Human*, 38.

116. The contribution of Augustine of Hippo, while not unimportant, does not bear any direct consequence to our thesis. He was typical of the Patristic era in emphasizing the role of the Logos while at the same time making partial space for the Spirit. See the standard texts as cited throughout, along with Kelly, "Spirit, Church and the Ecumenical Endeavour," in *Starting with the Spirit*, 153–76, for a brief overview.

lasticism) and even found a footing during the reformation period in regard to Christology.[117]

Inheriting their Christology from the Patristics, the theologians of the Byzantine, Roman Catholic, Reformation, and Protestant churches generally upheld the now long-standing Logos Christology that stresses incarnation over inspiration, ontology over function, and a methodology from above as opposed to one from below. The literature of this time highlights the fact that christological discussion is dominated by reflection on the hypostatic union of the Logos and the human reality of Jesus.[118] While these emphases are constitutive of Christology it is what is not examined that is of concern. What is neglected is the constitutive role of the Holy Spirit, especially when it comes to the relation between the Spirit and the Christ.

To conclude this section I can do no better than repeat the words of Philip Rosato when, in an article entitled "Spirit Christology: Ambiguity and Promise," he reflects on the loss of Spirit Christology from the Great Tradition:

> Had Spirit Christology's weakness not been so exaggerated, its strength would have remained a permanent legacy to the later Christological treatises of classical Scholastic and Protestant theology. Its weakness, of course, was its denial of the ontological significance of Jesus. But its strength was its ability, far superior to that of exclusively ontological Christology, to incorporate within it the essentially biblical, eschatological, and soteriological implications of the Christ-event. Ontological Logos Christology attempted in its own way to balance out the antimetaphysical excesses to which adoptionism had led. But, in doing so, Logos Christology lost sight of the genuine advantages which Spirit Christology, for all its faults, intended to retain.[119]

---

117. From my perspective this confinement of Christological development has only recently been circumvented.

118. A simple illustration of this is the definition of "Christology" given in the glossary of terms by McGrath, *Christian Theology*, 495, "The section of Christian theology dealing with the identity of Jesus Christ, particularly the question of the relation of his human and divine natures."

119. Rosato, "Spirit-Christology: Ambiguity and Promise," 435–36. In attempting to learn from the Adoptionists I am are not wanting to dilute truth by combing it with error. Rather, following the methodology proposed by Poythress, *Symphonic Theology*, 96, "we may sometimes add more truth to what truth we already have by listening carefully to doctrinal disagreements. Even when one party in a dispute is basically wrong and the other basically right, the party in the wrong may have noticed at least one or two things

CRITICAL ASSESSMENT

Several steps in the movement of Spirit Christology to the periphery of the Great Tradition have been reviewed.[120] The first step, taken in the Patristic era, was attributing the anointing of Jesus to the Logos as much as to the Holy Spirit. Interest in Jesus's baptism diminished rapidly and interest in the incarnation proper increased. The Logos was quickly identified as the anointing one along with the Holy Spirit. The second step was advanced considerably by the scholastics, both Roman Catholic and Protestant, in their philosophical analysis of Christology. Following Aquinas,[121] the hypostatic union is considered the *substantial* sanctification of Jesus and also that, subsequent to this substantial grace, Jesus's humanity had to receive an *accidental* habitual grace as distinct from the grace of union, which is the hypostatic union itself. Thus, the Holy Spirit's influence on Jesus is now viewed as merely *accidental* compared to that of the Logos which is *substantial*.[122] The third and final step in the eclipse of Spirit Christology in favor of Logos Christology is the scholastic theory of the appropriations. Under scholastic formulations of the doctrine even the accidental working of the Holy Spirit on/in Jesus is not considered properly his own work, but that which is common to the Trinity.

Considering the early church's attempts to construct a Christology culminating in the Chalcedonian Definition, it is accurate to conclude that Christology is continually faced with problems. In the attempt to hold onto the divinity and the humanity of Jesus (the two natures) in the one person (the unity), one christological method does not seem adequate to do justice to both natures equally. If a Spirit Christology is

---

in the Bible that have usually not been noticed by the opposite side. These one or two things become the basis for the plausibility of their own claims." He goes on to briefly examine the Adoptionist argument, ibid., 96–99.

120. Schoonenberg, "Spirit Christology and Logos Christology," 354–55.

121. Thomas Aquinas, *Summa Theologia*, III, q.6, a. 6.

122. See ibid., I q.7, a.1, and III, q.7, a.13. It may be noted that this is still the consistent teaching of the Roman Catholic tradition. See Ott, *Fundamentals of Catholic Dogma*, 170. For a radical departure from within Roman Catholicism the work of David Coffey takes on significant importance. Utilizing the insights of Spirit Christology (a Christology he is in favor of and a large contributor to), Coffey, "Theandric Nature of Christ," departs from Aquinas's distinction in Christ between substantial and accidental grace and now considers there to be "no room in this scheme for a habitual grace in Christ," ibid., 426. See further in Coffey, *Deus Trinitas*, and *"Did you receive the Holy Spirit when you believed?"*

followed in isolation from its complementary Logos Christology, then the heresy of adoptionism is forever lurking at the door. Adoptionism is clearly not consistent with biblical teaching and seeks to make Jesus into a mere model with no actual saving efficacy. Adoptionism makes Jesus less than divine and so has more in common with Jehovah's Witness doctrine (modern Arianism) than with traditional Christianity. It answers the soteriological necessity of *cur Deus homo* but ignores or rather dismisses the ontological dimension. Conversely, when Logos Christology dominates Christological method the opposite and equally dangerous extreme is the constant threat of Docetism (and/or subordinationism). While the divinity of Jesus is secured and so his preexistence as the Logos is maintained, what is lost is real humanity and in its place is a fleshy phantasmal shell. This is not only unbiblical but also contradicts the soteriological necessity that Christology must maintain. In commenting on the state of Christology today Wallace writes, "We seem at times to be confronted by an Arianism content to affirm that the Son is simply 'of like substance' with the Father, at times with a docetism for which the reality of the human nature is of little importance."[123]

Intended to cement unity within the church, the Definition of Chalcedon[124] became a dividing document, the West held unswervingly to it, but many in the East did not.[125] Among both Roman Catholic and Protestant traditions this Document has not been seriously challenged until the nineteenth century, first by Schleiermacher,[126] and then by the many since who have sought to attack the Chalcedonian Definition and either undermine or overturn it. As Anthony Lane writes, "[Schleiermacher] founded not a school but an era."[127]

But what are these objections to Chalcedonian Christology? Obviously they are many, and much of the debate does not concern us directly here. The following is a representative sample of objections that

---

123. Wallace "Christology," *EDT*, 227.

124. See the English text in Appendix 1.

125. The eastern wing of Christianity began to return to the much simpler concept of monophysitism. Jesus was conceived as one divine person whose divine nature had absorbed his humanity and thus he now possessed one nature. See Robichaux, "Pneumatic Person of Christ," 3.

126. Schleiermacher, *Christian Faith*.

127. Lane, "Christology Beyond Chalcedon," 262. See the article defending Chalcedon outright by Bray, "Can we Dispense with Chalcedon," 2–9.

Logos and Spirit

will provide a conceptual background to the case for a Spirit Christology.[128] The objections raised are common to those we have looked at already. While I certainly do not share all the following objections they must be heard nonetheless. I have not sought to defend Chalcedon point by point, or to answer any of the criticisms. What I seek to do is highlight the current objections, and posit a Spirit-Christology as a necessary *complement*, not *replacement*, to what I consider to be the very fine Chalcedonian Definition.[129]

The first criticism is that of an over-dependence upon Greek philosophy.[130] Many scholars claim that the biblical record has been polluted with Greek philosophy; non-biblical words such as *"person," "hypostasis," "nature,"* and *"substance,"* are given overly nuanced and extra-biblical authority.[131]

Second, functional versus ontological categories reign supreme. Chalcedon is often accused of presenting a predominantly ontological Christology as opposed to the predominantly functional Christology of the New Testament,[132] and it is said to distort biblical Christology considerably. A presupposition of this criticism is the attempt to divest Christian theology of all elements of Hellenistic philosophy (as if some pristine, non-philosophical conception of Divine revelation could be attained).

---

128. In addition see the summary of Newman, *Spirit Christology*, 1–27.

129. Bray, "Can we Dispense with Chalcedon," 2, implies that *any* objections raised against Chalcedon are calling for either a "complete overhaul" or "a recognition of theological pluralism in the area of christology." Neither view is advocated here. As Robichaux, "Pneumatic Person of Christ," 3, comments, "For all its propriety regarding the person of Christ, Chalcedon suffers from inherent weaknesses. These, probably more than complaints about Hellenic theology, motivate the new christologies."

130. Hooker, "Chalcedon and the New Testament," 73–93.

131. Rosato, "Spirit-christology: Ambiguity and Promise," 423–49, also rails against the philosophical language of Chalcedon. He lists doctrinal relevance and New Testament precision as the two main reasons for the rise of Spirit Christologies today.

132. This argument has been the most persistent amongst more liberal scholars. Many suggest that there is no ontological Christology in Scripture, and that the Gospel of John is historically unreliable and so inadmissible. See Robinson, *Honest to God*, 74 and Hick, *Myth of God Incarnate*, for the classic treatment of this theme. More conservative scholars merely claim that Chalcedon is overly ontological *if it is our only standard of Christological method*. What I am suggesting is a complementary emphasis on functional Christology alongside that of our dominant ontological Christology. Obviously, there can be *no* functional Christology without a corresponding ontological one anyway. See chapter 2.

Third, and a derivative of the second point, there is an imposed doctrine of immutability thrust onto God. Greek thought presents a fundamental distinction between the world of becoming and the world of being; the former being inferior, if not evil. To the Greek mind it was inconceivable that God could belong to the world of becoming, therefore God was immutable or incapable of any sort of change. To suggest change was to imply that either God became less perfect, hence ceased to be God, or that he was not perfect in the first place, hence he never was God. It is argued that the God of the Bible, based on its internal evidence alone, is not immutable. Many argue that the Chalcedonian Definition presupposes God's immutability and impassibility, said to be established *a priori* and taken to the Word of God, rather than being derived from it.[133] This trend was highlighted through the Apologists adoption of the Hellenistic *logos* concept into their Christology.[134]

A fourth criticism is Chalcedon's allegedly inherent dualism. This too is a direct consequence of the former point; if God cannot change or suffer then surely he cannot really become human. Lane, in suggesting this criticism, does not shrink from the paradox that the incarnation inevitably provides but he does state that "the paradox of impassable passion arises not from the Christian revelation itself but from its conflict with Greek philosophy."[135] To circumvent this paradox Chalcedon, and the Father's following the council, uphold Jesus as both active in the heavens as the divine Son and active on earth as the God-man. Even on earth the picture of Christ is dualistic—at times he acts as God, at other times he acts as man. This dualism is foreign to the New Testament portrait of Christ.

Finally, the charge of Docetism is frequently made.[136] "If the immutability and impassability of God inevitably led Chalcedon to a

---

133. This is the most serious challenge that Lane, "Christology Beyond Chalcedon," 265–67, makes against the Chalcedonian Definition.

134. This is not to imply that God is passible but that impassibility is not a philosophical predicate read into the economy. See the excellent treatment in Bloesch, *God The Almighty*, 203–40, along with Weinandy, *Does God Change?* and *Does God Suffer?*

135. Lane, "Christology Beyond Chalcedon," 265–67.

136. These two points, Docetism and dualism are abiding criticisms of the Definition. Olaf Hansen, "Spirit Christology," 173, writes, "the dilemma, constituted by Chalcedon's distinction between the 'who' as the personal object implied in the name and the 'what' as the qualities or specific personality traits, is that we are caught between dualism and docetism." Hansen rightly considers the Definition as safeguarding three vital dogmas: the unity of God, the divinity of Christ and the unity of Christ's person (ibid., 174).

dualistic portrait of Christ the most serious consequence of this dualism is the undermining of his true humanity."[137] Chalcedon succeeded in defending the true deity and humanity of Christ in the one person. Unfortunately, many believe Chalcedon did not succeed in maintaining a practical belief in Christ as *fully* human. The Definition makes a theoretical acknowledgement of the human limitations of Christ but in practice it denies them (in much the same way as we saw in the work of Athanasius). "The problem with Chalcedon is not that it affirms the biblical paradox of God accepting human limitations but that it effectively denies these limitations."[138]

Throughout our survey we have witnessed the truth of many of these criticisms. However, does this mean that Chalcedon must be abandoned in contemporary Christology? Surely not. Knox provides a good summary as to why Chalcedon is a good confession but not the definitive word on Christology.

> . . . if the gospel of God's deed in Christ had to be expressed as a metaphysical or quasi-metaphysical proposition, this formulation of it was as adequate as any could be; we may be persuaded that if we had been at Chalcedon we should have found ourselves heartily concurring with it. [However] the consequence is that innumerable Christians, loyal to the Church and its traditions find themselves utterly perplexed as to what they are expected to think—being told, as they understand it, that Jesus was ignorant as a man must be but at the same time omniscient as only God is; that he was both limited in power . . . and also omnipotent; that he was divinely impregnable and serene in goodness but was also tried and tested and tempted as a man must be and only a man can be.[139]

Implicit in the criticisms of Chalcedon by many of these authors is a critique of the underlying Logos Christology. The merit of Logos Christology, which had its origins with the Apologists of the second century and which prevailed against modalism, is that it is essentially biblical, and it asserts the differentiation of Father and Son within the

---

137. Lane, "Christology Beyond Chalcedon," 268–69.

138. ibid., 270. He goes on to say "The affirmation that the historical Jesus was omniscient and omnipotent, which undermines his participation in human weakness and limitations, is not one half of a biblical paradox but an alien intrusion foreign to the New Testament," (ibid., 270).

139. Knox, *Humanity and Divinity of Christ*, 100.

Godhead. The Logos doctrine of the Apologists, subsequently adopted by Patristic theology,[140] was able to show how the Son could be thought of as different from the Father and yet together with him as a single God. However, the use of Chalcedonian Christological definitions in interpreting the Gospel portraits of Jesus has tended to restrict the access of modern Christians to the man Jesus in his historical actuality. The church cannot deny the humanity of Jesus since it "remembers" Jesus and it cannot deny the divinity since it knows him as the divine Lord. But we experience Jesus with those two natures together, not abstracted apart or even philosophically explained.

Now we must broach the essential question: Are we to dispense with Logos Christology in the construction of a contemporary Christology? My answer is a resounding "NO," and for various reasons. Logos Christology can clarify Jesus's unity with the Father without blurring the distinction between them, or the surrender of monotheism. Furthermore, it made the divinity present in Jesus, familiar to Hellenistic society as a power that was decisive for its conception of the world. Logos Christology succeeded in explaining the role of the preexistent Son of God in mediating creation, to which the New Testament testifies. The universal significance of God's revelation in Jesus is the natural consequence when the Logos, the foundation of the world's being, has appeared in his fullness in Jesus. However, Logos Christology's subsequent reflection upon Divine self-revelation is not to be accepted without criticism.

The weaknesses of Logos Christology are many. First, the unity of the Logos with God cannot be so strictly conceived in the categories of Platonic cosmology as this tended towards subordinationism.[141] Patristic Christology, throughout the time of the Arian controversy, was occupied with the problem of how to establish the equality of the Logos' deity with that of the Father, and thus to counteract the subordinationist tendency of the Logos doctrine itself. The church Fathers were driven by soteriological reasons to affirm that Jesus possesses equal deity with the Father. But there was little possibility of doing justice to this soteriological concern within the framework of Logos Christology. The inner logic of the Logos doctrine supported Arius rather than Athanasius. "Because the

---

140. Pannenberg, *Jesus*, 160.

141. This was compounded in the scholastic era through the adoption into theology of Aristotelian epistemology. See Weinandy, *Father's Spirit of Sonship*, and for the legacy of Aristotelianism in Protestantism. Cf. Clifford, *Atonement and Justification*, 95–110.

procession of the Logos means the first step of creation and the Logos is thus the first creature, a subordinationist tendency belonged to the Platonically conceived Logos doctrine from the very beginning."[142]

Pannenberg identifies a second weakness of Logos Christology, the "precarious loosening" of the connection of the Son's divinity with Jesus of Nazareth, God's historical revelation.[143] He highlights Tatian's ability to develop his whole Logos doctrine without saying anything about Jesus Christ! Sadly this has been a tendency in much modern Christology as well as we shall have occasion to see.

Third, there is the unbroken influence that the philosophical concept of God, the conception of an unchangeable and simple origin (*archē*) of the world at hand, attained in the centre of Christian theology through Logos Christology.[144] The argument is not about developing a philosophical construct to explain God, which was necessary in the Hellenistic world into which the gospel went. The one God is revealed in the person and history of Jesus differently than he had been conceived by philosophy. This difference between the biblical God revealed in the history of Jesus, and Greek philosophy's concept of *god*, did not achieve decisive significance in Logos Christology. Rather, the Logos Christology contributed to the obscuring of this problem because of its thought structure which relied on patterns of philosophical questioning.[145]

Turning its attention away from the full deity of the Son as elucidated at Nicaea, Chalcedon concentrated on the historical life of Jesus and the problem of how the same person could be both God and man. Amid the many problems Chalcedon has been blamed for (many wrongly), perhaps the most serious problem with Chalcedonian Christology is that it has encouraged the wrong kind of Christology, exclusively from above. It

---

142. Pannenberg, *Jesus*, 164.

143. Ibid., 165.

144. Ibid.

145. Ibid., 165–66. Pannenberg goes on to discuss the impossibility of reviving the Logos Christology today—as the Fathers did. For that would entail contemporary analogies—i.e., Jesus Christ is the embodiment of Einstein's theory or of some other inclusive physical law, etc., ibid., 166. It must also be pointed out that Pannenberg does not consider any form of Spirit Christology to be a viable option as it inevitably, in his opinion, tends to adoptionism, (ibid., 120–21). This is largely due to his insistence on the resurrection as the sole determiner of Christ's identity. However, as we will argue, a Spirit Christology is entirely compatible with the resurrection as a starting point and retroactively working back (and forward) from there. See chapter 4.

has encouraged the church to start with the deity of the Son of God and then to fit the (problem of his) humanity into the divinity. At all costs the divinity must remain inviolate, while the humanity may be shortchanged.[146] The result is an inadequacy in the classic scholastic teaching of Christology. "All too often traditional presentations of Christology have grossly neglected or totally ignored the role of the Holy Spirit in their expositions of the mystery of Christ, who reveals himself both as the incarnate Word of God and as the glorified and exalted Son of Man."[147] The organic or "normative" link of pneumatology with Christology has been lost or ignored. It is this normative link that needs to once again be incorporated into contemporary Christology if it is to be both biblical and capable of speaking to today's culture. Spirit Christology proposes to be a paradigm that best suits the construction of this normative link.

Considering these criticisms the following chapter will present a broad outline of a new paradigm in contemporary Christology and indeed for the other *loci* of systematic theology by establishing its biblical foundations.

---

146. Fuller and Perkins, *Who is This Christ?* 126.
147. Bobrinskoy, "Indwelling of the Spirit in Christ," 49.

4

Interpreting the Evidence

Christology in New Testament Scholarship

> *For the presentation of Jesus in the New Testament is in fact itself a representation: it resembles a painting more closely than it does a photograph.*
>
> —Jaroslav Pelikan

> *His awareness of being uniquely possessed and used by divine Spirit was the mainspring of his mission and the key to its effectiveness.*
>
> —James D. G. Dunn

> *The Holy Spirit is the Spirit of Jesus and he comes to us clothed in Christ's humanity, not to make us super-spiritual saints, or ascetic anchorites, or miracle-mongering super-naturalists, or chandelier-swinging fanatics—but quite simply to make us men.*
>
> —Thomas A. Smail

AS WE NOW CONSIDER more closely New Testament Christology one question predominates: "Who is Jesus?" Or more specifically: "How is God's presence in Jesus of Nazareth to be understood?" The approaches to answering this question have been many and varied. As we have seen, foremost in determining the identity of Christ within the history of theology, has been the practice of a Christology from above. Hence a Trinitarian ontology is presupposed and read back into the accounts of Jesus's life. This is the classical approach of a Logos Christology. What this approach apparently ignores is how and why the earliest communities of faith came to a belief in the deity of Jesus Christ in the first place.[1]

---

1. An attempt to answer the why of early Christian worship of Jesus is the monograph by Turner, *Lord of the Spirit*.

This chapter surveys the ways biblical scholarship has developed to address and assess the biblical testimony to this answer. Specifically, the issues of doctrinal development are considered and a specific retroactive hermeneutic is proposed in order to best read the biblical testimony to Jesus's unique identity. In chapter Five key disclosure episodes in the life of Jesus are examined in detail.

In starting his Christology from below, specifically on the historicity of the resurrection, Wolfhart Pannenberg's approach has been hailed as ushering in a new era in European Protestant theology.[2] This basic program is shared by a Spirit Christology. Within New Testament scholarship the Christological enterprise has been approached differently. Given the almost universal acknowledgement that the resurrection changed the perspective of the early church considerably, New Testament scholarship asks, "How is the Jesus of history related to the Christ of faith?" The answer to this question is considered to be "the most critical issue in theology today—the question of the historical Jesus and the part that it plays in our knowledge of God."[3] Within the confines of this chapter it is impossible to outline, let alone analyze, the developments that are taking place in biblical studies so it must suffice to note a representative selection as I outline the thesis of a Spirit Christology. I shall begin with a brief review of some of the significant writing on Jesus within the last one hundred or so years. This story has been told many times and there is little to add to what has been written elsewhere.[4] However, an outline will show where my proposal fits on the theological map.[5]

2. Craig, *Assessing the New Testament Evidence*, xiii.

3. Brown, "Christology and the Quest of the Historical Jesus," 67, and Guelich, "Gospels," 117–25, who traces the change in perspective of Gospel scholars in terms of three artistic expressions, 1) the snapshot, 2) the portrait, and 3) the abstract painting. Also important here is Wright, *Challenge of Jesus*.

4. For an introduction to the literature see Schweitzer, *Quest for the Historical Jesus*; Meyer, *Aims of Jesus*; Tatum, *In Quest of Jesus*; Brown, *Jesus in European Protestant Thought*; and Wright, *Jesus and the Victory of God*.

5. While my primary concern is the theological presentation of the Evangelists as we find them in the canon and not the historical credibility of the canon *per se*, the one follows logically from the other. I am thus presupposing the historical accuracy of the New Testament witness and refer the reader interested primarily in the historicity of the New Testament to a few of the excellent resources available. All of the following contain extensive bibliographies to refer the reader further: Craig, *Assessing the New Testament Evidence*; Blomberg, *Historical Reliability of the Gospels*; Barnett, *Jesus and the Logic of History*; Barnett, *Is the New Testament History?*; Bruce, *New Testament Documents*; Marshall, *I Believe in the Historical Jesus*; France, *Evidence for Jesus*; Hagner,

APPROACHES TO CHRISTOLOGY
IN NEW TESTAMENT SCHOLARSHIP

How has New Testament scholarship understood the relationship between the Jesus of history and the Christ of faith?[6] The simple answer is by recognizing a development of understanding within both the New Testament itself, and the community of faith.[7] Witherington, following a diachronic survey of the New Testament, argues that any similar approach will inevitably come up with a development within New Testament Christology.

> It should be clear from what we have said to this point that whenever one talks about the development of New Testament christologies, one is conceding at the outset that the full significance of Jesus did not just dawn on Christians immediately after the Easter experiences. That awareness came gradually to full fruition.[8]

New Testament scholarship now almost universally no longer speaks of *a* New Testament Christology. Instead it speaks of multiple Christ*ologies*.[9] "There was a wide variety of terms and concepts used by the writers of the New Testament to bring out the significance of Jesus, and so we must speak of Christologies of and in the New Testament."[10]

While the fact of development is not in dispute, the precise nature of this development is. The term "development" lends itself to two very different interpretations. By development and Christologies we may be

---

"Interpreting the Gospels," 23–37. For a concise survey of the historical question and an evangelical response, see Macleod, *Person of Christ*, 109–20. I also presuppose what has come to be termed the critical realist position. On critical realism in addition to the above, see Wright, *New Testament and the People of God*, 15–16, 31–36, 61–64; Meyer, *Critical Realism and the New Testament*; Erickson, *Word Became Flesh*; Bockmuehl, *This Jesus*; and Schwarz, *Christology*.

6. See a survey of the three "Quests" in Brown, "Person of Christ," vol. 3, 781–801.

7. Dunn, *Unity and Diversity in the New Testament*, 205–6f., provides a brief review of the situation regarding the continuity between the historical Jesus and the kerygmatic Christ.

8. Witherington, *Many Faces of the Christ*, 8.

9. There is a narrative character to much of the Christological discussion of the New Testament. Brown, *Introduction to New Testament Christology*, 105, points out that Christological terms and ideas tend to cluster around certain moments in the career of Jesus. He speaks of Parousia Christology, Resurrection Christology, Ministry Christology, and Birth Christology.

10. Witherington, *Many Faces of the Christ*, 3.

saying that there is a clear development of ideas concerning the person of Christ witnessed in the Gospels in the form of an *evolutionary* movement or, a development by accretion, from one Christology to another, repeated several times. An evolutionary hypothesis was taken up and applied by the original Quest for the historical Jesus,[11] and is again finding new support amongst New Testament scholars, ranging from advocates of the Jesus seminar to James Dunn.[12] Or we may simply be saying that multiple Christologies merely imply multiple *perspectives* on one cohesive theme, an unfolding in later works of what was already present although implicit in earlier works.[13] This unfolding or organic development has been taken up by conservative scholars.[14] After surveying the differences between these two views of development I will show how and why a Spirit Christology works with the concept of unfolding rather than accretion.[15] This will enable us to consider several episodes in the life of Christ in order to bring out the force of the Gospels's presentation of the person of Jesus Christ, from the perspective of a Spirit Christology.

Within New Testament scholarship three approaches have been adopted to account for the historical Jesus and the Christ of faith. First, the latter nineteenth century was content to let the Jesus of history and the Christ of faith fall apart and to abandon the latter to the former. Liberal Protestants followed this line settling for the gospel *of* Jesus—a gospel where Jesus himself played no role such as was ascribed to him by post-Easter faith. The gospel of Jesus that they believed in was one in which

---

11. Starting in the late 1800s and developed with Schweitzer's work, *Quest for the Historical Jesus*. For a full survey and critique, see Brown, *Jesus in European Protestant Thought*, and Wright, *Jesus and the Victory of God*.

12. See *Five Gospels*; Mack, *Myth of Innocence: Lost Gospel*; and Crossan, *Historical Jesus*. For a very different treatment, see Dunn, *Christology in the Making*; *Unity and Diversity in the New Testament*; and "Making of Christology—Evolution or Unfolding?" 437–52.

13. The concept of "unfolding" was first put forward by Newman, *Essay on the Development of Christian Doctrine*.

14. See C. Moule, *Origin of Christology*; Marshall, *Origins of New Testament Christology*; and Hengel, *Son of God*.

15. While our investigation is concentrated on Christology and specifically the Gospels a similar line of investigation of development has been pursued within Pauline studies. See the seminal work of Sabatier, *Apostle Paul*; Hurd, *Origin of 1 Corinthians*, 8–9 ns. 2, 3; 11, n. 1; Wrede, *Paul*; Wiles, *Remaking of Christian Doctrine*; and Longenecker, "On the Concept of Development in Pauline Thought," 195–207.

Jesus was simply the first or the foremost to proclaim and live by ideals that the nineteenth century considered to be of abiding value. Jesus was the great exemplar, the first Christian.[16]

The second attempt tried to blur the distinction between the gospel of Jesus and the *kerygma* of Paul. This was achieved by claiming the *kerygmatic* Christ is the only one with whom we have to deal. It is not necessary or possible to get behind the *kerygmatic* Christ to a historical Jesus. Martin Kähler argued for this basic position, and he had considerable influence on the biblical theology movement which dominated the first half of the twentieth century.[17] The alternative way was the attempt to demythologize the *kerygma-(ta)* of the early church-(es). The *kerygma* of Christianity becomes a form of all purpose message whose proclamation of Jesus is ultimately an accident of history.[18]

The third alternative was the attempt to uncover or trace the development from the message of Jesus to the *kerygma* about Christ. Advocates of this approach are confident that enough about the historical Jesus is available to trace the broad outlines or contours of his identity and mission, and then endeavor to discover whether any of these are sufficient to explain some or part of the characteristic Christological emphases of the early *kerygma*. Within this approach there is a broad spectrum which may be further broken down into the radical, conservative, and new perspectives.[19]

16. The classic treatment being that of Harnack, *What is Christianity?*

17. Kähler insisted that the real Christ is the Christ of faith and condemned approaches to get behind the tradition. He was one of a number of scholars who were somewhat ahead of their time. He shares this distinction with Newman whom we have already mentioned and Johann C. K. von Hofmann who developed *Heilsgeschichte* theology, a conservative alternative to an evolutionary development of doctrine. Hofmann founded the Erlangen School which has found something of a renaissance since the 1970s.

18. Bultmann's, *Theology of the New Testament*, provides the zenith of this approach. His work is anti-historical in the traditional sense of history, and presents a development by accretion. He proposes the now debunked Gnostic-redeemer myth as the background to the development of the Christ of faith. He goes so far as to exclude Jesus himself from the subject matter of New Testament theology. Bultmann is joined by Lessing and Kierkegaard. Their minimalist answers leave little if any real knowledge of the historical Jesus. Furthermore, they consider this knowledge to be inconsequential to faith. Lessing's famous phrase to summarize his position is "accidental truths of history can never become the proof of necessary truths of reason."

19. For a complete survey, see Wright, *Jesus and the Victory of God*, and on a more popular level Witherington, *Jesus Quest*.

Of the three approaches above the first two have given up any hope of establishing the *kerygma* of Christianity in the historical Jesus. The first opts for a Jesus whose significance at the end of the day is less than that characteristically ascribed to him by Christianity. The other opts for a *kerygmatic* Christ who in his central significance has no discernible connection with the historical Jesus. "Only the third alternative offers the possibility of a more positive answer—of a continuity between the message of Jesus and the kerygma of earliest Christianity which provides an anchor point for the early church's claims about Christ in the history of the man Jesus of Nazareth, of a unity between kerygmatic Christ and historical Jesus which alone can hold the diverse forms of Christianity together as one."[20] We shall consider this third alternative in more detail later, as a Spirit Christology is one of the many new perspectives this "third Quest" offers.[21] However, before we turn in more detail to a Spirit Christology in Scripture we shall consider the issue of the development of doctrine, particularly Christology.

DEVELOPMENTAL THEORIES

Before presenting my own contribution to Christology I must first engage in some grateful and critical dialogue with my predecessors. Such a critical dialogue necessarily involves being selective. The material from the Bible, exegetes, philosophers, and theologians is complex and often controversial.[22] The following introduces various contributions to Christology with the aim of finding my own tiny accents in a systematic Christology which finds its primary interpretative key in the relationship between Jesus and the Spirit, and not with the aim of writing a complete history of Christology.

Evolutionary Development—The Radical Spectrum

For many scholars divinity is a predicate imposed upon the earthly Jesus by the post-resurrection community of faith. Hence, the Christ of

---

20. Dunn, *Unity and Diversity in the New Testament*, 209.

21. I am using the term "third Quest" in a much broader sense than the original narrow sense that Wright meant when he coined the term. See his *Jesus and the Victory of God*, 83, and *New Testament and the People of God*.

22. In the preface to *Origins of New Testament Christology*, 7, Marshall rightly speaks of Christology as being "a subject vast in scope, unencompassable in its bibliography and daunting in its problems."

faith is read back into the Jesus of history; the historic accounts of Jesus Christ have really become "mythical stories" that have more in common with the second century community of faith than with the earthly Jesus of Nazareth.[23] Accordingly, the New Testament is said to evidence a considerable amount of development by accretion when it comes to Christology.

A major modern proponent of this view of development is the New Testament scholar James Dunn[24] who, for example, rejects seeing John's pre-existence of the Son as simply the fuller apprehension of what had always been true, the making explicit of what had always been implicit in earlier formulations.[25] In addition, he rejects the Trinitarianism of the orthodox councils as being the inevitable progressive unfolding of what had always been, in fact, integral to the whole of New Testament theology. This, Dunn believes, creates a canon within the Canon. In order to recognize the diversity of development within the Canon he argues against a development along any single trajectory, presenting this development less like a pipeline and more like successive radii added to a sphere, or branches growing out of the one trunk. Thus, Dunn is presenting a development by accretion derived from a single source, the Canon. This canon, however, evidences a variety of symbols, pictures, and representations of the identity of Jesus Christ, and each of them is worthy of development, even when the subsequent developments are mutually exclusive. Dunn accuses orthodox Christianity of canonizing certain developments to the relative neglect of others.[26]

Dunn sees the unity between the Jesus of history and the *kerygmatic* Christ residing in the many religious experiences shared by Jesus

---

23. For instance Harnack, *What is Christianity?*; Bousset, *Kyrios Christos*; Bultmann, *Theology of the New Testament*, 1.§15; and Casey, *From Jewish Prophet to Gentile God*. Although not all of the same school, they each proposed an evolutionary development of Christology.

24. Dunn does not consider his position to be the same as Newman's. He seems to consider Newman's thesis as organic development more than evolutionary though. Dunn, *Unity and Diversity in the New Testament*, 380.

25. Dunn, *Christology in the Making*, 264. See a critique of Dunn's views on Johannine Christology by Gruenler, *New Approaches to Jesus and the Gospels*, 98.

26. I agree to a point. Logos Christology has tended to gain canonical status while Spirit Christology has traditionally been viewed as heterodox even though both are present in the Canon itself. However, this does not mean the two are incompatible.

and the earliest communities.[27] This unity is not merely a post-Easter theological creation, but has firm anchor points in the pre-Easter history of Jesus. In no way does this intimate that the post-Easter community merely parroted the pre-Easter message of Jesus; rather the Easter event was the central significance in decisively determining and shaping the post-Easter *kerygma*. The resurrection event was the vindication Jesus looked forward to and what the early church needed. As Dunn says, "there are sufficiently clear foreshadowings of the centrality of the kerygmatic Christ in the self-understanding of Jesus during his ministry for us to recognize the kerygmata of the early churches as a development from Jesus's own proclamation in the light of his resurrection."[28]

More specifically, Dunn finds the unifying strand of this development to be the unity between the historical Jesus and the exalted Christ.[29] That is "the recognition that the divine power through which they now worshipped and were encountered and accepted by God was one and the same person, Jesus, the man, the Christ, the Son of God, the Lord, the life-giving Spirit . . . the cohesive focal point was Jesus, the man, the exalted one."[30] He sees differing patterns of belief woven into the unifying strand of the person of Jesus Christ in differing settings and communities. These differences were by no means complementary, in fact, they frequently clashed. Thus, Dunn can claim that "there was no single form of Christianity in the first century."[31] While all Christianity centered on Jesus Christ, not all expressed his humanity and divinity in the same way. Often these diverse presentations collided with each other, as seen between Jewish and Hellenistic Christianity. In many instances the result was a synthesis or amalgam of Christologies. Dunn sees irreconcilable diversity within the New Testament at many points. In this regard he believes:

---

27. He outlines this development in his book *Unity and Diversity in the New Testament*, along with his earlier work *Jesus and the Spirit*.

28. Dunn, *Unity and Diversity in the New Testament*, 216. This is an important point, for the resurrection in itself, contra Pannenberg's thesis, is insufficient to count for the worship of Jesus. The entire incarnation, being the accounts of the historical Jesus, is also vital. This point is expressed succinctly by Wright, *Challenge of Jesus*, 52–69.

29. Ibid., 369.

30. Ibid.

31. Ibid., 373.

Christology should not be narrowly confined to one particular assessment of Christ, nor should it insist on squeezing all the different NT conceptualizations into one particular "shape," but it should recognize that from the first, the significance of Christ could only be apprehended by a diversity of formulations which though not always strictly compatible with each other were not regarded as rendering each other invalid . . . if the NT does serve as a norm, the truth of Christ will be found in the individual emphasis of the different NT formulations as much as in that which unites them.[32]

Accordingly, Dunn views these early Christologies as a kind of spectrum, highlighting the diversity of each presentation. He goes so far as to conclude, "if the distinctive unifying strand running through the NT and first-century Christianity is narrow, the surrounding diversity is broad and its outer margins are not always readily discernible. An identifiable unity, yes; but orthodoxy, whether in concept or actuality, no."[33] Dunn views this diversity as residing within the Canon itself, therefore he is pressed to discuss the relevancy or otherwise of the Canon for today.[34] He finishes up affirming the value of a Canon but it must be normative for Christianity in the sense that if the Canon models a diversity within a unity, albeit a diversity unable to be reconciled, then Christianity, and especially Christology, must also be characterized by diversity.[35]

This diversity reveals the need for the continued development of doctrine. By this Dunn means contextualization, but he speaks of reinterpreting Christ for new situations. By development he does not mean a straight line of development, of one idea growing out of another, as in Newman's thesis,[36] and he is not advocating the idea of an unfolding

32. Dunn, *Christology in the Making*, 267.
33. Dunn, *Unity and Diversity in the New Testament*, 374.
34. Ibid.
35. One wonders how Dunn can find it acceptable for himself and others to engage in biblical-systematic theology at all! Surely this is to place a straight-jacket fit on the New Testament witness in his view. It must be said that Dunn is faithful to his method. Gruenler, *New Approaches to Jesus and the Gospels*, 104–5, has a page of quotations from Dunn's *Christology in the Making* highlighting the diversity of statements made in his book with no attempt to clarify the many contradictions. What these seem to amount to is an uncertainty on Dunn's part as to what he believes can and cannot be said to be authentic sayings of Jesus. Therefore Dunn's insistence against all ideas of preexistence is seriously weakened.
36. Dunn, *Unity and Diversity in the New Testament*, 380. Cf. Newman, *Essay on the Development of Christian Doctrine*. See Toon, *Development of Doctrine in the Church*,

development, where, one might argue, the Johannine Christology of personal pre-existence is making more explicit what was implicit in earlier formulations.[37] Dunn concludes that the New Testament developments are no more authoritative or binding for us than our own "branching out" of Christological ideas and developments![38] "The more we believe that the Spirit of God inspired the writers of the NT to speak the word of God to people of the 60s, 70s, 80s or 90s of the first century AD, reinterpreting faith and life-style diversely to diverse circumstances, the more acceptance of the NT Canon requires us to be open to the Spirit to reinterpret in similar or equivalent ways in the twentieth century."[39]

These comments need to be read in light of his earlier work, *Jesus and the Spirit*. Dunn investigates the origins of the doctrine of the incarnation, attempting to go back to the New Testament itself and hearing its Christology untainted by the Christological developments of the first five centuries, which so greatly influence our reading of the New Testament (a difficult task at best). To achieve this he examines titles and conceptions used by the New Testament authors to describe the significance of Jesus (for example: "Son of God"; "Son of man"; "last Adam"; "Spirit"; "Angel"; "Wisdom"; and "Word"). He claims that the earliest Christianity traced Jesus's sonship to his resurrection, with each writer pushing sonship back into the life of Jesus; Paul—to Jesus's death, Mark—to Jesus's baptism/anointing, Matthew and Luke—to Jesus's supernatural conception, the writer of Hebrews—to Jesus's impersonal pre-existence

---

where he surveys the developmental ideas from John H. Newman to James B. Mozley, Benjamin B. Warfield, Karl Rahner, and Edward Schillebeeckx (among others). God's revelation in Scripture is the paradigm; doctrinal formulations are successive elaborations of that paradigm in different historical and cultural contexts, (ibid., 115). Toon goes on to give his own Evangelical view of development which accords well with what I am advocating here. Also of considerable use are Pelikan, *Historical Theology*, and *Development of Christian Doctrine*.

37. "Or that the orthodox Trinitarianism of the Councils was simply the inevitable progressive unfolding of what had always been in fact integral to the whole of NT theology," Dunn, *Unity and Diversity in the New Testament*, 380.

38. Although Dunn earlier made the point that the diversity of the New Testament indicates the boundaries or extremes of allowable diversity. An inherent contradiction is evident here. He apparently resolves the contradiction in his own mind by referring to the Canon as the fixed pole of the dialogue between past history and present experience. Dunn, *Unity and Diversity in the New Testament*, 381–82.

39. Ibid.

(i.e., Philo's Platonism),⁴⁰ and finally John—to Jesus's pre-existence/incarnation, personal Logos.⁴¹

In tracing this line of development, Dunn stands within a long tradition that views pre-existence as ideal, as opposed to real. The Enlightenment mindset and Schleiermacher became some of its most able proponents.⁴² Schleiermacher's Christology was one of pure inspiration, not incarnation:⁴³ Jesus is the God-filled man not the God-man. The History-of-religions school looked for Hellenistic parallels of pre-existent and incarnational myths and explained Christianity in light of them; hence the preexistent attributions to Jesus are merely an attempt to push his divine status earlier and earlier.⁴⁴ Bultmann popularized this theory particularly in relation to the Gnostic-redeemer myth which he identified with the origins of the New Testament Jesus story.⁴⁵ John Knox does acknowledge pre-existence even as early as Paul but this, he argues, is not literal but "story," language used to convey the idea that in *some vague sense* God was in Christ.⁴⁶ More recently John Macquarie has argued for ideal pre-existence—Jesus was foreknown in the mind of

---

40. It is difficult not to conclude that Dunn has fallen into his own trap and reinterpreted the book of Hebrews in light of Platonic philosophy rather than letting the book speak for itself. As the Church has read Hebrews the overwhelming consensus has not been a belief in an impersonal pre-existence but in a dynamic and relational God.

41. In this way Dunn is squarely committed from the outset to an evolutionary view of development. See his *Christology in the Making*, 248ff. Dunn believes New Testament Christology develops from the abstraction of the "message" to the personalizing of Word as Christ himself. See the critique of Gruenler, *New Approaches to Jesus and the Gospels*, 88f.

42. Along with Romanticism. See Packer, "Modern View of Jesus' in *Collected Shorter Writings of J. I. Packer: Volume 1*, 65–72.

43. Schleiermacher, *Christian Faith*.

44. This despite the fact that there simply was not enough time for this kind of development to occur.

45. Hengel, *Son of God*, refutes the Gnostic redeemer myth and other theories of the history-of-religions school. Also of use is France, "Worship of Jesus," 19–23. France begins with an overview of the idea of the search for "parallels" to the cultural background of the New Testament. Taking his cue from the presidential address of Samual Sandmel he gives four ways in which parallels can be abused. His point is that even if these "parallels" are found, how do we know if they actually influenced the New Testament writings? Did they come from a relevant culture? Are they real parallels? And is a parallel necessarily a source or influence? He uses the idea of Wisdom as an example.

46. Knox, *Humanity and Divinity of Christ*, 107–8. In Knox's developmental scheme there are four movements, 1) adoptionism, 2) kenoticism, 3) docetism, and finally 4) incarnationism.

God eternally.[47] One radical exponent of this development is John Hick[48] who follows the lead of Schleiermacher, Strauss and Harnack (liberal Protestantism).[49] Jesus's importance lies in his words not his works: his words were not terribly unique so neither was Jesus. Jesus is merely the model of Godly ethical activity. Clearly Dunn's position is not identical to those above, however it must be understood as residing within the broad category of an evolutionary development of Christology.[50]

Organic Development—The Conservative Spectrum

While diversity and development within the New Testament is acknowledged by all biblical scholars, we may argue against Dunn and others that this diversity and development need not, and should not, imply contradiction or correction of earlier statements made by later ones.[51] This account considers the development of Christology within both Scripture and history to be that of an organic development, or more correctly an organic unfolding as summed up by David Wells:

> Indubitably there is a development in the way that Jesus, as a human and divine, is treated in the New Testament . . . it is not a development from one kind of Christology to another, more exalted kind. There is one Christology for which different terms and conceptualities are employed. There is a terminological and theological diversity within a doctrinal unity.[52]

---

47. See his *Jesus Christ in Modern Thought*, 57.
48. Hick, *Metaphor of God Incarnate*.
49. Strauss, *Life of Jesus*; and Harnack, *History of Dogma*.
50. See his treatment of the texts such as Phil 1:6–11 in Dunn, *Christology in the Making*, 114. In response to Dunn's interpretation of these texts, see Rowden, *Christ the Lord*. Also worthy of note is Cullmann, *Christology of the New Testament*, 321, who constructs a three step process in the development of New Testament Christology, or what he calls the Christological *Heilsgeschichte*. He argues that the New Testament offers no Christological synthesis, however the various concepts are not contradictory but cyclic, or rather, spiral in method. For a similar treatment see the developmental theory of Grant, *Introduction to New Testament Thought*.
51. Witherington, *Many Faces of the Christ*, 227, also comes to the conclusion that there are various Christologies in the New Testament which do not all blend or dovetail together nicely. That does not mean that they are contradictory. Rather, they show diversity.
52. Wells, *Person of Christ*, 65.

David Wenham recognizes diversity, but within an overall unity.[53] He says the case for unity is not as shaky as Dunn and others would suggest and points to the following: Jesus did have a unique filial consciousness evidenced by his use of "Abba" (Mark 14:36; cf., Gal 4:6; Rom 8:15). The synoptic Gospels are not as far from John as is alleged. Matthew and Luke include the so-called "Johannine bolt from the blue" (Matt 11:27/Luke 10:22). While this language is not common it is not totally foreign to either evangelist (cf., Mark 13:32). The evolutionary line of development toward Johannine Christology is upset by the saying of Matthew 11:27/Luke 10:22, and even more so by Paul's Epistles. Dunn rejects pre-existence in Paul but his objections are overstated.[54] In these earliest books of the New Testament the community already exhibits a firm belief in the complete deity of Jesus of Nazareth (i.e., Phil 2:5–11; Col 1:15–20; 2 Cor 8:9).[55] This argues against the mistaken idea that the silence of an author must be equated with ignorance of an idea.

Recent New Testament scholarship has used a variety of means to discern the identity of Jesus Christ.[56] These include the use of titu-

---

53. Wenham, "Unity and Diversity in the New Testament," in Ladd, *Theology of the New Testament*, 684–719.

54. Again I refer the reader to the exegesis of these passages in refutation of Dunn in Rowden, ed. *Christ the Lord*. Particularly France, "The Worship of Jesus: A Neglected Factor in Christological Debate?" 34, 35, who writes: "These are not seen as brilliant *tours de force*, formulating hitherto unheard-of ideas, but as the explicit theological working out of an estimate of Jesus which was already established in Christian devotion," and further: "Thus when Jewish Christians ultimately reached the stage of calling Jesus 'God,' in spite of all the inhibiting traditions of their culture, this was not a brash new doctrine, but the eventual outcome of a process of Christological development which can be traced throughout New Testament Christianity right back to the teaching and impact of Jesus himself." Also consult Hurst, "Re-Enter the Pre-Existent Christ in Philippians 2:5–11," 449–57, and Fuller, *Foundations of New Testament Christology*, 236 n. 10, for whom "the preexistence-incarnation christology is so widespread that it can hardly be called specifically Pauline." See also the discussion in *Where Christology Began*.

55. Bauckham, *God Crucified*, 27, writes, "I shall be arguing . . . that the highest possible Christology, the inclusion of Jesus in the unique divine identity, was central to the faith of the early church even before any of the New Testament writings were written, since it occurs in all of them." He does not deny some form of development in understanding Jesus's identity but makes the point clear that Jewish monotheism and high Christology were not in tension as many would argue. See the discussion in Torrance, *Space, Time and Resurrection*.

56. See Doriani, "Deity of Christ in the Synoptic Gospels," 333–50, what Blomberg, *Jesus and the Gospels*, 403–5, calls "indirect evidence."

lar Christology,⁵⁷ the miracles of Jesus,⁵⁸ worship in the early church,⁵⁹ opposition,⁶⁰ and more recently the Judaism of the time.⁶¹ While each of these approaches has its merits, none of them has proven to be comprehensive enough to act as an integrative framework that is capable of presenting all the New Testament teaching on the identity of Jesus in a balanced fashion. Indeed, it is difficult for any one framework to do so. This does not mean, however, that such a framework is not to be found. By presenting Spirit Christology as a new paradigm in systematic theology to complement our existing Logos Christology, such an integrative framework is now thought to be closer at hand. This claim will be investigated by utilizing a pneumatological hermeneutic.

---

57. See the defense of titular Christology in Hahn, *Titles of Jesus in Christology*. It was a mistaken idea of the place of titular christology that led Taylor, *Names of Jesus*, 1, to write "the question, who Jesus is, is approached best by considering how men named him, for it is by His names that He is revealed and known." It is now generally recognized that meaning does not reside in words alone, but rather in sentences. See Barr, *Semantics of Biblical Language*, 234. See the five-point critique of titular christology in Keck, "Toward the Renewal of New Testament Christology," 369–70.

58. For instance, see Betz, "Jesus as Divine Man," 114–33; Hengel, *Charismatic Leader and his Followers*; Kee, *Miracle and the Early Christian World*; and the fine work of Brown, *Miracles and the Critical Mind*, which contains an extensive bibliography, and Twelftree, *Jesus the Miracle Worker*, and ibid., *In the Name of Jesus*.

59. Scholars who are pursuing worship as a meaningful Christological insight include France, "Worship of Jesus," 50–70; Torrance, "Vicarious Humanity of Christ," 127–47, ibid., *Worship, Community, and the Triune God of Grace*; Wainwright, *Doxology*; and Hurtado, *One God, One Lord*; ibid., *Lord Jesus Christ*; and ibid., *How on Earth did Jesus Become a God?* Worship has not been overlooked by those who follow a Spirit Christology as evidenced by the work of Clark, "Spirit Christology in the Light of Eucharistic Theology," 270–84.

60. Dunn moved in this direction in his work *Partings of the Ways*. Colin Brown takes up this concept in *Miracles and the Critical Mind*, 293–325, and "Synoptic Miracle Stories," 55–76. He is also following a model of Spirit Christology by which he sees John's prophecy (Mark 1:8) as fulfilled by Jesus through the Spirit within his earthly ministry of exorcisms and miracles. See also the exhaustive contribution by Twelftree, *Jesus*.

61. See Sanders, *Jesus and Judaism*; Vermes, *Jesus the Jew*; Hagner, *Jewish Reclamation of Jesus*; Hengel, *Charismatic Leader and His Followers*; and Bauckham, *Jesus and the God of Israel*.

Interpreting the Evidence

PNEUMATOLOGICAL HERMENEUTICS AND DOCTRINAL DEVELOPMENT

A Retroactive Hermeneutic

Given the complexities involved in understanding the way to approach New Testament texts, the nature of doctrinal development, and the place of the Holy Spirit in relationship to Jesus Christ, a revised and nuanced hermeneutic is required. I propose such a nuanced hermeneutic here and then relate this to a way to understand doctrinal development. I have restricted myself to Johannine theology in order to keep the proposal concise.[62]

The role of the Holy Spirit has long been a neglected factor in contemporary hermeneutics. Major textbooks on biblical interpretation fail to address the role of the Holy Spirit, simply allude to pneumatology, or at best, offer one—or two-page summaries. Most biblical interpreters, however, intuitively grasp the significance of the Holy Spirit in the process of interpretation but struggle to articulate it. The present proposal contributes a partial articulation of the role of the Holy Spirit in interpretation and, in turn, doctrinal development, by adopting something I call a retroactive hermeneutic.[63] While the language is clumsy I trust the hermeneutic is robust.[64] A retroactive hermeneutic recognizes that the experienced presence of Christ in the Spirit, post-Easter, brought to mind the life of Jesus; thereby reawakening remembrances of his life, words, and deeds. In this sense, the present and the past correspond such that the present does not contradict the past, nor vice-versa. This same retroactive process is available for the exegete today.

We see this retroactive hermeneutic clearly illustrated in the Johannine literature. John brings the dialectic between the historical

---

62. An alternate version of this proposal was first published as Habets, "Developing a Retroactive Hermeneutic," 77–89.

63. Advocating similar views to my own are Anderson who labels his a christological hermeneutic, *Ministry on the Fire Line*, 111, and his *Dancing with Wolves While Feeding the Sheep*, chapter 3, where it is described as a hermeneutic of "eschatological preference." Another close example is the "Christotelic" hermeneutic being developed by Enns, *Inspiration and Incarnation*. This merely highlights the reciprocity between Christ and Spirit. See Klooster, "Role of the Holy Spirit in the Hermeneutic Process," 453, who prefers "the pneumatically christological theocentric" motif.

64. I toyed with the idea of replacing *Hermes* the messenger/interpreter of Zeus with *Janus* the two faced god who oversees beginnings and endings and naming this approach *Janusneutics*. Thankfully good sense (and good taste) prevailed.

words of Christ (Gospel) and the present experience of the Spirit into sharp focus.[65] In John 14:26 and 16:12, the other (*allos*) Paraclete fulfils two functions. The first is to continue the ministry of revelation already given: "he will teach you everything," and second, to "remind you of all that I [Jesus] have said to you." Hence, the new illumination has the continual ministry of the original revelation: "he will guide you into all truth" is balanced by "He will not speak on his own" (16:13). And again "he will declare (*anangelei*) to you the things that are to come," (16:13, cf. 16:15) is balanced by, "he will glorify me for he will take what is mine and declare it to you" (16:14). The key word or concept here is *anangelei*, for it can have the force of *re*-announce or *re*-proclaim. The force of the action is understood by John 16:13 to include some further information or meaning.[66] That further meaning is in effect drawn out of the old by way of reinterpretation.[67] Consequently, this word presents both inspiration in the present and interpretation of the past as bound up in the framework of illumination.[68] What this interpretive work of the Spirit meant for John is that he would undoubtedly regard his own gospel as the product of this inspiring Spirit. His own work was in direct fulfillment of these very promises; in fact those promises may constitute an implicit *apologia* for his gospel.[69] Dunn writes, "the way in which John handles the words and deeds of the historical Jesus is typically the way in which the Spirit interprets Jesus to a new generation, guides them into the truth of Jesus."[70]

In 1 John 2:27 the same thought is expressed in the following: "the anointing (that is, the Spirit) abides in you, and so you do not need any-

---

65. Dunn, *Jesus and the Spirit*, 351. Cf. the similar theme in Paul—2 Cor 1:22, Rom 8:23, and 1 Pet 1:12.

66. Commenting on John 16:13 Newbigin, *Gospel in a Pluralist Society*, 78, writes, "To the Church, however, the work of the Spirit will be 'to declare the things that are to come,' to interpret coming events, *to be the hermeneutic of the world's continuing history*" (italics mine).

67. On the retroactive perspective of John, see Thompson, *Humanity of Jesus in the Fourth Gospel*, 123–28. Thompson uses the term "retrospective" but means the same as my use of "retroactive," (ibid., 125).

68. See the same conclusions in Fowl, *Engaging Scripture*, 99–100.

69. What is true of John is also shared by the other evangelists. For example, Matthew 13:52 echoes this thought when it relates the teaching of Jesus about the bringing forth of old and new together; the one informing the other, the one anticipating and the other unfolding and unpacking as well as revealing new thoughts and concepts.

70. Dunn, *Jesus and the Spirit*, 352.

one to teach you . . . his anointing teaches you about all things," and thus the prophecy of Jer 31:34 is fulfilled. But the parallel in 1 John 2:27 implies that the Spirit's teaching is actually a continual reinterpretation of the original message of faith.[71] Again, in 1 John 4:2-6, present inspiration is expected and known, but a right understanding of Jesus is normative. Finally, in 1 John 5:6-12, we see this same dialectic between the remembrance of the life of Christ (*kerygma*) and the present communicative role of the Holy Spirit. The Spirit testifies to the truth of the humanity of Christ (vv. 6-7), and the Spirit continues to bear testimony to the anti-docetic *kerygma* (vv. 9-10). The last book of the Canon, Revelation, also points to this forward orientation or development as the Spirit catches John of the Apocalypse up and is commanded to write down what he sees and hears and what is to come (Rev 1:10, 19). This is, of course, a natural extension; for in the Gospel of John, the Spirit cannot come until Christ is ascended (John 14:12). Again in Revelation we read, "let anyone who has an ear listen to what the Spirit is saying (*legei*, present tense) to the churches" (Rev 2:7). The canonical authors are consciously writing to and for Spirit-inspired readers.[72]

This last point has been recognized by Markus Bockmuehl and forms the fifth thesis of his proposals for New Testament scholarship.[73] He writes, "The implied reader is drawn into an act of reading that involves playing an active role on stage rather than the discreet spectator on the upper balcony."[74] It is the Spirit of Light who illuminates the sig-

71. On the Spirit's role as biblical interpreter, see McCartney and Clayton, *Let the Reader Understand*, 75–80.

72. In this sense the neo-orthodox and existentialist schools are correct in realizing that the moment of understanding is at once the moment of response. The words of Scripture in this sense do *become* the Word of God. In the words of Barth, "revelation *is* reconciliation." According to Barth "Revelation takes place in and with reconciliation; indeed, the latter is also revelation. As God acts in it he also speaks . . . Yet the relationship is indissoluble from the other side as well. Revelation takes place as the revelation of reconciliation" (*CD* IV/3, 8), cited in Hunsinger, "Karl Barth's Christology," 137. Following Barth the other major presentation of this theology has been by Torrance, especially in his work *Mediation of Christ*.

73. Bockmuehl, "'To Be Or Not To Be," 271–306.

74. Ibid., 300. This is similar to the approach advocated by Torrance, *Christian Doctrine of God*, 37, who borrows an idea from Manson in which we must *indwell* the New Testament as a whole in such a way as to look *through* the various books and passages of Scripture and allow the message to be interiorized in the depths of our mind. For this reason his approach is called "depth exegesis." He also draws heavily from the work of Polanyi, *Belief in Science and in Christian Life*.

nificance of the Christ event (*retro*); it is the presence of the Spirit of Life that moves the church on (*active*); and it is the Spirit of Truth who brings the word of God into new situations (*retroactive*).[75] The Holy Spirit, therefore, is the one who moves the Church through history. We see this vividly in Acts, as we see the Spirit enabling the Church to make radical counter-cultural innovations in its missionary activity, encapsulated in the slogan of Acts 15:28: "It seemed good to the Holy Spirit and to us."[76]

This retroactive motif parallels to some degree what Anthony Thiselton has been writing about for some time—the so-called *two horizons*.[77] The first horizon is the text and its world and equates to my *retro*. The second horizon is that of the reader and their world, and equates to my *active*. In the words of Stephen Fowl:

> The Spirit's role is to guide and direct this process of continual change in order to enable communities of Christians to "abide in the true vine" in the various contexts in which they find themselves ... Because the Spirit speaks this "more" in unison with the Father and the Son, believers can act in ways that are both "new" and in continuity with the will of God.[78]

Traditional scholarship has been good at working in the first horizon—that of the text. However, if one spends one's life looking backward then bruises are sure to form on the head! While retrospection is crucial, it cannot be the totality of biblical hermeneutics. We need to spend more time, Clark Pinnock and others argue, in the world of the second horizon—with how the text is to be interpreted and applied today—and this refers to the *active* element of interpretation which relies on the Holy

---

75. This terminology has been used by Rosato, "Spirit Christology: Ambiguity and Promise," 444. Anderson, *Ministry on the Fire Line*, 35, speaks of theology as being both historical (backward or retro) and contemporary (future or active) due to Christ and the Spirit.

76. Brown, *Gospel According to John*, vol. 2, 716, describes this as "interpreting in relation to each coming generation the contemporary significance of what Jesus has said and done." Also see the similar hermeneutical insights of Anderson, *Soul of Ministry*, 29–30. He speaks of theological innovation not unrelated to theological antecedent or precedent. In this way he achieves what I have labeled a retroactive hermeneutic. Fowl, *Engaging Scripture*, 99–100, provides two examples from the Gospel of John where this "remembering" in a theological way (retroactive reading) is evidenced, in John 2:22 and 12:16. Fowl goes on to use the convincing and rather helpful historical case-study of Acts 10–15.

77. Thiselton, *Two Horizons*.

78. Fowl, *Engaging Scripture*, 101.

Spirit.[79] And it is here that a Spirit Christology has much to contribute. As Pinnock writes:

> The Spirit's goal in the illumination of the Word for the Church is to shed light on her pilgrim way ... Here [Acts 15:28] the Spirit led the community to an important corporate decision, not insight into the faith so much as insight into the mission. The Spirit was guiding the Church to move beyond the confines of Judaism and learn to adapt to a mission among Gentiles. All through Acts the ministry of the Spirit is to direct believers in what to think and where to go.[80]

Pinnock adds that,

> Evangelical theology has to be a "pilgrim theology." We never pass beyond the necessity of reconsidering our traditional interpretations until the return of Christ. We continually ask where the deep structures of Biblical revelation are pointing. A theology that is not restlessly probing and exploring is not serving the Church well. A theology that takes the path of discovery requires the Spirit's illumination most urgently.[81]

The Spirit Christology presented here seeks to heed this call and walk faithfully in the direction the Spirit points.

The Exegete and the Spirit

Having established a retroactive hermeneutic that accounts for the mission of the Holy Spirit, we are left with the task of briefly pointing out some of the implications of a pneumatological hermeneutic for the biblical exegete.

There are generally two approaches to the role of the Holy Spirit in interpretation. One focuses on what the Spirit does with the *text*, the other on what the Spirit does with the *exegete*.[82] The first approach, while

---

79. See Pinnock, "Role of the Spirit in Interpretation," 491–97.

80. Ibid., 495.

81. Ibid., 496. Pinnock has put this theory into practice in his recent theological works. A very good example in my opinion is his constructive proposals for pneumatology in *Flame of Love*. Very bad examples, again in my opinion, are his constructive proposals for Theology proper and soteriology as developed in Pinnock, *Wideness in God's Mercy*; *Openness of God*; and ibid., *Most Moved Mover*.

82. A third approach is now becoming more popular—the role of the Spirit in the communicative event of reading Scripture and then seeking to apply it. See the perceptive work of my colleague and former golfing partner Meadowcroft, "Relevance as

becoming a popular option in contemporary hermeneutics, is rejected by a retroactive reading of Scripture.[83] Proponents of the first approach aver that the Spirit enables the text to be read in a way which would not have been obvious to the first recipients (a "Spiritual" reading) and so in this way renders Scripture of continuing relevance to the Church. On this view the Spirit is the creative power behind the fusion of the text's and the reader's horizons, with the second horizon exerting a clear dominance over the first. The second approach, the one adopted here, appeals to the Spirit as the minister of the Word, the one who leads the community into a correct interpretation of the text. The locus of the Spirit's re-creative work is not the letter of the text; this is fixed and hence forms our *retro*. Rather the Spirit's re-creative work centers on the life of the interpreter, who, as sinner, is inclined to distort the text insofar as its message is perceived as threatening the *status quo*.[84] Given this distortion, the Spirit guides and leads the interpreter to the truth of the text and its correct application into new situations and hence forms our *active*.[85]

Having articulated the difference between these two approaches it remains to further explicate the actual mission of the Holy Spirit as it relates to the interpreter of Holy Scripture. Roy Zuck provides fourteen propositions related to the Spirit and interpretation which culminate in five elements necessary for properly interpreting the Bible: "salvation, spiritual maturity, diligent study, common sense and logic, and humble dependence on the Spirit of God for discernment."[86] A nice illustration of this in practice is that of William L. Lane who, in the preface to his commentary on the Gospel of Mark, writes:

> Only gradually did I come to understand that my primary task as a commentator was to listen to the text and to the discussion it has prompted over the course of centuries as a child who needed to be made wise. The responsibility to discern truth from error has been onerous at times. When a critical or theological decision

---

Mediating Category in the Reading of Biblical Texts," 611–27; and "Between Authorial Intent and Indeterminacy," 199–218.

83. See Vanhoozer, *Is There a Meaning in this Text?* 415, for a brief survey.

84. Ibid.

85. For Vanhoozer, the formula is not retro + active but "biblical relevance = revelatory meaning + relative significance." Ibid., 423.

86. Zuck, "Role of the Holy Spirit in Hermeneutics," 130.

has been demanded by the text before I was prepared to commit myself, I have adopted the practice of the Puritan commentators in laying the material before the Lord and asking for His guidance. This has made the preparation of the commentary a spiritual as well as an intellectual pilgrimage through the text of the Gospel. In learning to be sensitive to all that the evangelist was pleased to share with me I have been immeasurably enriched by the discipline of responsive listening.[87]

Lane, like Pinnock, appeals to the concept of *pilgrimage* as the best way to describe the way in which the exegete receives this ministry of the Word by the Holy Spirit. This pilgrimage, however, is not simply that of the individual exegete but involves the entire faith community. The work of the Spirit is thus a work *in* community and *for* community and so an examination of the communal nature of the of the Spirit's role in interpretation is required.

The Community and the Spirit

Of special importance is the communal aspect of the reading and interpreting of Scripture.[88] On the basis of Acts 2, James McClendon argues that Scripture is addressed directly to readers *today*: Peter declares "this" (the event of Pentecost) is "that" (the meaning of the prophecy of Joel).[89] Such an interpretation is not merely Peter's human projection but a product of the Spirit's guidance. Only his sharing in the life of the believing community allowed Peter to see "this" as "that."

In a similar way to McClendon, Kevin Vanhoozer notes that when Ezra the scribe opened up the Scripture, the people literally "stood under" the text (Neh 8:5).[90] Their response to the reading showed that they understood and, as a result, worshipped. Contrast their response with that of earlier kings and priests who had failed to understand or to follow the law (Neh 9:34). A habit of disobedience had made it difficult to understand or to follow the biblical text. Under Ezra, by contrast, there was a week-long feast of reading, followed on the eighth day by a solemn

---

87. Lane, *Commentary on the Gospel of Mark*, xii.
88. See Fee, *Listening to the Spirit in the Text*, 15.
89. McClendon, *Ethics*, 1, 31–33. Following McClendon's position would be Hays, *Echoes of Scripture in the Letters of Paul*, and Hauerwas, *Unleashing Scripture*.
90. Vanhoozer, *Is There a Meaning in this Text?* 408. He also uses Acts 2 as a case study. Fowl, *Engaging Scripture*, 115, uses Acts 10–15 as his case study and comes to similar results.

assembly. The Scriptures were read and the people responded in confession and worship (Neh 9:2–3). Here was no dead letter, no tired book, but a text that spoke directly to the people's hearts and minds.[91] Their reception of the text was the occasion for reformation and renewal, both communal in nature.

While a communal reception of the text under the guidance of the Holy Spirit is acknowledged, when this approach is taken to an extreme it reveals a problem, notably: How can the church know what God is saying through Scripture if what God is saying fails to coincide with the verbal meaning of the text? Hauerwas appeals to the leading of the Spirit.[92] But is this sufficient? The solution has problems. First, the Spirit's leading is often difficult to discern or to distinguish from merely human consensus. Second, it relocates the Word of God and divine authority from the text to the tradition of its interpretation.[93] When individualized, there is the constituent problem of subjectivity. However, when this is done in the context of ecclesial community it is perhaps similar to the early church and their use of the "rule of faith" (*regula fidei*). For Tertullian and Irenaeus, Scripture is rightly understood only in the context of the living tradition handed down through apostolic succession; tradition being both the content and context. Ultimately the criterion for right interpretation is the consensus of the catholic Church, best represented by the earliest creeds. On this view, the arbiter of right interpretation is the church, which enjoys not canonical but "*charismatic authority, grounded in the assistance of the Spirit: for it seemed good to the Holy Spirit and to us.*"[94] The function of the *regula fidei* is thus not overturned but placed within its proper context: the community which "stands under" the text of Scripture and the Spirit of Truth.

These issues are only a problem when a pneumatological hermeneutic is not at the same time a retroactive one. A retroactive hermeneutic seeks to hold together the plain sense of Scripture ("what it meant") with its use by the Spirit in the community ("its significance today"). We

---

91. This relates to Fee's words in his *Listening to the Spirit in the Text*, 14: "During the process of exegesis we momentarily reverse these roles, so that we act as subject with the text as object. I would argue that the exegetical process is not completed until we return to the proper posture of objects being addressed by the subject."

92. See for instance Hauerwas, "Moral Authority of Scripture," 356–70.

93. All criticisms made by Vanhoozer, *Is There a Meaning in this Text?* 411.

94. Cited in ibid.

may now go back to Nehemiah 8 and look again at what was going on. Amidst a community that had departed from the Spirit, the Word held no great attraction for them. However, amidst the missionary work of the Spirit inhabiting the Word of the Law, the people were convicted, revived, and reformed.[95] Here, as Vanhoozer states: "The Spirit's role in bringing about understanding is to witness to what is other than himself (meaning accomplished) and to bring its significance to bear on the reader (meaning applied)."[96]

Utilizing speech-act theory,[97] Vanhoozer outlines three aspects of the Spirit's work in bringing readers to understanding. First, the Spirit *convicts* believers that the Bible is divine as well as human locution (and thus to be read as a unified text). This relates to the *testimonium internum Spiritus Sancti* by which the reader comes to receive the Bible as the Word of God. Second, the Spirit *illuminates* the letter by impressing its illocutionary force upon the reader. Under the influence of the Holy Spirit believers see and hear the text of Scripture as warnings, commands, promises, and assertions. In so doing the Spirit does not alter but ministers the meaning. "The distinction between the 'letter' and the 'spirit' is precisely that between reading the words and grasping what one reads. Likewise, the difference between a 'natural' and an 'illuminated' understanding is that between holding an opinion and having a deep sense of its profundity."[98] Finally, what does the Spirit illumine, head or heart? Both! The Spirit's illumination of the mind is dependent on his prior transformation of the heart. Vanhoozer concludes:

---

95. This is why Fowl, *Engaging Scripture* 113, speaks about reading the Spirit and how that is crucial for the interpretive task. In fact, Fowl writes: "[the] experience of the Spirit's work provides the lenses through which Scripture is read rather than vice-versa. This is perhaps the most significant point the New Testament has to make about the hermeneutical significance of the Spirit; this point runs against the grain of modern interpretive presumptions," ibid., 114. Fowl goes on to elaborate on this controversial statement.

96. Vanhoozer, *Is There a Meaning in this Text?* 413.

97. Speech-act theory involves three constituent elements: the "locutionary act" is the bare fact of the utterance of the text; the "illocutionary act" is the intent of the utterance or text; and the "perlocutionary act" is the effect on the reader or hearer.

98. This relates back to points three and four on Zuck's list. Marshall, "Holy Spirit and the Interpretation of Scripture," 69, points to passages such as 1 Thess 1:5 and 2:13 to indicate that Paul's preaching was effective because the Spirit was active in and through the preaching of the Word to produce faith. By this he indicates that understanding Scripture is not only an intellectual task, it is also a spiritual one.

> Negatively, the Spirit progressively disabuses us of any ideological or idolatrous prejudices that prevent us from receiving the message of the text. The Spirit purges us, first, of hermeneutic sin, of that interpretive violence that distorts the otherness of the text. Positively, the Spirit conforms our interests to those of the text. To read in the Spirit does not mean to import some new sense into the text, but rather to let the letter be, or better, to let it accomplish the purpose, illocutionary and perlocutionary, for which it was sent: "[My Word] will not return to me empty, but will accomplish what I desire and achieve the purpose for which I sent it" (Isa 55:11). In short, the Spirit convicts, illuminates, and sanctifies the reader in order better to [sic] minister the Word.[99]

How do we foster this ecclesial context in which a Spirit-inspired hermeneutic or reading of Scripture takes place? For Stephen Fowl, the answer includes not only reading *with* the Spirit but also learning to "read the Spirit":

> If Christians are to interpret with the Spirit, they will also need to learn how to interpret the Spirit. Further, our prospects for interpreting the Spirit are closely linked to our proficiency at testifying to the Spirit's work, particularly the Spirit's work in the lives of others. Such testimony depends on the forming and sustaining of friendships in which our lives are opened to others in ways that display the Spirit's working. Welcoming strangers and the extension of hospitality become building blocks for such friendships. Finally, building such friendships, becoming people of the Spirit, and recognizing and interpreting the work of the Spirit all take time and demand patience from us.[100]

The Enrichment of Doctrine

The final issue which deserves some attention is the movement from Scripture, through exegesis, to doctrine. How do we speak of doctrinal development when a retroactive hermeneutic is applied? The correct development of doctrine is one involving a retroactive reading of the Canon. Moltmann calls this a "reverse movement,"[101] while Pannenberg

---

99. Vanhoozer, *Is There a Meaning in This Text?* 413.
100. Fowl, *Engaging Scripture*, 119.
101. Moltmann, *Way of Jesus Christ*, 75. In his work *Crucified God*, 112, Moltmann speaks similarly of holding together the reciprocal relationship between historical and eschatological method, the historical and eschatological history of Jesus.

labels it "proleptic."[102] Or, for Donald Bloesch, it is a theology of "Word and Spirit."[103] When Word and Spirit are kept together, theological construction emerges as both faithful and creative. But does it develop, change, or grow out of the original revelation preserved in Scripture? How do we articulate the relationship between exegesis and systematic theology when working within a retroactive hermeneutic?

The Synoptic evangelists unfold the apostolic preaching of Christ as they tell the life history of Jesus. In these histories the central event is Jesus's death on the cross and the experience of the presence of the risen One in the Spirit. Hence, we start with the past, with the deposit of faith left to us in the Canon, and then in successive generations we attempt to penetrate its truth or reality. Under the guidance of the Holy Spirit, and with advances in science and technology, we implement every means of inquiry in order to unpack and interpret the canon, not develop or improve on it. But within these tools of inquiry, the determinative principle of interpretation will always be the indwelling Holy Spirit.[104]

With Pinnock I assert that "God gives us freedom to operate within biblical boundaries by the Spirit, who inspired the witnesses and also opens the significance of scriptural words."[105] Or with Francis Watson I affirm that:

> It is crucially important to achieve a correct balance between the assertion that the disclosure of truth lies in the future and the assertion that it lies in the past. What lies in the future is a true apprehension of what has already happened in the past; and revelation is thereby tied irrevocably to the historicity and particularity of human existence within the world and prevented

---

102. Although Pannenberg's use of "proleptic" (derived, one would suppose, from the initial use by J. Weiss) includes a considerable amount of philosophical connotations we do not include in our term "retroactive." Pannenberg, *Systematic Theology*, vol. 2, 365, and *Introduction to Systematic Theology*, 53–69. See Moltmann's critique of Pannenberg's thesis in *Way of Jesus Christ*, 76 n. 9. See Fuller, "New German Theological Movement," 160–75.

103. See the pneumatic/Christological exegesis of Bloesch, *Holy Scripture*, 181, 200, 206–8, and "Christological Hermeneutic," 78–102, and more fully worked out in his initial volume of the Christian Foundations series *Theology of Word & Spirit*.

104. This would concur at many points with Peter Stuhlmacher's call for a "hermeneutic of consent." See his *Vom Verstehen des Neuen Testaments: Eine Hermeneutik*, 205–25

105. Pinnock, *Flame of Love*, 230. See further in his earlier works "Work of the Holy Spirit in Hermeneutics," 3–23 and "Role of the Spirit in Interpretation," 491–97.

from drifting away into gnostic fantasy. Conversely, however, the meaning of what happened in the past cannot simply be read out of that past, conveyed by means of an authoritative tradition.[106]

The late Colin Gunton provided the sort of model of doctrinal development I am proposing here. He thought of doctrinal development the terms of "enrichment" elaborated on earlier.[107] Development suggests a continuing process of change too easily mistaken for a form of *evolution*. *Enrichment*, in contrast, is a Spirit-inspired reading of the past from the vantage point of the future. It is a retroactive enterprise undertaken within the knowledge that we do not have the whole truth, but as the tradition passes through our hands, we seek to enrich it and, hence, it is not merely retrospective.[108] Utilizing Gunton's imagery of "enrichment" we may reject a view of an evolutionary development of doctrine in which its conclusions are patently different from its origins. Under this model of doctrinal development the original message has been transformed into something different. It is no longer related to the original Canon. One such example would be the suggested development from the earliest worship practices characterized as polytheism, to a developed monotheism of the later Hebrew and early Christian writers, to contemporary forms of panentheism and pantheism. The latter positions are of a different sort than the former from which they have moved away. The development model is a modernist one which claims that most teaching before the modern age is obsolete, so development involves being critical of it.

By contrast, Gunton's enrichment model or notion of "organic development," is intimately related to the Canon. It is not another gospel but the enrichment of the original. The model of enrichment treats history as significant but the original witness, the Canon, remains supreme.[109]

---

106. Watson, *Text, Church and World*, 260–61.

107. Gunton, *Theology Through the Theologians*, 48–49. This is similar to what Kelly, "Spirit, Church and the Ecumenical Endeavour," 175, terms "traditioning."

108. In this regard see the programmatic thesis of Poythress, *Symphonic Theology*.

109. Obviously we are raising the question of presuppositions in hermeneutics. See Polanyi, *Personal Knowledge*, who argues that we deceive ourselves when we think we can achieve truth by approaching an object of study, such as Jesus and the Gospels, in a spirit of critical doubt and "scientific" objectivity. He argues that tacit beliefs/commitments affect all interpretation. What we are acknowledging is that tacit knowledge is equivalent to fiduciary knowledge which in turn is equivalent to our pneumatological hermeneutic. This is why correct exegesis can only be achieved from "within" therefore,

An example of an organic development of doctrine would include the historical enrichment of the Christological and Trinitarian doctrines. In the fourth century, Gregory Nazianzen moved beyond the words of Scripture to further articulate Christological thought, using the term *perichoresis* to describe the intimate communion between the two natures of Christ. In the seventh century, Pseudo-Cyril used the same term to help illustrate the coinherence of the three persons of the Trinity.[110] In commenting on the theology enshrined in the orthodox creeds and definitions of Christendom such as Nicaea (AD 325), Constantinople (AD 381), and Chalcedon (AD 451), F. C. Grant writes: "these were not ventures in speculation, but, as their very language indicates, simply statements which *ruled out* various conceptions or attempted definitions which infringed or invalidated the language of Scripture and religious experience, especially of worship."[111] In this way, doctrine was enriched through the tradition and made relevant for contemporary audiences.

When we apply this hermeneutic to Christology, we see that while Jesus was misunderstood until after the resurrection and Pentecost, this very lack of understanding led to more reflection and deliberation on the actual life of Jesus, his words, and works (cf. John 16:4). Any rewriting of history in a quasi-mythological way would have devalued the benefit of Christ's life for the Christian community rather than enriching it.[112] As such, the Gospels must be read in light of these eschatological events and the reinterpretation of them in light of the Spirit's illumination.[113] "As Christianity could properly claim to be a legitimate interpretation of the Old Testament in the light of Jesus, so the *kerygmatic* Christ can claim to be a legitimate interpretation of the historical Jesus in the light of Jesus's

---

the Gospel writers, as committed followers of Christ, are the most reliable storytellers. Cf. Van Til, *Christian Theory of Knowledge*. Polanyi's insights have been developed and applied forcefully by Newbigin when he speaks of "indwelling" the Story of the Bible in *Gospel in a Pluralist Society*, and "Truth and Authority in Modernity," in *Faith and Modernity*, 60–115.

110. On the use of *perichoresis* see Egan, "Toward Trinitarian *Perichoresis*," 83–93.

111. Grant, *Introduction to New Testament Thought*, 243.

112. Hoskyns and Davey, *Riddle of the New Testament*, 170. Also see Pinnock, *Flame of Love*, 243, where he lists four points for evaluating claims to illumination and discernment.

113. What has been termed "a hermeneutic from within," by Gruenler, *New Approaches to Jesus and the Gospels*, 129.

resurrection."[114] What the Gospels evince is the reinterpretation of Jesus, his identity and mission. It is a theological-biographical-historical account of the Messiah—the Christ, and a retroactive reading of his life and ministry.[115] Cullmann summarizes saying that,

> The problem of Jesus in its full theological scope was recognized only in the light of the new events of his death on the cross and the experience immediately following his resurrection. These events caused those momentary glimpses of recognition during Jesus' earthly life to stand out in the bright light of perception, and at least a few came to understand those indirect references of his which had found no open ears during his lifetime.[116]

As we approach the Gospels we also must employ a retroactive reading. We come already with an awareness of how the story ends—with the resurrection-exaltation of the Christ and his presence with us in the Spirit. But the Gospel writers start with Jesus's birth and historical life not with the exalted Christ.[117] They choose to take us along with them in this double movement that nevertheless ascends from below to above.[118] In their accounts they include Messianic indicators throughout in order to arrest the reader, to bring to the reader's mind the Old Testament anticipation of the promised Messiah and the fulfillment in Jesus of Nazareth. As they were led to write by the Holy Spirit they were reminded of Messianic intimations prevalent throughout the life of

114. Dunn, *Unity and Diversity in the New Testament*, 216.

115. Gunton, *Yesterday and Today*, 61, speaks of Jesus's "suprahistorical significance" for the evangelists. For Moltmann, "the past can be narrated, and every narration, like enumeration, begins at the beginning and proceeds to the end. But in the direction of eschatological anticipation, the last must come first, the future precedes the past, the end reveals the beginning and objective time-relationships are reversed. 'History as recollection' and 'history as hope,' within the 'hope in the form of recollections' which is the determining element of Christian faith, are not contradictory, but must be complementary," *Crucified God*, 113.

116. Cullmann, *Christology of the New Testament*, 319.

117. While John does start from above "In the beginning was the Word, and the Word was with God" (John 1:1) his point is to ground the Word in the historical life of Jesus of Nazareth, "And the Word became flesh . . . dwelt among us . . . we saw his glory" (John 1:14). The Gospels open with the beginnings of Jesus, either with John Baptist or with Jesus's birth to Mary. But they tell the story of his life in the light of his resurrection and his presence in the Spirit of God. This is what defines, partly, a gospel and separates it from a biography or a secular history in the modern sense. See the comments made by Gunton, *Yesterday and Today*, 66.

118. See the discussion in Ibid., 46.

Jesus and they incorporated these into their theological presentations. They were selective in their material, (John 20:30; 21:25), choosing only those details that would enhance and clarify one thing—"that you may believe that Jesus is the Christ, the Son of God" (John 20:31).[119] As we read these Gospels we too must look for, recognize, and incorporate these Messianic indicators into our Christology. The supreme indicator is the Son's relationship to the Father in the Holy Spirit. This is what is presented in calling Jesus the "Christ" or "Messiah." Hence, pneumatology is the key to unlocking the identity of Jesus of Nazareth. At this point Moltmann's definition of Spirit Christology may be helpful:

> The whole thrust of the experience of the presence of the Spirit of the risen Christ is towards presenting his whole history as the history of the Spirit with him. This is the point of approach for the pneumatological christology of the earthly life, ministry and way of Jesus Christ: the remembrance of the life-history of Jesus discerns Jesus' endowment with the Spirit and the workings of the Spirit in him. This is the sphere of pneumatological christology. Jesus appears as the messianic human being in the history of the Spirit of God with him and through him.[120]

This is the hermeneutic of a Spirit Christology, a retroactive reading of the Gospels from a pneumatological perspective. This retroactive reading opens us up to an encounter with Jesus the Messiah. From here it will be germane to survey directly the New Testament witness to the identity of Jesus the Christ in the next chapter.

---

119. Moltmann, *Way of Jesus Christ*, 141, insightfully comments that "If we judge the matter historically, unprejudiced by dogmatic or humanist postulates, we have to assume that there is a correspondence between the community's remembrance of Jesus, and their Easter experience of the One risen. Inconsistencies would have destroyed either the remembrance of Jesus or the experience of the risen One, and would in either case have broken down the identity involved in the acknowledgement 'Jesus—the Christ.'" Also see Hagner, "Interpreting the Gospels," 30.

120. Moltmann, *Way of Jesus Christ*, 78.

5

Explaining Jesus

The Testimony of the New Testament Writers

> *In speaking about the part of the Spirit in the being and mission of Jesus, we are treading on the holiest of holy ground*
> —Tomas A. Smail

> What the apostles experienced at Pentecost was simply Calvary in its fullest dimension. It is not Pentecost but Calvary that we proclaim, but we must proclaim Calvary with the power of Pentecost.
> —Donald G. Bloesch

> *Christ and the Spirit act in unison to enable the relationship between Creator and the creature to be renewed for the sake of the creature. Thus, the prayer, Come, Creator Spirit is a prayer of commitment to what God has already done in Jesus Christ and a prayer of participation in the divine nature.*
> —Peter Lockhart

Having examined the various ways biblical scholarship has approached the question of Jesus's identity and proposed a doctrine of theological enrichment, allied to a retroactive hermeneutic, we are now ready to survey the New Testament testimony to Jesus's identity and mission. Through six disclosure episodes in the life of Christ his messianic identity and mission becomes clear and the biblical basis for a Spirit Christology is firmly established.

Due to the theological focus of this study it is not appropriate to entertain a full exegetical examination of the biblical text. However, it is necessary to recall, at least summarily, the biblical basics without which the development of theology cannot be comprehended. I will focus primarily on the most important and interesting exegetical details of the New Testament, giving special attention to the Gospels and Acts. While a full-fledged commentary on each episode from Jesus's life and ministry is not possible, it is within our compass to highlight main themes and patterns and focus on particularly crucial or controversial texts. I am well aware that the New Testament does not furnish one line of thought on the identity of Jesus Christ. Rather, it presents a kind of mosaic that is intertwined and complex.[1] We have already identified various aspects of this mosaic in the previous chapter. What I am offering is a broad and unifying strand of that mosaic—that of a Spirit Christology.

PAULINE CORPUS

While popular opinion tends to think of the Gospels as the first written documents of the Christian church and the Epistles as later, refined reflection, the opposite is actually the case. The Epistles represent the earliest Christian writings after which the Gospels were composed. This begs the question: Why have the evangelists structured their accounts the way they have? Already within the New Testament Epistles we see the relationship between Christ and the Spirit is highly developed. Gordon Fee has brought out many aspects of this relationship in the Pauline corpus.[2] While our investigation is primarily concerned with the Gospels and Acts, the following points from the Pauline corpus highlight the degree of early Christian reflection on Christ and the Spirit.

The relationship between the Spirit and Christ is of the utmost importance, and yet it has caused an untold measure of confusion when scholars came to define it in more precise terms.[3] Paul refers to the Spirit as the "Spirit of Christ" (Rom 8:9), and as the "Spirit of his Son" (Gal 4:6), and in Philippians 1:19 a third expression can be added, the "Spirit of Jesus Christ." These expressions have been understood in two opposing

---

1. This is the theme of Dunn, *Unity and Diversity in the New Testament*.

2. Fee, *Gods Empowering Presence*. On Christology in the Pauline corpus see the companion volume by Fee, *Pauline Christology*. No attempt to resolve the long-standing issue of Pauline authorship will be attempted here. In this study all thirteen of the canonical Epistles attributed to Paul are referred to as "Pauline." By using the name "Paul" or "Pauline" I am intending to mean either Paul the apostle himself (particularly the major ten), or of Pauline influence, however that be considered (particularly the Pastoral Epistles). I refer the reader to the discussion and bibliography in Fee, *Gods Empowering Presence*, xxi–xxii.

3. See Meyer, "Holy Spirit in the Pauline Letters," 5.

ways. The first misunderstanding has been in taking the genitive as one of definition, thus making the identification between Spirit and Christ ontological.[4] Other scholars such as Dunn have modified this view, but instead of ontology posit a functional identity.[5] Central to this position is that in the disciple's experience at least, there was no conscious difference between the internal presence of Christ and that of the Spirit. Advocates of this position consistently point to 2 Corinthians 3:17 and 1 Corinthians 15:45 in support of their argument.[6] However, neither text identifies Christ and the Holy Spirit in strict ontological or identically functional terms.[7] In Romans 8:9-10, another commonly appealed to text, there is no reason to equate the "Spirit of Christ" (Rom 8:9) with "Christ in you" (Rom 8:10) *simplicter*. The point is that the Spirit of Christ in believers develops "Christ" in them. "The Lord and the Spirit are not personally identified, but the Spirit is the mode in which the Lord works in the new dispensation,"[8] clarifies Ladd.

The second way to interpret these expressions is in a unitarian sense where the Spirit of God, immanent in believers, is the inspiration of Christ-like life in them.[9] This position takes Jesus's life to be a perfect model for our own as God, who is Spirit, was uniquely revealed in Jesus's life; subsequently God began to repeat in believers what he had inspired in Jesus.[10] The "Spirit of Jesus" is understood in the same way as "the Spirit

---

4. This view is traceable to Gunkel and followed by Deissmann and Bousset among others. For a survey and bibliography see Turner, *Holy Spirit and Spiritual Gifts*, 130.

5. Dunn, *Jesus and the Spirit*, 319–26. Contra Dunn and warning against collapsing the Spirit into Christ Badcock writes: "that Paul adopts a trinitarian formula in the benediction of 2 Corinthians 13:13, for example, is significant in this respect in that he sees no need, after 2 Corinthians 3:17, not to mention the Spirit because he has already mentioned Christ," *Light of Truth & Fire of Love*, 26.

6. See the review in Robichaux, "Pneumatic Person of Christ," 3–13.

7. For a fuller argument see Turner, "Significance of Spirit Endowment for Paul," 63–69. "The best evidence that we can put forward to support the view that there is some degree of functional identity is (a) that much of the work described in one context as attributable to the Spirit is in another context said to be performed by Christ and (b) the phrase 'in the Spirit' appears in some contexts to be a formal parallel to 'in Christ,' while at the same time 'Christ in you' appears hard to distinguish from 'the Spirit of Christ' in you," (ibid., 64). Also see Ladd, *Theology of the New Testament*, 531–34, and Badcock, *Light of Truth & Fire of Love*, 23–36.

8. Ladd, *Theology of the New Testament*, 532.

9. This position has found its most able advocate in Lampe, *God as Spirit*.

10. Without denying the resurrection, Dunn is an advocate of a modified form of this view. For an overview see Turner, *Holy Spirit and Spiritual Gifts*, 133.

of Elijah" (2 Kgs 2:9-10), meaning the Spirit with the character of Jesus. The result, however, is to reduce the S/spirit to an influence and Jesus to a uniquely inspired man rather than the Christ, the Son of God.

Rather than present the Spirit of Christ as an *absolute* ontological equivalent, or a *purely* functional identity, Paul stands more in the tradition of the Old Testament. When Paul speaks of the "Spirit of Jesus Christ" or the "Spirit of the Son" it is to affirm that the Spirit is Christ's executive power, or as Fee puts it "God's empowering presence."[11] Understood in this way, the Spirit is now related to Christ in exactly the same way as the Spirit was related to Yahweh in the Old Testament, expressed as "Spirit of the Lord" or "Spirit of God." In Philippians 1:19, Paul asserts that he expects to receive fellowship through the Spirit with Christ himself. The Spirit of Christ is the Spirit that now proceeds from Christ, as from the Father in the Old Testament.

Formerly, Paul was of the official Jewish opinion that Jesus was a false prophet and deserved to die. The official attitude of the Jerusalem hierarchy was encapsulated in the slogan "Jesus be cursed" (1 Cor 12:3). This was confirmed in the manner of Christ's death on a cross. But Paul had come to see that it was the cross that brought about redemption, reconciliation, and salvation (2 Cor 5:21; Rom 3:24-26). To curse Jesus is proof in itself that one does not possess the Spirit; conversely, one can only acknowledge Christ in the power of the Spirit (1 Cor 12:3). This new experience of Christ in the Spirit shows that Jesus is indeed the Spirit-inspired Christ and that the interpretation of Jesus's enemies is wrong. 2 Cor 5:16 (so often used to argue Paul had no interest in the historical Jesus!), is a condemnation of judgments about Jesus that are not prompted by the Spirit (1 Cor 2:1-16; 2 Cor 3:12—4:15). Paul claims to know nothing but Christ crucified (1 Cor 2:2), that is to know Jesus who was crucified for his claiming to be the Spirit-anointed Messiah. Paul's apostolic ministry focused on Jesus's death, resurrection, and bestowal of the Spirit. To Paul, therefore, Jesus is the vindicated Messiah. His identity is established beyond doubt by the Spirit; Jesus is "designated Son of God in power according to the Spirit of holiness by his resurrection from the dead, Jesus Christ our Lord" (Rom 1:4; cf. 8:1).[12]

---

11. Fee, *Gods Empowering Presence*.
12. Brown, "Person of Christ," in *ISBE*, vol. 3, 794.

GOSPEL PERSPECTIVE

With this evidence of early Christian reflection in mind we turn now to the Gospels. Central to the thesis of a Spirit Christology is that the Gospels all present the identity of Jesus in terms of a pneumatic—human relation. In the words of Colin Brown, "If Matthew, Mark, and Luke have an explicit Spirit Christology accompanied by an implicit Word Christology, John presents *an explicit Word Christology*, accompanied by *an implicit Wisdom and Spirit Christology*."[13] My claim here is simple: during key disclosure episodes in the life of Jesus the Spirit is seen as *the* interpretation of Jesus's identity. The relationship between Jesus and the Spirit thus becomes crucial to understanding Jesus.

What a Spirit Christology does not imply is that the presentation of Jesus's identity is uniform throughout the Gospels, or even that the emphasis on the relationship between Jesus and the Spirit is constant.[14] Each evangelist develops his Gospel in a unique way and in the following pages we shall survey a selection of the key moments in Jesus's life[15] where the evangelists identify him through his relationship with the Holy Spirit.[16] We shall treat these moments episode by episode rather than looking at each evangelist's presentation in turn. This is not to deny the differences between each presentation but to trace the broad contours of the source material and derive the most crucial teachings on the identity of Jesus.[17]

---

13. Brown, "Trinity and Incarnation," 95 (italics in original).

14. For instance the Spirit appears considerably more often in Luke than in Matthew or Mark, and John develops his pneumatology using the unique concept of *paraclētos*.

15. What O'Donnell, "In Him and Over Him," 44–45, calls "decisive *kairoi* of his life and ministry. Among the most significant of these *kairoi* were his baptism . . . and his death on the cross." See Congar, *Word and the Spirit*, 87, who uses similar language, "*kairoi*," "established times," "historical stages," and so forth to describe these disclosure episodes.

16. Welker, *God the Spirit*, 186.

17. There are three moments or *kairoi* in the life of Jesus that are consistently seen as of ultimate significance: the birth, baptism, and resurrection. McIntyre, *Shape of Pneumatology*, 44, surveys these three events or "points in the story of Jesus where his association with the Spirit is stated with clarity . . . they may be regarded as overtly significant expressions and identifiable foci for a relation which was to prove fundamental and continuous." In relation to Jesus's baptism, temptation, transfiguration, and in Gethsemane, Witherington, *Christology of Jesus*, 233–62, calls these "crisis moments" but not in the form of an identity crisis. Rather they are points of confirmation. Within the Gospels eight distinctive episodes clearly highlight the relationship between Christ

Disclosure Episode One: Jesus's Miraculous Conception and Birth

Both Matthew and Luke begin their account of the life of Christ with his unique birth (Matt 1–2; Luke 1–2).[18] What stands out in their infancy narratives is the pivotal role the Holy Spirit plays.[19] The conception and birth of Jesus contains many crucial insights into his identity but three key elements critical for both an understanding of the identity of Jesus Christ and to a Spirit Christology, stand out. In the first place we notice the prophetic activity that abounds around Jesus's birth in both Matthew and Luke. Second, the prominence of the Spirit in Jesus's birth as this points forward to Pentecost and the new creation, and back to his creative and providential activity in the Old Testament. More precisely Matthew and Luke present the virginal conception of Jesus through the Spirit. Finally, within the birth narrative we witness the deliberate explanation as to the true identity of both John the Baptist and Jesus of Nazareth, also explained in pneumatological terms.[20]

While Matthew and Luke differ in their narration both are in considerable agreement on the main details of the conception and birth of Jesus. Central to both evangelists narrative is the virginal conception of Jesus by the Holy Spirit and an explanation as to the true identity of both John Baptist and Jesus of Nazareth, also explained in pneumatological terms. While both are unique individuals on the stage of Jewish history, one of them stands out as supremely unique; and this is highlighted through Jesus's experience of the Holy Spirit.

Matthew (Matt 1:1–17) stresses the theological significance of Jesus from the outset. Jesus is the Jewish Messiah—the Christ—and the descendent of King David, and also of Abraham. "[Jesus] is born as the embodiment of the messianic history and the messianic sphere of hopes and expectations."[21] For Matthew it is Jesus's resurrection and his exaltation to be the Immanuel which are projected into the nativity story.

---

and the Spirit and in turn highlight his identity as complete God and complete man. These eight episodes are: 1) his birth; 2) baptism; 3) temptation; 4) ministry; 5) passion; 6) resurrection; 7) ascension; and 8) Pentecost, each of which deserves to be developed in its own right.

18. Shelton, *Mighty in Word and Deed*, chapter 2.

19. Turner, *Power from on High*, deals extensively with the theme of the Holy Spirit within the Lucan corpus. For the birth narrative see chapter 6 especially.

20. McFarlane, *Why Do You Believe What You Believe About the Holy Spirit?* 39, brings this emphasis out well.

21. Welker, *God the Spirit*, 188.

Joseph is at the centre of prophecy not Mary (as in Luke). To Joseph the angel speaks; the agency of the Spirit being the decisive factor. "Life in the Spirit of God and Jesus as the child of God are thought of as being so intimately connected—even in Jesus's very beginnings, in his mother's womb—that this suggested the notion that Mary was pregnant through the Holy Spirit."[22] Blomberg concludes that three key themes are presented in Matthew 1 and 2: first, Jesus is the hope of Israel, its long-awaited Messiah, and the fulfillment of the Old Testament. Second, through him blessings will be extended to the Gentiles and others who are ostracized. Third, Jesus is the legitimate king and ruler, not Herod, not the priests in Jerusalem, nor any other earthly authorities.[23] This is further confirmed as Matthew presents Jesus as far superior to John. Jesus declares that John Baptist is the greatest of all previous people, and yet Jesus ushers in the kingdom that will make its subjects greater still (Matt 11:11-12 par.). He calls John the Elijah who was to come (Matt 17:11-13 par.), but that leaves only a messianic "job description"[24] open for Jesus, his successor.

Luke's commentary of the birth of Jesus follows an elegant Greek literary structure commonly found as the preface to other historical and biographical works of the day.[25] Luke was both an accomplished historian and theologian as his preface suggests (Luke 1:1-4). "Whereas Matthew structures his infancy narrative around Old Testament 'prophecies,' Luke organises his to provide an overview of God's plan of salvation and to highlight the similarities and differences between John the Baptist and Jesus."[26] First the birth of John is foretold (Luke 1:5-25), then the birth of Jesus (Luke 1:26-28). John was born into a priestly family and from Zechariah's prophecy he was permanently filled with the Spirit "yet from his mother's womb" (Luke 1:15).[27] This was unprecedented, and linked John with a prophetic role of calling people to repentance and preparing the way of the Lord, like Elijah of old (Luke 1:15).[28] The birth of Jesus (Luke 1:26-38) is foretold by the angel Gabriel who came to Mary and

---

22. Moltmann, *Way of Jesus Christ*, 81.

23. Blomberg, *Jesus and the Gospels*, 202.

24. Ibid., 403.

25. See ibid., 202.

26. Ibid., 203.

27. On Luke's use of the Holy Spirit inspiring human beings to witness concerning Jesus within the infancy narratives, see Shelton, *Mighty in Word and Deed*, 15-32.

28. For an extensive list of parallels between Jesus and Elijah, see ibid., 28-29.

promised her a miraculous conception (Cf. Luke 3:23). The child Mary would bear was to be the "Son of the Most High," which in this context is a Davidic, regal, messianic title (Cf. Luke 1:32a with vv.32b-33). The angel cites Isa 7:14 and 2 Sam 7:12f, but says nothing about a virgin birth. It is only when Mary asks "how?" that the interpretation follows, with reference to her overshadowing by the Holy Spirit, and the conclusion, "Therefore, the holy one to be born of you will be called the Son of God" (v35). The link between the Easter enthronement and the title of Son is projected into the birth of Jesus in Luke (1:32, 35). The Jews understood the announcement of a messianic figure and in the Hellenistic context the Son of God interpretation would have made sense. Divine figures also have a divine birth. John will be the forerunner pointing to one greater than he, Jesus. Only Jesus is called "Savior," "Christ," and "Lord" (2:11).[29]

The two mothers come together to highlight how their respective stories intersect (Luke 1:39-56). Mary visits her relative Elizabeth and Elizabeth repeats the angel's blessing, and for the first time in Luke we have a reference to someone who boldly proclaims God's word as being "filled with the Holy Spirit." In utero John leaps for joy showing that he too is empowered with the Spirit. Then the birth and growth of John are narrated (Luke 1:57-80), and then that of Jesus (Luke 2:1-52). Throughout the birth and growth of Jesus we see Messianic indicators culminating in the aged prophet Simeon's last "swan song." He was promised that he would live to see the Messiah born. As Jesus's family take him to the temple Simeon lived to see that prophecy fulfilled and can now die in peace after he sings the *Nunc Dimittis* (Luke 2:29-32). Here appears the most explicit reference to the Messiah's ministry extending to the Gentiles (v. 32 alluding to Isa 42:6 or 49:6). Anna matches Simeon's prophecy.

In all Luke shows the similarities between the two, both born to godly Jewish parents who experienced miraculous conceptions involving the Holy Spirit and outward "signs," both heralds of the new age, both having an impact on Israel and then beyond offering deliverance in both spiritual and socio-economic realms. But it is also clear that Luke is presenting Jesus as greater than John. The miracle of virgin conception is greater than that of merely opening a once-barren womb.

---

29. For more similarities and differences between Jesus and John the Baptist see Nolland, *Luke 1—9:20*, 40-1.

Luke is not finished making his point. In his genealogy he goes well beyond Matthew's extending right back to Adam (Luke 3:23-28). By placing this genealogy between Jesus's baptism and temptation Luke seems to be highlighting the unique sense of Jesus as Son of God (Cf. Luke 3:22; 4:3). Luke's birth and growth narrative provides almost the same information as that of Matthew, although utilizing divergent stories in the process. Jesus is the Davidic Messiah coming as the consolation of Israel, but he is also "a light to enlighten the Gentiles." He will be both Savior and Lord, bringing spiritual and socio-economic liberty.[30]

The promise of Jesus's birth in both Matthew and Luke is intended to say that he is the Messianic Son of God and Lord of the messianic kingdom not only since his resurrection and enthronement at Pentecost, and not merely since his baptism by John, but from his earthly beginnings in relation to the Holy Spirit, and by his heavenly origin.[31] Not only was Jesus filled with the power of the Holy Spirit, but there was no time in his existence when he was not in total relationship with the Holy Spirit. Clearly, Jesus is the *Messiah* right from his beginning and as such he is filled uniquely with the Holy Spirit and, as the community already knew, was the one who brings about the out-pouring of the Spirit on "all flesh." As a consequence, Jesus was filled with the Spirit of God from the beginning, indeed, his whole being is the "warp and weft" of the Spirit.[32]

With John's prologue (John 1:1-18) we have an entirely different orientation to the appearance of Jesus, and yet one that yields the same conclusions. John starts with a theological assessment of Jesus and mentions his ontological identity in terms of pre-existence. Pannenberg objected that John's (and Paul's) preexistence Christology is incompatible with earlier conception Christology.[33] Burge identifies the Johannine

---

30. On the historicity of the birth narratives see Blomberg, *Jesus*, 208-9 and Cranfield, "Some Reflections on the Subject of the Virgin Birth," 177-89.

31. von Balthasar, *Theologik*, vol. 3, 167-68, and 187, speaks of a "soteriological inversion" in relation to the roles of the Son and the Spirit in the economy of salvation. In opposition to Mühlen's logical priority of the incarnation of the Logos over the anointing with the Spirit, he appeals to the life of the immanent Trinity. He concludes that the incarnation and the anointing with the Spirit are both contemporaneous and represent two aspects of the one event. See Mühlen, *Der heilige Geist als Person*, and *Una Mystica Persona*.

32. Moltmann, *Way of Jesus Christ*, 86.

33. Pannenberg, *Jesus*, 143.

prologue as a serious problem facing any study of the Spirit in John.[34] While it is true that John goes beyond the synoptic Gospels it can be said that both views are compatible as they are complementary answers to the same problem.[35] While we cannot enter into the debate over the structure, origins, or exact interpretation of the prologue or Logos concept in early Christian thought[36] we can say that for the synoptic Gospels the Spirit was used to explain the question of Jesus's origins; for John the Logos hymn answers this problem. The point of John's prologue is to stress that the origin of Jesus is not this worldly, but other-worldly, and has now come into history (John 1:14). Here we find the Johannine miraculous conception. Jesus's birth by the Spirit is substantially related to the incarnation of the Logos. Both speak, albeit in different ways, of divine origins and divine union with humanity.[37] While John does go one step further than either Matthew or Luke, their basic presentation is not dissimilar. By stressing the virgin conception in Matthew and Luke the tendency found within John is a logical development. "Both images portray a suprahuman divine connection which ... could be harmonized. The Spirit, just like the Logos, was believed to exist above history."[38] Both Spirit and Logos are preexistent, both refer to the personal presence of God, and both lead to the conclusion that Jesus is the Son of God (John 1:14, 18; Luke 1:32, 35). The Word, as John calls Jesus was with God at creation, in fact the "Word was God," not in the sense of being identical to God but rather the Logos fully shared in his divinity. The same Word is now revealed to all humanity in the person of Jesus.

The primary role of John the Baptist within John's presentation is consistent with the perspectives of Matthew and Luke, he is to testify about Jesus (John 1:6–8, 15). John makes it explicitly clear that John the

---

34. Burge, *Anointed Community*, 111.

35. "It would be simplistic to say that Jesus's Logos origins and Spirit birth are merely two sides of the same coin. There are vast differences. But at their heart they are wrestling with the same problem: How has God substantially expressed himself in the man Jesus?" ibid., 113.

36. Miller, "Johannine Origins of the Johannine Logos," 445–57, and "Logos was God," 65–77.

37. "Jesus's humanity has its origin in his conception by the Holy Spirit; it has its effectiveness from its anointing by the Holy Spirit. This new man, Jesus Christ, is the work of the Son of God opening in his own human nature the power and energy of the Holy Spirit," Smail, *Reflected Glory*, 64.

38. Burge, *Anointed Community*, 112.

Baptist is not the Messiah but a witness to him. His prologue thus alternates between the Baptist and Jesus in much the same way as Luke 1–2 (albeit for different reasons). While much has been made of the above nature of John's prologue the whole point is to boldly assert that the Word became flesh and is to be identified with Jesus of Nazareth (John 1:9–14). John uses the language of the Word "tabernacling" or "dwelling" because it contained the same consonants as the Hebrew for God's shekinah glory. The incarnation then harks back to when God's presence dwelt among the Israelites. John is thus stating that the presence of God now dwells in Jesus the "Only Begotten," and from the birth narratives we are led to believe that this presence was experienced in Jesus as the Holy Spirit.

While the virginal conception neither proves nor demands an interpretation in terms of incarnation it is a fitting way to reinforce the Christian conviction that Jesus is both fully God (divine paternity) and fully man (human maternity). In Luke the emphasis is on Jesus as God's gift, a reminder that salvation is by grace, in Matthew the emphasis is on Jesus as Immanuel, God in solidarity with us. Due to the little use made of the virginal conception in both the Gospels and the rest of the New Testament we should not make this the central crux of any doctrine, however, it is an important indicator to Jesus unique identity. It highlights his relationship to the Father through the Spirit and of God's presence in Jesus through the Spirit.

A Trinitarian perspective is already emerging throughout these narratives whereby we understand the divine-human identity, largely through Jesus's relationship to the Father through the Spirit. Divinity is communicated to humanity via the indwelling Spirit and humanity is communicated to divinity in the exact same way. In Moltmann's words, "If Christology starts by way of pneumatology, this offers the approach for a trinitarian Christology, in which the Being of Jesus Christ is from the very outset a being-in-relationship."[39] In the creating and filling of the Spirit, Jesus of Nazareth is set apart as God's anointed (Christ), his Son, the final eschatological prophet awaited for and predicted by the faithful prophets of old. Within the New Testament these testimonies narrate and proclaim the history of Jesus of Nazareth, God's Messiah. They tell the history of Christ, but they tell it as the history of the Spirit with Jesus; furthermore, they proclaim this history as Jesus's history with the Spirit.

---

39. Moltmann, *Way of Jesus Christ*, 74.

The synoptic Gospels begin with *a Spirit Christology*. Paul and John have this as their premise; but they themselves stress *a Christological doctrine of the Spirit*.[40] Moltmann can write:

> Spirit Christology is not set up in opposition to incarnational Christology, for every doctrine of the incarnation begins with the statement "conceived by the Holy Spirit." Nor is Spirit Christology leveled at the doctrine of the two natures. But it does make it possible to absorb the exclusive christomonism of a Christology of the God-human being into the fullness of trinitarian Christology, with its wealth of relationships. The notion that there is an antithesis between an adoptionist and a pre-existence Christology is a nineteenth-century invention.[41]

When considering the New Testament testimony about the person of Christ it is impossible to talk about Jesus without talking about his relationship with the Holy Spirit, and about his relationship to the God whom he called "Abba, my Father." From the beginning the historical account of Jesus's life is at heart a Trinitarian history of God.[42]

One major implication behind the virgin conception by Spirit birth is to highlight Jesus as the archetype to our birth in the Spirit.[43] John 1:12–13 speaks of our birth as children of God immediately before it speaks of the incarnation of the Word, (i.e., it is not the human process of procreation and conception, but the experience of the Spirit.)[44] In this sense Jesus is the divine archetype of the divine sonship in the Spirit. However, this does not mean that Jesus's Spirit birth is identical to that of believers. Only Jesus is described as the "only begotten." Only he is the "firstborn," unique from all others as the history of his primal and original birth from the Spirit of God brings out. Jesus is different from us in that we come into fellowship with God through the Christ, and in fellowship with the Christ through the Spirit. From the very beginning

---

40. Moltmann, *Spirit of Life*, 58 emphasis in original.
41. Moltmann, *Way of Jesus Christ*, 74.
42. See the treatment of Abba and filial consciousness in Witherington, *Christology of Jesus*, 215–28, where he critiques the theses of Vermes, Dunn, and others.
43. Pinnock, *Flame of Love*, 86. Pinnock operates from a soteriological framework of recapitulation. While this is a theme, I do not consider it to be the main theme. Moltmann, *Way of Jesus Christ*, 83, speaks of the theological significance of the Spirit birth of Jesus as being mythical in character. While he avers that it can be understood literally, (i.e., a gynaecological miracle) he dismisses this.
44. Rom 8:29 is our parallel.

God is the Father of Jesus Christ, not temporarily but essentially and eternally. This Fatherhood does not just extend to Christ's consciousness or ministry, but to his conception, and before, to his person and being (as John brings out so vividly). As a consequence the Messiah Jesus Christ is essentially God's Son. He does not become so at some point in his life (i.e., baptism, or exaltation). This distinguishes the incarnation from or out of the Spirit from the indwelling of the Spirit in human beings. This is one of the purposes behind describing the difference between John the Baptist and Jesus. Jesus Christ was incarnated through the agency of the Holy Spirit; believers are inhabited through the agency of the Holy Spirit. There is both a qualitative and quantitative difference between the two. "If incarnation is identified with inhabitation," writes Moltmann, "christology is dissolved in anthropology."[45]

The birth of the Son in the Holy Spirit is the beginning and the sign of hope for the rebirth of human beings, and eventually even the rebirth of the cosmos itself. That is the significance of the indwelling of the Spirit at the birth of Jesus Christ. To the Jews this was a deliberate sign. It was a messianic indicator that lit up the eschatological scene like a neon light of Vegas over the lowly stable of Bethlehem. As the divinely assigned star lit up the night sky of Bethlehem in order to give "light" to the wise men, so the birth of the baby Jesus in and through the Holy Spirit lit up the theological horizons of the Jews, giving them the true "Light" of salvation, and not the Jews alone but all nations, "all flesh." And so right from the beginning of the narrative we see that a pneumatological path will be trail blazed by Jesus Christ, deliberately highlighted by the Gospel writers in order to inform us that the risen and exalted Lord of the Spirit is none other than the lowly figure of the Galilean rabbi, Jesus of Nazareth. In these pivotal episodes in the life of Christ the evangelists

---

45. Moltmann, *Way of Jesus Christ*, 84. Moltmann takes John 1:12 as the point of comparison between the birth of the Son and the rebirth of believers to its logical extreme and posits the fact that "we do not have to assume any supernatural intervention [in Christ's birth] . . . Christ's birth from the Spirit is a statement about Christ's relationship to God, or God's relationship to Christ. It does not have to be linked with a genealogical assertion." Clearly Moltmann is applying the results of a mythical reading of Scripture, a practice of which I do not share. We gain nothing by a mythical reading of the birth narratives and in actual fact risk losing everything. A literal reading of these narratives supports the differences between Jesus Christ and believers, as the entire Gospels will go on to develop.

engage in a retroactive reading of his life, presenting him to us as the unique Messiah. The Coming One has indeed been heralded as Come.[46]

Episode Two: Jesus's Baptism in the Jordan River and Subsequent Wilderness Temptation

The second major disclosure episode in Jesus's life to concern us is his baptism and subsequent temptation. The baptism of Jesus has been seized upon by many as a key way to account for the identity and mission of Jesus Christ.[47] This is achieved through the emphasis on both the anointing of the Spirit and Jesus's filial relationship with God, *his* Father. Basic to Jesus's experience of God was a sense of sonship and a consciousness of Spirit, but what is the link between the two? The link is clear in the early church (for instance John 3:34-5; 20:21-2; Acts 2:33; Rom 1:3-4; Gal 4:4-6), but within the synoptic Gospels only one passage directly associates Son with Spirit—the baptism narrative (Mark 1:9-11/ Matt 3:17/Luke 3:22), an event described by one scholar as "a focal point of salvation history."[48]

The earliest mention of the Spirit in Mark is in connection with John the Baptist (Mark 1:8). Here again the essential difference between Jesus and other men is emphasized: the difference being his relation to God through the Holy Spirit. John was conscious of his role as forerunner of "One mightier than I." John baptized with water but the coming one would baptize "with the Holy Spirit."[49] Here John contrasts his own baptism in water, which cleanses Israel through repentance and forgiveness, with the much more powerful baptism or cleansing of Israel that will be effected by the Messiah, the agent of God's reign.[50] All the Baptist does is rich in symbolism and steeped in the context of Israel's covenant-

---

46. O'Donnell, "In Him and Over Him," 25–29.

47. For an overview of the pneumatological dimensions of the baptism narrative see Hawthorne, *Presence and the Power*, chapter 4, and Turner, *Power from on High*, chapters 7–9; and for the temptation narrative Smail, *Reflected Glory*, 90–103.

48. Toon, "Historical Perspectives on the Doctrine of Christ's Ascension: Part 1." 285.

49. Matt 3:11 and Luke 3:16 read "he will baptize you with the Holy Spirit and fire." This phrase is best understood as a hendiadys, one deluge consisting of Spirit and fire. Dunn, *Jesus and the Spirit*, 8–22.

50. Most probably John was echoing the familiar imagery and expectation of an eschatological messianic figure found in Isa 11:1–4; and 9:2–7. For parallels in Judaism see 1 Enoch 49:2–3; 62:1–2; Pss Sol. 17:37; 18:7.

al relationship to God. His message, symbolism and baptism constitute an "eschatological sacrament of repentance," to quote Moltmann.[51] The baptism he offered was not that of the ritual ceremony of the cult, but one of repentance within the context of the eschatological conversion of all Israel. John was the Elijah who had come to usher in the end-time (Matt 11:14). He was both the end of the old era, that of the torah and the transition into the new era of Christ and the Spirit. As such Jesus does not see John as merely the forerunner, but actually takes over his message and takes it to its messianic and eschatological conclusion (Matt 3:2; 4:17).[52]

The difference between Jesus and other men, especially John the Baptist, is intensified in the baptism narrative and is brought out through John the Baptist's use of the title "the coming one" for Jesus (Matt 11:3; Luke 7:20). Later John would himself ask this question of Jesus while he was imprisoned and awaiting death (Luke 7:20). But what did he mean by the coming one? Clearly John the Baptist did not see himself as this coming one (John 1:19-23). Within Old Testament and the intertestamental tradition various bringers of eschatological salvation were expected. Common to each of these figures was that they would be distinctive bearers of the Spirit of God: the Messiah of the last time (Isa 11:1f; Song 17:37), the Servant of Yahweh (Isa 42:1ff), the Son of Man and the eschatological prophet, the New Moses. "This is to be understood in the sense that the special capacity and function of the bearer of salvation at the end of time is the effect of the Spirit of God, of whom he will constantly partake."[53]

In those days there were three outstanding personages who were widely expected to appear in Israel—a great king (a second David), a great priest (a second Aaron), and a great prophet (a second Moses). We see in the person of Jesus the fulfillment of all three inspired ones to

---

51 Moltmann, *Way of Jesus Christ*, 88.

52. While the similarities between John and Jesus are obvious, the differences are too. John proclaimed the coming kingdom of God as judgment and wrath on an unrepentant generation. Jesus proclaimed it as grace to the poor and sinners. John left civilization for the wilderness. Jesus left the wilderness for an urban ministry. John lived on a starvation diet of the desert. Jesus ate bread and drank wine with anyone. John was an ascetic. Jesus was labeled a "glutton and a drunkard" (Matt 11:19). John baptized for repentance. Jesus did not baptize at all but forgave people their sins. I am indebted to Moltmann, *Way of Jesus Christ*, 89, for pointing out these differences.

53. Pannenberg, *Jesus*, 116.

come. "All the characteristics of the Spirit within the Old Testament now relocate in Jesus."[54] Regarding Jesus's Kingship it is significant to read in Luke 4:18 (and Acts 10:38) that in the temple Jesus reads from Isa 61, "The Spirit of the Lord is upon me . . ." It was to his baptismal anointing which he referred. So to identify Jesus as the Messiah is to put aside the military and political connotations implicit in the identity with David and instead to fill those terms with the meaning which Jesus gave them by being the person which he was and doing the things he did.

In relation to Jesus's priesthood Jesus could not be the Aaronic high priest, for he was not from the tribe of Levi, but he is identified as a priest in the order of Melchizadek (Heb 5:10 cf. Ps 110:4). In the Psalms God swears an oath to the Messiah of David's line. Jesus performs priestly functions in other writers also; Paul speaks of him interceding for his people (Rom 8:34), and John calls him our advocate with the Father (1 John 2:1). Finally in relation to his prophetic role we see here a realization in Jesus that is direct and obvious (cf. Deut 18:15). The people readily recognized in Jesus this greater prophet, when he fed the multitude in the wilderness and in the temple court called all those thirsty to come and drink, some of the people said "This is indeed the prophet!" (John 6:14; 7:40). They remembered how in the wilderness Moses had fed the people with bread from heaven and refreshed with water from the rock. Again at the transfiguration when the Father said "listen to him" (Mark 9:7), they recalled the fulfillment of Moses's words "you must listen to him." Similarly on two occasions in Acts Moses's words about the coming prophet are quoted and applied to Jesus, once by Peter and once by Stephen (Acts 3:22–23; 7:37). Throughout Mark Jesus is thought to be John the Baptist himself, Elijah, or one of the prophets (Mark 8:29; 9:12f). All three possibilities indicate that Jesus is thought of as one identified by his anointing by the Spirit. Peter rejects these labels and confesses Jesus as the Christ. "By what or by whom is Jesus anointed as the Christ?" asks Colin Brown. "The answer has already been given: Jesus was anointed by the Spirit at his baptism and identified as the messianic Son of God."[55]

The Baptist's message was of the "coming one" who would baptize with the Holy Spirit in fulfillment of prophecy; Jesus heard him preach and responded. In Luke 3:21–22 Jesus receives the Holy Spirit. This was

---

54. McFarlane, *Why Do You Believe What You believe About The Holy Spirit?* 43.
55. Brown, "Person of Christ," in *ISBE*, vol. 3, 790.

his anointing as "Messiah."[56] For John, this shift from water baptism to Spirit anointing begun in the synoptic Gospels is completed. Through the testimony of John the Baptist, Jesus's experience of the Spirit is described while his water baptism is not mentioned. "[John] has certainly elided from the tradition all but what is of chief importance for his own purposes. For John, then, Jesus's anointing with the Spirit and the revelatory significance of this anointing for the Baptist are all that matter."[57] When we inquire further into what this significance was for John the Baptist we see that Jesus's identity is revealed to the Baptist only in the Jordan River, not through water baptism but through Spirit anointing. John witnessed this anointing (John 1:34) and came to the same conclusion given in the synoptic Gospels: "This is the Son/Chosen of God" (John 1:34; cf. 1:14, 18). John's gospel deliberately sets John the Baptist up as the interpreter of Jesus identity.[58] In John 1:33 the Spirit is noted as the sole signal of the Messiah's identity. The Spirit thus becomes "the revelatory key which will tell the Baptist when his expectation has been fulfilled."[59] This is further strengthened by John's reference to the Spirit coming to settle or remain upon Jesus (John 1:32–33), implying the permanent residence of the Spirit with Jesus. This separates Jesus from other prophets, and other men; this Jesus is the Chosen One, the Son of God.[60] This is further confirmed by the allusions to Isa 42 which underscores Jesus's unique Messianic status. Jesus is the Chosen One precisely because he possesses the Messianic endowment, and this will enable him to anoint in power

---

56. For Barrett, *Holy Spirit and the Gospel Tradition*, 115, the baptism narrative "is essentially the solemn appointment of the Messiah to his office, the installation of the Son of God, and it stands in the Gospel tradition as an indication of how the ministry ... was to be understood ... the baptism details which as they stand refer to inspiration by the Spirit are in fact subordinated to the intention of the writers to set forth Jesus as the Messiah." See Dunn, *Jesus and the Spirit*, chapter 2, and his *Baptism in the Holy Spirit*, 32–37.

57. Burge, *Anointed Community*, 52.

58. Burge (ibid.) argues that John the Baptist had a supplementary revelation that provided him with the interpretation of what would happen at the Jordan. Cf. Jonge, "Jewish Expectations About the 'Messiah' According to the Fourth Gospel," 253.

59. Burge, *Anointed Community*, 53.

60. Ibid., 59, writes; "As John completed the shift in emphasis away from the water baptism to the Spirit, his use of the dove tradition to that end may have inspired later reflective writers to elaborate their Spirit Christologies within the Jordan event." On Dove imagery, see further in Keener, *Spirit in the Gospels and Acts*, 60; and Hildebrandt, *Old Testament Theology of the Spirit of God*, 37–39.

those who believe. As the rest of the gospels will highlight, Jesus fulfils his Sonship by giving himself completely as Servant in the power of the Holy Spirit.[61]

Within the baptism itself there are three Messianic indicators that attest to Jesus's unique identity,[62] and in these we see the interpretative keys for the synoptic Gospels's presentation of the baptism of Jesus as the Messianic figure that has come.[63] The three indicators are the descent of the Spirit as a dove, the open heavens, and the divine audition.

All four Gospels refer to a dove, but all use a simile to clarify that the Spirit's descent on Jesus was "like" a dove (Matt 3:16; Mark 1:10; Luke 3:22; and John 1:32). Doves in the ancient world symbolized peace, love, and even dignity itself, but the most obvious reference is to the activity of God's Spirit in creation, just as Gen 1:2 spoke of him "brooding" over the waters.[64] All four evangelists focus the return of the Spirit on Jesus (i.e., Matt 3:16; Mark 1:10; Luke 3:22; John 1:32–33). Mark's presentation of the Spirit descending on Jesus agrees with the function of the Spirit in Jewish thought.[65] The other evangelists, relying presumably on Isa 42:1, record that the Spirit came "upon him" (*ep auton*). But Mark says the Spirit entered "into him" (*eis auton*), intensifying the union of the Spirit and Jesus.[66] So in answer to the question: What accounts for the difference between Jesus and others? (prophets, David, even Moses), the answer is evident in the unique baptism of Jesus. His baptism was not one of repentance,[67] as others were, but uniquely, one of the Spirit who descended upon him like a dove (Mark 1:10, Acts 10:38). Jesus's anointing is without measure (John 3:34), and as the Spirit rested on him, the

61. See Cullman, *Christology of the New Testament*, 14, and Torrance, *Theology in Reconstruction*, 246.

62. Edwards, "Baptism of Jesus According to the Gospel of Mark," 43–57, speaks of these three indicators in kingdom terms. He also writes that "The baptism functions as the cornerstone of Mark's Christological understanding—a stone that is not undressed, as we shall see," (ibid., 43).

63. Edwards cites *Testimony of the Twelve Patriarchs* 18.2 in support, ibid., 44. Cf. Keener, *Spirit in the Gospels and Acts*, 53–60.

64. See Blomberg, *Jesus and the Gospels*, 222 n. 15 and Turner, *Power from on High*, 188.

65. See Edwards, "Baptism of Jesus," 46–47, for bibliographical details.

66. Keener, *Spirit in the Gospels and Acts*, 51, does not see Isaiah 42 behind Mark's narrative but it is behind Matthew's.

67. I do believe Jesus's baptism was for repentance but only if this is understood vicariously. The vicarious baptism of Jesus is a rich stream of thought but not one that is our immediate concern here.

Shekinah found its abiding dwelling place;[68] the self-restriction and self-humiliation of the eternal Spirit (a *kenosis* of the Spirit?) identifying with Jesus's person and embracing the history of his life and suffering. Hence, this poses indisputable evidence of Messianic endowment and identification.

Along with this Spirit endowment was the corresponding vision of the open heavens and the divine audition: "Thou art my beloved Son, with whom I am well pleased" (Mark 1:11 pars; cf. Ps. 2:7; Isa 42:1, and the legitimization of Israel's kings).[69] In the *bat qol* (Mark 1:11; Matt 3:17; Luke 3:22; John 1:34) Old Testament themes are highlighted.[70] In light of Old Testament usage "'son of God" works on the first level, not initially as a divine title but a designation for a creature, indicating a special relationship with God, in particular, God's representative or vice-regent. Therefore, at the baptism, the title "Son of God" refers to the affirmation of Jesus as God's Son-king in virtue of his anointing by the Spirit.[71] "The title expresses the intimate relationship which Jesus had through the Spirit with the Father as the Father's anointed representative."[72] However, this usage quickly worked its way onto the second level of meaning, where Jesus's uniqueness made him not only a

---

68. Writing about the significance of Pentecost Torrance, *Theology in Reconstruction*, 241, writes, "In the birth and life of Jesus on earth human nature and divine nature were inseparably united in the eternal Person of God the Son. Therefore in him the closed circle of the inner life of God was made to overlap with human life, and human nature was taken up to share in the eternal communion of the Father and the Son and the Holy Spirit. In this one Man the divine life and love overflowed into creaturely and human being, so that Jesus, Man on earth, received the Spirit of God without measure, for the fullness of the Godhead dwelt in him bodily. Jesus became the Bearer of the Holy Spirit among men."

69. Turner, *Power from on High*, 197–98.

70. Adam is called "Son of God" in Luke's genealogy of Jesus (Luke 3:38), Hosea 11:1, cited in Matt 2:15, alludes to Israel as God's son, in Wisdom 2:18 the righteous man is God's son, Nathan's prophecy to David contains the promise to his successor that "You are my son, today I have begotten you" (2 Sam 7:14; cf. Ps 89:26–27), and Ps 2:7 in reference to the anointed king (cited in Acts 13:33; Heb 1:5; 5:5 cf. 2 Pet 1:17). Ps 2:7 is also behind the *bat qol* at Jesus's baptism. Also called the "Ordeal Narrative."

71. This is also true of the trial scene of Mark 14:61.

72. Brown, "Trinity and Incarnation," 88. Brown goes on to comment on the ancient view that the spirit of a god resides in his representative thus setting apart that person as the "image" of the god. In the case of Jesus he is the one in whom God's Spirit dwells, who is given stewardship and authority to act on God's behalf. In support Brown cites Clines, "Image of God in Man," 53–103.

son of God but *the* Son of God, the King, the eschatological prophet, the one true Messiah/Christ. "According to the tradition of Israel's messianic promise, it is self-evident that all this leads to the divine Sonship of the one so anointed and endowed."[73]

With the anointing of the *ruach* of God, Jesus's relationship to God is clearly authenticated as one of Sonship, and God's relationship to Jesus, as one of Father. The Father's declaration of pleasure in his Son, of both "Son" and "Servant," seems to have been understood in a messianic sense by important segments of pre-Christian Judaism.[74] "Therefore it would appear that God is forthrightly declaring Jesus to be both kingly Messiah and suffering Servant. There is also an incipient Trinitarianism in this baptism: God speaks and the Spirit descends on the man Jesus."[75]

The baptism of Jesus by John appears to have awakened within Jesus the call or drive to messianic function. It is definitely the inauguration of his public ministry that is cast by the evangelists in messianic terms, when Jesus experiences himself publicly (objectively?) as the messianic "child." While this filial relationship was implicit since birth, it may be that for Jesus it was publicly ratified, for the first time, at his baptism. Moltmann has it right when he states:

> In the Spirit [Jesus] knows himself to be the beloved Son. So the Spirit is the real determining subject of this special relationship of Jesus's to God, and of God's to Jesus. Therefore it is the Spirit who also "leads" Jesus into the mutual history between himself and God his Father, in which "through obedience" (Heb. 5:8) he will "learn" his role as the messianic Son.[76]

Traditionally, the baptism of Jesus is seen as a revelation of the Trinity, a being-in-relation; the Father acknowledging the Son and sending the Spirit. But a neglected factor has been the realization of the significance for Jesus himself of the Spirit directing his life in a specific way, a messianic way (as the temptation narrative will develop). At conception and birth, the Spirit created a human; a creature. At baptism, the Spirit

---

73. Moltmann, *Way of Jesus Christ*, 90.

74. "Because Jesus is son of Abraham . . . as well as son of David . . . but especially because Jesus is the suffering servant . . . Jesus's mission includes suffering as well as reigning," Keener, *Spirit in the Gospels and Acts*, 98.

75. Blomberg, *Jesus and the Gospels*, 222.

76. Moltmann, *Spirit of Life*, 61.

anoints Jesus for the messianic ministry;[77] a ministry first to Israel and then to "all flesh"; a ministry that exercises at once the threefold offices of the anointed—Prophet, Priest and King.[78]

As a result the baptism narrative, following from the conception-birth narrative and preceding the temptation narrative, presents two aspects of the relationship between Christ and the Spirit. One is the accommodation of the Spirit to Jesus's life as a human person (economic), while the other is the eternal relationship which exists within the inner life of the Trinity (immanent).[79]

The baptism of Jesus forms an important part of synoptic pneumatology: this event, marked by the visible appearance of the Spirit as a dove and the audible accreditation by God,[80] marks out the beginning of the new age of God. Taken as a whole, the baptism and reception of the Spirit by Jesus is significant in alerting the reader that from this time forward the Spirit will be with Jesus as the power to exercise the messianic task;[81] a task that was couched in Davidic and Mosaic motifs based on an Isianic New Exodus theology (Mark 1:3).[82] The reception of the Spirit by Jesus at his baptism does not conflict with the previously narrated account of his Spirit conception.[83] As has been mentioned, these

---

77. Gunton, *One the Three and the Many*, 189, who refers to Basil of Caesarea *On the Spirit* 16.39.

78. "The distinctive work of the Spirit is, through Christ, to perfect the creation. The function of the Spirit in relation to Jesus is, accordingly, as the perfecter of his humanity. Just as the enhypostasia reminds us of the origin of our salvation in the eternal love and action of God, so attention to the Holy Spirit reminds us of the way in which the saving action of Jesus is accomplished humanly in time," Gunton, *Christ and Creation*, 50.

79. See further in Lockhart, "Spirit, Christ, and Worship," 4–5.

80. Turner believes the dove and the voice to have been a vision seen and heard by Jesus, *Holy Spirit and Spiritual Gifts*, 28. Swete, *Holy Spirit in the New Testament*, 44–47, emphasizes the fact that the vision was seen by only Jesus (and John the Baptist, John 1:32), and so did not function as a public annunciation of Jesus person or ministry.

81. In no way does the *pericope* suggest any adoptionist Christology. Baptism is another stage of Jesus's unveiling or revelation as the Messiah. See Hodgson, *Jesus—Word and Presence*, 177–78.

82. John prepared the way in the "wilderness" against the backdrop of Isa 40.3. The Messiah of this imagery, strengthened in intertestamental times, would destroy Israel's enemies (mostly spiritual forces) and lead the people through a transformed wilderness to a restored Zion where he would rule. To Israel, this was both "joy" and "comfort" and "salvation." Keener, *Spirit in the Gospels and Acts*, 51–53, and Bauckham, *God Crucified*, 55–56.

83. Dunn, *Jesus and the Spirit*, explains Jesus's reception of the Spirit at this point as a paradigmatic sonship and only secondarily as empowering for ministry. This view fails

accounts rule out all adoptionist theories.[84] What is significant in the synoptic accounts of the baptism is that they secure the baptism of Jesus in anointing terms, by shifting the emphasis away from the baptism to the anointing of Jesus by the Spirit.[85] For Luke, the chief interest is not the baptism *per se* but the event of the Spirit (Luke 3:21-22).[86] The baptism was the preliminary participation in an event of the old aeon about to end, but the pivotal event on which the dawning of the eschaton was about to turn would be the emergence of the Spirit (cf. Acts 2:17; Joel 2:28). This is confirmed in Acts 10:38, when Luke records Peter's account of the salvation-historical events in Jesus's life and the baptism with water is omitted entirely—"God anointed Jesus of Nazareth with the Holy Spirit and power."

Within this context the temptations of Christ in the wilderness naturally act as the trial of calling to the offices of prophet, priest, and king. The human relevance of Christ's temptations is clear and is spelt out in Hebrews; Jesus is human and so identifies with his creation in the same way as us, yet without sin. The significance of the temptations resides in the fact that they are *messianic* in character and that is why it follows and is associated with his baptism.[87] As the Augustinian tradition teaches, freedom is not an inherent quality for humanity. But in Jesus alone we see freedom, for he alone is totally obedient to the will of the Father,

---

to take into account Jesus's Spirit conception and also later receptions of the Spirit. The context of the baptism would more clearly indicate that the Spirit was for an empowering for messianic mission, as seen by the temptation narrative to follow and Christ's defeat of Satan. O'Donnell, "In Him and Over Him," 31, makes it plain that Spirit reception is never a static affair, not even for Jesus: "Hence even if Jesus had the full indwelling of the Holy Spirit from the moment of the Incarnation, it is also true to say that the Holy Spirit did not indwell him in a static way. The Spirit's presence was dynamic and made itself felt in the humanity of Jesus at significant moments of his life and ministry."

84. This again emphasizes a retroactive reading of the Gospels. "If there was at any time an adoptionist christology, it gave way to the 'incarnational Christology' which prevails in the New Testament. Possibly what obtained was a working back from the death-resurrection. The Resurrection was the unmistakable evidence that he was the son of God. This gave foundation to the faith of the earliest Christians . . . Mark shows that Jesus was the Christ at his baptism. Luke and Matthew show that he was the son of God at his birth. John showed that he was God from the beginning" [Stagg, "Holy Spirit in the New Testament," 135–47]. See Edwards, "Baptism of Jesus According to the Gospel of Mark," 55.

85. See Dunn, *Baptism in the Holy Spirit*, 33–37.

86. See further in Burge, *Anointed Community*, 50–51.

87 See Shelton, *Mighty in Word and Deed*, chapter 5.

submitted to the Spirit. Gunton helpfully talks of Jesus's "freedom."[88] He remained free by remaining committed to the Father through the Spirit. Freedom is not an absolute but something exercised in relation to other persons, and that means in the first instance that it is the gift of the Spirit, God in personal otherness enabling us to be free. It is in our relatedness that we are free or not, and this is as true for Jesus as it is for us. The link is found in the Holy Spirit.

Jesus exercised this freedom as prophet, priest and king. Edward Irving, one theologian who reflected deeply on the relationship between Christ and Spirit, limited Jesus's priestly activity to his post-resurrection state.[89] But that is too narrow a scope of his ministry. While it retains the important insight that Jesus's relation to the Spirit changes as a result of glorification, it fails to recognize the important priestly activity of Jesus in his active obedience. Already in Jesus's baptism and temptations we see a human priestly action of offering to the Father; the perfection of a true human life (Heb 9:14). That is, the Spirit perfected Jesus humanity, and that perfecting work consists of both his life laid down and the whole pattern of a life leading to his passion and death[90] (both his active and passive obedience).[91]

The temptation narratives[92] follow immediately after the baptism narratives and are intimately related (Mark 1:12–13; Matt 4:1–11; Luke 4:1–3). The synoptic Gospels relate Jesus's testing with his baptism chronologically. Mark makes this especially clear with his customary expression, "at once" (*kai euthus*) after baptism, the Spirit compelled (*ekballei*) Jesus to enter the wilderness.[93] The Spirit leads Jesus into the

---

88. Gunton, *Christ and Creation*, 50.

89. Irving, *Collected Writings of Edward Irving*, 5.236f.

90. Pinnock, *Flame of Love*, 87–89, brings this to the fore in his pneumatic theology. He brings discussion of the *kenosis* of Christ into focus at this point. For Pinnock the *kenosis* is the decision of the Son not to make use of divine attributes independently but experience what it would mean to be truly human. Therefore he depended on the Spirit for power to live his life and pursue his mission. See further in Hawthorne, *Presence and the Power*, chapter 7.

91. See further below.

92. Also called the "Ordeal Narrative."

93. While Mark only devotes two verses to the temptation narrative compared to Matthew's eleven and Luke's thirteen, it is now widely accepted that the whole of Mark relates to Jesus's temptation narrative; his entire ministry was one continuous encounter with the Satan. See Wessel, "Mark," in *Expositor's Bible Commentary*, vol. 8, 623; Lane, *Gospel According to Mark*, 206.

wilderness, Satan tempts him there, the angels minister to him, and he is said to have been among beasts. The baptism and temptations converge at two prominent junctures: the reception of the Spirit and the voice from heaven. In Jesus's mission we cannot ascribe priority to Jesus's experience of God as Son or in the Spirit.[94] The Son obeys the Father's will; the Spirit drives him forward. The two statements describe the same inward compulsion that found expression in Jesus's deeds and words. It is not surprising then that the wilderness temptations (Mark 1:12) which were directed at his consciousness of sonship ("if you are the son of God …") are temptations to prove his sonship by means of miraculous power ("command these stones to become bread").

For Mark (1:12) the temptations are set within an Old Testament understanding of the Spirit being the compulsive power of God coming upon him, while Luke makes Jesus the "subject of an action in the Holy Spirit"[95] (Luke 4:1). While Mark stresses the fact that Jesus was the inspired man, Luke emphasizes the fact of Jesus's lordship over the Spirit.[96] For both Jesus is fully equipped to enter into the battle of the spirit-world. His temptations are the first confrontation of this kind and are clearly Messianic in character. The rest of Jesus's ministry will also evidence Jesus victory over Satan and his spiritual hoard. Only after this does he go in the power of the Spirit to Galilee (Luke 4:14). The temptations were not leveled at his human weakness but rather aimed at his relationship to God; hence they follow upon his baptism.[97] Presumably the power of the new age, the salvation bearing Messiah, would be tested and found worthy. The temptations echo those of Israel in the wilderness.[98] While Israel rebelled and grieved the Holy Spirit (Isa 63:10), their new representative, Jesus Christ, proves faithful and overcomes.[99] While the Spirit's

---

94. Kimball, *Jesus's Exposition of the Old Testament in Luke's Gospel*, 90, "Many scholars interpret the typology solely at the point of Jesus's relationship to God (i.e., at his sonship) rather than also at the point of his messiahship because they fail to see the messianic character of the temptations."

95. Isaacs, *Concept of Spirit*, 121.

96. Turner, *Power from on High*, 204.

97. Moltmann, *Spirit of Life*, 61.

98. See Exod 4:22–23; Deut 8:3; 6:13, 16. Strauss, *Davidic Messiah in Luke-Acts*, 215–56.

99. In this way only are the wilderness temptations a paradigm for all believers by virtue of the fact that the Spirit with which Jesus was endowed with at his baptism committed him to an irreconcilable conflict with evil. Mark 1:10 calls it "The Spirit," Matt

role is not explicitly described in the temptation encounters,[100] it is right to infer that the Spirit afforded Jesus "new depths of charismatic wisdom and insight, which is the basis for the hoped for Messiah's redoubtable righteousness."[101] For believers living in the milieu of first-century Judaism it was axiomatic that the Son of God had the Spirit of God, particularly in view of the fact that the Spirit was active at the time of the Exodus and Israel's wilderness wanderings (Isa 63:14).[102] While Mark emphasizes the Spirit's action of driving Jesus to the desert Matthew is equally clear that the wilderness wanderings were Spirit directed, as were those of Israel earlier (Matt 4:1ff; cf. Isa 63:14). Matthew stated that Jesus was "led up by the Spirit to be tempted" (Matt 4:1), an infinitive of purpose, so that the testing of Jesus's obedience became the purpose of the Spirit's leading into the wilderness. Luke is equally clear when he wrote that Jesus was "full of the Holy Spirit" (Luke 4:1). The synoptic Gospels thus confirm the fulfillment of Isa 11:2, that Jesus would face his opponent equipped with divine power. However, Jesus was not anointed with the Spirit only for the forty day period in the wilderness, but his entire ministry was characterized by the power of the Spirit (Luke 4:1, 14, 18).

To clarify things further we must remember the *bat qol* asserting intimate sonship. This sonship becomes paradigmatic for everything that follows in the temptation narratives because all the Adam/Israel/Messianic attributes of Jesus in the wilderness are undergirded by the concept of his Sonship. The whole temptation narrative is therefore about the testing of the Son of God in the power of the Spirit.[103] Just as

---

3:16 has "God's Spirit," and Luke 4:1 "the Holy Spirit." The Spirit is "Holy" because the primary function is not to perform (miracles, manifestations, etc.), but to equip for the battle against evil. The Spirit is "power," not nude power but "holy power," ethical, God's power of salvation. "If you like Jesus is the funnel through whom the Spirit becomes available to men. Jesus transposes the Spirit into a fully personal key. Jesus is the prism through whom the diffused and fitful light of the Spirit is concentrated . . . What follows is that the Spirit is forever afterwards marked with the character of Jesus," Green, *I Believe in the Holy Spirit*, 42.

100. Swete, *Holy Spirit in the New Testament*, 54–55, and Turner, *Power from on High*, 208–11.

101. Turner, *Holy Spirit and Spiritual Gifts*, 29. This view is strengthened by the fact that includes the note in 4:14 that Jesus returned "in the power of the Spirit." It is power that was granted by the Spirit at the baptism of Jesus.

102. See Davies and Allison, *Critical and Exegetical Commentary on the Gospel according to Saint Matthew*, vol. 1, 355.

103. The divine voice from heaven is steeped in Old Testament allusions (Deut 4:36).

Israel was called by the voice of God to be his people, so Jesus was called by the voice from heaven to undertake his mission as the ideal "Israel" of God.¹⁰⁴

> The temptations can be viewed as the transition into the entire Gospel story of Jesus, who is said to be greater than all the possessors of the Spirit, holy people and places of Judaism, and the various contenders for messianic recognition . . . The question comes down to this: Who is the Son of God? And the answer of these authors is unambiguous: Jesus of Nazareth.¹⁰⁵

In the temptation narrative Jesus's messianic kingship is put on trial and this kingship is also defined. It is a kingship devoid of economic, political, and religious methods of forcible rule. It is a kingship of weakness and suffering. This is the way the Spirit leads Jesus, the way he is assured of his Messiahship. Under the direct guidance of the Spirit, Jesus rejects all offers of messianic function that Satan tempts him with. Instead he chooses the way of helplessness. Here his passion is prefigured; his victory comes through suffering and death. God the Father, through the Spirit defines the messianic function, not Satan. From the story of the temptations the way to the cross follows. What the synoptic Gospels are clear to relate is that the way to the cross is the way of the Spirit and the way of the Spirit is that of the cross. Moltmann develops this idea of the Spirit being the Shekinah hence the "companion" of Jesus through his earthly sojourn. The Spirit is drawn into Christ's sufferings. The Spirit is the transcendent side of Jesus's immanent way of suffering. Moltmann says this leads to a progressive *kenosis* of the Spirit, together with Jesus.¹⁰⁶ "Although the Spirit fills Jesus with the divine, living energies through

---

See Thompson, "Called-Proved-Obedient: A Study in the Baptism and Temptation Narratives of Matthew and Luke," 1–12.

104. For background material on Jesus's relationship to Adam, Abraham, Israel, Moses, and Elijah, see Garlington, "Jesus, the Unique Son of God," 287. Luke emphasizes an Adam Christology through inserting a genealogy between the baptism and temptations.

105. Garlington, "Jesus, the Unique Son of God," 306. Best, *Temptation and the Passion*, 168, echoes the same theme when he writes: "The Gospel is not a mystery story in which the identity of the main character has to be guessed; from the outset it is made clear who this is—the Son of God."

106. Moltmann, *Spirit of Life*, 62. Moltmann possibly adapted this concept from the original proposition of Wheeler-Robinson, *Christian Experience of the Holy Spirit*, 83. In that work Wheeler-Robinson uses "kenosis" to mean the acceptance of the "lower" (physical) as the medium of the "higher" (spirit).

which the sick are healed, it does not turn him into a superman."[107] By so identifying with Jesus, while remaining a separate entity (*hypostasis*, person), the Spirit of God becomes definitively the Spirit of Christ and from this time onwards can be invoked in Christ's name.[108]

The oldest attempt to express God's presence in Jesus is by appeal to the presence of the Spirit.[109] The significance of God's Spirit in primitive Christianity is to be understood primarily from the perspective of Old Testament and Jewish tradition and only secondly from Hellenistic ideas that modified this perspective. The Spirit of God has been bestowed upon the charismatic leaders and the prophets of ancient Israel, as well as upon those with a special commission from Yahweh. The Spirit then departed from Israel with the last of the prophets in order to be "poured out" on all flesh in the eschaton (cf. Joel 2:28–32; Zech 6:1–8; Isa 44:3). Against this background early Christianity understood Jesus as the Coming One, the eschatological prophet, the bearer of the Spirit.

Episode Three: Jesus's Messianic Vocation

Through a survey of critical events in Jesus's public ministry his identity is clearly presented upon the backdrop of his relationship with the Holy Spirit. Throughout the accounts of Jesus's ministry we see Jesus the *pneumatiker*. Jesus weaves amongst the spiritual realm of satanic adversaries, healing, exorcising, commanding demons and nature with unprecedented authority, the Spirit playing a crucial part in each encounter.[110] But Jesus is not presented as a mere magician or super-man;[111] his acts of

---

107. Moltmann, *Spirit of Life*, 62.

108. Moltmann further develops the theme of the *kenosis* of the Holy Spirit under the discussion of the crucifixion. I shall postpone discussion of this theme until then also.

109. Indeed the reciprocal relations between Word and Spirit are developed throughout the Bible. Congar, *Word and the Spirit*, 19, could conclude his little biblical survey with these words, "Scripture, then, from Genesis to Revelation, that is, from the first to the last verse, bears witness to the intimate connection between the word and the Spirit!"

110. Twelftree, *Jesus*, is one of the most useful and exhaustive treatments of this aspect of Jesus ministry.

111. The evangelists were not particularly interested in presenting Jesus as a mere miracle worker, or even as a *theos aner*; such men were too common to attract attention in Jesus's day. In a few pages of Acts we read of Simon magus and of Elymas, of the woman ventriloquist at Philippi, of the seven sons of Sceva, and of a multitude of Christians with spiritual gifts who dealt in ecstatic phenomena. Rather, the evangelists

power clearly point beyond themselves to his person and message. His powers are chiefly Christological as they unveil his messianic identity. The mighty works of Jesus were portals through which the presence of the Spirit might be viewed; they point to who Jesus is and demand a response in light of this revelation. Jesus's ministry demanded faith, not in the works themselves, but in the person doing the works, Jesus the Christ.[112] There are too many such events in Jesus's public ministry to mention here so I have restricted the study to several key events which highlight the link between Jesus and the Spirit and as such show forth Jesus's messianic identity.

For our purposes we shall survey those texts that stand out as paradigmatic for the evangelist's presentation of Christology proper. We shall look at Jesus's answer to John the Baptist's question as to his true identity, was he the coming One? In the answer recorded by the synoptic Gospels we shall see into the heart of their understanding of his identity with Isaiah 61 as the conceptual background. We shall then examine the Beelzebub controversy. Within this accusation from the religious establishment of the day the evangelists present Jesus's eschatological identity in terms of his being the Messiah and the first embodiment of Israel's mission empowered by the Spirit in the new era. Finally we shall note the place of a Spirit Christology within John's Gospel, and the understanding of Jesus as the Prophet of God.

Are you really the Coming One?

As Jesus was full of the Holy Spirit then the Spirit is the power behind all his works. Where the Spirit is not active, Jesus is not active either. The Spirit is the creative energy of God and the vital energy of everything that lives. The Spirit is saving power, first for Israel but ultimately for all nations. "In the Gospels Jesus is consistently portrayed as one whose ministry was empowered by the Spirit—that is, as one whose effectiveness is to be explained in large part by a unique measure of divine power which he experienced himself and the impact of which others experi-

---

were presenting Jesus as the Messiah who fulfils all the messianic functions both expected and unexpected. While all aspects of his argument are not shared in this study, see the discussion in Barrett, *Holy Spirit and the Gospel Tradition*, 117. See the discussion in Carson, *Matthew*, vol. 8, 289.

112. Burge, *Anointed Community*, 67.

enced through his words and deeds."[113] As such the presence of the Spirit in Jesus implies the beginning of the end-time deliverance of humanity, the new creation and the manifestation of God's glory. It is the beginning of the kingdom of God. In this power Jesus drives out demons, heals the sick and restores spoiled creation. The presence of the Spirit is the authority behind his proclamation. In the first chapters of the synoptic Gospels the Spirit is presented as the divine determining subject of Jesus actions. The Spirit leads him into the wilderness and leads him out of the wilderness into his public ministry. In the Spirit God experiences Jesus as the Messianic child, and Jesus experiences God as "Abba." In light of this amazing beginning we see that "what being filled with the Spirit meant for Jesus's proclamation and his life is described on every page of the Gospels."[114] The Gospels present the history of Jesus in the light of his messianic mission, which was inaugurated through his baptism. His mission embraces his proclamation and acts, acts and suffering, life and death. To some of these acts we now turn our attention.

We focus once more on the relationship between John the Baptist and Jesus. Already in the birth and baptism narratives these two end-time figures have been contrasted by the evangelists and repeatedly they present John as the herald of the eschatological prophet, the end-time Messiah, Jesus. Once more the Baptist and Jesus are brought into focus and now, shortly before John's beheading, both he, all Israel, and indeed all flesh will again have Jesus's true identity revealed to them. Behind the answer of Jesus to John in Matt 11:2–19/Luke 7:18–28 is Isa 61. Isa 61 is alluded to in a number of passages (Luke 4:18f; 6.20f/Matt 5:3–6 and 11:2–6/Luke 7:18–23), and is a central text placed on the lips of Jesus to explain the nature of his ministry.[115] From Jesus's reply to the Baptist he evidently thought his ministry to be self-evident in its nature.[116] The evangelists then make this implicit interpretation explicit with the references to Isa 61 along with Jesus's Nazareth Manifesto at the beginning of his ministry. Luke 4:18f is the only direct quotation of Isa 61.[117] This

---

113. Dunn, *Christology in the Making*, 139.

114. Moltmann, *Way of Jesus Christ*, 93.

115. See Isa 11 and 42. Welker, *God the Spirit*, 191, acknowledges the centrality of these texts and highlights a form of Spirit Christology.

116. Moltmann, *Crucified God*, 98–102. Cf. Jesus's question to the disciples "but who do you say I am?" in Matt 16:13ff.

117. Matt 12:15–17 (cf. 11:10) may function in Matthew's Gospel as the parallel to Luke's Nazareth Manifesto. In this episode Jesus quotes Isa 42:1–4. In response to the

synagogue speech can be seen as a secondary expansion of the original narrative by the Christian apologists.[118] This is not to say that Jesus did not say these words, but it is to emphasize the obvious retroactive reading of the Gospels the evangelists wished to create. The question to ask is why did Luke insert this story right here at the beginning of Jesus ministry?, and why did he wish to highlight the role of the prophet and the Spirit?[119] The only appropriate answer would appear to be that Jesus's subsequent words and deeds must be seen as the fulfillment of this text.[120] Luke opens Jesus ministry by presenting him as a Spirit-anointed healer and teacher (Luke 4:16–44). The ensuing two sections of his first teaching (Luke 4.16–30), and then stories of healing (Luke 4:31–44), are introduced similarly. Luke is clearly presenting Jesus's relationship with the Spirit as the power of his ministry[121] and thus a key to a correct understanding of his identity.[122] John does the same thing with his version of the Nazareth Manifesto, "For the one whom God has sent speaks the words of God; to him God gives the Spirit without limit" (John 3:34).[123] With the quotation of Isaiah in Luke 4:18–19, Luke most emphatically presents his view of the nature of Jesus and the significance of the mir-

---

Pharisees decision to kill Jesus prompted by his Sabbath healings Jesus responds in messianic terms. Jesus is clearly identified as the bearer of the Spirit. Welker, *God the Spirit*, 192.

118. Dunn, *Jesus and the Spirit*, 54, argues this is the case based on the presumed idea that an announcement with messianic import simply could not have been made this early on in Jesus's public ministry. On different grounds see Turner, *Power from on High*, 233.

119. For the various interpretations of this disputed passage such as seeing Luke's presentation of Jesus as anointed as a prophet, as the eschatological prophet (Elijianic or Mosaic), as the Davidic Messiah, as a priestly Messiah, the Servant of the Lord or a combination of these views see Schreck, "Nazareth Pericope," in *L'Evangile selon Luc—The Gospel of Luke*, 399–471.

120. See the function of Acts 1:8.

121. "This suggests that the introductory statement of 4:14–15 (about Jesus's returning in the power of the Spirit) relates both to the teaching and to the miracles. The readers could be expected to conclude that each equally arises out of Jesus being motivated by the Spirit of the Lord," Twelftree, *Jesus*, 145. Cf. Shelton's, *Mighty in Word and Deed*, 102–9.

122. These verses have long been recognized as paradigmatic for Luke-Acts. See Turner, *Power from on High*, 213ff; and the extensive bibliographical details in Menzies, *Development of Early Christian Pneumatology*, 161 n. 8.

123. The stress in this Johannine text would appear to be that Jesus was speaking the words of God because the Father was giving him the Spirit in unlimited fashion.

acles he performs. Twelftree writes; "primarily we must note that Luke sees the ministry of Jesus arising out of his being anointed by the Spirit. This episode is the public introduction of Jesus."[124] Clearly Luke himself was influenced by Isa 61 in his understanding of Jesus's ministry and was thoroughly convinced it applied to Jesus. This is further confirmed by the second usage of Isa 61 which occurs in Luke 6:20f/Matt 5:3–6, forming the conceptual background to various beatitudes.[125] By the use of the specific classes of the "poor" and to "weep/mourn," Jesus is thus claiming to be the one who fulfils the role of the Spirit-anointed figure of Isa 61:1. So Jesus had been anointed by the Spirit of God, commissioned to proclaim the good news of the end-time kingdom of God.

However, it is Matt 11:2–6/Luke 7:18–23 that concerns us here. John the Baptist is in prison and sends word to ask if Jesus is the "coming one." Prison was not part of the Baptist's plan and his apocalyptic message of judgment did not seem to be coming to fruition, Jesus was becoming known more for his compassion for his enemies. It appears that Jesus does not answer the question directly. Instead, he turns attention to his ministry; his miracles and concern for the poor (Matt 11:4–6), an allusion to his Nazareth Manifesto (Luke 4:16–19), which in turn echoed the servant passage of Isa 61:1–2. In so doing, Jesus not only tacitly acknowledges his messianic ministry but redirects the Baptist's attention to its true nature.[126] In Jesus's answer to John the Baptist there is this direct allusion to Isa 61; but Isaiah does not mention "the dead are raised." One of the Dead Sea Scrolls, 4Q521 however, written in Hebrew, dates back to thirty years before Jesus was born. It contains a version of Isa 61 that does include this missing phrase. This phrase is unquestionably embedded within a messianic context referring to the wonders the Messiah would do when he comes and when heaven and earth obey him. "4Q521 makes it clear that [Jesus's] appeal to Isaiah 61 is indeed messianic. In essence, Jesus is telling John through his messengers that messianic things are happening. So that answers [John's] question: Yes, he is the one who is to come."[127]

---

124. Twelftree, *Jesus*, 146.

125. Note the cautious comments by Welker, *God the Spirit*, 194 n. 27, and the more assured conclusions of O'Donnell, "In Him and Over Him," 33.

126. Blomberg, *Jesus and the Gospels*, 220.

127. Miller, "War of the Scrolls," 44, quoting Evans.

Clearly this text in the Gospels is from a post-resurrection point of view (as are the entire Gospel record), and so again we have to ask why it is included here, what does it mean?[128] One thing at least is clear, this text has been deliberately included for a specific effect—to reveal the true identity of Jesus. In John the Baptist's question to Jesus we see Luke's view of Jesus and his ministry (Luke 7:18–23/Matt 11:2–6). Against the background of who this "coming One" was, Luke understands John the Baptist's specific question not to be in exclusive relation to any particular tradition of messianic expectation but to relate to a collection of all hopes to be fulfilled in Jesus.[129] From v. 21 Luke understands Jesus to be the Messiah. The poor having good news brought to them would recall the words of Isaiah read by Jesus earlier, and this is the first mention in Luke of the giving sight to the blind. In both these activities the Spirit anointed Messiah is plainly in view.[130] Luke could not have said it any clearer had he written "Jesus of Nazareth is the long awaited Messiah, the end-time prophet anointed by the Spirit of God." John the Baptist received his answer and with it the assurance he was so obviously longing for.

The key to interpreting this passage is to see how the answer of Jesus relates to the question of John the Baptist. The Baptist's question is really: Where is the fiery judgment that we all expected? Are you the one to do that or will another come? Jesus's reply is: Look, the end has come now in my works. In addition to Isa 61:1 Jesus's reply alludes to Isa 35:5f; 29:18f. Each passage contains an equal promise of blessing and judgment. So in alluding to these passages Jesus says that despite the absence of judgment, the blessings of the end-time prove that it is already here. The day of God's vengeance is not yet; the year of the Lord's favor is now (cf. Luke 4:19).[131] The "stumbling block" is first of all the already/not yet

---

128. Dunn, *Jesus and the Spirit*, 54, believes this text to be a post-resurrection perspective but agrees that it is original.

129. This reasoning also forms the content of the answer to Wrede's problem with Mark's gospel and the so-called "messianic secret" motif. It is not that Jesus is not the Messiah—rather, he is not the Messiah *entirely expected* by the Judaism of the day. His first and second comings were part of the "mystery" of his ministry, separating his atoning work from his final judgment. Wrede, *Messianic Secret*.

130. For further exegetical comment, see Twelftree, *Jesus*, 154–55.

131. There is evidence that Isa 61:1–2 functioned in Judaism as an organizing framework for a host of Jubilee associations linked to the coming Messiah. This messianic Jubilee would consist of a period of release from cosmic and political oppression,

nature of this end-time, and secondly Jesus himself. Can John the Baptist and the disciples see that in Jesus the kingdom is present, albeit in an unexpected way?

Other aspects of Jesus's ministry deserve brief mention at this point. Demon expulsion and the healing of the sick are the mark of Jesus's ministry from the very beginning.[132] They also belonged to the messianic mission of his disciples (Mark 3:15).[133] What do they mean? Miraculous healings and exorcisms were quite common in the ancient world. But in Jesus's case their context is unique, for the context is the dawn of the lordship of the divine life in this area of Godless death. The lordship of Jesus drives the demonic out. With the coming of the kingdom of God is salvation, and salvation comes to the whole creation, thus resulting in the health of body and soul, individual and community, human beings and creation. Immediately following Jesus's first preaching in Capernaum Mark presents a story about demons (Mark 1:2–28) in order to show the *exousia* of Jesus's new teaching—its "authority". He preaches with *exousia* and with *exousia* commands unclean spirits and they obey him. His teaching effects what it says. Following the baptism of Jesus, Mark makes it clear that the first to recognize who Jesus is in the eyes of God is the demons or unclean spirits (Mark 1:24; 3:11). He is the "Holy One of God," the "Son of God." Luke is even more emphatic stating that when demon possessed people acknowledged Christ it was *en masse* (Luke 4:40–41). When God sets up his rule over the world it is not extraordinary that the sick should become well and devils should be expelled; it is a matter of course. It is one of the tell-tale works of the Messiah. "Healing the sick and driving out demons are important signs that Jesus of Nazareth is the Messiah promised in the Old Testament traditions, on whom the Spirit of God rests, and that Jesus is the servant of God who bears people's sorrows and sicknesses."[134] With the coming of Jesus the sick come to the fore. They appear from the dark recesses of

---

as gleaned from such texts as Lev 25:9–13; Deut 15:2; Isa 52:7; and Pss 82:1–2 and 7:8–9. See Sanders, "From Isaiah 61 to Luke 4," 75–106, and for the association with the text of 11QMelchizedek see Turner, *Power from on High*, 226f, and De Jonge and Van der Woude, "11Q Melchizedek and the New Testament," 301–26.

132. On the Spirit's role in relation to demon possession see Welker, *God the Spirit*, 196–203.

133. Although significantly they drive out demons in the name and authority of Jesus.

134. Welker, *God the Spirit*, 196.

their social banishment to be exposed by the light of Jesus Christ and healed by the great physician. In the Gospels those who gather round Jesus are more often termed the "sick" than "sinners." They are suffering people who come for healing. The healing ministry of Jesus is not some additional messianic magic but is in fact part and parcel of the message. In this sense the medium is the message. As Dunn rightly stated;

> Luke is quite justified therefore when he depicts Jesus as opening his public ministry in the full conviction and inspiration of the Spirit upon him. The power which he experienced in himself, the power which became evident in his healings (in his exorcisms in particular) and especially in his proclamation of the good news to the poor, was in Jesus's view the eschatological Spirit operating in and through him—the power which brought God's forgiveness and acceptance effectively to his hearers. This power was the rule of God; to experience it in the ministry of Jesus was already to share in the kingdom of God (Luke 6:20).[135]

THE BEELZEBUB CONTROVERSY

In light of the messianic ministry of Jesus, the healings, the teaching with authority, the forgiveness of sins, and particularly the exorcisms, the Pharisees confront Jesus and ascribe the power behind his ministry as being that of the Beelzebub (Mark 3:22ff/Matt12:24ff/Luke11:15ff).[136] It is here that the crux of Jesus's identity is to be either veiled or revealed.[137] As such, this controversy forms one of the most significant passages within the synoptic Gospels for any interpreter wishing to discern the true identity of Jesus.[138] The issue in Mark over the identity of Jesus

---

135. Dunn, *Jesus and the Spirit*, 61.

136. Beelzebub refers to the prince of the demons and is identified with Satan. See Carson, *Matthew*, 253, and Wright, "Satan, Beelzebul, Devil, Exorcism," *NIDNTT*, vol. 3, 468–76.

137. Note the similar function of the various texts that question Jesus's sanity. There seems to be a development in the attitudes of the people; he is first of all thought to have "gone out of his mind" (Mark 3:21), then he is thought to be "crazy," finally he is charged with being "demon possessed" (John 8:48; 10:20–21).

138. The Beelzebub controversy involves four sayings that help to understand Jesus's own view of his ministry and that of the evangelists. The first is the actual Beelzebub charge (Mark 3:22–26/Matt 2:24/Luke 11:15–18), second, the Spirit/Finger of God saying (Matt 12:27–28/Luke 11:19–20), third, the strong man saying (Mark 3:27/Matt 12:29/Luke 11:21–22), and finally, the Blasphemy charge proper (Mark 3:28/Matt 12:31, 32b). See Boring, "Unforgivable Sin," 258; and O'Neil, "Unforgivable Sin," 37.

comes to a crisis point in the argument between Jesus and the religious leaders over the source of his authority (Mark 3:19b–30, cf. 12:24.). In this later reference, Jesus uses "power" with the qualifier "of God" thus obliquely affirming the divine origin of his miracles,[139] which for Mark is from God, specifically the Holy Spirit (Mark 3:28–30).[140]

> In other words, the title Christ carries with it an implicit reference to the Holy Spirit. Thus each use of the title Christ contains an allusion to the Spirit's unique manifestation in the life of Jesus. The confession of Jesus as the Christ stands in direct contradiction to the religious leaders claim that Jesus is possessed by Satan.[141]

The Beelzebub controversy highlights the response to Jesus that is required; a person is either on the side of Satan or on the side of Christ. One cannot reside in two kingdoms at once. Thus, the Pharisees are squarely within the camp of Jesus's enemies, as are all those who charge his ministry as being empowered by the Devil.[142] Hence, to reject Christ and his message *in this particular way* is to be found guilty of blasphemy against the Holy Spirit. To reject Jesus is to reject the Holy Spirit who anointed and works through him.

Then follows the strong man saying (Mark 3:27/Matt 12:29/Luke 11:21–22). Jesus is not just presented as a healer, but as the healer who has the power to bind the evil powers, a binding that was the inauguration of the end of the age. Satan was being routed (Luke 10:18).[143] The kingdom

---

139. Twelftree, *Jesus*, 67.

140. Mark then goes further and relates Jesus walking on the sea (Mark 6:47–53). "In Jesus's intention to pass by the disciples, Mark was portraying Jesus not simply as God's Son or divine, nor only acting for God . . . he is God himself uniquely present," Twelftree, *Jesus*, 94. He sees continuity between the identity of Jesus presented by Mark and that of Paul's presentation. Mark includes almost all of his miracle stories in the first half of his gospel. This clearly establishes Jesus as the Messiah—God himself at work, who gives himself to die for others. Jesus is the Son of God in his powerful miracles as well as in his powerless death. In this Mark's christology is seen to mirror that of Paul's in describing Jesus as being in the form of God yet emptying himself, becoming obedient to the point of death (Phil 2:5–8); ibid., 95.

141. Brown, "Person of Christ," in *ISBE*, vol. 3, 790.

142. Carson is justified in going even further in writing, "Neutrality to Jesus is actually opposition to him (v30); and therefore Jesus gives this warning regarding those who blaspheme against the Spirit, since the self-professedly neutral person may not recognize the inherent danger of his position" (Carson, *Matthew*, 292).

143. Within Luke's perspective Jesus is the victor of a cosmic struggle. He drives out demons by the finger of God, he thus brings in the kingdom in its initial form as

of God is present because the Spirit is uniquely present in the unique Jesus of Nazareth.[144] In these exorcisms the promised end-time Spirit is operative in the Messiah. This was evidence that the drought of the Spirit had finally come to an end (Heb 6:5).[145] Jesus and those affected by his ministry were experiencing the powers of the age to come. The sign of the kingdom of God is the manifestation of the power of God.

The final saying in the Beelzebub controversy is the concluding blasphemy charge (Mark 3:28–29/Matt 12:31–32). By concluding the Beelzebub controversy with the blasphemy saying proper, the evangelists emphasize what we have already discussed in regard to this passage, to blaspheme the Spirit is to reject Jesus as the Messiah. Here pneumatology and Christology are found in an essential unity that characterizes Jesus's entire life as pneumatological and hence forth would characterize the Holy Spirit as Christological. Matthew presents the distinction between the Son of Man and the Spirit as merely incidental. It is not that the two are ontologically one (as previously considered), nor that the two have an identical ministry (also previously considered), but rather it is the case that the two are bound together in one essential ministry: initiated at birth, ratified in baptism, worked out in ministry, and vindicated in death-resurrection-exaltation. The Son is anointed by the Spirit to live a perfect human life and the Spirit identifies with Christ so that where Christ is, so too is the Spirit of Christ.[146]

> Here indeed is a consciousness of Spirit without real parallel at the time. Here we see coming to clear expression Jesus's sense of the awfulness, the numinous quality, the eschatological finality of the power which possessed him. In him, in his action, God

---

evidence that Satan can be overrun, and ultimately, through death, resurrection and exaltation Jesus forever deals with evil. Bock, *Luke*, 15–25.

144. Dunn, *Jesus and the Spirit*, 46–49, overstates his Spirit Christology at this stage with the comment, "the eschatological kingdom was present for Jesus only because the eschatological Spirit was present in and through him. In other words, it was not so much a case of 'Where *I* am there is the kingdom,' as, 'Where the *Spirit* is there is the kingdom.'"

145. Some Jewish expectation looked forward to the final binding of Satan in the Messianic age (Moses 10:1; cf. Rev 20:2). Jesus thus declares that his ministry is evidence that he is binding Satan, thus, he is the strong man, the Messiah of the end-times.

146. These themes are developed in the Johannine *Paraclete* sayings along with Acts and the rest of the New Testament writings, especially the Pauline corpus.

was present and active in a decisive and final way—to reject his ministry was to reject God and so to reject forgiveness.[147]

The Role of Miracles in Revealing Jesus's Identity

While John does not relate the Beelzebub controversy he does give the highest profile to Jesus's miracles and yet has the fewest miracles recorded of any Gospel. For John the opposite is true from that of Matthew; John sees the miracles of Jesus as taking center stage. The miracles are presented as "signs" (*sēmeia*),[148] in much the same way as the synoptic Gospels use the parables as symbols, pointing to something beyond the event to the true identity of Jesus and his relationship, even identity, with the Father through the Spirit.[149] The miracle stories in John's construction build up and rise to a crescendo in the raising of Lazarus. This final miracle-sign of Jesus both prefigures the great sign of the death and resurrection of Christ himself and acts as the prism through which to look back at the other signs and forward to the Parousia. In all this "the great sign anticipates the final earthly sign of the return to the Father, which itself is an anticipation of the return of the Spirit and the parousia (John 13–14)."[150] John uses the same word to describe the entire ministry of Jesus as the LXX uses for the salvific work of God *ergon* ("work"). Thus John conveys the idea that God is to be understood as the author of Jesus's miracles. John includes miracles in his narrative[151] and calls them "signs" saying that they were recorded "so that you may come to believe that Jesus is the Messiah" (John 20:31). This functions in an equivalent way to Luke's miracles being attributed to the Spirit of the Lord being upon Jesus (Luke 4:18).

For all the evangelists the miracles of Jesus were not just performed for novelty or to get attention. They conveyed meaning. In light of our survey of Jesus's ministry it is clear that the evangelists thought Jesus was the anointed figure, the Messiah from God.[152] This conclusion is further enhanced when we consider the choices of the kinds of miracles

---

147. Dunn, *Jesus and the Spirit*, 53.
148. See Thompson, *Humanity of Jesus in the Fourth Gospel*, 119ff.
149. Twelftree, *Jesus*, 340.
150. Ibid.
151. Ibid., 221ff, believes the miracle stories form the centrality of John's presentation of the identity of Jesus.
152. Twelftree comes to the same conclusions in his exhaustive study, ibid., 346ff.

Jesus conducted and the methods he used. The choice of exorcism as his principal miracle category highlights his ministry as a battle with Satan. His healing of paralytics and cripples would have been understood to reflect the messianic hopes of the Old Testament. In the raising of the dead Jesus shows that he saw himself as doing the work of God (a similar conclusion is reached based on the nature miracles). Twelftree concludes his study of the meaning of the miracles of Jesus by saying:

> [I]t seems to me that despite the general hesitation of contemporary scholarship, we are bound to conclude that through the experience of the presence of the Spirit of God in him that enabled him to perform miracles, Jesus was uniquely aware that he was God's anointed individual or Messiah, who was at the same time at the center of these eschatological events that were expressions of God's reign or powerful presence.[153]

The Identity of Jesus as The Prophet of God

One final aspect of Jesus's ministry will be surveyed, the function of Jesus as prophet. The office of prophet was one that required the anointing of the Spirit. In particular, the final end-time Prophet would be uniquely anointed with the Spirit and would be the eschatological agent that shares the Spirit with "all flesh." In this way miracles and prophetic ministry overlap in revealing Jesus's Messianic identity. Was Jesus understood to be this prophet? It was thought prophecy had ceased within Israel largely due to the citation of Tosefta Sotah 13:2: "From the death of Haggai, Zechariah and Malachi, the latter prophets, the Holy Spirit ceased from Israel." But this view has been successfully challenged. It now seems clear that there was no such universal dogma.[154] Rather there was a nostalgic belief that there were no longer any prophets *like the prophets of old*. 1 Maccabees expected *a* prophet, so too Philo (*De Spec. Leg.* 1.65). But at some stage hope for the future appears to have been more narrowly defined and to have focused on a particular figure. In the Qumran material we learn that the Community was expecting *the* prophet, together with the Messiah's of Aaron and Israel (I QS 9.11). Evidence for this expectation is found in John 1:21; 6:14; and 7:40. In these passages a popular expectation of a prophet like Moses but greater than him to appear has been fulfilled in Jesus's ministry. We have already

---

153. Ibid., 347.
154. Hooker, *Signs of a Prophet*, 6.

seen this through our comparison of John the Baptist and Jesus. The Baptist was a prophet, a great prophet but he was always looking forward to the greater one to come. Jesus looked no further than himself. Within Jesus mission and person *the* prophet has come. As such Jesus is unique—in Jesus's mission alone resided the final and ultimate authoritative revelation, the end-time had come (Matt 13:16f/Luke 10:23f; Matt 12:41f). This is bolstered by Jesus's sayings in which he utilized the various concepts and terminology of "I was sent" and "I came,"[155] clearly placing himself within the atmosphere of the expected end-time prophet. With these words the evangelists were unambiguously claiming Jesus to be the end-time Messiah.

Jesus had the reputation of a prophet even during his life (Mark 6:15; 8:28; 14:65; Matt 21:11, 46; Luke 7:16, 39; 24:19). This was a conclusion drawn from his inspiration and authority. This prophetic power was in turn understood as the presence of the Spirit, God's personal empowering presence. In this way the miracles of Jesus are related to his prophetic activity. Mark places almost all the miracles of Christ in the first half of the Gospel, not as some have suggested to present a false Christology but to persuade his readers that Jesus is superior to the prophets who have gone before him. Mark tells us of Jesus's authoritative actions, including miracles, then raises the question of the source of his authority: in the Beelzebub controversy Jesus affirms he is acting in the power of the Holy Spirit and not Satan, or in other words he is a true prophet not a false one. There follows a series of more remarkable miracles, all reminiscent of those performed by Moses, but interpreted as greater than his ones. "Jesus's actions go beyond the actions which might be expected of a prophet, and therefore pose the question 'Who can this be, since even the wind and sea obey him?'"[156] Already we are forced to think of Jesus as greater than a prophet. Twice we are told that Jesus is a prophet but at Caesarea Philippi Peter acknowledges Jesus as Messiah. In this context the opening of blind eyes inserted into the text at strategic points takes on additional meaning (Mark 8:22–26; 10:46–52). These stories are dramatic signs of what will happen after the resurrection, particularly at Pentecost.

Matthew is very similar to Mark's picture. Joseph gives the name "Jesus" to the child of Mary—meaning YHWH saves, for he will save

---

155. Mark 2:17; Matt 11:19/Luke 7:34; Luke 12:49; Mark 1:38; 10:45; 5:17; 10:34ff.
156. Hooker, *Signs of a Prophet*, 55.

his people from their sins. Matthew also sees the miracles as signs of who Jesus is. When John the Baptist sends messengers to ask if he is the One Jesus replies in language reminiscent of various passages in Isaiah (Matt 11:2–6; Isa 29:18; 35.5f; 42:7,18; 26:19; 61:1). As we have already seen, Jesus is the end-time prophet, but he is at the same time more than that, he is the Messiah, the Son of God. For Luke the naming of Jesus is also significant as spelt out in the *Magnificat* and the naming of John in the *Benedictus* (Luke 1:46–55; 68–79). Also Jesus reads from Isa 61 and announces its fulfillment in himself; he is the prophet in whom God's Spirit is at work. The following chapters spell out the ways in which Isa 61 is fulfilled. Luke in particular is fond of describing Jesus as a prophet (Luke 7:16, 39; 13:33; 24:19), and Matthew and Luke both develop elements of Moses typology in their presentation of Jesus. Matthew by his clearly implied parallel between the "slaughter of the innocents" in Matt 2:16–18 and Exod 1:22, and by his gathering of Jesus's teaching into five blocks (Matt 5–7; 9:36—10:42; 13:1–52; 17:22—18:35; 23–25). Luke does this by presenting Moses and Elijah as speaking with Jesus on the Mount of Transfiguration about his "exodus" (Luke 9:31), and by his allusions to Deuteronomy in his "travel narrative." Even in John we still have an echo of the "prophet like Moses" language (John 7:52; 12:47f.-Deut 18:18f; cf. John 14:10; 17:8; 18:37).

Matthew and Luke go to lengths to present Jesus as acting in the power of the Spirit in fulfillment of Jewish prophecy.[157] Both emphasize not only his ministry but his whole life was a manifestation of the power of God (Matt 1:18, 20; Luke 1:35). Also of significance is that Jesus regarded himself as a prophet. He was aware of his anointing and empowering by God's Spirit from birth and especially from baptism. His ministry of exorcism and definitive apprehension of God's will were evidence of his prophetic charisma. This is confirmed in the reaction and hostility of the Jews, both professional and townsfolk.[158] We may also say that in light of his understanding of Isa 61:1 and the various fulfillments of eschatological prophecies Jesus clearly stood in the line of the prophets, and as would become increasingly clear to himself and others, he was in actual fact *the* eschatological Prophet. Jesus's mission can be

---

157. See Matt 12:18; Luke 4:18; 4:14; 10:21. See Dunn, *Christology in the Making*, 140.

158. See Mark 6:4, rejected in his own home, Luke 13:33; Matt 23:31–36/Luke 11:47–51; Matt 23:37f/Luke 13:34f.

described as prophetic in its proclamation, its reaction to the formalism of contemporary religion (Judaism) and in its ministry to the "poor." Also, we see this more clearly in his prophetic insight into the thoughts and motives of others. This ability is well attested to as distinctive of a prophet (1 Cor 14:24f) and was regarded as a mark of prophecy by Jesus's contemporaries also (Luke 7:39). This activity is frequently attributed to Jesus and would have gone a long way in authenticating his identity and mission as the Prophet.[159] Other prophetic insights revolve around his predictions about his death and vindication, amidst the wider apocalyptic expectation—that the consummation of the kingdom was at hand.[160]

In all the miracles Jesus performed as the end-time prophet Hooker reminds us that they are to be seen as "prophetic drama's" that present manifestations of God's power, pointing to something as yet hidden but which is certainly going to happen.[161] Healings reveal God's life-giving power, but Jesus's message to John the Baptist reminds us that they are pointers to the fact that Jesus is the One whose coming heralds salvation (Matt 11:4ff/Luke 7:22). Elsewhere she argues that his exorcisms are a sign that the Kingdom of God is bursting into this world, and that Satan's kingdom is crumbling (Matt 12:25–29/Luke 11:17–22; cf. Mark 3:23–27). The stories about Jesus feeding the crowd and controlling the sea demonstrate that God is about to save his people by means of an even greater Exodus than he achieved through Moses. "All the miracles, therefore, can be seen as pointing beyond themselves: they are *signs* as well as *wonders*."[162] To the religious leaders of the day Jesus exhibited all the signs that were to accompany the coming One. However, they chose to reject him as a false prophet. The disciples however, saw in Jesus the unique God-man, the messiah.

Moltmann speaks of the three-dimensional person of Christ.[163] To confess Jesus as the Christ of God means he is firstly, the eschatologi-

---

159. Mark 2:5, 8; 3:4, 16; 9:33; 10:21; 12:15; 12:43; 14:18; Matt 12:15/Luke 11:17; Luke 7:39ff; 19:15; John 1:47; 2:24f; 4:17f; etc.

160. Mark 8:31; 9:1; 14:22ff, 27; Matt 23:37–39; Luke 13:33; 22:35–38. Dunn, *Jesus and the Spirit*, 84, also lists the following as representative of cases where we do not see logical corollaries drawn from wider expectations but the partly detailed partly obscure premonitions in respect to particular individuals or places which are the mark of charismatic and inspired prophet, Mark 10:39; 13:2; 14:8; 14:25; 14:30; Mark 5:36, 39.

161. Hooker, *Signs of a Prophet*, 37ff.

162. Ibid.

163. Moltmann, *Way of Jesus Christ*, 149.

cal person: in him are present Israel's Messiah, the Son of man of the nations, and the coming Wisdom of creation itself. He is the kingdom of God in person, the bearer of hope for the world. In him believers recognize the messianic human being. Secondly, the theological person: he is the child of God, the God whom he calls "Abba." He lives wholly in God and God wholly in him through the Spirit. He opens this unique relationship with God to all who believe. They participate in Jesus's joy. In him believers recognize the childlike human being. And thirdly, the social person: brother of the poor, comrade of the people, friend of the forsaken, sympathizer with the sick. In him believers recognize the brotherly and sisterly human being. Moltmann warns us that to take only one of these dimensions leads to fatal consequences.

Traditional Christology has stressed the theological person of the God-man Jesus Christ. Classic Christology has been all too ready to appreciate the divine nature of Jesus, without also appreciating his humanity. To remedy this Moltmann proposes an addition to the Nicene Creed by way of elaboration not alteration as follows: Following "born of the virgin Mary" we should add something along the following lines:

> Baptized by John the Baptist,
> filled with the Holy Spirit:
> to preach the kingdom of God to the poor,
> to heal the sick,
> to receive those who have been cast out,
> to revive Israel for the salvation of the nations, and
> to have mercy upon all people.[164]

In so doing we would retain the Gospel emphasis on the pneumatic ministry of Jesus. In the synoptic Gospels the empowering Spirit is essential in defining Jesus's identity and mission as God's servant rather than the devil's. So too in contemporary Christology we must reclaim this biblical paradigm of a Spirit Christology. Dunn stated his case strongly when he wrote of Jesus; "His awareness of being uniquely possessed and used by divine Spirit was the mainspring of his mission and the key to its effectiveness."[165] I could not agree more. But what I am laying greater stress on is the proleptic element of Jesus's ministry and the subsequent

---

164. Ibid., 150.

165. Dunn, *Jesus and the Spirit*, 54. The same expression is used by Burge, *Anointed Community*, 63: "The presence of the Spirit would be the mainspring of Jesus's power and would express itself in works of power and words of authority."

retroactive reading of his life by the evangelists. As Hooker commented; "Whether we treat them as fundamentally historical or as later creations of the community, these stories confirm that Jesus was seen as a prophet, whose actions were understood as manifestations of divine power."[166] Hence the Spirit Christology of the synoptic Gospels is not an accidental feature of the Gospel record but one of the more important interpretative keys to Christology proper. A key fashioned and shaped originally by Jesus and his historical mission, and later used effectively to open the door into a more thorough comprehension of who Jesus is and the significance of what he said and did. To separate pneumatology from Christology is to separate the ministry of Jesus from a correct understanding of that ministry and the nature of the miraculous activity as signs and pointers to the identity of Jesus. Jesus is who he is because of the Spirit. To the Jews of his day the Spirit was the definitive confirmation that this man was different, unique. He alone was the Messiah. His ministry bore the messianic stamp all over it. For this reason the religious leaders of the day committed the unpardonable sin—blasphemy against the Holy Spirit, which was synonymous with a rejection of God's Son—Jesus the Christ. To side step a Spirit Christology is to fall foul to the temptation of Spirit blasphemy.

Episode Four: Jesus Crucified

Through the ministry of Jesus as we have surveyed it we come face to face with *the* tragedy of the human situation: the more God offers himself in love, the more humankind refuses the offer. This became most evident in the various accounts and sayings of the Beelzebub controversy. This clash between God's offer of Jesus, including the Kingdom of God, and human resistance leads inexorably to the cross. Two consequences followed for the ministry of Jesus. In the first place, Jesus had to accept the failure of his human mission. Due to the hardness of the human heart Jesus's offer of the kingdom was not accepted based on his active obedience alone; it required the way of the cross. And so Jesus would go to his death in total dependence on the same Spirit who had created, empowered, comforted and driven Jesus throughout his life. He would go to his death in total submission to his Father's will in the power of the Spirit. "In the death of

---

166. Hooker, *Signs of a Prophet*, 36.

Jesus, the Son surrenders himself totally to the Spirit, entrusting it to the Spirit to rescue his mission after his death."[167]

The second consequence is that Jesus promises to pour out his Spirit anew upon the believing community after his death. This is what links the death-resurrection of Jesus with the exaltation-Pentecost event. They are two aspects of the one eschatological drama. "As most scholars agree, there was originally no material distinction in the early Christian mind between resurrection, ascension and exaltation."[168] Jesus is aware that for the new covenant to become effective people's hearts must be softened from the hardness of their unbelief, and in continuity with Old Testament prophetic expectation, that is properly the work of the Holy Spirit, or as Paul could say, "Christ in you." The gift of the Holy Spirit is made possible only in the paschal mystery when Jesus gives to his Church another *Paraclete* who breaks down human hearts and interprets to the world the meaning of Jesus which it could not grasp during his own life-time (John 7:38–39).

While the death, resurrection, and exaltation of Christ have been extensively dealt with in the history of Christology, the role that the Holy Spirit plays has been grossly overlooked. What a Spirit Christology seeks to achieve is to bring the role of the Holy Spirit back into focus in all of the manifold expressions of his relationship to Jesus and the Father. A good example of this can be seen clearly through Christ's work on the cross and beyond. Jesus would go to his death in total dependence on the same Spirit who had created, empowered, comforted, and led him throughout his life, he would go to his death in total submission to his Father's will in the power of the Spirit. "In the death of Jesus, the Son surrenders himself totally to the Spirit, entrusting it to the Spirit to rescue his mission after his death."[169] It is at this juncture that the Christ of the Spirit is functionally transformed into the Spirit of Christ. Upon the cross the ages turned: the old age came to a climax and the new age was ushered in. Up until the cross, the Spirit empowered Jesus both in his

---

167. O'Donnell, "In Him and Over Him," 35.

168. Dunn, *Jesus and the Spirit*, 120. He cites in support Acts 2:32f; 13:33; Rom 1:3f; 10:9; Phil 2:8ff; Col 1:18; Heb 1:3–5. Lampe, "Holy Spirit and the Person of Christ," in *Christ, Faith and History*, 116, is just as clear, "Pauline theology points towards the possibility of understanding Easter, Ascension and Pentecost, which Luke presents as distinct events, as three aspects of one and the same reality, or even as three ways of talking about the same thing."

169. O'Donnell, "In Him and Over Him," 35.

person and in his ministry, but now, as a result of the death, resurrection, and ultimate exaltation, the Christ would be the Lord of the Spirit and would gift him to his church. This gift is, in Barth's words, "in order that [Jesus's] relationship to the Father may be repeated in us."[170]

Jesus's life was lived out in the power of the Spirit, and it is this which provides the context for a *theologia crucis*, the end to which the Priesthood of Jesus is directed from the very beginning.[171] The cross is the outcome of Jesus's humanity—as the Son obedient to the Father's will, and as representative man led by the Spirit, and as human priest. For this reason the life of Christ, empowered by the Holy Spirit, provides the context for a *pneumatologia crucis*. Rather than treat them separately or to disregard a *pneumatologia crucis* altogether, as has been common in classical Christology, a Spirit Christology holds them together, for one without the other is a distorted view of the cross work of the Trinitarian God (cf. Rom 5:10).

> A Christology is inconceivable without being complemented by a theology of the Spirit. Christ is misunderstood, there is no inkling of the depths of his being, if he is detached from the Spirit through whom he is conceived, through whom he acts, through whom he rises from the dead and who is at his service.[172]

As the drama reaches its climax, Mark again highlights the role of the Spirit through the Gethsemane account. The prayer which ends with the Son's embracing of the Father's will, "not my will but yours" (Mark

---

170. Barth, *CD* II/2, 780.

171. On the background to, and development of the *theologia crucis* of Martin Luther, see McGrath, *Luther's Theology of the Cross*, and Forde, *On Being a Theologian of the Cross*. It is from the *theologia crucis* that Moltmann derives the title for his book *Crucified God*. Following closely in Moltmann's footsteps is Dabney, "Naming the Spirit," 28–58, and a whole host of theologians such as Jüngel, *God as the Mystery of the World*, Paul Fiddes, *Creative Suffering of God*, along with the works of Heribert Muhlen, Hans Urs von Balthasar, Hans Küng, Walter Kasper, François-Xavier Durrwell, Sebastian Moore, and Anne Hunt.

The *crux probat omnia* of the *theologia crucis* is that the Christian is forced by the very existence of the crucified Christ to make a momentous decision. Either they will seek God elsewhere, or they will make the cross itself the foundation and criterion of their thought about God. A Spirit Christology seeks to complement and inform a *theologia crucis* with a *pneumatologia crucis* and in the process add something significant to our *theologia crucis*, our understanding of God. The cross is a Trinitarian event. What I highlight is the pneumatological dimensions of that event as related to the Christological dimensions.

172. Durrwell, *Holy Spirit of God*, 31.

14:36), begins with the words, which the early church identified as the witness of the Holy Spirit, that one is a child of God; "Abba" (cf. Mark 14:36; Rom 8:15; Gal 4:6).[173] In light of the fact that this practice was widespread in the early church, why is it only here, in Gethsemane, that Mark records Jesus addressing his Father by the Spirit-inspired words "Abba"? Moltmann rightly concludes that this means Mark is giving a pneumatological interpretation to Jesus's passion.[174] What began with his conception and baptism through the Spirit now ends in his passion through the Spirit.[175] The Spirit that led Jesus into the wilderness is still beside him now in this time of trial and temptation.[176] While the disciples are willing in Spirit their bodies are weak. The willing Spirit evidently rests on Jesus. At his baptism God calls Jesus his beloved Son, here in Gethsemane, Jesus responds by addressing him as Abba, "dear Father." Both the call to "life" and the response in "dying" are given "in the Spirit." Jesus goes in and through the Spirit to his death, thus fully aware that he is the messianic Son of God. As Leonhard Goppelt remarked, "this immediacy of devotion to God did not come from innate human capacity but from the Spirit."[177] It is Jesus, empowered by the Spirit, whom Mark presents as freely taking up the suffering of the cross.[178]

According to Mark (and the other evangelists), Jesus is defined by the Holy Spirit, he is empowered for mission and, now, his death on the cross is enabled by the Holy Spirit. Throughout his life it was his obedi-

173. "In Gethsemane [Jesus] experienced a crucifixion of will before his execution," and later "The cross happened because of the Son's fidelity to God's call by the power of the Spirit," Pinnock, *Flame of Love*, 90–91.

174. Moltmann, *Spirit of Life*, 64.

175. Luke shares this perspective and uses consistent metaphorical language in Luke 12:50, "But I have a baptism to undergo, and how distressed I am until it is accomplished." Here Luke links his water baptism with the cross. Paul develops this theme in many of his letters when he writes of the Christian's baptism symbolizing Christ's death (e.g., 1 Cor 12:13; Gal 3:27; Eph 4:5; Col 2:12). From baptism Jesus knew his mission as the divine servant was to suffer, hence it would lead to the cross. This is the shape a life led by the Spirit of God would have to take in a fallen world. O'Donnell, brings this out in his article "In Him and Over Him, 32–33.

176. On the temptations of Jesus and the anthropological aspects of his mission see Palmer, *Active Life*, 99–119.

177. Goppelt, *Theology of the New Testament*, vol. 2, cited in Dabney, "Naming the Spirit," 51.

178. If Jesus is defined by the willing Spirit then he stands out markedly from his disciples who are characterized as sleeping while he prays, fleeing while he dies, and denying authorities while he stands true to his mission (Mark 14:38ff.).

ence to the Father that became Jesus's own will, and this was motivated and empowered by his relationship with the Spirit. "A Christology is inconceivable without being complemented by a theology of the Spirit. Christ is misunderstood, there is no inkling of the depths of his being, if he is detached from the Spirit through whom he is conceived, through whom he acts, through whom he rises from the dead and who is at his service."[179] Mark tells the history of Jesus as the history of the Spirit with Jesus. Any "messianic secret" motif is reversed or rather unveiled in Jesus's sufferings and dying.[180] The true Messiah, regardless of popular expectation, would be a dying Messiah. The fact of Jesus's Messiahship was derived from his Spirit baptism, the content of which is defined through the vista that stretches forward to his death.[181] The effect of this divine empowering of the Spirit enabled Jesus to maintain the messianic mission without giving in, failing or faltering; on the road to Jerusalem (Mark 9:30; 10:1, 3, 23, 46; 11:1–11), in Gethsemane (Mark 14:36, 39, 41–42), at the trial (Mark 14:61–62; 15:2, 5), and finally on the cross (Mark 15:23, 30–32).[182]

As Jesus is brought before the Sanhedrin for trial Mark records Jesus's reply to their questions about who he is; Caiaphas asks Jesus "Are you the Christ, the Son of the Blessed One?" (Mark 14:61). He wants to know if Jesus really claims to be the Messiah. Jesus answers with "I am" (Mark 14:62a). Matthew and Luke give more evasive replies (Matt 26:64/Luke 22:67), "You say that I am" or "You have said it" may be more literally correct.[183] But Jesus goes on to add, "And you will see the Son of man sitting at the right hand of Power, and coming with the clouds of heaven" (Mark 14:26b). Clearly his reply includes allusions to Dan 7:13 and Ps 110:1. In this context, as is now generally held, "Son of man"

---

179. Durrwell, *Holy Spirit of God*, 31.

180. As far as the messianic secret is concerned, the only reason Jesus did not publicize some of his actions was because the people did not have the Spirit and thus could not perceive who he really was. This accords well with the retroactive reading of Scripture I advocate. Because the people do not have the Spirit, they cannot comprehend. This is what Gruenler, *New Approaches to Jesus and the Gospels*, 115, calls the inability to perceive three-dimensionally, or with a "new third dimension depth of field in stereoscopic fashion."

181. Moltmann, *Spirit of Life*, 63.

182. I am indebted to both Moltmann, *Spirit of Life*, and Dabney, "Naming the Spirit," for these insights.

183. See Catchpole, "Answer of Jesus to Caiaphas (Matt 26:64)," 213–26.

means far more than simply a human being. He is referring to the Son of man in the Daniel vision who is "coming on the clouds of heaven" and "approached the Ancient of Days and was led into his presence" and was given authority and power over all humanity, leading to universal worship and everlasting dominion (Dan 7:13–14). Jesus was claiming to be more than a mere mortal, and it was most likely this that elicited the verdict of blasphemy by the Jewish high court.[184] Throughout Mark's passion story Jesus becomes increasingly explicit in his Messianic identity, culminating with the confession before Pilate (Mark 15:2), an acknowledgement which leads to his execution. This growing certainty of his messiahship is a clear sign of the presence of God's Spirit in the absence of the hidden, absent, even rejecting Father which Jesus experienced. In the strength of the Spirit Jesus endures this God-forsakenness vicariously, on behalf of the God-forsaken world; and by so doing, he brings into this God-forsaken world the Spirit of God, now also the Spirit of Christ, who also intercedes for us, as he does for Christ, with groanings and sighs too deep for words (Rom 8).

But what of the pneumatological dimensions of the cross? How do we develop a *pneumatologia crucis*? Why is it essential that Jesus have the Spirit in death?[185] The answer is obvious when asked in relation to the resurrection and the exaltation, but death? In death because without the Spirit Jesus could not endure the wrath of God. In death he was cut off in some sense from the experience of the Fatherhood of Yahweh. In death he threw himself wholly on the Spirit's power and ministry. In death the Spirit also underwent a *kenosis* whereby he committed himself totally to the Son.[186] The Spirit accompanies Jesus to the cross and indwells him in his suffering for he is the strength of Jesus, the divine enablement to submission. The Spirit of Christ endures the passion with the crucified one. When we turn to the literature of the early church we see this *pneumatologia crucis* repeated. The letter to the Hebrews emphasizes this point when it says of Jesus, "who through the eternal Spirit offered himself unblemished to God" on the cross (Heb 9:14). Here Jesus is both the high priest and the sacrifice. The Spirit is

---

184. Blomberg, *Jesus and the Gospels*, 343 n. 29.

185. Hawthorne, *Presence and the Power*, chapter 6.

186. In no way am I taking the idea of a *kenosis* of the Spirit to mean he empties himself of his distinct personality as Vladimir Lossky and Paul Evdokimov insinuate. See Congar, *I Believe in the Holy Spirit*, vol. 3, 5, especially n. 12.

that power that makes Jesus Christ ready to surrender and obey and at the same time sustains this surrender. Christ himself is the truly active one in his passive obedience through the operation of the divine Spirit who acts in him. "In 'the theology of surrender,' Christ is made the determining subject of his suffering and death through the Spirit of God."[187] The Letter to the Hebrews thus declares what the Gospel of Mark narrates: the Spirit of God is the Spirit of self-sacrifice, the power by which Jesus Christ was offered up on the cross.[188]

Jesus's death was not like other holy martyrs. He is said to have been "greatly distressed" (Mark 14:33 pars.), and his soul was immensely sorrowful. Hebrews testifies that Jesus died with loud cries and tears (Heb 5:7), confirmed by Mark's account that he died with a loud cry (Mark 15:37). Jesus clearly died as one in agony, and profound horror. How can this be explained? Jesus's death in this way can only be explained in light of his relationship to his God and Father, Abba. Mark records Jesus words of Ps 22 (Mark 15:34), the cry of dereliction—"My God. My God, why have you forsaken me?" Immediately following this cry Jesus dies and the centurion at the foot of the cross says "Surely this man was the Son of God" (Mark 15:39). Faithful to his purpose, Mark continues to present Jesus as the Messiah. In his life he was rejected, and now in his death this rejection is pushed well beyond the human realm and extends into the very being of God himself. In some sense, Jesus died with all the signs and indicators of a profound abandonment by God.

When the cross is viewed in the context of Jesus's ministry we can begin to understand the dynamic of this feeling of abandonment by Jesus; "it is the experience of abandonment by God in the knowledge that God is not distant but close; does not judge, but shows grace. And this, in full consciousness that God is close at hand in his grace, to be abandoned and delivered up to death as one rejected, is the torment of hell."[189] Jesus's entire ministry had been one of proclaiming the neces-

---

187. Moltmann, *Spirit of Life*, 63.

188. Dabney, "Naming the Spirit," 56.

189. Moltmann, *Crucified God*, 148. Abandonment is thus not understood ontologically, but rather within the context of Ps 22, the abandonment is the delivering up of the Son to death on the cursed cross. There is no warrant to overextend this abandonment metaphor and conclude that there existed an actual separation of the Son from the Father in the ontological realm of the Godhead (the immanent Trinity). The Trinitarian implications of this position would be immense resulting in the conclusion that God ceased to be God for a time! Rather here I am discussing the cross in terms of the

sary closeness between himself and God his Abba-Father. In his life Jesus was seen to be the unique Son, the indwelt man, the greatest and final prophet. Now, on the cross these suppositions were to be put to the test. Here, in his greatest hour of need, the Son experienced a fatherlessness that he had hitherto not encountered. Yes he knew he was in the will of the Father as the Gethsemane account confirms.[190] But that does not diminish the agony of the cross. There was never a time in Jesus's conscious existence whereby he did not experience the fatherhood of God, the Abba—Son relationship of intimate communion created and sustained through the Spirit. Now, for the first and last time, on the cross, this experienced relationship was severed. And the implications for both Christology and pneumatology (*theologia crucis* and *pneumatologia crucis*) were immense. For the Father a loss of paternal experience, for the Son the loss of filial experience, for the Spirit a loss of experienced community.[191] The *kenosis* of the Son was most fully realized on the cursed cross as the *eikōn* ("image") of God (Col 1:15), the Word made flesh (John 1:14), was now made sin for us (2 Cor 5:21; Gal 3:13). In this moment of abandonment Jesus was most fully "made lower than the angels" (Heb 2:7ff.) and in every way "made like us" in order to become our high priest and make atonement for us (Heb 2:17). But this could not have happened without the indwelling of the Holy Spirit.[192] And so too the Holy Spirit experiences the greatest and most complete *kenosis*. Through the ministry of Jesus the Spirit was the inspirer, comforter, Paraclete and presence of God. On the cross the Spirit empowered Christ to maintain his obedience, to remain faithful, to overcome sin and death. In the abandonment of the Son by the Father the Spirit was also, for the first time, to desist in communicating (experientially at least) the fatherhood

---

economic Trinity. Moltmann overstates his case when he mentions a separation within God—"God against God," using the concept of *stasis*, see ibid., 154ff. See further in Habets, "Putting the 'Extra' Back into Calvinism."

190. Along with the entire sending motif throughout the New Testament. The Father sent the Son to redeem those under the law (Gal 4:4f.). But he also gave him up on the cross (Rom 8:32; Gal 2:20; John 3:16; Eph 5:25).

191. Pinnock, *Flame of Love*, 102–8, describes the atonement by the motif of participation amidst his broader Last Adam theology.

192. Taylor, *Go-Between God*, 102, recognized the role of the Holy Spirit at the cross when he wrote, "What was the Holy Spirit doing at Calvary? First, in a mystery that we cannot plumb, he must have been about his eternal employ between the Father and the son, holding each in awareness of the other . . ."

of God (Abba consciousness) to Jesus and the beloved sonship of Jesus to the Father (filial love).[193] Or, more profoundly, the Spirit mediated the absence of the Son to the Father and the absence of the Father to the Son and in that mediatorial absence assured both of their presence. A profound *Deus absconditus* was at work before which we are better to bow in humble adoration than attempt to dissect. And so we are led to a fuller *pneumatologia crucis*. However, if the cross of Christ had of ended on this note then the life of Jesus ends with an open question concerning God.[194] While the abandonment of Jesus by God must be and will be recapitulated through resurrection-exaltation, on the cross itself we are given a brief foretaste of what will happen.

Through so identifying and casting himself on the sustaining power of the Spirit, the Spirit most fully indwelt and filled Christ. But in that movement of the Son's total surrender, will and identity, the Spirit also committed himself wholly to the Son to achieve the purposes of God. In the other evangelists accounts of the crucifixion Jesus's last words are recorded variously as: "'Father, into your hands I commit my spirit.' When he had said this, he breathed his last" (Luke 23:46);[195] "and when Jesus had cried out again in a loud voice, he gave up his spirit" (Matt 27:50);[196] and "When he had received the drink, Jesus said, 'It is finished.' With that, he bowed his head and gave up his spirit" (John 19:30). Here in these last words of Jesus we see the completion of his atoning work. With his last breath he hands back over to his God the Spirit that was sent by the

---

193. Are we then valid to also posit on the cross a form of *kenosis* of the Father? On the cross the Father emptied himself of his current experience of the Son's filial presence. By choosing the way of the cross the Father committed himself to *a form* of suffering in the suffering of the Son, see 2 Cor 5:19ff. (although not the same as the incarnate Christ and thus not open to the charge of patripassianism). By adopting the way of the cross only the Son suffered, humanly speaking, but the Father and the Spirit were present and involved, and so they too are affected (and thus not open to the charge of modalism). While it was only the incarnate Son who offered himself up on the cross for the atonement of sins a thorough *theologia crucis* must acknowledge the Trinitarian implications of this event; God was *in* Christ and so was the Holy Spirit. My thesis is only concerned with the implications of a *pneumatologia crucis* and how it affects our *theologia crucis*. In no way am I implying an abandonment of divine immutability or impassability (although Moltmann does so explicitly). See Muller, "Incarnation, Immutability, and the Case for Classical Theism," 22–40; and Weinandy, *Does God Suffer?* This deserves a through treatment but that shall have to await another publication.

194. As Moltmann contends it does, *Crucified God*, 153.

195. Alluding to Ps 31:6.

196. Could this cry have been that recorded in Mark 15:37?

Father to empower his ministry and mediate the Father's presence to him.[197] But what does this handing of the Spirit over refer to? How is it to be understood? Once again a retroactive reading of these texts alert us to the fact that this narrative is the retroactive result of the inspired evangelists. The fledgling church would soon experience both the resurrection of Jesus and the Pentecostal outpouring of this self-same Spirit of whom Jesus spoke (see John 14–17). Integral to all later Christian experience was the fact that Jesus would, from this time forward, be experienced in and through the Holy Spirit. The Holy Spirit, sent by the Father to indwell Christ, would now indwell those who trust in Jesus the Christ. The Spirit who strengthened Jesus for faithful obedience to the Father's will would soon be given to the followers of Christ to enable them to follow Jesus and in turn fulfill the Father's will. Because of the cross work of Christ the Spirit would be granted to the church to create a Christ-like life out of a new redeemed humanity. On the cross a transition took place; the Christ of the Spirit became the Spirit of Christ. "So what the Spirit 'experiences'—although we must not over stress the metaphor—is surely that the dying Jesus 'breathes him out' and 'yields him up.'"[198] The Spirit yields Christ up to the Father from whence he came; up to the Father's will and power and wisdom to await the exaltation of the Son from the grave. The Spirit yields Christ up to the Father to await the new nexus of his ministry, to be the Spirit of Christ poured out, first of all on the church and then eventually on all flesh. And as we shall see, the Spirit yields Christ up to the Father in order to be sent back as the power of resurrection, to again be Christ's breath of life and empowering force.[199]

Through the "eternal Spirit" and the "indestructible life" (Heb 7:16; 9:14) Jesus offered himself up to suffer God-forsakenness. On this basis we are compelled to look beyond Jesus death to his rebirth from this same divine, quickening power of the Spirit. "Looked at pneumatologi-

---

197. That the Spirit mentioned here is to be understood as the Holy Spirit has been forcefully argued by De la Potterie in "Gesu e lo Spirito secondo il Vangelo di Giovanni," 124, as quoted by O'Donnell, "In Him and Over Him," 36.

198. Moltmann, *Spirit of Life*, 64. Again the metaphor refers to the economic Trinity and not the immanent Trinity.

199. In this giving back of the Spirit by the Son to the Father, O'Donnell, "In Him and Over Him," 37, sees a way beyond the classic *filioque* controversy of East and West when he writes, "as the mutual love of Father and Son, the Spirit proceeds from the Father *per Filium* and also *Filioque* in such a way that the perichoresis is established: the interpenetration of the divine persons."

cally, Christ's death and rebirth belong within a single moment. They are one event. They are not two different acts performed by God in Jesus."[200] As the Spirit led Jesus throughout his life, even into and through death, so now he is also with Christ as the power of his resurrection.[201]

Episode Five: Jesus's Resurrection

There is no single answer to the question: "Who raised Jesus from the dead?"[202] In one sense it is and can only be God, a Triune act. Yet the common activity of the Triune God, according to the venerable formula, *opera Trinitatis ad extra sunt indivisa* ("the external works of the Trinity are undivided"), does not preclude, and if true to Scripture, requires, the ascription of certain acts as being peculiarly the work of a particular Person *servato discrimne et ordine personarum* ("the distinction and order of the persons being preserved"). Throughout Acts, the resurrection of Christ is presented in terms of "you [the Jews] killed him, God raised him up" (Acts 2:23; 3:15; 4:10 etc.). These texts say that God raised Jesus from the dead and thus vindicated him (Rom 8:11; 1 Cor 15:15). Nevertheless, a Spirit Christology looks to the "Trinitarian" dimensions of the resurrection.[203] Moltmann distinguishes between "raising" and "resurrection."[204] In the resurrection God *raised* Jesus from the dead, but Jesus had to respond and so we speak of his *resurrection* from the dead. The difference between the two is that in the symbol "raising" the dynamic comes from above, in the symbol "resurrection" the dynamic comes from below. When the two symbols are put together systematically we come up with a reciprocal relationship of raising and resurrection. God has raised Christ from the dead but also God was in Christ who has been raised from the dead.

---

200. Moltmann, *Spirit of Life*, 65. Moltmann makes the connection between the cross and resurrection, an integrally related event, "Christ's death and resurrection are the two sides of the one single happening which is often termed "the Christ event," Moltmann, *Way of Jesus Christ*, 213–14. See Durrwell, *Holy Spirit of God*, 41.

201. Käsemann, *Commentary on Romans*, 129. This has important soteriological consequences discussed later.

202. Gunton, *Christ and Creation*, 62.

203. Moltmann develops a Spirit Christology in relation to the resurrection under the heading *the rebirth of Christ from the Spirit*. Something he seems to call an ecological Christology. Moltmann, *Way of Jesus Christ*, 247.

204. Moltmann, *Way of Jesus Christ*, 247.

While there is no question that the Son was active in his resurrection (John 2:19–21; 10:17–18) we are led to ask if he was the determinative force of the resurrection. Thomas Torrance stresses that it was the Son alone, without the Spirit.[205] Torrance is partly right in ascribing the work of resurrection to the Son. However, Paul likens the resurrection of Jesus to that of his church; he describes Christ's resurrection as being the "first-fruits" and as being first from the dead. That implies a measure of passivity as we can not raise ourselves. What Torrance lacks is the pneumatological dimension to the discussion. Gunton comments, "here the pneumatological dimension is crucial."[206] As the one who perfects the Father's word in creation, the Spirit is the agent of the eschatological act of resurrection in the midst of time. If the resurrection is designed to do, as well as to show, something (as Scripture maintains), then we must view it as the beginning of an eschatological redemption (see Rom 4:25).[207] Through the resurrection, Jesus's particular humanity becomes the basis of universal redemption. So what of the Holy Spirit? Christ offered himself up through the eternal Spirit (Heb 9:14) and he lives "in the 'life-giving Spirit' (1 Cor 15:45). He endured the sufferings and death through the power of the Spirit and was born again to eternal life by the Spirit (Rom 8:11; 14:9; 1 Cor 15:45; 2 Cor 13:4); hence, the pneumatological-Trinitarian paradigm.[208] The Spirit gives birth to Christ once more, this time to eternal life, through and beyond his death. In Christ's re-birth it is the Spirit who is active, as in Christ's conception.[209] That is why the living Christ is present in this Spirit, and the experience of the Spirit's presence gives life.

Early Christian testimonies see the raising of Christ from the dead as the first-fruits of the end time operation of the Spirit (Rom 8:23; 1 Cor 15:20, 23). Christ has been raised from the dead ahead of all others as their representative, as such the Spirit that raised Jesus is our earnest or down-payment guaranteeing our future resurrection as well (2 Cor 1:22; 5.5; Eph 1:14). "The close connection that existed for Paul between the *pneuma* and the reality of the resurrection that appeared in Jesus

---

205. Torrance, *Space, Time and Resurrection*, 53.

206. Gunton, *Christ and Creation*, 64.

207. See the important work of Dabney, "Justification of the Spirit," 59–82.

208. Moltmann, *Way of Jesus Christ*, 248. I prefer the much simpler designation of "Spirit Christology."

209. Without implying any inactivity of the Son or the Father.

and is hoped for by Christians is demonstrated by the Old Testament understanding of the Spirit as the power of life."[210] That is why Jesus was raised through or by the Spirit (Rom 1:4; 8:2, 11, see 1 Pet 3:18). Not only does the Holy Spirit produce life and sustain it in resurrection, but as the fulfilment of Old Testament prophecy, he rests or remains on people. Thus the resurrection life of Jesus has a certain identity between Jesus and the Holy Spirit (1 Cor 15:44f.). From this it is understandable that "all genuine, theologically pregnant statements about the Spirit in the principal Pauline letters are Christologically stamped."[211] Early Christian faith in the resurrection was not based solely on Christ's appearances. It was just as strongly motivated by the experience of God's Spirit. Therefore Paul calls this Spirit "the Spirit or power of the resurrection." Luke follows the end of the ascension with the Pentecostal outpouring of the Spirit. Believing in the risen Christ means being possessed by the Spirit of the resurrection. In the Spirit the presence of the living Christ was experienced.[212] The New Testament uses the Old Testament words "appeared" and "see" to interpret the appearances of Jesus Christ (Mark 16:7; John 20:18; 1 Cor 6:9; Luke 24:34; Acts 13:31; 1 Cor 15:3–8). In so doing they are affirming the theological interpretation that the revelation of God has arrived and the messianic era has been inaugurated. As God appeared to Moses and the Patriarchs so he now appears to all flesh in the risen person of the Son.

The Spirit of God is the eschatological *Spiritus Vivificans,* active on both sides of the cross and it is precisely here, in the resurrection, that we come face to face with the *pneumatologia crucis* that so informs our *theologia crucis*. This is who the Spirit is;[213] the Spirit of God, the power of resurrection, *the Spirit of Jesus Christ*, soon to be the Spirit of Christ's Church. The Spirit, who freely entered into the suffering and

---

210. Pannenberg, *Jesus*, 171.

211. Hermann quoted in ibid.

212. Moltmann, *Way of Jesus Christ*, 218, uses this argument to suggest the resurrection was a mythical event. "Believing in Christ's resurrection therefore does not mean affirming a fact. It means being possessed by the life-giving Spirit and participating in the powers of the age to come." But this is in serious disagreement with Paul. For Paul (1 Cor 15:14) and earliest Christianity God's raising of Christ was the foundation for faith in Christ. In fact the Christian church itself stands or falls with Christ's resurrection.

213. Hence the name of Dabney's paper "Naming the Spirit." I am indebted to Dabney for introducing me to many of these themes in a systematic way and look forward to the further fruits of his own labors in this area.

death of Jesus, is the same Spirit who led Jesus throughout his earthly ministry, and this same Spirit is the Spirit of the cross, the Spirit of the self-sacrifice and resurrection of Jesus Christ.[214] The early church could now identify Christ and the Spirit without collapsing one into the other.[215] Christ, the new human being, became the life giving Spirit. This means that the risen Christ lives from, and in, the eternal Spirit, and that the divine Spirit of life acts in and through Christ. "Through this reciprocal perichoresis of mutual indwelling Christ becomes the 'life-giving Spirit' and the Spirit becomes 'the Spirit of Jesus Christ.'"[216]

The Spirit of God becomes the Spirit of Christ (Rom 8:9), the Spirit of the Son (Gal 4:6), and the Spirit of faith (2 Cor 4:13), so that Christ becomes the determining subject of the Spirit: he sends the Spirit (John 16:7); he breathes out the Spirit (John 20:22). The Spirit experienced by the community of believers now and forever bears the impress of Jesus Christ.[217] The resurrection establishes the representative status of Jesus Christ as "first-born" (see Rom 8:29; Col 1:18). He becomes the means whereby through the Spirit, other created reality becomes perfected. This also gives coherence to the concept of the church as the body of Christ, with Christ as the Head. The church consists of persons in relation to Father, Christ, Spirit and each other. The Spirit, by relating people to the Father through the crucified and risen Jesus, moves toward perfecting those first created in the image and likeness of the Creator.

The resurrection represents the transition from the Christ of the Spirit to the Spirit of Christ. The resurrection represents Jesus's power in the Spirit to vivify. The transition from Christ of the Spirit to Spirit of Christ by way of the theology of the cross (and a *pneumatologia cru-*

---

214. In Dabney's words, the Holy Spirit is *"the self-sacrifice and resurrection of Jesus Christ made manifest in the Trinitarian kenosis of God on the cross . . ."* He describes this *kenosis* as the sacrifice of the Father, the forsakeness of the Son, and the abnegation of the Spirit, ibid., 58 (italics in original).

215. Dunn mistakenly conceives of this relationship as: Christ is Son to the Father and Spirit to believers. But this fails miserably to represent the Pauline material. Dunn, *Christology in the Making*, 149, "It is presumably in this indeterminate intermediate role of the exalted Christ between men and God as Son and between God and man as Spirit that we find the uncomfortable dynamic which was an important factor in pushing Christian thought in a Trinitarian direction." For Dunn this Trinitarianism would not be reached until the early theologizing of the church, the only hints of which, in the Bible, are parts of the prologue of John.

216. Moltmann, *Spirit of Life*, 67.

217. Ibid., 68.

cis) is not an automatic or clear cut transition though. It is a Trinitarian event that begins with something initiated by the Father (John 14:16, 26; 15:26) and ends with the Son handing all things back over to the Father in total completion of his will (1 Cor 15:24). Throughout the gospel of the incarnation the Spirit is with the Father; he is sent by the Father in Jesus's name; he proceeds from the Father and is sent by Jesus. The origin of his existence is with the Father but the cause of his coming is with the Son. "Between Christ, the recipient of the Spirit, and Christ, the giver of the Spirit, stands the hearing of Christ's plea by the Father and the sending into time, through the Father and the Son, of the Spirit who in eternity proceeds from the Father."[218] With the resurrection of Jesus Christ we are confronted with the heart of theology, we are confronted with God himself (a *theologia crucis*) and as we have seen, with the Spirit himself (a *pneumatologia crucis*). And yet it is not the Spirit by himself, but the Spirit in relation to the Son and the Son in relation to the Holy Spirit that is in focus.

Clearly then the resurrection is the central tenet of Christian belief, both in the early church and today. As I noted earlier, the resurrection forms the proleptic starting place for Pannenberg's entire theology[219] and in principle many would agree. Moltmann calls his retroactive reading an eschatological reading of Jesus's history.[220] The Christian faith essentially reads the history of Jesus back to front: his cross is understood in the light of his resurrection.[221] In this sense the evangelists set in place a method of a retroactive reading for all to follow. Moltmann calls this back to front reading one in which we relate the ontic-historical and the

---

218. Ibid., 70. It is at this stage that I, as Moltmann does, would need to venture off into an investigation of the Trinitarian mutuality between God's Spirit and his Son, see ibid., 71ff. Not that I would share much of Moltmann's theology at this point.

219. Pannenberg, *Jesus*, 135–41. Pannenberg suggests that it is the resurrection event which realizes the oneness of Jesus with God, but this creates logical contortions. It appears to say that before the resurrection Jesus was not uniquely one with the Father. It also appears to rule out the pneumatological dimensions stressed throughout the present study. Durrwell, *Holy Spirit of God*, 43, seems to make the same mistake. He even presents the possibility of post-mortem salvation, ibid., 49. Gunton, *Christ and Creation*, 66 n. 23, writes: "Is not the Holy Spirit the one by whom we understand Jesus to have been from the beginning one with the Father?" Gunton accuses Pannenberg of being characteristically western in his Christology by failing to give constitutive significance to the part played by the Spirit in the life and ministry of Jesus.

220. Moltmann, *Crucified God*, 164.

221. Ibid., 162.

noetic-eschatological to each other and identify the results we achieve.²²² What I have termed and defend throughout my study a Spirit Christology based upon a retroactive reading of Scripture. Rudolf Bultmann once made the intriguing suggestion that:

> Events or historical figures are not historical phenomena in themselves, not even as members of a sequence of cause and effect. They are "historical phenomena" only in the way in which they are related to their future, for which they have significance and for which the present bears the responsibility.²²³

I am sympathetic to a certain application of this principle. If this is followed, then Jesus can only be correctly understood historically in the way in which he is related to his future. Faith in the cross work of Christ is thus an evidence of this. The cross work of Christ is seen to be effective due to the resurrection of Jesus Christ. The resurrection vindicates the claim that Jesus is both Christ/Messiah and Lord (Acts 2:36).²²⁴ "If Christ is not risen, then our preaching is in vain and your faith is in vain," wrote Paul in 1 Cor 15:14. The historical title "Jesus of Nazareth" binds Jesus to his past; the eschatological title "Christ" binds him to his future.

With Colin Gunton I am inclined to affirm that "Here, if anywhere, we may speak of retroactive force."²²⁵ However, retroactive force is not confined to the resurrection and may be better applied to the completed exaltation of Jesus (Pentecost) than to the initial exaltation (resurrection), for it is Pentecost that publicly relates Jesus in a new way to the Father and the Spirit and so realizes for the entire world the work of Christ. While we shall survey the exaltation of Christ shortly, for now we must realize that the death and resurrection are the initial phase of the exaltation of Jesus. Already in his life there was an understanding that in his death he was being exalted or "lifted up." John particularly presents this perspective with increasing impetus (John 3:14; 8:28; 12:32). The resurrection of Jesus Christ is one of the crucial events in his life on earth upon which the significance of his entire identity and mission hang. This

---

222. Ibid.

223. Bultmann, *Glauben und Verstehen* III, 113, quoted in ibid., 164. Bultmann would regretfully abandon this approach in his subsequent work.

224. For a survey of the theme of resurrection in the New Testament writers see Jansen, *Resurrection of Jesus Christ in New Testament Theology*, and the definitive work of Wright, *Resurrection of the Son of God*.

225. Gunton, *Christ and Creation*, 61.

is what Pannenberg, Moltmann, and Gunton are emphasizing. However, resurrection is the first step in the exaltation of Christ in fulfillment of the prophecy of Psalm 16:10, as well as Christ's own predictions of His resurrection (Mark 9:9; 14:28; Matt 16:21; 20:19; 26:32; John 2:19).[226] The final step before the ultimate consummation (1 Cor 15:28) is the event of Pentecost.

Episode Six: Jesus's Two Stage Exaltation

As important as the resurrection is for understanding Jesus's identity, it is not the only event of significance. The activity of Jesus continued after his resurrection for it was a resurrection to something: to life, to rule, to exaltation and glorification. While this exaltation was initiated on the cross it was further confirmed in the ascension and consummated in the event of Pentecost. Without these two events a Christology is seriously hamstrung as it would miss the final chapter of the earthly career of Jesus. These events are also crucial for the connection between Christology and soteriology with ecclesiology and eschatology.

The earliest titles applied to Jesus have their foundation in the resurrection event. Formulas of adoption were used for this act: by his resurrection Jesus was adopted as the Son of God (Rom 1:4). Enthronement formulas were also used: by the resurrection Jesus was exalted and appointed to be Lord. On the use of the term *Christos*, Fuller and Perkins say that this term was the easiest to retroject into the earthly life of Jesus. Beyond all doubt he was crucified as a messianic pretender, and his friends used this title for him, although in a somewhat different sense than he would have used it of himself. Easter demonstrated that he who had died was accepted and recognized by God as Messiah. At Easter God vindicated Jesus as the bringer of eschatological salvation. Hence it was an easy step to say that Jesus died as *Christos*, as Messiah (1 Cor 15:3). Early Christians thought in terms of Acts 2:36 and held that God had enthroned Jesus as Messiah. Jesus was already seen as a charismatic prophet-healer due to the anointing (*chrio*) of the Spirit (Acts 4:27; 10:38). In saying this the early church must have been thinking of his baptism especially. Hence the title *Christos* would fittingly cover the whole of Jesus's ministry, his eschatological preaching, his exorcisms,

---

226. Walvoord, "Earthly Life of the Incarnate Christ," 298.

and healings, and above all his death.²²⁷ What is important to note is the fact that this retrojection of a title, originally applied in the full Christian sense to Jesus at his resurrection and applied to his earthly life, is not the christologizing of a life that was originally non-Christological. We have distinctly seen that this is not the case. Rather, the title *Christos* took over the functions of the earlier titles, "Servant," "Holy One," "Righteous One," "Prophet." As Fuller and Perkins point out though, "Neither the self-understanding of Jesus nor the earliest post-Easter kerygma is falsified or altered by this retrojection."²²⁸ Also, the term *Christos* is still being used in its functional sense.²²⁹ It does not imply that Jesus is now something other than what he believed himself to have been during his earthly life. It is merely the communities "catching up" with the fuller significance of this man Jesus, and so it is a retroactive description of Jesus ministry and hence identity.

The purpose behind these titles was to say that by his resurrection it was not just that one man was raised from the dead before all others. It was to distinguish Jesus from other men, all other men. We all shall be raised, but none of us shall be exalted as was Christ. The titles of Christ are first of all related to his function, and then from his function to his identity and status. It is Christ alone who is the mediator, Christ alone who offers himself up as an atonement for sins, Christ alone who in his active and passive obedience has the salvific quality to ensure our eternal salvation.

> The Christ of God represents God himself in a still unredeemed world. The Son of God represents the Father in a godless and forsaken world. The Kyrios is the mediator between man who is passing away and the God who is coming . . . the adoption and enthronement of Jesus through his resurrection from the dead defines his actual temporal role as the mediator between God and man.²³⁰

227. Fuller and Perkins, *Who is This Christ?* 44f.

228. Ibid., 44. The authors go on to discuss the retrojection of the titles *Lord,* and *Son of God*, ibid., 45ff. On the development of the Son of God title see Hengel, *Son of God*. In this work he refutes the Gnostic redeemer myth and other theories of the history-of-religions school.

229. But as was pointed out earlier, function always presupposes being.

230. Moltmann, *Crucified God*, 179. Dunn, *Christology in the Making,* takes these titles and descriptions as purely functional and does not adequately move onto the ontological conclusions; ibid., *Parting of the Ways*. See the response to Dunn's lack of

And if Moltmann had of been more comprehensive he could have added:

> the exaltation and enthronement of the Messiah through the ascension and Pentecost was a public display of his vindication by God thus acting as a final chapter to his earthly history and the opening chapter of his new relationship to his kingdom as Lord of the Spirit.

On the resurrection-exaltation link Dunn writes that "Such identification as there is in the NT between Christ and the Spirit begins with Jesus's resurrection, stems from Jesus's exaltation,"[231] and elsewhere, "In his life on earth Jesus was a man determined by the Spirit—he lived 'according to the Spirit' (Rom 1:3f); but in the resurrection the relationship was reversed and Jesus became the determiner of the Spirit."[232]

Though allusions in Scripture to the ascension of Christ are much fewer than to his resurrection, the accounts as given demonstrate the bodily departure of Christ from earth and his arrival at the right hand of the Father. The ascension plays a prominent role in Luke-Acts (Luke 24:44-52; Acts 1:2, 8-11, 22). In Matthew the ascension is not described and in Mark only a passing mention is made at the end of the book (Mark 16:18). For Luke the ascension forms a kind of transition from the Gospel into the Acts. The ascension triggers the release of the power of the Holy Spirit upon Jesus's followers. In addition to the accounts given in Mark, Luke, and Acts, the epistles refer to the ascension as a fact (Eph 4:8–10; Heb 4:14; 1 Pet 3:22). The arrival of Christ in the heavens is also repeatedly stated in Scripture in more than a score of passages (see Acts 2:33–36). It was a fitting climax for the life of Christ on earth and in fulfillment of his own declaration that he would return to the Father. The historical facts as they recount the birth, life, death, and resurrection of Christ and culminate in his ascension to the right hand of the Father give a solid basis for theological consideration of the person and work of Christ. The historical narratives are fully in keeping with the theological implications which are drawn from them in the Epistles. Upon these

---

divine Christology by Turner, "Spirit of Christ and 'Divine' Christology," 413–36; and ibid., "Spirit of Christ and Christology," 168–90. Turner specifically seeks to explore the contribution to Christology made by the New Testament church's understanding of Jesus's relationship to the gift of the Spirit poured out on believers.

231. Dunn, *Christology in the Making*, 160.

232. Dunn, *Jesus and the Spirit*, 325.

facts rest our Christian faith and our hope of life to come.[233] The ascension acts as a bridge between heaven and earth, God and humanity. The ascension brings out the character of mediation Jesus represents and is. "As the resurrection opens the creation upwards to the holy God, so the ascension completes what comes first, the earthwards movement of the Son, the opening of heaven to earth."[234]

The ascension acts as an important aspect of Christ's kingly office as it is ascension to the "right hand of God" (Mark 16.19).[235] It proclaims Christ's triumph (1 Pet 3:22; Heb 2:9; Phil 2:9; Eph 4:8; fulfils Pss 8; 115; Is 40:28). The man of Nazareth is now Lord over all (1 Cor 12:3; Eph 1:22ff.). His reign is not confined to the church but to "all things" (*ta panta*)[236] The ascension acts as the first stage of exaltation. It is the path to the throne, the road to the destination. It is the antecedent to Pentecost. Pentecost is the official ceremony, the public coronation; the ascension is the final parting glimpse on earth of the Word made flesh, the light of the world, the final drama of the incarnation proper. It also means the high priestly ministry of Christ will continue in the heavenlies. It speaks of Christ's final rule in glory. It thus looks forward to the final day of the Lord—when he has subjected all enemies under his feet once and for all (1 Cor 15:25), and returns on the clouds of heaven from which he departed (Matt 26:64; Mark 14:62). As Bauckham stated, "It is this radical novelty which leads to all the other exalted christological claims of the New Testament texts."[237] For Paul "the last Adam became a life-giving spirit" (1 Cor 15:45). Here "Spirit" is best identified as Holy Spirit.[238] Christ on his ascension came into such complete possession of the Spirit who had so associated himself with Jesus through the incarnation, that an economic equivalence of sorts resulted. The resurrected

---

233. Walvoord, "Earthly Life of the Incarnate Christ," 300.

234. Gunton, *Christ and Creation*, 67.

235. See the significance of the exaltation in Bauckham, *God Crucified*, 28–35. He clearly makes the point that no intermediary figure could sit on God's throne as this right is reserved for God alone. Therefore, Jesus is clearly being identified with God. On the theological significance of the ascension more generally see Farrow, *Ascension and Ecclesia*.

236. This phrase carries considerable theological weight. See Bauckham, *God Crucified*, 31–32.

237. Ibid., 29. See his further exegesis of Psalm 110:1 in the New Testament as applied to Jesus Christ.

238. Gaffin, *Perspectives on Pentecost*, 18–19.

Christ and the Spirit are now experientially one (although not undifferentiated). From the ascension and then Pentecost the Spirit is now the *alter Christus* to us, and ministerially he is the *allos paraclētos* (see John 14–16).[239] To confirm this further Paul states that "the Lord is the Spirit" (2 Cor 3:17–18). The most natural reading of this verse is that Jesus Christ is Lord *of* the Spirit.[240] Here we see the consequences of the cross being worked out by Paul. The ministry of the Spirit post-resurrection is in increasing identification with Jesus so that the Spirit is now understood to be the messianically shaped Spirit and Jesus is now the Lord of the Spirit who will send his Spirit to reshape believers to be like him (2 Cor 3:17–18).[241] This sending of the Spirit was initiated at Pentecost.[242]

While the ascension is spoken of relatively little the Pentecost event becomes a central episode for the early church, "As Jesus's announcement of his Spirit-anointing in Luke 4:18–19 . . . is programmatic for Luke, Acts 1:8 and 2:16–21 . . . are programmatic for Acts."[243] Pentecost stands

---

239. These are the words of Ferguson, *Holy Spirit*, 54. This does not imply that there is an ontological fusion between them. Paul consistently retains the personal distinctions of the three Persons of the Godhead. Neither do I intend the use of *equivalent* to be taken as a complete functional equivalence, merely that there is now a considerable overlap and complementarily in the external operations of the Son and the Spirit so that they must be thought of as together.

240. Ferguson, *Holy Spirit*, 55. This would be supported by two other passages where Jesus is given the Divine Name YHWH; Heb 1:4 and Phil 2:9. While these texts are debated it seems that the divine name YHWH is in view. On 2 Cor 3:17, see the difference of opinion in Fee, *Gods Empowering Presence*, 309–20, where "Lord" equals the "Spirit," and Dunn, "2 Corinthians 3:17—'The Lord is Spirit,'" 309–20 where "Lord" equals "Yahweh."

241. Dunn, *Jesus and the Spirit*, 322.

242. There is the issue of the so-called "Johannine Pentecost" of John 20:22. While many scholars see this as a rival tradition to Luke-Acts as to when the Spirit was definitely given, I do not take it to be such. Clearly Jesus received the Spirit on a number of occasions in his life as did the disciples. For a survey of the various views and a defense that John 20:22 acts as a climacteric in the resurrection appearances which bring the disciples to authentic faith (cf. John 20:22 with 17:18) see Turner, "Concept of Receiving the Spirit in John's Gospel," 24–42.

243. Keener, *Spirit in the Gospels and Acts*, 190. Keener describes Pentecost as "one of the most unique moments in salvation history," ibid., 192. While I cannot detail here the many ways in which Pentecost is seen to be of universal significance I just mention at this stage the parallel to Babel (Gen 3). Pentecost is a reversal of this chaos. This is confirmed by the presence of the table of nations and the speech-phenomena that Luke records. See Davies, "Pentecost and Glossolalia," 228–31. Marshall does not agree, see "Significance of Pentecost," 351ff. and ibid., *Acts of the Apostles*, 64, while for Turner, *Power from on High*, 267, this passage has a greater claim than Luke 4:16–30 to be called the programmatic text of Luke-Acts.

as the gateway from the old age to the new.²⁴⁴ Pentecost inaugurated the new era of the eschatological age (1 Cor 10:11).²⁴⁵ Through the event of Pentecost three things resulted: first, the identity of Jesus was further clarified and so our Christology was advanced, second, the identity of the Spirit was further clarified, and once again it is in relation to both God the Father and the Son, and third, the community dimensions of the Christ-event would be spelt out in more detail.²⁴⁶ With Pentecost came the birth of the church.²⁴⁷ While the various phenomena and occurrences of Pentecost have been the focus of much modern discussion²⁴⁸ the central point of Pentecost is the Christological dimensions, or to be more accurate the Spirit Christological dimensions.

In Peter's pivotal speech he provides for us a supernatural explanation as to the significance of Pentecost.²⁴⁹ He says that "exalted to the right hand of God, he [Christ] has received from the Father the promised Holy Spirit and poured out what you now see and hear" (Acts 2:33). Here two promises are seen to be fulfilled. The first is the general Old Testament promise that the Spirit would be poured out on all flesh in the end time (see Ezek 36:27; Gal 3:14).²⁵⁰ The second promise was the more

---

244. The feast of Pentecost came to be considered a celebration of the giving of the law at Sinai. Hence it is no coincidence that the birth of the church occurred on this day also. Luke is clearly presenting a new epoch of salvation history, the age of the Spirit, as beginning on the anniversary of the law giving at Sinai. It was the feast of covenant renewal, the most obvious, and next feast on the calendar that brought the disciples to Jerusalem, for the decisive eschatological intervention of God. See this worked out in 1 Cor 15:27–28; Eph 1:22; Phil 3:21; Heb 1:2; 2:8; Eph 1:10, 21–23; 4:10; Col 1:20, etc.

245. Turner, *Power from on High*, chapter 10.

246. Community dimensions such as the human participation in God's action in the creation initiated through the reception and dispensing of the Spirit by Christ. See Lockhart, "Spirit, Christ, and Worship," 1–21, who discusses this aspect around an interpretation of the sanctification Jesus offered in John 17:19.

247. McFarlane, *Why Do You Believe What You believe About the Holy Spirit?* 48–51.

248. For instance the debate concerning what baptism in the Spirit means, are tongues for today, is Pentecost a repeatable event, etc.

249. Accompanied by supernatural phenomena such as wind (Acts 2:2), tongues of fire (2:3) filling with Spirit (2:4) and speaking in tongues (2:4). For the background and meaning of these phenomena see Keener, *Spirit in the Gospels and Acts*, 193. Also see his literary structure of Peter's sermon, ibid., 217.

250. In one sense the pouring out of the Spirit is a continuing event as Acts shows. However, Pentecost does give a "determinative orientation for the recognition that in each case it is *the Spirit of God* that is poured out," Welker, *God the Spirit*, 229.

specific, that the Spirit was promised to the Christ and that he would pour out the Spirit on his people (see Isa 52:15; 53:12). Pentecost could only be realized after the death and resurrection and then exaltation of Jesus Christ (Ps 2:8).[251]

> The hidden reality revealed publicly by Pentecost is that the ascended Christ had now asked the Father to fulfill his promise, had received the Spirit for his people, and had now poured him out on the church so that the messianic age begun in the resurrection of Christ might catch up in its flow those who are united to him by participation in the one Spirit.[252]

"In other words, the dispensation of the Spirit in the church and in the world which found glorious initial expression at Pentecost depends utterly on the triumph of Jesus (Jn 7:39),"[253] writes Bruce Milne. Luke affirms this by deliberately commencing the story of the church's birth and beginnings under the impact of the Pentecost event (Acts 2:1ff.), with an account of the ascension of Jesus (Acts 1:9–11), despite already having recounted the ascension at the conclusion of his gospel (Luke 24:50f.).[254] The exaltation of Jesus following his resurrection proves that Jesus is not only David's Son, the Christ, as implied by Ps 16, but also his "Lord" as in Ps 110 (Acts 2:36). Pentecost was the public coronation of the one and only Messiah. In response to this message the crowd was deeply convicted (Acts 2:37) and asked how to be saved (Acts 2:37, cf. 16:30). Peter's response: "call on the name of the Lord" (Acts 2:21).[255]

See Turner, "Significance of Receiving the Spirit in Luke-Acts," 131ff. Amazingly Welker does not once mention Christ throughout his treatment of Pentecost! (However, note Welker, *God the Spirit*, 240 n. 25.)

251. Hence the Spirit as *Paraclete* could only be given at Pentecost and not in John 20:22.

252. Ferguson, *Holy Spirit*, 59–61. See Torrance, *Theology in Reconstruction*, 248, and Pinnock, *Flame of Love*, 93–98.

253. Milne, *Know the Truth*, 179.

254. See Dunn, *Baptism in Holy Spirit*, chapter 4, for Luke's understanding of Pentecost.

255. Bauckham, *God Crucified*, 31, recognizes the significance of the exaltation of Christ and concludes that "the exaltation of Jesus to the heavenly throne of God could only mean, for the early Christians who were Jewish monotheists, his inclusion in the unique identity of God, and that furthermore the texts show their full awareness of that and quite deliberately use the rhetoric and conceptuality of Jewish monotheism to make this inclusion unequivocal."

Paul is totally consistent with Luke in setting forth the propinquity of the Spirit's gifts within the context of Christ's exaltation (Eph 4:8-10). "The gifts of the Spirit are the spoils of the victorious Christ, the fruits of triumph."[256] This means the Spirit is the one to apply the benefits of Christ's atonement to us. But more importantly for my argument it "underlines the folly of any attempt to separate the work of the Spirit from the work of Christ."[257] There is an indissoluble link between the ministry of the Spirit and the glorification of Christ. The Spirit is the Spirit of Jesus (Acts 16:7). The Spirit is Jesus in the sense that he seeks to bring Christ to us and bring us to Christ. Welker attempts to make this clear by speaking of the Spirit as a Public Person when he writes; "the Spirit is the public person corresponding to the individual Jesus Christ."[258]

The question Pentecost answered was how the experience of salvation that Jesus came to inaugurate was to be continued and deepened when Jesus had departed? How was God to be more powerfully, self-revealingly, universally and transformingly present among his people when Jesus was taken away?[259] The answer: by God's Spirit who was above all God's powerful, self-revealing and transforming presence, the Spirit of Jesus. *Kyrios* and *pneuma* belong together. "Wherever there is a reference in any way to the reality of the resurrected Lord, as it is established through hearing the message of Jesus's resurrection, there one is already in the sphere of the Spirit's activity."[260] In Luke 24:47–49 and Acts 1:1–8, the promise of the Spirit as power from on high is not only for missionary activity but first and foremost power for the transformation and restoration of Israel, by making salvation a reality thus making Israel a light to the nations and establishing the Church (Gen 12:3; Gal 3:13–14).[261] These themes of salvation being realized in the power of the Spirit are elaborated on in Acts 1–3. Luke 1:32–33, promises that Jesus would receive the throne of his father David and rule over Jacob. Jesus's entire ministry is about this Kingdom of God and the rule he had come to establish. However, Jesus is crucified as an impostor and only then ascends to his (for now heavenly) throne. On the day of Pentecost Peter

---

256. Milne, *Know the Truth*, 180.
257. Ibid.
258. Welker, *God the Spirit*, 314.
259. Turner, "Spirit in Luke-Acts," 89.
260. Pannenberg, *Jesus*, 172.
261. Cf. the backdrop of Isaiah 49.

draws the threads of Jesus teaching together. According to Acts 2:24–36, Jesus has been exalted to the eschatological throne seen by David and now begins to effect his (God's) rule as Messiah by pouring out God's Spirit on his people (see Heb 1:1–5).

The Spirit is said to be the fulfillment of Joel's prophecy (Joel 2:28–32). Joel prophesied the gift of the Spirit to all who repent and are baptized, to all God's people. The key thing to notice here is that for Joel there was no time delay between a repentance baptism and the reception of the Spirit. The Spirit would then equip and empower the whole of the believers walk before God.[262] We see this new age of the Spirit lived out in the rest of the book of Acts. In his gospel Luke wishes to present Jesus as the Messiah, endowed with the Spirit as a unique individual, and then in Acts to present the early church as a unique, historical manifestation of the accomplishing of the Messiah's salvation. Both are clearly unique and non-repeatable. Turner summarizes Lucan pneumatology with a warning:

> Above all, we need to resist the temptation to read Luke-Acts as though we can re-live the experiences of the disciples, first experiencing salvation through Jesus, and then receiving the Spirit as a *donum superadditum* . . . Beyond the ascension there is simply no way to "experience Jesus" and his salvation except through the Spirit . . . who is given precisely to make him "accessible."[263]

By emphasizing the proper work of the Holy Spirit in ecclesiology an important complement to a Spirit Christology is achieved. Union with Christ results in both personal re-creation and then trans-creation as well as the corporate reality of incorporation into the Body of Christ—the church. "Everything that stands in relation to the reality of the resurrected Lord is filled with the power of life of the divine Spirit."[264] This is true for the apostolic message, along with the special tasks and services of the members of the new community. The Spirit incorporates believers into the body of Christ, he himself is the unity of that body composed of the bearers of the gift of the Spirit (1 Cor 12). And the Holy Spirit

---

262. It is only after the reception of the Spirit at Pentecost that the community of believers was transformed from a community of faithless and ineffective people to a powerful band of loving, united, and effective Christians. Acts 2:42–47 is as a direct consequence of the Pentecostal gift of the Spirit.

263. Turner, "Spirit in Luke-Acts," 97.

264. Pannenberg, *Jesus*, 172.

will bring about the resurrection of the dead. Pentecost was a unique event that ushered in a unique manifestation of the Spirit's activity in the world but especially in the Church (and the believer). Now the filling and the baptizing work of the Spirit are normative for *all* Christians, and accompany gifts of the Spirit for the building up of the body of Christ. In this way a solid ecclesiological pneumatology is wedded to a secure Spirit Christology. With the coming of Christ the Christological and ecclesiological programs of God became unified.[265] The Pentecostal outpouring of the Spirit stands as our interpretative hinge unifying these two *loci* of theology.[266] Pentecost was a once for all event because it was an historical event.

> This becomes all the clearer when we view Pentecost as an aspect of the work of Christ, not a Spirit event separate from it and in addition to it. It is the visible manifestation of a coronation. The events of the Day of Pentecost are the public expressions of the hidden reality that Christ has been exalted as the Lord of glory and that his messianic request for the Spirit, made as Mediator on our behalf, has been granted.[267]

With the phenomenon of Pentecost the church was born; one that was given the mandate of Acts 1:8, "but you will receive power when the Holy Spirit has come upon you; and you shall be my witnesses both in Jerusalem, and in all Judea and Samaria, and even to the remotest part of the earth." Evangelism itself was a gift of the empowering Spirit; without the inspiration and empowering of the Spirit the mission of the church would have no impact on the hearers (Acts 4:8, 31; 6:10; 16:6; 18:25; 1 Cor 2:4f.; 14:24f.; 1 Thess 1:5; Eph 4:11). However, the content of the

---

265. In the history of redemption Jesus Christ came not only to redeem his people but also to establish them as a unique entity—his Church, his body, his sphere of *resonance* in this world through the sending of "another comforter." See Welker, "Holy Spirit," 18ff., where he develops a social model of the Trinity to comment on the concept of *resonance* as characterizing that social sphere both in the life of the Trinity and the life of the people of God—the church.

266. This is really a hermeneutical point. See McDonnell, "Determinative Doctrine of the Holy Spirit," 142–61. "Being the point of entry into Christology and the doctrine of the Trinity, and the point of contact between God and history, the Spirit is the horizon where the meaning of Christ and history are made manifest. One respects this horizon not necessarily by making the Spirit the specific object of theological reflection, or by continual talk about the Spirit, but by recognising this role of point of entry and contact and its consequences for the whole theological process," (ibid., 153).

267. Ferguson, *Holy Spirit*, 86. See Dawe, "Divinity of the Holy Spirit," 737.

proclamation of the early church was none other than Jesus Christ (Acts 2:32; 4:2, 33; 10:40ff.; 13:30ff.; 17:18; 1 Cor 15:3–8, 11; cf. Rom 1:3–4; 2 Tim 2:8).[268]

CONCLUSION

Working from Old Testament expectations, primitive Christianity understood Jesus as the bearer of the Spirit. It is clear that the community recognized, in the activity of the pre-Easter Jesus, the eschatological prophet, the New Moses, the end-time Servant of Yahweh. And yet it would take his death, resurrection, and exaltation to confirm and convince them that, in short, in Jesus they were confronted with the Messiah. The evangelists then structured their respective Gospels so as to bring out the full identity of Jesus the Christ. This was borne out of his conception/birth, baptism, and ministry, and confirmed in his death, resurrection-exaltation, and was finally lived out in the experience of the church. It was this life story that enabled the early church to make the connection between Jesus as the eschatological prophet and the title *Christos*, which at first was only used eschatologically for the function of the One who would return in power, but which was soon also connected with the earthly Jesus through the passion tradition, and could designate his whole activity.[269] With the resurrection-exaltation of Jesus of Nazareth, the early Christian community came to the realization that this Jesus of Nazareth was both Lord and Christ. From that time on Jesus was worshipped as God; he was proclaimed as Savior and he was heralded as the King. Throughout the incarnation we have seen that the Spirit is the eschatological dimension integral to an understanding of Christology. The incarnation is a Trinitarian event that climaxes at the cross and culminates in the exaltation of the Son to the right hand of the Father in order to be Lord of the Spirit at Pentecost.

Through this biblical survey of Spirit Christology I have traced one way of looking at the identity of Jesus Christ. He is both anointed man, full of the Spirit, and Spirit dispenser; Lord of the Spirit. He is both Jesus of Nazareth and Christ of faith, the two are indeed one. While I have attempted to confine myself to a biblical survey in this chapter, theological questions have been raised and partly dealt with. In the next chapter I

---

268. Dunn, *Jesus and the Spirit*, 155.
269. Pannenberg, *Jesus—God and Man*, 117.

turn attention to what may be called a Spirit Christology proper. I shall inquire into the Trinitarian implications of a Spirit Christology and present a coherent Spirit Christology in a systematic fashion. In so doing I will draw together the methodological and biblical material that we have so far acquired, and harness the results into a coherent unity. We now move from economic considerations to the ontological.

6

And Then There Were Three

Spirit Christology and the Trinity

> *We have to look at Jesus' humanity in order to know his divinity, and we have to contemplate his divinity so as to know his humanity.*
>
> —Jürgen Moltmann

> *Jesus' uniqueness, the specific form of his existence that makes him who he is, is that he unites in himself both a "katabatic" and an "anabatic" movement, that is, from God to the world, and from the world to God. In Christ, the two are one.*
>
> —Gary D. Badcock

> *On the Trinity—I possess the reality although I do not understand it.*
>
> —Hilary of Poitiers

OVER THE PAST TWO decades or more calls for reclaiming a Spirit Christology have increased in their frequency and fervor. Representatives of Protestantism, Roman Catholicism, and Eastern Orthodoxy have joined the chorus of voices calling for a more robust integration of pneumatology with Christology. As many have realized, this also entails rearticulating the doctrine of the Trinity and reconceiving the mission of the church. While calls for a Spirit Christology show no sign of abating, what is evident in the literature is the amount of presumption involved in what a Spirit Christology is, involving a considerable amount of misunderstanding, allied to a veritable dearth of comprehensive and constructive theological interrogation of a Spirit Christology and its implications.

In this chapter a Spirit Christology proper is defined, one which is distinctly Trinitarian in line with the Great Tradition, as opposed to being post-Trinitarian and unorthodox. As David Coffey remarked, "Spirit Christology provides our best mode of access to the theology of the Trinity."[1] After detailing the criteria for Christology, a survey of various proposals for a Spirit Christology will be presented highlighting the differences between those who advocate replacing Logos Christology with Spirit Christology from those, like me, who propose complementing Logos Christology with Spirit Christology. Finally, a Trinitarian Spirit Christology will be provided.[2]

CRITERIA FOR CHRISTOLOGY

Due to the pluralistic nature of contemporary Christology, it becomes necessary to briefly outline certain necessary criteria for what can be considered an orthodox Christology.[3] In an effort to advance the propriety of my proposal, the crucial question is how to introduce Spirit Christology to the theological community? What criteria must be followed to both allow and to highlight the orthodoxy of Spirit Christology alongside Logos Christology?[4] Harold Hunter, writing in 1983, surveys ten prominent authors on the subject of Spirit Christology and concludes that no unanimity regarding a definition of the term can be found.[5] My own survey of a further sixty five works published since 1983 bears the same testimony.[6] While Hunter concedes that Spirit Christology could be constructed in line with classical orthodoxy, he wrongly reserves the term "Spirit Christology" for what I label post-Trinitarian construc-

---

1. Coffey, "Spirit Christology and the Trinity," 315. Later in the same work Del Colle concurs, "A Response to Jürgen Moltmann and David Coffey," (ibid., 339).

2. An alternate version of this proposal was first published as Habets, "Spirit Christology," 199–234.

3. For an introduction to the pluralistic nature of contemporary Christology see Bloesch, *Jesus Christ*, 15–24, Haight, *Jesus Symbol of God*, 425–31, and Jacqes Dupuis, *Toward a Christian Theology of Religious Pluralism*. Pluralism can be both good and bad in theology. "If one must rightly caution against an indiscriminate and undiscerning pluralism, one should not thereby impugn the validity of an authentic and enriching pluralism," writes Imbelli, "New Adam and Life-giving Spirit," 238.

4. Schoonenberg, "Spirit Christology and Logos Christology," 360–61.

5. Hunter, "Spirit Christology (1)," 127.

6. See the bibliography for the sources consulted.

tions.⁷ In so doing he gives the impression that *all* Spirit Christologies are by their very nature, unorthodox.⁸ That is clearly not the case as my own proposal will show.⁹

For a Christology to be adopted by the wider church it must fulfill certain requirements. The number of criteria selected is not meant to be exhaustive but basically constitutive.¹⁰

A first criterion for Christology is the need to be faithful to the testimony of Scripture. It must be faithful to the biblical language about Jesus. This is no more than the general premise that Scripture is normative for the church. Clearly based on chapters 5 and 6 my proposal for a Spirit Christology is firmly rooted in the biblical witness. This supreme requirement has had an explicit role in the development of almost all proposals for a contemporary Spirit Christology.¹¹

---

7. Specifically, Hunter, "Spirit Christology (1)," 127–28, believes Spirit Christology to have five distinguishing marks: 1) an orientation from below, 2) no ontological distinction between the Spirit and the risen Christ, 3) classical Trinitarianism is not accepted, 4) it claims to reject the influence of philosophy, particularly Platonism, and 5) there is an explicit denial of the hermeneutical principles associated with systematic theology. The criteria I develop should clearly separate my proposal for a Spirit Christology from those that Hunter critiques.

8. The following authors make the same faulty assumption: Weinandy, "Case for Spirit Christology," 173–88, and Wright, "Roger Haight's Spirit Christology," 729–35. Significantly, both are interacting with Haight's post-Trinitarian Spirit Christology. Bloesch, *Holy Spirit*, 222–24, suffers from the same defective definition of Spirit Christology.

9. One example bears this out. Several years ago when I pitched the idea for this book to a prominent Evangelical publishing house it was rejected on the grounds that it was too controversial a proposal for evangelicals at this time. However, I was told that had Clark Pinnock authored the work the publishing house would have been happy to proceed to publication! Clearly the editor had not read my draft manuscript very closely at all.

10. For a similar list of criteria, some of which overlap with mine, see Schoonenberg, "Spirit Christology and Logos Christology," 360–61; Newman, *Spirit Christology*, 62–67; Haight, "Case for Spirit Christology," 260–62, and *Jesus Symbol of God*, 47–51; and Tracy, *Analogical Imagination*.

11. Schoonenberg, "Spirit Christology and Logos Christology," 360, a modern Roman Catholic advocate of Spirit Christology, writes: "decidedly I want to make more room for Spirit christology. My reason is simply that here, as in all my theological efforts, I want to introduce more of the Bible's own theology into dogmatics. I find it intolerable that a main theme of Paul's, Luke's and even John's christology remains either banished from our christological treatises or confined to some *scholion*." I am in full agreement with Schoonenberg's motivation for introducing Spirit Christology, as a renewed paradigm, for Systematic theology.

A second criterion for Christology is: Does it adequately presents the full divinity and humanity of Jesus Christ? This is an extension from the biblical material. It must be shown that our Christology is neither docetic nor adoptionist in both its theological formulation and practical application. While a Logos Christology can fulfill this criterion (although with explicit tension on the full humanity of Jesus Christ), for many it remains to be seen if a Spirit Christology can do it to the same degree or better than a Logos Christology.

Does the orientation of Christological method diminish either of these two natures?[12] This question forms the third criterion. Many object that when a Spirit Christology begins with a supposition describing the man Jesus as filled with the Holy Spirit, what we are left with is merely an inspired man, something short of divinity. They claim that a Spirit Christology shows a man in whom God is present (*anthropos theophoros*) rather than an "enfleshed God" (*theos sarkotheis*) as with Logos Christology. This is the debate surrounding a Christology from below considered in some detail earlier where it was shown that a Christology from below to above (one that begins with Jesus as a human person) is more than sufficient to account for the identity of Jesus and does not make him any less divine than the classical Logos Christology does. Schoonenberg correctly notes that:

> Because the Spirit is equally divine as the Logos, the Spirit too is not only present in Jesus, but also embraces, contains and sustains his human reality, although we do not say that it is *enhypostatic* in the Spirit. In Spirit christology as well, the Spirit is connected with Jesus not only functionally but also ontologically, because function is the expression of being and being includes function ... Once again I come back to the conclusion formulated above: in both christologies Jesus can be seen as fully divine and fully human.[13]

---

12. Del Colle, *Christ and the Spirit*, 182, notes that the utilization of this method is undeveloped and new with respect to constructive proposals and therefore calls for careful consideration.

13. Schoonenberg, "Spirit Christology and Logos Christology," 365. Note the objections to this method and to Schoonenberg's method by Kasper, "Christologie von unten?" 141–70. "Ours is a historically conscious period," wrote Haight, "Case for Spirit Christology," 257. Because of this historical consciousness a Christology that does not betray this will scarcely be credible. As a consequence of this fact contemporary Christology begins overwhelmingly with a consideration of Jesus and proceeds throughout to underline his humanity. This point of departure lies, Haight says, in the

The fourth criterion asks: Can this Christology adequately conceive of the divine person (unity) of Jesus Christ? By the use of "adequately conceive" I mean that it must be both intelligible and coherent, especially on this crucial point.[14] As Jesus is the center of Christian faith then Christology—the way we understand and interpret the identity of Jesus Christ—must be coherent, not just in the sense of intelligibility to the church and the wider community, but also coherent within the theological interpretations of other doctrines. This is a basic tenet of all *systematic* theology. Together, these aspects of coherence and intelligibility will be seen to contribute to a Spirit Christology in a positive way.

Fifth, is it consistent with the accepted creeds of Christendom? (Nicaea and Chalcedon), and specifically for our thesis, how is it related to Logos Christology?[15] This is an extension of the fourth criterion above. Christology must be faithful to the great Christological achievements that are universally accepted by the church. The councils of Nicaea and Chalcedon set the parameters within which Christology can unfold, what Haight terms "a certain equilibrium of historical norms."[16] That is, Jesus is truly divine and truly human; Jesus is consubstantial with God (Nicaea) and consubstantial with us (Chalcedon). The Ecumenical Creeds and standards establish a perimeter within which the orthodox theologian may delve into deeply. Without such a perimeter constructive theology inevitably tends to become wide and shallow rather than focused and deep. Because of this criterion the Spirit Christology presented here is purposely designed to be complementary to, not a replacement of, our existing and inherited Logos Christology.

The sixth and final criterion of contemporary Christology is that it must respond to contemporary issues; it must be truly contemporary and culturally relevant; it must be intelligible in today's world and empower the Christian life.[17] Adrian Thatcher makes the point that there are twin temptations confronting Christology today. The first is to reduce the full

---

data of the Synoptic Gospels in which Jesus is portrayed as a human being related to God uniquely.

14. Haight, "Case for Spirit Christology," 260–61.

15. "A typically important question for Spirit-christologies is whether they propose to replace or complement the traditional Logos-christology," Del Colle, *Christ and the Spirit*, 182.

16. Haight, *Jesus Symbol of God*, 49.

17. Ibid., 47.

divinity of Christ to something more manageable (liberalism) and the second is to repeat the ancient formulae without regard for the vastly different thought-world of today (conservatism).[18] This again is a basic tenet of all systematic theology and especially Christology.[19] The Spirit Christology I am proposing is borne out of the biblical record (economy), the theological coherence and richness that it adds, and finally, the cultural relevance for today. This view is shared by Philip Rosato for whom Spirit Christology "might well allow Christian theologians to present Jesus Christ in a way more understandable to contemporary secular culture and also more appropriate to the current spiritual and pastoral needs in the Christian community."[20] There is strong biblical warrant for a Spirit Christology and an even stronger theological warrant, due to the neglect of the Spirit in systematic theology, especially for Christology and even the Trinity. And culturally there is a need for, a hunger, openness to Spirit talk that will facilitate the presentation of a Spirit Christology. As Rosato has said, "A new Christological model is necessary; though valid in itself, the prevailing Logos model of dogmatic Christology is not totally adequate to the pressing issues which face fundamental and pastoral theology."[21]

These methodological criteria, when taken together, represent a first effort to explain the logic underlying the need to incorporate a comprehensive Spirit Christology into our contemporary theology. Each of these requirements provides, in its own way, a reason for thinking of the identity of Jesus in terms of the presence and operation of the Spirit of God in him.

CONTEMPORARY PROPOSALS

In the nineteenth, twentieth, and twenty-first centuries, various proposals have been made in reaction to the dominant Logos Christology of classical Christology. Confining ourselves to the various proposals to reclaim some form of Spirit Christology it is right say that we are cur-

---

18. Thatcher, *Truly a Person, Truly God*, 1. The labels, "liberal" and "conservative" are his. See Haight, "Case for Spirit Christology," 271. We could also add another pair of temptations constantly facing the church—fideism and fundamentalism.

19. "This forms an *a priori* context for Christological thinking," writes Haight, "Case for Spirit Christology," 261.

20. Rosato, "Spirit Christology," 423.

21. Ibid.

rently amidst a renaissance of proposals with divergent emphases and assumptions. Haight visits a range of contemporary Christological proposals and concludes:

> This range of theologians . . . testifies to the strain that began to afflict classical patristic language in the modern period. All who criticize patristic language do not necessarily turn to the symbol Spirit. But it provides a way of remaining faithful to the scriptural and doctrinal language while meeting today's exigencies.[22]

Amongst the various advocates for a Spirit Christology the proposals largely fall into two distinct categories: those that seek to *complement* Logos Christology with a Spirit Christology,[23] and those that seek to *replace* Logos Christology with a Spirit Christology.[24] These two approaches indicate two very different directions. The first is toward a thoroughly Trinitarian orthodoxy while the second is towards a post-Trinitarian or non-Trinitarian theology.[25] As these various proposals have attracted considerable critique it is not my intention to survey all of them in detail, but rather, to trace the sweep of revisionist Christology in order to set my own proposal within the wider theological landscape.

Replacing Logos Christology

Early Christianity exhibited a robust Spirit-Christology that utilized the concept of Spirit in a rather flexible fashion.[26] Today many are returning to this model for a way forward. Various proponents of a Spirit Christology

---

22. Haight, *Jesus Symbol of God*, 447.

23. In place of my "complementarity" Haight, (ibid., 424), speaks of the "pluralism of Christologies" both in Scripture and today. "Pluralism marks contemporary christology both in fact and principle."

24. Corresponding to these two categories Schoonenberg, "Spirit Christology and Logos Christology," 356, writes that "since the 19th century we find [Spirit Christology] clearly in two forms, a re-working of the scholastic theory under the influence of a Patristic renaissance, and a fresh start in search of new models."

25. Newman, *Spirit Christology*, 172ff., presents two alternative Spirit Christologies—the "interpersonal model" and the "intrapersonal model." The first relates to what I have labeled post-Trinitarian while the latter corresponds to the sort of Spirit Christology I advocate. The key difference for Newman is that the interpersonal model that he adopts is founded upon an exclusive monotheism while the intrapersonal model he rejects is founded upon a Trinitarian monotheism.

26. See the comprehensive summary in Wolfson, *Philosophy of the Church Fathers*, 183–91.

contend that "Spirit" identifies the divine element in the incarnation. This pneumatic emphasis has been preserved in one form by Eastern Orthodoxy.[27] It is now becoming popular amongst Roman Catholic and Protestant scholars alike. Since the early 1970s, theologians have been searching for a way to further Christological thinking. Today many new Spirit Christologies refer to the pre-Chalcedonian period and the biblical witness in proposing a revisionary non-Chalcedonian alternative to classical Christologies. At least twelve authors representing twenty-nine works written over the past thirty years are included in this category.[28] While the nuance of each writer varies, the fundamental thrust remains consistent. There is a general rejection of Chalcedonian Christology and, with it, the Logos Christology that it enshrines. This is evidenced in the definition given by Roger Haight, "by a Spirit Christology I mean one that 'explains' how God is present and active in Jesus, and thus Jesus' divinity, by using the biblical symbol of God as Spirit, and not the symbol Logos."[29] Along with this rejection of Chalcedon is its corollary; the rejection of any incarnational Christology at all. This obviously has serious affects for Christology, pneumatology and Trinitarian doctrine, affects that these writers are well aware of.

A common theme found within this model of Spirit Christology is the denial of any real preexistence of Jesus,[30] as it equates the risen

---

27. For a survey of Eastern Orthodox distinctives see Del Colle, *Christ and the Spirit*, 8–33. He includes extensive references to eastern writers.

28. Amongst whom are included: Berkhof, *Doctrine of the Holy Spirit*; Lampe, *Seal of the Spirit*; and "Holy Spirit and the Person of Christ," in *Christ, Faith and History*, 111–30; Schoonenberg, *Christ*; "Spirit Christology and Logos Christology," 350–75; "Christ and the Spirit," 29–49; Dunn, see especially *Christology in the Making, Unity and Diversity in the New Testament*, and *Jesus and the Spirit*, and for his collected essays see *Christ and the Spirit*, vol. 1: *Christology, Christ and The Spirit*, vol. 2: *Pneumatology*; Hook, "A Spirit Christology," 226–32; Newman, *Spirit Christology*; and Haight, "Case for Spirit Christology," 257–87. Haight states that his point is not to affirm that a Logos Christology has been or is wrong but to characterize a Christology that is more adequate to our situation. However, he ends up with the same basic conclusions as Lampe.

29. Haight, "Case for Spirit Christology," 257. Lampe does not just reject pre-existence, but also seeks to demythologize the New Testament and thus do away with the post-existence of Jesus, the incarnation, resurrection, ascension, session and Parousia. In its place is the activity of God as Spirit. Lampe, *God as Spirit*, 162–75.

30. In place of a real pre-existence some opt for "ideal preexistence." "Ideal means that whoever or whatever is deemed preexistent was in the mind and intent of God before it appeared on earth. Ideal preexistence had roots in Judaism, where some of the rabbis taught that seven things existed in the mind of God before they appeared on

Lord with the Spirit in an overly functional way and eventually into an ontological unity.[31] The Logos is interpreted as a functional notion of God's activity in the same way as S/spirit and wisdom are interpreted in the Old Testament,[32] and they are accurately labeled "post-Trinitarian."[33] The broadest definition of Spirit Christology is one which posits Spirit as the divine element in the person of Christ. The Spirit may then be identical to, or a substitute for, the divine Logos. In this way modern proposals echo those of the early church already reviewed, intending to displace Logos Christology in order to reach an alternative metaphysical understanding of the operation of divinity in Jesus. By abandoning Chalcedon's insistence on two natures within one person, a Christology of pure inspiration is achieved.

In light of these comments, those who wish to replace Logos Christology with a Spirit Christology are, properly speaking, post-Trinitarian.[34] They do not agree with traditional Trinitarian language of "person" (*prosopon, hypostasis, persona*), "nature" (*natura*), and "essence" (*ousia, physis, substantia*) in the orthodox understanding of Jesus Christ and the triune God.[35] Amongst the post-Trinitarian Spirit Christologists

---

earth, including Torah and the Messiah . . . The problem with ideal preexistence is not that it is untrue but that it is trivial. Ideal preexistence is merely another name for divine foreknowledge. This teaching says nothing about Jesus of Nazareth that it does not say about any other human. It is really a statement about the relationship between God and his creation, not Christology" (McCready, "Preexistence of Christ Revisited," 424).

31. This is why Lampe rejects an understanding of Jesus as "adjectively" or "substantively God." He is only prepared to allow Jesus to be "adverbially God." See Lampe, "Holy Spirit and the Person of Christ," 124. In his essay "Case for Spirit Christology," 257–87, Haight accepted this position. However, in his later release he agrees with the critique of this position claiming that "one cannot separate God's function in such a way. Jesus *is* divine dialectically, because the presence of God as Spirit pervades his being and action" (*Jesus Symbol of God*, 455 n. 59).

32. Consult the works of Dunn already cited and the critique by Del Colle, *Christ and the Spirit*, 141–94.

33. Del Colle traces the roots of this development back to the debate over the priority of the Jesus of history or the Christ of faith for Christian experience starting with D. F. Strauss, and developed by R. Bultmann, W. Hermann, and M. Kähler. He sees Dunn as the latest exegete to comprehensively examine the relationship between the historical Jesus and the Christ of faith in light of New Testament testimony to the experience of the Holy Spirit. Del Colle, *Christ and the Spirit*, 141.

34. Del Colle, "Spirit-Christology," 98, is correct when he states that their positions are "triadic but not a trinitarian construction. Neither Jesus nor the Spirit are considered to be divine persons."

35. The use of "person" in Christological and Trinitarian theology has occasioned

the most prominent advocates have been Piet Schoonenberg, Hendrikus Berkhof, Geoffrey Lampe, James Dunn, and recently Paul Newman.[36] Within the various works of each author a common strand of teaching can be ascertained. Berkhof is representative of the others in equating an exact identity between Christ and Spirit. He says we must think of the Spirit in strictly Christocentric terms.[37] He sees the Pauline expressions "in Christ" and "in the Spirit" as synonymous.[38] Berkhof affirms that "Christ and the Spirit are identical" and is aware that this goes beyond orthodox trinitarianism, what he calls the "traditional connection between Christ and the Spirit."[39] In summary, this revisionary Spirit Christology conceives that the Spirit is now the function of the risen Christ. Berkhof is explicit when he writes:

> how do we have to conceive of this identity of the Spirit with the exalted Lord? Traditional theology would avoid the word "identity" or merely speak of an identity in functions of the Son and the Spirit. This position is untenable, however, if we face the fact that the Spirit in Scripture is not an autonomous substance, but a predicate to the substance God and to the substance Christ. It describes the fact and the way of functioning of both.[40]

---

much debate in our post-Lockean, post-Kantian milieu as "person" seems to require three subjective individual consciousnesses and is said by many to lead to tritheism when applied to God. As regards Christology, to call Jesus a divine person has been seen by many to deny the attribution that he is an authentic human person, and it is here that the implications for Trinitarian theology are evident. On the concept of "person" in contemporary theology, see Fatula, *Triune God of Christian Faith*, Gaybba, *Spirit of Love*, Galot, *Person of Christ*, Schwöbel, and Gunton, *Persons, Divine and Human*, Wojtyla, *Acting Person*, and Zizioulas, *Being as Communion*.

36. This is not to suggest there are no differences in their respective Christologies. For instance, I note Coffey's remarks that "Schoonenberg is in a class of his own. While he does not replace Logos Christology with Spirit Christology, he has the Logos becoming a person in the human person of Jesus at the Incarnation ... He also has the Holy Spirit becoming a person at the glorification of Jesus. Prior to these personalizations the Logos and the Holy Spirit are for Schoonenberg only extensions of the single personhood of God" ("Spirit Christology and the Trinity," 336 n. 6).

37. Berkhof, *Doctrine of the Holy Spirit*, 24.

38. Ibid., 25. Here he is following the essay of I. Hermann (see references in his text).

39. Ibid., 26.

40. Ibid., 28. Berkhof does acknowledge some differentiation between the risen Christ and the Spirit however. Taking note of passages such as John 14:18; 2 Cor 13:14; and Rev 22:17, Berkhof wishes to retain a form of transcendence for the risen Christ as well but does not sufficiently develop this distinction.

In his reformulation of Christology along pneumatic lines Berkhof is aware of the Trinitarian implications of his proposal. "We must ask the question whether a radical return to a pneumatic Christology would not do more justice to the biblical message, and be more relevant to the modern mind, than our traditional categories. *It is clear that such a rethinking would not leave the trinitarian dogma unaffected.*"[41] The Spirit Christologies of the various revisionist proponents offer two alternatives to orthodox Trinitarianism. Returning to pneumatology as a resource for Christological construction may result in either an abandonment of the ascription "personhood" to the Holy Spirit (and/or the risen Son), or its continued affirmation, although along vastly revised lines.[42] The former proposal limits the identity of the Spirit to a description of the activity and presence of God while the latter alternative maintains the "personal" nature of the Spirit as hypostatically distinct from the Father and the Son but only and exclusively within the economy.[43] As such, they both diverge considerably from the biblical testimony and orthodox Trinitarianism. While these proposals are substantially different from one another, they both raise the question as to whether a pneumatic Christology can contribute meaningfully to Trinitarian theology or whether it finally results in a unipersonal theology with a Christological component.[44]

Presenting "S/spirit" as the saving presence of God in Jesus and the church means that the incarnation is not viewed as the assumption of

---

41. Ibid., 21 (italics mine).

42. As in the case of Schoonenberg's post-incarnational Trinitarianism as espoused in his work *Christ: A Study of the God-Man Relationship in the Whole of Creation and in Jesus Christ*, and developed in his essay "Spirit Christology and Logos Christology," 365–71.

43. This is in fact the thesis of LaCugna, *God With Us*. Her central axiom is that "*theologia* is fully revealed and bestowed in *oikonomia*, and *oikonomia* truly expresses the ineffable mystery of *theologia*," (ibid., 221). This collapses the Trinity into the economy to the point where the Trinity does not exist ontologically apart from the economy. Thus the Trinity is not three persons of Father, Son, and Holy Spirit but rather an impersonal theological principle of revelation. It also comes perilously close to a form of panentheism. See the critique of LaCugna's Trinitarianism in Molnar, *Divine Freedom and the Doctrine of the Immanent Trinity*, 1–25, 84–85, 253–56.

44. Del Colle, *Christ and the Spirit*, 181. When the Jesus of history is separated from the Christ of faith and the latter is interpreted according to a pneumatic construction then a modalistic identification between Christ and Spirit has been achieved. This is evident throughout the work of James Dunn, see for instance: *Partings of the Ways, Christology in the Making, Unity and Diversity in the New Testament, Jesus and the Spirit*, and *Baptism in the Holy Spirit Today*.

a human nature by a pre-existing divine person (Logos/Son) but as a mere human being inspired by God the S/spirit.[45] Thus, the Spirit is defined as the active presence of God, but not as a person of the Godhead. Spirit is the divine outreach that has taken on the form of Jesus. Under this construction neither Jesus nor the Spirit are divine persons. Rather, God is present in Jesus as S/spirit. Although mistaking this form of Spirit Christology as the only model, Harold Hunter[46] can correctly apply the logic that "there are no classical trinitarians among the Spirit christologists [he reviews] because it is claimed that Jesus is not a divine person, but is inspired by divine influence. Those who claim that the Hebraic concept of *ruah* is reducible to divine influence are modalists. If that influence is hypostatized, then the author is binitarian."[47] Hunter is correct of course, except for the fact that this is not constitutive of a Spirit Christology generally, only of a *post-Trinitarian* Spirit Christology.

This logic finds clear expression in the work of Paul Newman. His model of Spirit Christology stresses the relational unity of Christ to God without any ontological corollary. He is explicit when he writes, "adoption is a useful and appropriate term to describe the covenantal relationship of the children of God, including Jesus to God."[48] Newman, Berkhof, Lampe, and Dunn are representative of the extreme functionalists discussed in Chapter Two and have a basic *a priori* premise—that for Jesus to be divine is to negate his humanity;[49] the two are seen as entirely

---

45. See Del Colle, "Spirit-Christology," 98.

46. Hunter, "Spirit Christology (1)," 127–40, and ibid., "Spirit Christology (2)," 266–77.

47. Hunter, "Spirit Christology (2)," 271. See Mackey, *Christian Experience of God as Trinity*, 246, and Dunn, "Rediscovering the Spirit," 12, "This naturally raises the question as to how appropriate it is to speak of a *Trinity* rather than a *Binity*. Before the incarnation Logos and Spirit were hardly to be distinguished. After the incarnation the divinity of Jesus was a function of the Spirit. And after the resurrection the risen humanity of Jesus was a function of the Spirit." More accurately than binitarian may be the classification of "strict monotheists." See for example Newman, *Spirit Christology*, 215ff., and Lampe, "Holy Spirit and the Person of Christ," 123, and *God as Spirit*, 228, whose Spirit Christology amounts to an affirmation of monopersonal theism.

48. Newman, *Spirit Christology*, 215. He is even more explicit when he writes, "The uniqueness is better established on Jesus' vocational role than on ontological uniqueness," (216).

49. Lampe claims that Chalcedonian Christology tends to debilitate the two natures of Christ, *vere Deus, vere homo*, resulting in an explicit subordinationism of humanity to deity. In answer to this objection he presents his Spirit Christology where the humanity is safeguarded at the expense of divinity. Lampe, *God as Spirit*, 13, 132, 140,

incompatible outside of the notion of inspiration.⁵⁰ What all of these revisionist Spirit Christologies propose is a functional identity between the risen Christ and the Spirit that equates to a denial of any hypostatization to either the Spirit or the Son. Hence, the Son is now experienced as Spirit, the active presence of God.⁵¹ As such, all non-Chalcedonian proposals for a Spirit Christology fail the essential criteria of Christology outlined above.

Complementing Logos Christology

In the wake of what can only be termed a Trinitarian revolution within contemporary theology, propositions for the recovery of the ancient paradigm of Spirit Christology have been advocated across the theological spectrum. This includes at least fifty authors,⁵² representing more than

---

and "Holy Spirit and the Person of Christ," 123. This form of Spirit Christology has roots directly or indirectly in the work of the Scottish theologian Edward Irving. See Irving, *Collected Writings of Edward Irving*, Strachan, *Pentecostal Theology of Edward Irving*; and the comprehensive assessment of Irving's Spirit christology by McFarlane, *Christ and the Spirit*.

50. "If Jesus was human he could not at the same time be deity. His relationship with God had to be adoptive," Newman, *Spirit Christology*, 217. This assumption seems to be the impulse behind the proposals of Lampe to displace Logos Christology with his form of Spirit Christology. He writes, "Christology could then avoid this conclusion only by developing the idea of *kenosis* to the point where, in order to become incarnate as true man . . . the divine Person has virtually divested himself of the deity" (Lampe, "Holy Spirit and the Person of Christ," 120).

51. While Dunn has a more nuanced position than we are able to present in this brief overview (i.e., he does allow that there is more to the risen Jesus than life-giving Spirit) he equates the Spirit with the risen Jesus, the only personal element of the Spirit being Jesus himself. Dunn, *Jesus and the Spirit*, 325f., 351ff. He characterizes Paul's pneumatology as "immanent christology" ("1 Corinthians 15:45—Last Adam, Life-giving Spirit," 139).

52. These authors include: Mühlen, *Una mystica persona*; Coffey, "Gift of the Holy Spirit," 202–33, "'Incarnation' of the Holy Spirit in Christ," 466–80, "Proper Mission of the Holy Spirit," 227–50, "Holy Spirit as the Mutual Love of the Father and the Son," 193–229, "Theandric Nature of Christ," 405–31, "Spirit Christology and the Trinity," *"Did You Receive the Holy Spirit When You Believed?"*; Moltmann, *Crucified God, Triunity and the Kingdom, Way of Jesus Christ, History and the Triune God, Spirit of Life, Source of Life*, "Trinitarian Personhood of the Holy Spirit," 302–14; Smail, *Reflected Glory, Giving Gift*, "Doctrine of the Holy Spirit," 87–110; Kasper, *Jesus the Christ, God of Jesus Christ*; Rosato, "Spirit Christology," "Spirit Christology as Access to Trinitarian Theology," 166–76;. Clark, "Spirit Christology in the Light of Eucharistic Theology"; McDonnell, "Determinative Doctrine of the Holy Spirit," 142–61, "Trinitarian Doctrine of the Holy Spirit," 191–227, "Can Classical Pentecostals and Roman Catholics Engage

eighty works written over the past fifty years.⁵³ Again our purpose is not to summarize the various proposals, but rather, to state in general terms what the content of these calls for complementarity consist of and then to present my own nuanced position.

In contradistinction to replacement Spirit Christologies, an orthodox Spirit Christology that I propose preserves the Trinitarian distinctions in correlation with the classical understanding of the incarnation of the divine Son/Word become flesh in Jesus. Thus, it would guard against any modalism of the Second and Third persons of the Godhead, especially at the point of the relationship between the exalted Christ and the present Spirit.⁵⁴ The Spirit Christology presented here acknowledges the pneumatological dimension of Christology but does not displace the existing Logos Christology and its Trinitarian outcome. Ralph Del Colle stated: "it is a question of complementarily and enrichment rather than wholesale reconstruction and revision of traditional Christology."⁵⁵ As was pointed out in Chapter Two, a post-Trinitarian Spirit Christology is rejected in favor of a form of pneumatic Logos Christology, or a Spirit Christology that is compatible with and enriches Logos Christology, one that "makes impossible a Christology that is not wholly theocentric and pneumatological, and a pneumatology which is not genuinely christocentric and theocentric."⁵⁶ In Peter Hodgson's words:

---

in Common Witness?" 97–106.; O'Donnell, "In Him and Over Him," *Mystery of the Triune God*; Hawthorne, *Presence and the Power*; Del Colle, "Spirit-Christology: Dogmatic Foundations for Pentecostal-Charismatic Spirituality," 91–112, *Christ and the Spirit*, "Oneness and Trinity," 85–110, "Response to Jürgen Moltmann and David Coffey," 339–46; Badcock, *Light of Truth & Fire of Love*, Pinnock, *Flame of Love*; and Studebaker, "Integrating Pneumatology and Christology," 5–20.

53. It is noteworthy that many Roman Catholics have proposed some form of complementary Spirit Christology as they have an inherent respect and awareness for the Great Tradition. As such they are less want to diverge significantly from the received dogma of the church. Evangelical Protestants, in comparison, hold unswervingly to the formal and material principle of the Reformation and so are capable of holding multiple perspectives in theology if it is so warranted from Scripture. Poythress, *Symphonic Theology*, calls this "symphonic theology."

54. Spirit Christology advocates a more robust pneumatology than Western Christology has generally exhibited and it guards against any modalism of the second and third persons in the relationship between the *Christus praesens* and the *Spiritus praesens*. I am indebted to Del Colle, "Spirit-Christology," 98, for this succinct insight.

55. ibid.

56. Hunter, "Spirit Christology (2)," 270. See Del Colle, "Spirit-Christology," 98, who shares the same view. Zizioulas, *Being as Communion*, 127, raises the question of priority: should Christology be made dependent on pneumatology or should it be the other

> A Spirit-Christology essentially holds that Jesus was a man so totally possessed by the Spirit that the outcome of his life and ministry was a revelation of God as full and complete as can be expressed in a finite human life . . . It is convinced that the Gospels tell the story of a human life, a life full of meaning and significance, but that humanity is not the last word about it . . . Spurred by the inadequacy of the traditional Logos-Christology, it essays a re-interpretation of our Lord's Person that will be expressive of the church's conviction that indeed in him we meet with nothing other than God himself.[57]

Spirit Christology as a complementary paradigm with Logos Christology has been advocated in both Roman Catholic and Protestant traditions, with somewhat of a convergence appearing in contemporary proposals, as I trust my own work attests to. Prominent Roman Catholic theologian David Coffey is adamant that the two approaches are complementary in nature and both have significant contributions to make to Christology.[58] Coffey writes:

> A Spirit Christology that successfully incorporates Logos Christology will, then, be superior to one that does not. This is because it will do greater justice to the total data of the New Testament about Christ and therefore to the person of Christ himself. For the same reason a Spirit Christology that incorporates Logos Christology will be superior to a Logos Christology that does not incorporate Spirit Christology.[59]

Likewise, Protestant theologian Gary Badcock states that "Spirit Christology and Logos Christology are surely no more incompatible than Spirit and Logos themselves. According to strict Trinitarian orthodoxy, after all, the two are one as much as they are distinct."[60]

---

way round? He rightly concludes that the question of priority only arose when the two aspects were separated from one another both theologically and then liturgically. As I state repeatedly throughout this study, Word and Spirit are not mutually exclusive. See Torrance, *Christian Doctrine of God*, 1, 147–55.

57. Hodgson, *Jesus—Word and Presence*, 184.

58. Coffey, "Holy Spirit as the Mutual Love of the Father and the Son."

59. Coffey, "Spirit Christology and the Trinity," 316, 317.

60. Badcock, *Light of Truth & Fire of Love*, 161. He goes on to speak of the relationship between the two as a "coincidence of opposites," (ibid., 161).

Roman Catholic Proposals

Modern Roman Catholic proposals have been significantly influenced by two figures,[61] Matthias Scheeben (1835–1888)[62] and Heribert Mühlen.[63] While Scheeben merely introduced pneumatology into the discussion of Jesus's person, Mühlen elaborated on the role of the Spirit in the incarnation, particularly the scholastic doctrine of the "habitual" or "accidental" sanctification of Jesus.[64] He stated that the Logos relates to the human *nature* and personalizes it; the Spirit relates to the *person* of Jesus and sanctifies him through created gifts of grace. Mühlen attempted to develop a salvation-historical role for the work of the Holy Spirit in the life of Christ drawing on the heterodox teachings of the Ebionites but, importantly, he corrected their overly functional metaphysic with the ontological propositions of Logos Christology.[65] For Mühlen, the role of the Holy Spirit in the life of Christ was not accidental but essential. The Spirit created in Jesus such graces as were essential for his Messianic task, graces that increased throughout time. These graces, while deriving ultimately from the hypostatic union, were also more immediately derived from the "unction" of the Holy Spirit. "The total history of grace in Jesus's life, according to Mühlen, from his conception to his death, resurrection, and exaltation must be understood as a history also of the Spirit

---

61. Schoonenberg, "Spirit Christology and Logos Christology," 356, traces contemporary proposals of a Spirit Christology within Roman Catholicism back to the seminal works of Petavius (1583–1652) and Thamasinus (1619–1695) along with the Tubinger schools of the nineteenth century in that they diverged from the appropriations theory and meaningfully reintroduced pneumatology into their theology.

62. For a discussion of Scheeben's theology, see Coffey, *Grace*, 93–95.

63. Mühlen, *Una mystica persona*. For a more extensive bibliography consult Badcock, *Light of Truth & Fire of Love*, 147. We could also add to this list of seminal Roman Catholic theologians the contributions of Rahner, *Trinity*; ibid., *Theological Investigations,*, and von Balthasar, *Theodramatik*.

64. See further in Badcock, *Light of Truth & Fire of Love*, 146f.

65. Mühlen, "Das Christusereignis als Tat des Heiligen Deistes," in *Mysteruim Salutis*, III/s, 513–45, quoted in Badcock, *Light of Truth & Fire of Love*, 151. O'Donnell, "In Him and Over Him," 26, seeks to integrate a Spirit Christology with the dominant Logos Christology. In this, he follows Mühlen and more recently Congar, *La Parola e il Soffio*, 111. O'Donnell writes, "a descending Christology of the Incarnation needs to be complemented by an ascending Christology of the Spirit, which reveals how the Father, through the Spirit, acted in new and diverse ways upon Jesus . . . Such a theological reflection, while in no way contradicting the ontological mode of thinking, would be based rather upon a salvific-historical perspective" ("In Him and Over Him," 26).

who bestowed the grace."[66] Even so, Mühlen's theology still made the work of the Spirit posterior to that of the Logos.[67] The role of the Holy Spirit in the life of Christ was a secondary implication of the hypostatic union as was worked out by subsequent theologians.

Following Mühlen, the Roman Catholic tradition produced numerous attempts to further elaborate the relationship between Christ and Spirit in some form of complementary (orthodox) Spirit Christology.[68] Most prominent in their attempts at formulating a Spirit Christology of an orthodox nature have been Piet Schoonenberg, Walter Kasper, Philip Rosato, David Coffey, and Ralph Del Colle.[69] As previously stated, Philip Rosato says, "a new christological model is necessary; though valid in itself, the prevailing Logos model of dogmatic Christology is not totally adequate to the pressing issues which face fundamental and pastoral theology."[70] He adds that, "setting Christology in a pneumatic framework is a clear and challenging mandate of present-day theology."[71] In the theology of these writers the relationship between Christ and Spirit[72] is taken further than in Mühlen's enterprise and the Trinitarian implications have been explicated. Rosato and Kasper concur that, "it appears from the New Testament's point of view that Christology is a function of

---

66. Badcock, *Light of Truth & Fire of Love*, 151.

67. For further elaboration on Mühlen's Christology see Congar, *I Believe in the Holy Spirit*, vol. 1, 22–25, Schoonenberg, "Spirit Christology and Logos Christology," 357–58, and O'Donnell, "In Him and Over Him," 27f.

68. I have estimated seventeen theologians representing approximately thirty-five monographs so far.

69. Schoonenberg's thesis is the less orthodox of these proposals and has been discussed elsewhere. See his proposal in "Trinity—The Consummated Covenant," 273–82.

70. Rosato, "Spirit-christology," 423. Hook, "Spirit Christology," 226–32, concurs although he believes the Western philosophical language for the Trinity and Christology is "outmoded and long since discredited," (ibid., 226).

71. Rosato, *Spirit as Lord*, 179. Rosato also adds that it will be no easy task. As far as the relationship between Logos Christology and Spirit Christology goes, Rosato is squarely within the complementarity camp although he does raise the question, "must Spirit Christology be viewed simply as an appendage to Logos Christology, and not as an independent theological model which might better explain the uniqueness and universality of the Christ event?" (ibid., 174).

72. Coffey calls this relationship in the economy the "incarnation" of the Holy Spirit in Christ, see "'Incarnation' of the Holy Spirit in Christ," while Del Colle calls this the "*Christus praesens*" and the "*Spiritus praesens*," in his *Christ and the Spirit*.

an overarching pneumatology."[73] Coffey equally insists that, "Christology and pneumatology can no longer be regarded as independent studies; they are interdependent."[74] Yves Congar is in total agreement when he develops his theology of the "Pneumatised Christ."[75] Why? For two reasons: first, on the economic level, because this is the New Testament's view; Jesus came into a Jewish context as bearer of the Spirit and mediator of the Spirit. Second, on the immanent level, because this is the revelation of intratrinitarian communion; this is who God is.

In Kasper's proposal he makes the bold assertion that the hypostatic union is not the presupposition of Jesus's anointing with the Spirit but is instead its consequence. In this move Kasper has made Logos Christology a consequence of a Spirit Christology, thus reversing the received tradition.[76] Following Kasper, most advocates of this paradigm of Spirit Christology concur that Spirit Christology logically precedes that of Logos Christology. For Coffey, "the bestowal model is thus more basic than the procession model, for it arises from the phenomenon from which the Christian religion itself takes its origin, and not, as with the procession model, from something consequent upon this."[77]

Just as the adoption of believers is the work of the Spirit, Kasper argues, so it is the same for Christ. Without excluding the idea of the assumption of the flesh by the Logos, Kasper argues that Jesus can only be the Christ by virtue of the anointing of the Holy Spirit. In this sense then, the Spirit mediates the incarnation continually. In the work of David Coffey and Del Colle this theme is further elaborated upon.

73. Rosato, "Spirit-christology," 424.
74. Coffey, "Theandric Nature of Christ," 431.
75. Congar, *Word and the Spirit*, 101ff.
76. Kasper, *Jesus the Christ*, 230–74.
77. Coffey, "A Proper Mission of the Holy Spirit," 233. In a later work, "Holy Spirit as the Mutual Love of the Father and the Son," Coffey writes more forcefully that, "the descending method remains valid but, like the major and minor notes in music, seems now to be exhausted, and Christology, and theology generally, like contemporary music, now need to explore other modes to meet the incessant demands on the human spirit." While Badcock, *Light of Truth & Fire of Love*, 169, is in essential agreement he writes convincingly that "the movement from below cannot take place without the prior movement from above, but equally, the movement from above exists only for the sake of the corresponding movement from below." Congar, *Word and the Spirit*, 86, schooled in the Christology of Thomas Aquinas (*Summa Theologiae* IIIa), now finds Thomistic Christology unsatisfactory as "[Aquinas] gave more attention to the aspect of descent, that is, the incarnation of the Word, than to the aspect of reascent, in which the action of the Holy Spirit is involved."

Coffey speaks of the divinization of the humanity of Christ and to the question: how this may be so? he answers, "through the anointing of Jesus by the Father with the Spirit."[78] Hence, Coffey and the other advocates of a Spirit Christology of this category (including me) see the incarnation as a distinctive work of the Holy Spirit, the Spirit of Sonship. "In the one act of nature and grace the humanity of Christ was created by the triune God and so radically sanctified by the Holy Spirit, sent thereto by the Father, that it became one in person with the eternal Son, and so Son of God in humanity."[79]

Adhering fully to Nicene-Chalcedonian Christology, Kasper wishes to reappropriate its meaning in more relational or personal terms.[80] He argues that the received view in the West is overly metaphysical and static, showing little concern with Jesus's historical, human relation, not to his divine nature as the Son, but to the Father. Kasper is heeding Mühlen's call for a more elaborate incorporation of the salvation-historical witness into our received Christology, and by direct implication, into our Trinitarian doctrine.[81] This is why Christology must begin with the humanity of Jesus and from there, rise above to ontological conclusions. To answer the question, "how it is possible for the divinity and humanity, though distinct, to be one in Jesus?" Kasper utilizes a distinctly pneumatologically oriented Christology.[82] Jesus's humanity is filled by the Holy Spirit in such a way that a mould for God's self-communication results. The Spirit is God's personal freedom which sanctifies Jesus, enabling him to be obedient and an incarnate response to God's self-communication.[83]

Each of the authors under review attempt to incorporate their Christology into a fully developed Trinitarianism. The dogmatic issue for Spirit Christology, as identified by Del Colle, is the Trinitarian one;

---

78. Coffey, "'Incarnation' of the Holy Spirit in Christ," 469.

79. Ibid., see his discussion of the *enhypostasia* understood alongside a dynamic conception of the *communicatio idiomatum* in Coffey, "Theandric Nature of Christ," 405–31. Coffey now sees the term "theandric" as the most beneficial for Christological discussion as it expresses the fact that the focus of Jesus's unity resides in the humanity from the divinity by which the latter is clearly seen to be actualized in the former.

80. Kasper, *Jesus the Christ*, 236–38.

81. Badcock, *Light of Truth & Fire of Love*, 156, also notes the influence on Kasper of Karl Rahner.

82. Kasper, *Jesus the Christ*, 240ff.

83. Ibid., 251.

namely, the convergence and distinction between the Son and the Spirit in the person and work of Christ,[84] and then in the immanent Trinity itself. On the Trinitarian level, the various Roman Catholic theologians look to Augustine's model of the Spirit as the bond of love for inspiration.[85] Coffey notes that Augustine postulated two models for the Trinity, the *filioque* or "procession model," and the so called "bestowal model" or (his now-preferred term) the "mutual-love" theory; an alternate way of conceiving the Trinity in which the Holy Spirit appears as the mutual love of Father and Son.[86] However, they do not accept his mutual-love theory uncritically.[87] Going beyond the Augustinian scheme, Kasper posits that the Spirit is the "surplus and effusion of freedom in the love between the Father and the Son,"[88] whereas, in the Augustinian paradigm the Spirit is the bond of love between Father and Son *in se*. For Kasper the Spirit is also the "extra" or "surplus" of that bond that is exercised outward, *ad extra* to the world. Coffey, taking his cue from Augustine and Richard of St. Victor, affirms that the Holy Spirit is the "bond" rather than the medium between Father and Son. This bond has a two-way communicative affect: the Holy Spirit is the bond of love not just from the Father to the Son but also in return from the Son to the Father.[89] Coffey identifies this as a "bestowal model" as opposed to a "procession model."[90] For Coffey these models are ultimately complementary, but due to the neglected nature of the bestowal model or mutual love theory and its suitability to Spirit Christology, he highlights it alone. In his earlier work Coffey makes it clear that the Spirit is the means of Jesus's response to the Father and the Father to the Son.[91]

---

84. Del Colle, "Spirit-Christology," 103.

85. All of Coffey's Spirit Christology is rooted in the Augustinian model of the mutual-love theory and as a follower of Coffey, so is Del Colle's model of Spirit Christology.

86. Coffey, "Holy Spirit as the Mutual Love of the Father and the Son," 193, and ibid., *"Did You Receive the Holy Spirit When You Believed?"* 47.

87. Coffey has a full critique of Augustine's trinitarianism in "Holy Spirit as the Mutual Love of the Father and the Son," 194–201, and *"Did You Receive the Holy Spirit When You Believed?"* 38–42.

88. Kasper, *Jesus the Christ*, 250.

89. Coffey, "'Incarnation' of the Holy Spirit in Christ," 478f.

90. Ibid., 478–80. In his later works, he now prefers over "bestowal model" the terminology "the model of return," "Holy Spirit as the Mutual Love of the Father and the Son," 228, and "mutual love" theory, *"Did You Receive the Holy Spirit When You Believed?"* 47.

91. See Coffey, "Gift of the Holy Spirit."

Del Colle, who advances the basic position of Coffey, explicitly states what this orthodox model of Spirit Christology entails;

> By Spirit-Christology I mean envisioning the constitution and mission of the person of Christ in terms that establish an interrelationship between the filiological and the pneumatological dimensions of Christology. In other words, reference to Jesus Christ is true to the gospel only when the christological event is understood to be a thoroughly trinitarian event, an event in which God effects salvation through the Son and in the Spirit. In terms commensurate with the earliest strata of the canonical Gospels we can state that Jesus is revealed as one who stands in a unique relationship to the God of Israel, that is, his "Abba relation," and as one who is filled with the Spirit without measure (Jn 3:34).[92]

He goes on to add, "the most succinct definition of Spirit Christology is that the Holy Spirit is attributed a constitutive role in the theological and soteriological reality that we identify as the person and work of Jesus Christ."[93] Del Colle wishes to assert more than the fact that the Holy Spirit plays a role in the work of salvation or is related to Jesus Christ. "Rather I am insisting that who Jesus Christ is and the salvation that he brings proceeds from a basic and foundational pneumatological orientation."[94] In this I am in total accord.

Protestant Proposals

Corresponding to the Roman Catholic proposals of a Spirit Christology has been the Protestant contribution. We have already mentioned the impact of Barth on the call for a pneumatic Christology. Before considering the responses to Barth we must make note of the proposals of two prominent theologians, both from the Reformed tradition, whose theology is currently undergoing a renaissance, and whose pneumatic emphasis in Christology act as important examples of attempts to construct a Spirit Christology. I am referring to the magisterial Puritan theologian, John Owen (1616–1683) and the renegade Scottish pastor, Edward Irving (1792–1834). While neither would identify themselves

---

92. Del Colle, "Spirit-Christology," 93.

93. Ibid., 95. In his monograph, Del Colle, *Christ and the Spirit*, 78, adds that "Spirit-Christology affirms the constitutive agency of the Holy Spirit in the confession of Jesus Christ and in those homologies and eventual doctrinal constructions that express the meaning of his person and deed."

94. Del Colle, "Spirit-Christology," 95–96.

as espousing a Spirit Christology (this term was not available to them anyway), they present us with two very important case studies of Spirit Christology. Both attempted to formulate a pneumatic Christology while holding to Nicene and Chalcedonian orthodoxy and, as such, their insights can lead into a more fully informed contemporary articulation of Spirit Christology.

John Owen sought to defend Christ's uniqueness as the God-man without limiting his humanity in any way, a tendency susceptible to the Western tradition as we have seen. Owen sought to present Christ as the Scriptures do, as the prototype of Christian existence, continually empowered, comforted, and sanctified by the Holy Spirit. He argued that the eternal Son of God assumed human nature into personal union with himself, but—and this was the distinctive insight of his Christology—he held that all direct divine activity on that assumed human nature was that of the Holy Spirit.[95] Prior to this time it was held that the Logos, the Son, determined the human life of Jesus directly, rather than indirectly, through the Holy Spirit as Owen maintained. This is a crucial insight in the formulation of a Spirit-Christology. Owen sought to defend this position from Scripture, raising extensive testimony in support.[96]

Against a rising Socinian view that the Son of God acts directly on the human nature (a Patristic distinctive that we have observed), Owen identified ten operations of the Holy Spirit in reference to Jesus Christ to prove his point. These included all the various *kairoi* or divine disclosure episodes already identified in Chapter Five.[97] Importantly for Owen, initial sanctification of Jesus Christ in the womb was accomplished by the Holy Spirit, and Jesus was filled with grace according to the measure of his receptivity.[98] This forms an important step in Owen's argument. As Jesus Christ was divinely conceived in the womb of the virgin Mary by the Holy Spirit, so Jesus Christ was also filled with the Holy Spirit from conception in order that his human nature could not fall prey to the hu-

---

95. Spence, "Christ's Humanity and Ours," 75–76. Spence has become a standard interpreter of Owen on this point. See his "Incarnation and Inspiration," 52–55, and ibid., "John Owen and Trinitarian Agency," 157–73. Also see Kapic, *Communion with God*, 84–88, especially.

96. Owen, "Work of the Holy Spirit," 159–88.

97. McFarlane, *Why Do You Believe What You believe About the Holy Spirit?* 103–6, identifies four areas especially where Owen articulated the relation between Christ and Spirit; 1) birth; 2) sanctification; 3) power; and 4) death and resurrection.

98. Owen, "Work of the Holy Spirit," 210.

man condition—the propensity to sin (Isa 11:1–3). Owen does not mean to say that upon conception and initial sanctification the Son was filled with *all* grace and *all* knowledge, rather "the soul of Christ, from the first moment of its infusion, was a subject capable of a fullness of grace, as unto its habitual residence and in-being, though the actual exercise of it was suspended for a while, until the organs of the body were fitted for it."[99]

Second, the Spirit carries on the work of progressive sanctification.[100] This point relates to the modern quest to determine Jesus's self-understanding. Owen is content to read Scripture at face value and to give full weight to the man Jesus, growing in grace and knowledge (Luke 2:40, 52). He writes, "his divine nature was not unto him in the place of a soul, nor did it immediately operate the things which he performed, as some of old vainly imagined; but being a perfect man, his rational soul was in him the immediate principle of all his moral operations even as ours are in us."[101] Owen is advocating here the view that Jesus Christ is *autokineton*—a self-determining spiritual principle, fully self-conscious and as creature, open and responsive to God, not determined by the Logos immediately. Owen's argument was that if this were not so then Christ would not be truly human.

Without at any point denying classical orthodoxy, Owen's formulation stands in stark contrast to the long tradition received in the West through Chalcedon.[102] The experience of God for the man Jesus is indirect; it is through the Holy Spirit thus it is voluntary rather than natural.[103] In Christ there is both continuity with humanity and discontinuity, for after all, he is the God-man. From where did Christ gain his source of knowledge and revelation of God the Father? As the eternal Word, he was privy to the entire council and wisdom of the Father from all ages. However, in the incarnation he restricted himself to the mediation of that knowledge and wisdom through the Spirit. Hence, he stood in continuity with the prophets of old as they were inspired by the Holy Spirit

---

99. Ibid., 211.

100. Ibid.,

101. Ibid.

102. Spence, "Christ's Humanity and Ours," 74–97, compares Owen's Christology to that of Apollinarius, and then through Athanasius and Chalcedon.

103. This is worked out in Owen's exegesis of Hebrews, especially Heb 5:7. See Owen, *Exposition of the Epistle to the Hebrews*, vol. 4, 507.

to both foretell and forthtell the things of God. What distinguishes the revelation in Christ from that of these prophets is "the infinite excellency of his person above theirs,"[104] due to his person being identical to that of the everlasting Son.[105]

According to Owen, it is not possible or convincing to acknowledge the divinity of Christ from any of his incarnate works for all his operations in the incarnation were those of a true human being. Although in his person he was truly God and truly man, his work of mediation was carried out through his human nature. For Owen, if we reject Apollinarianism, there is no place for identifying any part of Christ's incarnate life as being totally that of God and not of man; not his miracles, his resurrection, nor even his conception. These are insufficient grounds for the claim to divinity. So what evidence does Owen find as proof for divinity from the Scripture? As I have highlighted already in this study, it was by his relationship with the Father in or by the Holy Spirit; it was the Spirit that bore witness to Christ that he was the Son of God, the true Messiah. It was the Spirit that bore witness to his miracles as being the works of God almighty; it was the Holy Spirit who convinced the followers of Christ that his death as a criminal was actually the propitiation for sins offered to the Father by the Son; it is the Holy Spirit who convicts of sin, and it is the Holy Spirit to whom is committed the work of illumination, bringing to light the truth of Christ's divinity to his followers and the world in general.[106]

In Owen's Christology he was able to account for the real humanity of Jesus Christ, including his growth in grace and separation from the Father on the cross, while not diminishing his total status as the second Person of the eternal Trinity, the Son now Incarnate. In his own way Owen was able to affirm what I am currently labeling as an orthodox Spirit Christology. However, due to his overriding concern for the basis of the assurance of salvation Owen did not pursue this enterprise

---

104. Owen, *Exposition of the Epistle to the Hebrews*, vol. 3, 31.

105. This is fully consistent with the traditional doctrine of the *enhypostasia* and the *anhypostasia*. In this way Owen argues for an ontological uniqueness to Christ not just a functional one. See Davidson, "Reappropriating Patristic Christology," 225–39, and ibid., "Theologizing the Human Jesus," 129–53. For an overview see Muller, *Dictionary of Latin and Greek Theological Terms*, 35, 103.

106. This corresponds to what we have termed a retroactive reading of Scripture based on a pneumatological hermeneutic.

in any greater detail or investigate the Trinitarian implications of his Christology.[107]

Almost two-centuries later another seminal Spirit Christology was proposed, this time by the Scottish pastor, Edward Irving.[108] What marks Irving out for mention is that, unlike Owen, he did incorporate his distinctive pneumatic Christology into an understanding of the Trinity.[109] Throughout his ministry, Irving developed a unique Christology particularly in relation to the humanity of Jesus Christ. While he intended to remain true to his tradition he was considered to have transgressed the lines of orthodoxy and to have imbibed the wine of heresy. It is only recently that the significant insights of some of Irving's theology have come into serious consideration. His insights on the nature of Christ's humanity offer particularly fruitful study in relation to the formulation of a Spirit-Christology, although there are some aspects of his Christology that, while interesting, are not essential to a Spirit Christology.[110]

Irving found himself amidst a Copernican shift from the theocentric to the anthropocentric in Christology. Alongside the abiding temptation towards Docetism which depreciated Christ's humanity Irving was confronted by a rampant theological novelty led by Schleiermacher, where the divinity of Christ was all but denied and the humanity was all that remained.[111] In response, with McFarlane, Irving "does not entail a

---

107. This is most regrettable, especially given the fact that Owen is typically exhaustive in his treatment of almost every other subject he treats!

108. Irving, *Collected Writings of Edward Irving.*.

109. "He took the Cappadocian view of the Trinity and married it to Owen's insights about the Spirit and his relationship to Jesus. The net result was a helpful response to the issues of his day," McFarlane, *Why Do You Believe What You Believe About the Holy Spirit?* 115.

110. Such is the case with Irving's doctrine of the sinful humanity of Jesus Christ. Following Irving, a number of theologians adopted his thesis on the fallen humanity of Christ. See the discussion in: Barth, *CD* I/2, 147–59; Cranfield, *Critical and Exegetical Commentary on the Epistle to the Romans*, vol. 1, 379ff.; Torrance, *Mediation of Christ*, 48; James B. Torrance, "Vicarious Humanity of Christ," 141, Weinandy, *In the Likeness of Sinful Flesh*; Strachan, *Pentecostal Theology of Edward Irving*, 25–54; McFarlane, *Christ and the Spirit*, 139–47; Macleod, *Person of Christ*, 221–30, Kapic, "Son's Assumption of a Human Nature," 154–66; Crisp, "Did Christ Have a *Fallen* Human Nature?" 270–88, "Was Christ Sinless or Impeccable?" 168–86; and Davidson, "Pondering the Sinlessness of Jesus Christ," 372–98.

111. See for instance Schleiermacher, *Christian Faith*, Barth, *Theology of Schleiermacher*. An illegitimate form of Spirit Christology that neglected the unique way

flight from the divine. Rather, he reappraises the relationship between the divine and the human within the context of incarnation."[112] In order to account for the divine and human in the one person of the incarnate Son Jesus Christ, Irving sought to identify the place of the Spirit within the incarnation. He pursued a Trinitarian interpretation of the incarnation. Irving believed that in this way we would come to a greater understanding of the person of Jesus Christ. Irving followed Calvin's lead in establishing the fact that Christ's existence explains ours.[113] Knowledge of Jesus Christ supplies knowledge of both God and humanity.

While Adam is thought of as the *archē* Jesus is said to be both *archē* and *telos* in that he alone is the perfect *imago Dei*. The Son is the perfect image of God in the sense of being a reflection-in-dependence. This dependence was most intimately with the Father but importantly realized and experienced through the Spirit, both in the economic and immanent Trinity. The Son is a pneumatic-being-in-dependence from all eternity, depending upon the Holy Spirit to reveal the Father. So, for Irving, the incarnation would provide the clearest revelation of this image of God in a Trinitarian fashion. Irving's anthropology challenged the prevailing archaeological interpretation with a teleological one. He incorporated the Pauline emphasis of eschatological progression into his anthropology. In creation humanity is to image God, just as Jesus Christ would do in perfection. So our creation was teleological from the beginning. Adam was not the perfect state but the type of which Christ was the anti-type. In this sense then, Christ alone is the perfect human and we are to conform to his image by the work of the Holy Spirit.[114]

---

in which the Spirit is united with Christ is found within the Christologies of Kant, Schleiermacher, Ritschl, and von Harnack, hence Barth's reaction against them. They created a spiritual universalism which undercut the church's true relevance and led theology into disarray. Logos Christology received its impetus originally as an apologetic in light of faulty adoptionism and so too the modern impetus to Logos Christology from Barth was also occasioned by a reaction against a faulty adoptionism. So it seems that Logos Christology is complementary to Spirit Christology in that it acts as a protective hedge.

112. McFarlane, *Christ and the Spirit*, 71. Following the work of Strachan, *Pentecostal Theology of Edward Irving*, McFarlane is most responsible for the renaissance of Irving's Christology, although he is critical of it at many points. In addition to the above see ibid., "Strange News from Another Star," (98–119).

113. Calvin, *Institutes of the Christian Religion*, 1559 edition, 1.1.1.

114. McFarlane, "Strange News from Another Star," 98–119, and *Christ and the Spirit*, 70ff.

Within his Christology Irving incorporates a Trinitarian structure at every point and thus creating a more dynamic understanding of the Spirit in relation to Christ than had previously been the case. Irving develops a pneumatic understanding of incarnation, identifying the link between incarnational and inspirational Christologies. Between the two poles of the being of God as Trinity and the becoming of human being, Christ and the incarnation makes space for an incarnational, inspirational Christology without pitting Christ against the Spirit. He offers a possible *via medians* through the Christologies of Logos and Spirit.

It is here that Irving provides us with our most helpful information regarding the relationship between Christ and the Spirit. Christ was not merely filled with the Holy Spirit but the Spirit was the author of his bodily existence. For Irving, like Owen, the Spirit was united to the human soul of Jesus and so, due to his presence and control of the soul, Jesus was tempted but never assented to an evil suggestion.[115] So the soul is the central location of the incarnation; the Son unites himself to a human soul, which is assumed by the Holy Spirit; the Holy Spirit possesses and anoints the soul, but it is the Son who wields the Spirit. McFarlane explains:

> What is possessed is by the Son: what is empowered is by the Spirit. In this way the humanity is one that requires the Spirit's enabling, even when assumed by the Son. It has to be so both from the divine perspective where God's being as Father, Son and Spirit is such that the Son always relates to the Father's will through the Spirit, and from the human perspective where it is the Son's prerogative to obey and reveal the Father, but it is the Spirit's to sanctify. By means of both considerations Irving crosses the Rubicon that has so vitiated understanding of the Son's relation to the Spirit in previous generations.[116]

This is Irving's major point for our consideration: that both in his divine and human natures the Son is unable *of himself* to procure salvation. Such a claim stands in line with any Trinitarian interpretation of incarnation. It is not the prerogative of the Son to procure salvation in and by himself. Rather, he is the one sent by the Father and empowered

---

115. Along with the soul of Jesus the will also plays a prominent part in Irving's pneumatic Christology. The Spirit occupies the will of Jesus to superintend it, in this way Jesus is both sinless and remains sinless. See McFarlane, *Christ and the Spirit*, 168ff.

116. Ibid., 159.

by the Sprit, both in his divine and human existence.[117] The cross is a Trinitarian work just as the incarnation is a Trinitarian self-revelation.

Within Irving's theology only the Spirit sanctifies and empowers the humanity of Jesus. In this regard Irving is similar to Owen.[118] In Jesus's divine nature the Father's glory is communicated and revealed by the Son through the Spirit; in his human nature the Father's plan of salvation is effected through the Son in the power of the Spirit. In his glorified nature the Father's will is executed through the Son by the same Spirit who is now given to the church. In summarizing Irving's Christology MacFarlane explains:

> We can identify the Spirit's place in two ways here. Firstly, with regards to the person of the Spirit, any act of God the Father and Son always involves the Spirit. It is the triune God who mediates himself in the act of mediation. Secondly, with regards to the work of the Spirit within the economy of salvation, the work of the Spirit in relation to the Son who takes on fallen humanity, the Spirit empowers the Son to perform the Father's will and overcome "sin in the flesh" . . . In his understanding of the Son's relationship to the Mediator both as God and man, and of the Spirit's place in this filial role, Irving redressed the imbalance so prevalent in Western Christology which stressed the divinity of the Son at the expense of his humanity.[119]

While the particulars of Irving's Christology are still being debated his central concern is clear enough: to integrate the proper place and mission of the Holy Spirit into Christology and thus Trinitarian orthodoxy. That is, he presented an initial attempt at a Spirit Christology.[120] In

---

117. Ibid.

118. Although no where does he indicate an awareness of Owen's Christology. Gunton asks this very question, "Did Irving read Owen?" and answers "There seems little reason why he should not have done," Gunton, "Two Dogmas Revisited," 375. Gunton then asks the more important question, "why neither Owen nor Irving has been read seriously during the last century and a half?"

119. McFarlane, *Christ and the Spirit*, 178.

120. Gunton, "Two Dogmas Revisited," 373, argues that "[Irving's] christology is sometimes referred to as a "spirit christology," but that is precisely what it is not, as a glance at that jejune genre will demonstrate." However. Gunton only glances at non-Chalcedonian, post-Trinitarian literature which I agree is jejune. A more comprehensive reflection on the literature would have indicated a mellifluous genre to which Irving's theology certainly fits and to which his work can quite accurately be labeled as Spirit Christology.

the wake of these seminal attempts at a pneumatic Christology, Barth's radical call for a theology articulated through the Third Article, and in light of the Roman Catholic proposals already examined, it remains to mention contemporary Protestant contributions to a Spirit Christology. These include the works of Jürgen Moltmann, Tom Smail,[121] Colin Brown, Gerald Hawthorne, and Gary Badcock.

A conscious follower of Irving, Tom Smail has advocated a Christological ground for a new emphasis on the Spirit. Working from the relations between Christ and Spirit in the economy, particularly the baptism narratives of the synoptic Gospels, Smail presents a pneumatic Christology alongside the traditional incarnational Christology; "the Son is Son, not solely because he shares the divine nature, but because he is in constant interaction with his Father receiving and giving the Spirit."[122] Like the Roman Catholic proposals we have already examined, Smail and the various Protestant presentations are united in attempting to reclaim the complete humanity of Jesus without any depreciation of his divinity. Thus, a Spirit Christology fulfils this crucial criterion of Christology.

Christoph Schwöbel has also espoused elements that contribute to a Spirit Christology. For Schwöbel the *locus* of the divinity of Christ is not simply the possession of a divine nature but the relationship of Sonship to the Father, mediated in the Spirit and vice-versa. This is confirmed by the Gospels. Jesus's life is constituted divine on the basis of his Spirit inspired life and intimate communion with the Father created by the assumption and the filling.

> [The Gospels] present . . . the story of Jesus as the story of a life constituted by and conducted in the Spirit which is obedient to God the Father to the death on Calvary and to the resurrection on the third day and which in this way is the coming of God's Kingdom for the salvation of his creation. One element of this story is here of special significance. The obedience of Jesus as the Son to the Father is over and over again from his birth to his resurrection described as one that is enabled from the Father by the Spirit and exercised in response to the Father in the Spirit. Trinitarian Christology is always pneumatological Christology and vice versa.[123]

---

121. Smail, *Giving Gift*, and more specifically *Reflected Glory*.
122. Smail, *Giving Gift*, 97.
123. Schwöbel, "Christology and Trinitarian Thought," 140–41.

Although he has yet to produce a comprehensive model, noted New Testament theologian Colin Brown has advocated a complementary Spirit Christology on a number of occasions.[124] For Brown "Spirit Christology draws attention to the Holy Spirit's anointing of Jesus as the Christ and the Spirit's activity in and through Christ. Word Christology focuses on Jesus as the one who not only speaks the Word of God but *is* the Word of God incarnate . . . These approaches are ultimately complementary";[125] a reciprocal picture is presented of both the Trinity and the Incarnation, presenting one God who manifests himself as the Father, speaking his Word or wisdom through his life giving Breath. On the Trinitarian level, Brown insists that we are not speaking about three divine beings, nor are we speaking about a mere inspiration in the sense of enlightenment: we are speaking about the threefold God in human life, the God who always exists and acts in his threefoldedness.[126]

Over the last three decades Moltmann has been developing and advocating a robust pneumatological dimension to Christology, and at the same time has sought to integrate these insights into a fully Trinitarian theology.[127] I have already critically utilized many of his insights in my own exposition of Spirit Christology. For Moltmann, the Trinity consists of reciprocal relations that are Trinitarian in character.[128] Del Colle points to Moltmann as a leading exponent of Spirit-Christology, commenting that he has taken the discussion further; arguing not for a reciprocal relation between pneumatological Christology or Christological pneumatology only, but between all three members of the Trinity.

---

124. These include Brown, "Christology and the Quest of the Historical Jesus," 67–86; "Historical Jesus, Quest of," 326–41; "Trinity and Incarnation," 83–100, "Synoptic Miracle Stories," 55–76; and "Person of Christ," in *ISBE*, vol. 3, 781–801.

125. Brown, "Person of Christ," 800–801.

126. Brown, "Trinity and Incarnation," 83–100. Brown is squarely against the rising number of theologians who advocate some form of social Trinity. In his opinion New Testament theologians on the whole reject a social construct while more and more systematic theologians prefer a social Trinitarian construct. How true this statement is remains to be seen.

127. Moltmann, *Source of Life*; *Spirit of Life*; *Way of Jesus Christ*; *Trinity and the Kingdom*; *Crucified God*. See also the work of Dabney, "Naming the Spirit," 28–58, and "Advent of the Spirit," 81–107.

128. Pannenberg also speaks of reciprocal relations as against the traditional opposition of relations in "Father, Son, Spirit," 250–57, and an evaluation by Olsen, "Wolfhart Pannenberg's Doctrine of the Trinity," 175–206, and Jenson, "Jesus, Father, Spirit," 245–49.

What Moltmann calls "reciprocal trinitarian efficacies in God, which are multiple in kind."[129] Moltmann is careful to distinguish his Spirit Christology from that of the non-Chalcedonian revisionary type when he distinguished between the incarnation "*from* or *out* of the Spirit from the indwelling of the Spirit *in* human beings. If incarnation is identified with inhabitation, Christology is dissolved into anthropology."[130] This incarnation *from* the Spirit was from the very beginning, from his physical birth as recorded in Matthew and Luke and even before this, as the eternal Son of the Father. Hence, the Spirit was the agent of both the sonship of Jesus of Nazareth and the very self-same person of the eternal Christ, the Son of God.

Finally in this section I note the contribution of Gary Badcock. In a popularized form of his doctoral dissertation, Badcock surveys the role of the Holy Spirit in contemporary theology and makes some important contributions to the future of Spirit Christology.[131] Like the theologians we have already surveyed, Badcock recognizes the contemporary demise of the effectiveness of classical Logos Christology.[132] What he seeks to do is to highlight the reciprocal relations (Moltmann) or perichoretic identity of Christ and Spirit within our contemporary Christology and Trinitarian constructions.[133] "What is required," writes Badcock, "is a developed and integrated pneumatological Christology and christological pneumatology that can be taken up in their reciprocity into trinitarian theology."[134] What this means initially is that, in now familiar terms, there can be no conception of Christ that does not encompass an understanding of the Christ-event as thoroughly pneumatological in itself, and conversely, there can be no adequate pneumatology where the centrality of Jesus is lost from sight. Badcock is combining, as I seek to do here, the best of the various Roman Catholic and Protestant proposals for a

---

129. Moltmann, *Spirit of Life*, 59, 70–71, and *History and the Triune God: Contributions to Trinitarian Theology*, 57. See Del Colle, "Spirit-Christology," 99.

130. Moltmann, *Way of Jesus Christ*, 84 (italics in the original).

131. Badcock, *Light of Truth & Fire of Love*.

132. This demise consists of the fact that Logos Christology is now religiously unsustainable due to developments in Western intellectual culture and due to the sheer numbers of non-Western Christians in the world today. Badcock, *Light of Truth & Fire of Love*, 268.

133. Ibid., 266–67.

134. Ibid., 232.

comprehensive and orthodox Spirit Christology within a Trinitarian perspective.[135]

On the salvation-historical level, Badcock realizes that this results in a Christology where the humanity of Christ comes to the fore. When Spirit Christology is complementary to Logos Christology then Jesus as Logos is not only the eternal Son and hence revealer of God (in Barth's terms), he is also something more, due to Spirit Christology; the one anointed by the Spirit who loves to the end and who so fulfils his calling is also model man; our brother who meets us from within our humanity and our history as the one with, and in whom, we share the life and love of God and neighbor.[136] In terms reminiscent of Coffey's model of return, Badcock ventures, "the descending movement by which God reaches out to the world through the Word and Spirit thus reaches its goal in the point of return, or ascent, in which the creature raises its face to God and responds to his voice and calling."[137]

Given this salvation-historical reciprocity of Christ and Spirit, Badcock then suggests that these insights might profitably be taken up into a theology of the immanent Trinity.[138] After examining three differing conceptions of immanent Trinitarian reciprocity; that of von Balthasar's "Trinitarian inversion" model, the Eastern doctrine of the Trinitarian *energeia*; and the traditional doctrine of *perichoresis*, Badcock concludes that a form of social understanding of the Trinity where the priority of persons is accepted must be advanced in order for the idea of reciprocity to be fully developed.[139] Like the Roman Catholic exponents whom we have already examined, Badcock sees the contribution of Richard St. Victor as of great significance.[140] What Richard's Trinitarianism lacks however, is a clear grounding in the economy and it does not take sufficient notice of the reciprocity between the Holy Spirit

---

135. Specifically, Badcock builds upon what he identifies as "Barth's doctrine of divine self-communication, Jüngel's theology of the cross, and Moltmann's understanding of eschatology as a trinitarian history, together with the 'christology of ascent' developed by Mühlen and Kasper," (ibid., 233).

136. Ibid., 270–71.

137. Ibid., 271.

138. Ibid., 236.

139. Ibid., 241. Note that only a form of social Trinity is adopted. In my opinion Moltmann takes the model of the social Trinity too far and tends towards a tritheistic understanding.

140. Ibid., 246.

in Christology and Christ in pneumatology. When sufficient notice is taken of these relations it becomes possible, in the immanent Trinity, to say that the Spirit and Son relate mutually to each other in the fellowship of the divine intratrinitarian life, but they do so in distinct ways not sufficiently articulated by the Augustinian doctrine of "opposition of relations" derived from Anselm. Because of the relationship revealed in the economy between Son and Spirit within the immanent Trinity "each has active and passive relations to the other, so that within the trinitarian life a relation of reciprocity exists between the Spirit and the Son, not a relation that is identical on each side, but a relation of activity and passivity that is appropriate to each."[141] Or taken one step further, the distinct relations of each Person must also be understood in terms of the relations of each, not only to one another, but also to the Father in their respective relations with each other. This calls for is a new Trinitarian model. I shall address this presently.

Ultimately, Badcock confesses correctly that any Trinitarian relation that is taken up from the economy into the theology of the immanent Trinity, must be understood under a kenotic qualification so that the apophatic character of the immanent Trinity is preserved.[142] While this does not preclude our speculative investigations it does remind us of the limits of humanness. For Badcock, contemporary theology has provided a new way towards understanding the Trinitarian life of God as relational and, in turn, has opened up a fruitful basis for further theological reflection.

A TRINITARIAN SPIRIT CHRISTOLOGY

I am finally in a position to offer an account of the Trinitarian dimensions of an orthodox Spirit Christology. We have already had occasion to survey the criteria for Christology and have seen that a Spirit Christology more than adequately fulfils them. What is left to examine is the crux of the argument which is: "How does the new paradigm of Spirit Christology, presented here, alter our Trinitarian conceptions?"[143]

141. Ibid., 254.

142. Ibid., 255.

143. It is not my intention to present a history of Trinitarian studies, nor to present a comprehensive critique of contemporary Trinitarianism. Rather, I will only look at and comment on those aspects of Trinitarianism that directly relate to the immediate proposal. For a brief review and critique of Trinitarianism in relation to Spirit Christology, see Badcock, *Light of Truth & Fire of Love*, 236–56.

Or as Haight has said, "Bluntly put, can one still have a doctrine of the trinity if one adopts a thoroughgoing Spirit Christology?"[144] In each of the various proposals for a Spirit Christology we have seen that there is an explicit movement from the economic Trinity to the immanent Trinity. This is because a Spirit Christology works on two levels—the Christological and the Trinitarian. Schwöbel notes correctly that the theologian will have to be aware that "developing a Christology within the framework of the trinitarian logic of God has side-effects which seriously change established modes of reflection in Christian theology."[145] Similarly, O'Donnell writes about the "fecundity" that a recovery of the Spirit dimension of Jesus's life has for theological reflection.[146] Having already surveyed some varieties of this fecundity, we shall now briefly examine the Trinitarian enrichment that a Spirit Christology offers.

The Spirit Christology offered here differs considerably from that of the replacement paradigm in that the giving of the Holy Spirit by the Father constitutes the basis of both Jesus's mission in the world and his filiological relation to the Father. So instead of substituting the filiological relation of Jesus to Father, as does a replacement Spirit Christology (adoptionism), I propose that pneumatology enhances the Trinitarian relations.

The Trinitarian argument of Spirit Christology is founded on several related presuppositions. First, the three persons of the Trinity, as they reveal themselves in the economy of salvation, manifest their inner-Trinitarian life and relationships in accord with the axiom that "the economic Trinity is the immanent Trinity."[147] We thus proceed from God's revelation in the world to his being; from Christology to filiology; from the economy to the immanent Trinity.[148] Hence, we can say that

---

144. Haight, *Jesus Symbol of God*, 468.

145. Schwöbel, "Christology and Trinitarian Thought," 145.

146. O'Donnell, "In Him and Over Him," 39.

147. But not vice-versa as this would contradict what we have said about an apophatic reticence regarding the ontological Trinity.

148. Since the publication of Rahner's *Trinity*, the theological community has basically accepted his *Grundaxiom* that "the economic is the Immanent Trinity" and vice-versa (ibid., 21–22). This has led to one of the most significant advancements in Trinitarian study in recent decades. As is obvious from the present study, I agree with the basic orientation of the economic to the immanent Trinity and with a degree of identity between the two but I have serious reservations in adopting the "vice-versa." There is a metaphysical identity between the immanent and economic Trinity, whereby

Jesus is related to God as Son because of his relation to the Holy Spirit as the anointed One. Hence, Spirit Christology maintains the twin concepts of both the filiological and the pneumatological aspects of Christology.

Second, the economic Trinity is primarily expressed in functional terms in the Bible, yet inherent in these functional categories lies a Trinitarian ontology as discussed in Chapter Two. "The *pro nobis* manifestation of the Father, the Son and the Holy Spirit innately contains and naturally unveils *in se* ontological reality."[149] I have already had occasion to investigate and assess these presuppositions. Now, on the basis of this evidence, I am attempting to reconcile the immanent Trinity in light of a Scriptural Spirit Christology. Thus, the real movement is between the economic Trinity and the immanent Trinity, where the categories mentioned in Chapter Two of above-below, inspirational-incarnational, and functional-ontological, come into clearer focus. However, they are only useful as general identification labels, what is really at stake is the character of the Trinity.

In a work which has had a profoundly positive affect on my own Trinitarian theology, Fr Thomas Weinandy presents a reconceived doctrine of the Trinity in *The Father's Spirit of Sonship*.[150] In this work he builds upon the contributions of F. X. Durwell,[151] Leonardo Boff,[152] and Moltmann,[153] presenting a comprehensive thesis for a Trinitarian model,

---

the two are not two different Trinities. But the epistemological identity is different. The economic is part of the immanent Trinity epistemologically, but it does not exhaust it. The Rahnerian axiom only becomes a problem if the identity of the two is pressed. Pannenberg, *Systematic Theology*, vol. 1, 330. Congar also challenges the reverse aspect in *I Believe in the Holy Spirit*, vol. 3, 15, as does Kasper, *God of Jesus Christ*, 275, amongst many others. Amongst the vast literature on this theme see Jenson, "Jesus, Father, Spirit," 245–49, for Pannenberg's "principle," Badcock, *Light of Truth & Fire of Love*, 212–28, Moltmann, *Trinity and the Kingdom*, 160ff.; LaCugna, *God With Us*, whose entire book is a critique of this axiom, and "Re-conceiving the Trinity as the Mystery of Salvation," 1–23. See the critique of LaCugna by Weinandy, "Immanent and Economic Trinity," 655–66.

149. Weinandy, *Father's Spirit of Sonship*, 22.

150. Ibid., 6ff. This work has unfortunately not received the wider audience it deserves. See Habets, "Little Trinitarian Reflection," 80–81. In my opinion Fr Weinandy's Trinitarian proposal is the most profound and fruitful I have yet encountered. Cf. Ormerod, "What is the Goal of Systematic Theology?" 38–52.

151. Durrwell, *Holy Spirit of God*, 133–59.

152. Boff, *Trinity and Society*, 6, 84, 146–47, 204–5, 236.

153. Moltmann, *Trinity and the Kingdom*, 169–70, 182–85; ibid., *Spirit of Life*, 306–9. I also identify this theme in ibid., *Way of Jesus Christ*, 84.

compatible with the Spirit Christology I am developing here.¹⁵⁴ In light of the perceived inadequacies of the received Trinitarian tradition (East and West), Weinandy shares similar conclusions to my own that the weakness of the Trinitarian constructions of both East and West lies in an inadequate, even flawed, conception of the role and function of the Holy Spirit within the Trinitarian life.¹⁵⁵ In the West, the Father and Son play active roles while the Spirit assumes a passive function as merely the Love or Gift shared by the Father and the Son.¹⁵⁶ Under this presentation, how is the distinct personality of the Holy Spirit identified? In the East the opposite problem exists but the result is the same. The *monarchia* of the Father is so pervasive that the notion of *perichoresis* is undermined and an implicit subordinationism results. The appeal to the *energeia* of God does not really help.¹⁵⁷

A proper understanding of the Trinity can only be attained if all three persons, logically and ontologically, spring forth in one simultaneous, nonsequential, eternal act in which each person of the Trinity subsistently defines, and equally, is subsistently defined, by the other persons.¹⁵⁸ This compels him to present the thesis, that, as Weinandy articulates it, "may seem subtle, yet one that I believe radically trans-

---

154. I came to Weinandy's monographs late in my research and had the experience of being both delighted to find someone who shared my Trinitarian model and disappointed that it was not as unique as I had at first thought. Now with more reflection I thank God for the twin lessons of humility and community. I am also aware that Fr Weinandy's immense wisdom has meant his model is more developed than mine would otherwise have been.

155. Weinandy, *Father's Spirit of Sonship*, 8.

156. In no way am I or Weinandy denying that the Spirit is both Love and Gift. Our common thesis is that this in itself is not a sufficiently comprehensive statement about the identity of the Holy Spirit. I get the distinct impression that Augustine himself had these same reservations. See Augustine, *De trinitate* 8.5.

157. If the immanent Trinity is in danger of being regarded as a speculative construct of the theologian then the concept of *energeia* is even more open to this charge as it is based neither upon the economy of redemption nor on speculation alone. It is a consequence of a distinctively Eastern conception of the Trinity derived from their overly apophatic immanentalism.

158. Weinandy, *Father's Spirit of Sonship*, 15. The phrase "subsist" is used deliberately at this point to clearly indicate the propriety of describing Father, Son and Spirit as "Persons." See Calvin, *Institutes*, 1.14.4. Barth preferred to speak of *seinweise* or "modes of being," which ultimately led to wrong-headed but repeated charges of Christomonism. Barth, *CD* III/1, 196.

forms and revolutionizes the Christian understanding of the Trinity."¹⁵⁹ The thesis is simply that:

> the Father begets the Son in or by the Holy Spirit. The Son is begotten by the Father in the Spirit and thus the Spirit simultaneously proceeds from the Father as the one in whom the Son is begotten. The Son, being begotten in the Spirit, simultaneously loves the Father in the same Spirit by which he himself is begotten (is Loved).¹⁶⁰

Thus, the Spirit proceeds from the Father and is identified as the one through whom the Father begets the Son; in this double movement the Father is defined (personed) as the Father of the Son and the Son also is defined (personed) as the Son of the Father. In short, all three persons of the Trinity, within their relationships, help constitute each other. This is clearly an insight derived from the biblical text and is consistent with classic Trinitarian and Christological orthodoxy of East and West; thus, it is truly ecumenical. Here again another criterion for Christology is fulfilled.

This Trinitarian proposal does not denigrate the *monarchia* of the Father; rather, it highlights the *monarchia* without any subordinationist/emanationist tendencies, one of the main criticisms of Logos Christology. This is achieved through the mutual co-inherence or *perichoresis* of action within the Trinity that takes place whereby the persons are who they are because of the action of all three. While the Son and the Holy Spirit come forth from the Father, this is not some prior ontological action but rather, in the coming forth, all three persons become who they are doing so precisely in reciprocally interacting upon one another; simultaneously fashioning one another into themselves.¹⁶¹ By utilizing this model of the Trinity we have a loosely conceived social model of the Trinity, as Badcock and Moltmann are adamant we need, but we are also able to account meaningfully for the *taxis* that so clearly is present within the intra-Trinitarian relations and expressed in the economy.

What makes this *perichoresis* intelligible is the active role of the Holy Spirit within the Trinity. The Father begets the Son in the spira-

---

159. Weinandy, *Father's Spirit of Sonship*, 17.

160. Ibid.

161. Moltmann deals with this under his discussion of the reciprocal Trinitarian efficacies which are multiple in kind. Moltmann, *Spirit of Life*, 70–71. See Weinandy, *Father's Spirit of Sonship*, 78–79.

tion of the Spirit so the Spirit makes the Father to be the Father of the Son and the Son to be the Son of the Father. The Spirit thus proceeds from both Father to Son and Son to Father and so becomes distinct in his mutual relation to them as the Love by which they come to be who they are for one another. This conception advances beyond existing Western and Eastern models. In the West the Holy Spirit is Love shared between the Father and the Son and as such he is passive and impersonal (despite Augustine and Richard of St. Victor's protests). In the East, the Son and Spirit proceed out from the Father in a linear fashion. When Spirit Christology is raised to the Trinitarian level, the Holy Spirit is given an active role within the Trinity that guarantees him a personal distinction.

Within the Trinity the distinction of the persons is ordered upon both action and origin. From these are established the mutual relations by which the persons of the Trinity subsist and are distinguished. The *monarchia* of the Father must be maintained within the one being of the Trinity and not prior to, or outside it. In the East the tendency has been to see the Godhead as residing in the Father alone and he mediates divinity to the Son and Spirit. In the West, there is the particular impression that the Godhead is distinct from the three persons and is an independent but apophatic *ousia* of oneness.[162] Both are incompatible with the biblical revelation. The Godhead is neither the Father alone nor a solitary substance separate from the three persons. The Godhead is the Trinity. The one Godhead is the action of the Father begetting the Son and spirating the Spirit, thus sharing with them the whole of his deity, constituting them as equally divine. Thus, the *monarchia* of the Father is maintained but within the Triunity of persons.[163]

Because the Son is begotten from the Father, he is the Son, and he proceeds by way of generation, so filiation is ascribed to the Son alone. Each of the terms "Father" and "Son" presuppose the other and the relationship between them. But this action, traditionally understood, is a

---

162. This does not mean a denial of the ultimate apophatic nature of the Trinity. I agree with Badcock, *Light of Truth & Fire of Love*, 255, when he states that "the task of developing a theology of the inner-trinitarian relations from the economy has to reckon seriously with the paradox that an adequate doctrine of the immanent Trinity is only possible when an apophatic reticence about it is embraced." What is rejected is the god of the philosophers. This can be directly attributed to the Logos theologians and especially to Augustine's over reliance on Plotinus and Porphyry.

163. See the Trinitarian reflection on "person" in Gunton, *Promise of Trinitarian Theology*, 54, and Zizioulas, *Being as Communion*, 40.

passive one whereby the Son is Son due to his begetting from the Father. Is there a sense in which he also has an active role of a reciprocal nature which equally constitutes his being the Son in relationship to the Father? This question can only be answered in light of the role of the Holy Spirit.

In order to differentiate the Spirit from the Son, the early church spoke of the Son's generation and the Spirit's spiration. But exactly what the difference was, the early church was at odds to adequately explain.[164] Working with existing Trinitarian paradigms we have no adequate explanation as to why the Spirit is not another Son or at the very least a grandson to the Father. The reason provided by this paradigm of Spirit Christology is that, "the Father is the Father in that he begets the Son in the Spirit. The Father spirates the Spirit in the same act by which he begets the Son, for the Spirit proceeds from the Father as the fatherly Love in whom or by whom the Son is begotten."[165] This understanding of the Trinity maintains the *monarchia* of the Father as the *fons divinitatis* from whom came both the Son and the Spirit, without also positing any subordination within the Trinity (an Eastern tendency) or dividing *de Deo uno* from the treatise *De Deo trino* (a Western tendency attributable ultimately to Augustine and consolidated by Aquinas). [166]

In this way the comprehensive paradigm for Spirit Christology holds together a theology of Word and Spirit within a Trinitarian construct. As the Word of God, the Father breathes forth the Son which implies impulse and motion. This impulse or motion is the breath of God, the *pneuma*, hence Word and Spirit together go out from the Father in a mutual, co-inhering relationship with each other. In the economy, as in the immanent Trinity, God is revealed as the Father who begets the Son *in* or *by* the Holy Spirit. The Son responds to the Father in reciprocal fashion as the obedient Son *in* or *by* the Holy Spirit. Jesus was anointed by the Spirit and enabled therewith to utter "Abba," Father. There is an inner coherency in the anointing and utterance; the one informs the other. The Spirit creates the filiological relationship as well as empowering its

---

164. Gregory Nazianzus *Theological Orations* vol. 7, 31, 8.

165. Weinandy, *Father's Spirit of Sonship*, 69.

166. Rahner, *Trinity*, 17–18. Pannenberg, *Systematic Theology*, vol. 1, 281ff. For the same practice see the Greek Orthodox dogmatics of Dumitru Staniloe, *Orthodoxe Dogmatik* (Guterson, 1985). Also see the discussion in Rahner, *More Recent Writings*, 77–102.

response. Del Colle notes in Chalcedonian fashion that "only by development of each of these dimensions of Jesus' relation to God—i.e., his 'Abba' relation and his Spirit-anointing, without confusion or separation—can we speak of Jesus' relation to God as Son in the Spirit."[167] The pneumatological relation of Jesus to God intensifies rather than substitutes for Jesus's filial relation in much the same way as the Spirit's presence in believers makes them sons and daughters in the Son.[168]

The reciprocity of Christ and Spirit evidenced throughout Scripture and within recent theology, argues strongly that there can be no conception of Christ that does not encompass an understanding of the Christ event, as thoroughly pneumatological in itself. There can be no study of the identity or mission of Christ in abstraction from the mission and identity of the Holy Spirit. In the economy, the Spirit is prior to the Son hence the rationale for starting with the Spirit, but the Son is always preeminent. Where the Spirit is today there is also knowledge of the Son; where the Son is, there the power of the Spirit is present also.

What is left to examine is the wider theological implications of the Spirit Christology presented here. Specifically, we shall ask and answer the question in the next chapter: How and why is Starting with the Spirit now our task?

---

167. Del Colle, *Christ and the Spirit*, 168.
168. See further in Coffey, "Gift of the Holy Spirit," 219.

7

"Justified by the Spirit"?

Developing a Third Article Theology

> *This third Person is called, in technical language ... the "spirit" of God. Do not be worried or surprised if you find it (or Him) rather vaguer or more shadowy in your mind than the other two. I think there is a reason why that must be so. In the Christian life you are not usually looking at Him. He is always acting through you. If you think of the Father as something "out there," in front of you, and of the Son as someone standing at your side, helping you to pray, trying to turn you into another son, then you have to think of the third Person as something inside you, or behind you. Perhaps some people might find it easier to begin with the third Person and work backwards. God is love, and that love works through men—especially through the whole community of Christians. But this spirit of love is from all eternity, a love going on between the Father and the Son.*[1]
>
> —Clive S. Lewis

THEOLOGY IS NOT FORMED in a vacuum, nor does a theology exist in one. Spirit Christology is no different. If theology is to be systematic, and that is one of my goals, then doctrines must cohere. As John Webster has reminded the guild, "as the adjective suggests, 'systematic' theology is especially interested in the scope, unity, and coherence of Christian teaching."[2] What then is the wider context (scope) within which the Spirit Christology I am arguing for fits? How does Spirit Christology relate to dogmatics more generally (unity)? And is this theology consistent with other aspects of the theological task (coherence)? This chapter seeks to

---

1. Lewis, *Mere Christianity*, 175–76.
2. Webster, "Introduction: Systematic Theology," 1.

answer these questions with reference to a Third Article Theology and the illustration of soteriology.

A THIRD ARTICLE THEOLOGY

Mapping the Landscape

Spirit Christology is one specific attempt to follow through on Barth's suggestion, cited at the beginning of chapter 1, to begin dogmatics from a theology of the Third Article of the creed, the Holy Spirit.[3] Three works have attempted to truly start with the Spirit in theology and work within a Trinitarian framework; these are the systematic theology of Stanley Grenz, *Theology for the Community of God*,[4] the pneumatology of Clark Pinnock, *Flame of Love*,[5] and the occasional papers of D. Lyle Dabney.[6] Hence this is a new field of inquiry and the ground ahead is largely unplowed. Having witnessed the renaissance of Trinitarian theology in the latter half of the twentieth century, an application of that theology is now working its way into all the traditional *loci* of systematic theology in the twenty-first century, and, as a result, enriching the received tradition in numerous ways. One such enrichment is in what has come to be known as a Third Article Theology, by which pneumatology assumes first place in terms of theological methodology.

Until recently the Spirit was considered the "Cinderella of the Trinity. The other two sisters may have gone to the theological ball; the Holy Spirit got left behind every time," as Alister McGrath famously wrote. However, the quotation continues with these three important words: "But not now."[7] More than a decade after that claim was first made, the situation is very different. In the wake of the old man from Basel the Trinity now occupies centre stage in contemporary systematic theologies. Rather than rehearsing the well-worn path of describing how the Trinity came to reoccupy centre stage in theology I settle for a few

---

3. Barth, *Theology of Schleiermacher*, 278.
4. Grenz, *Theology for the Community of God*.
5. Pinnock, *Flame of Love*.
6. Dabney, "Advent of the Spirit," 81–107; "Otherwise Engaged in the Spirit," 154–63; "Jürgen Moltmann and John Wesley's Third Article Theology," 140–48; "Starting with the Spirit"; "Naming the Spirit"; "Justification of the Spirit"; and "Nature of the Spirit," 3–27; 28–58; 59–82; 83–110.
7. McGrath, *Christian Theology*, 307.

selective highlights. The social doctrine of the Trinity has been adopted by many, albeit with significant nuance and critique, ranging from the works of Moltmann through to Cornelius Plantinga.[8] The influence of Cappadocian trinitarianism is evident in many works ranging from Colin Gunton through Stanley Grenz, two theological statesmen taken from us too early.[9] In addition new models of the Trinity are being advocated, old models are being critiqued and often rejected, and countless numbers of monographs have appeared on our shelves articulating the biblical, historical, and theological contours of orthodox Trinitarianism.

While the Trinitarian renaissance has been a welcome feature of contemporary theology more recently thinkers have begun to turn their attention to the difference the doctrine of the Trinity makes to constructive systematic theology. As Colin Gunton once remarked, "In the light of the theology of the Trinity, everything looks different."[10] Specifically, if the Trinity is the ground and grammar of theology, as many rightly claim, then what difference does it make to the traditional *loci* of systematic theology? What is a *Trinitarian* theology of creation, Christology, and ecclesiology, for instance? Questions such as these have begun to be offered by many in the theological fraternity, and to good effect.[11]

As good as this Trinitarian renaissance is there is still a further development we should note. A number of constructive theologians wish to go further and are asking a more specific question—what happens when we intentionally start the task of systematic theology with pneumatology? In April 1999 the Australian Theological Forum ran a conference entitled: Task of Theology Today II: Starting with the Spirit, in Canberra, Australia, at which the keynote speaker, Professor D. Lyle Dabney presented four lectures, subsequently published, along with the other conference papers, as *Starting with the Spirit*.[12] The essence

---

8. See Moltmann, *Trinity and the Kingdom of God*; Plantinga, "Gregory of Nyssa and the Social Analogy of the Trinity," 25–352; "Threeness/Oneness Problem of the Trinity," 37–53; and ibid., "Social Trinitarianism and Tritheism," 21–47.

9. See Gunton, *Promise of Trinitarian Theology*, ibid., *One, The Three and the Many*; Grenz, *Rediscovering the Triune God*; Zizioulas, *Being as Communion*, ibid., *Communion and Otherness*; Torrance, *Trinitarian Faith*; and ibid., *Christian Doctrine of God*; and Ludlow, *Gregory of Nyssa*, 13–95.

10. Gunton, *Promise of Trinitarian Theology*, 7.

11. One such exemplary effort includes *Trinitarian Soundings in Systematic Theology*.

12. Pickard and Preece, *Starting with the Spirit*.

of Dabney's addresses was a plea for contemporary constructive theology to literally "start with the Sprit" and thus develop a Third Article Theology relevant for the twenty-first century. Christian theology should begin its task, that is to say, with an account of the Spirit, and thus that should now be first which has traditionally been last. Following Dabney a spat of works has appeared which heed his call to start with the Spirit and develop a Third Article Theology. These are, however, occasional in nature and as yet no comprehensive Third Article Theology exists.[13] Due to the fact that Dabney has initiated the move towards a Third Article Theology, briefly retracing his proposal here will afford me the opportunity to make my own contribution.

Constituent Features of a Third Article Theology

Dabney calls his approach a "theology of the third article" and argues that priority must be given to the Spirit in contemporary theology. I happen to think Dabney is right and I am indebted to him for his programmatic theses, even when I do not totally agree with some of his theology.[14] Western Christianity has inherent two great theological traditions—as a heuristic device they may be termed respectively a theology of the First Article and a theology of the Second Article of the creed. A First Article theology is typified by medieval scholasticism, a Second Article theology by Reformation theology. These two trajectories have dominated the theological landscape. The dilemma is that these theologies offer inadequate resources for answering the question of faith in Christ in today's postmodern world. We must utilize, according to Dabney, a theology of the Third Article.

To speak meaningfully into our contemporary context Christianity must speak not just of continuity between creature and Creator, nor simply of contradiction between the Redeemer and creatures in need of redemption. Rather, theology must learn to speak both of continuity *and* discontinuity, of both grace *and* sin, of both the free grace of nature *and* the free nature of grace. Thus it must articulate an account of faith in Christ that can enable the Christian community both to socially and

---

13. Dabney is rumored to be working on a four-volume systematic theology based on a Third Article Theology. I eagerly await the publication of such a work!

14. Lyle Dabney kindly examined my MTh thesis (Laidlaw College, New Zealand) on Spirit Christology for which I am very grateful (along with my other examiner, Dr. Graham McFarlane).

intellectually affirm some, and contradict other, aspects of the age in which we live. Christian theology must address itself both to the church and to society in general, speaking to the question of the identity of the one and to the issue of engagement with the other.

According to Dabney, a Third Article Theology has at least four characteristics: first, it starts with the Spirit; second, it unfolds the story of the Trinitarian mission of God in the world; third, it finds its focus in the center of that story—in the life, death, and resurrection of Jesus Christ; and fourth, it is a thoroughly ecumenical theology.[15]

In an age which rejects the universal for the particular, a Third Article Theology begins not with a universal claim for human capacity nor incapacity, but with an utterly particular claim: in and through Jesus Christ a quite particular community finds itself in and through the centuries moved in unlooked-for ways to new and transforming relationship with God, with one-another, and with all God's creation. The possibility of that redemptive relationship, that community claims, is the Spirit of God. More than this a Third Article Theology seeks to facilitate Christian mission in the world. It seeks to be a theology for a global Christianity, helping Christianity to, "act its age," in the time and place it now finds itself. With Welker, such a theology claims to be "realistic" and to get at the "thing itself" by means of the Holy Spirit. But "realism" is now eschatological in orientation, the eschatological reality of God's presence and activity in the world and the thing itself is to be understood as mission, the task of witnessing in word and deed to Jesus Christ in the world in which we find ourselves today.

A Third Article Theology is a theology of God's mission of a transforming recreation of creation, a theology of continuity in God's presence and purpose in creation and re-creation through the discontinuity of human sin and death. It is a theology of neither continuum nor of contradiction, but rather of transformation. Such a theology finds its focus—that is, defines what it means by Spirit—in the center of the story of God's mission: in the life, death, and resurrection of Jesus Christ. As a summary of this approach Dabney writes:

> [V]oices are being raised in the current discussions of pneumatology that would claim that we must start with that which is first: we must start, that is to say, with the Spirit ... Christian theology has never come to grips with the fact that relationship to

15. Dabney, "Starting with the Spirit," 24–26.

God through Jesus Christ starts with the Spirit. There may have been good reasons for that in the past. But now, a host of voices suggest, there are good reasons for beginning our theologizing where we begin our discipleship. In doing so, we may find that we can now begin to bring together what we have so often let slip apart: worship and theology, service to God and service to God's world, the honouring of God's creation and the proclamation of God's redemption. But if we are to do that, we must start with the Spirit. And thus at last, the last will be first.[16]

A Third Article Theology does not claim that starting with the First Article, the Father, or with the Second Article, the Son, is incorrect, or that starting with the Spirit is the only legitimate way to do theology today. That would be a gross reactionary move. Rather, the claim is that a Third Article Theology has not yet been attempted in any systematic or sustained way and that it is high time attempts were made in this direction. The goal is not to overturn the Great Tradition but rather, as will now be a familiar claim if you have read this far, to enrich the received tradition with additional insights that may be more suited to the contemporary milieu.

While Dabney is the most explicit he is not alone in attempting a Third Article Theology. In *Flame of Love* Clark Pinnock attempts the first explicit systematic theology that starts with the Spirit.[17] Reacquainting ourselves with some of the more important decisions Pinnock makes in his book is worthwhile.

According to Pinnock, a Third Article Theology (although he does not use that term), brings to the fore the Sprit in creation, thus creation becomes a dynamic unfolding of God's relationship with all of creation. There is thus a universal and cosmic scope to the Spirit's operations which moves creation towards its completion. When Pinnock deals with Christology he explicitly develops a Spirit Christology, which he labels a "last Adam Christology." Drawing on Irenaean insights, Pinnock suggests "Jesus is empowered by the Spirit to recapitulate the human journey and bring about humanity's fulfilment."[18] His creative proposal is to view "Christ as an aspect of the Spirit's mission, instead of (as is more

---

16. Ibid., 27.
17. Pinnock, *Flame of Love*.
18. Ibid., 80.

usual) viewing Spirit as a function of Christ's."[19] The force of Pinnock's Christology is that in Christ what was intended in creation is accomplished by incarnation.

Soteriology is addressed in both the chapter on "Sprit and Christology" and the chapter on "Spirit and Union."[20] In both chapters Pinnock's position is clear, "When we look at salvation from the standpoint of the Spirit, we view it in relational, affective terms."[21] According to Pinnock, the goal of our union with Christ is participation in the Triune communion. It comes as no surprise therefore, when Pinnock settles on a doctrine of *theosis* as the motif of his pneuma-soteriology. According to Pinnock, "Salvation is the Spirit, who indwells us, drawing us toward participation in the life of the triune God."[22] Basing his view around the theme of the *beatific vision* we read that "The Spirit summons as to a transforming friendship with God that leads to sharing in the triune life,"[23] and, "the category invites us to think of the goal of salvation as participation in the divine nature, in a way that preserves distinctions proper to Creator and creature without losing sight of their union."[24] In both chapters—Christ and salvation—Pinnock highlights the category of union as the central motif in a Third Article soteriology as is made clear in the following statement: "Spirit Christology helps us to take seriously the motif of the last Adam's tracing of our human path and directs our attention to a participatory model of atonement, in which the central motif is union with Christ."[25]

For our purposes a final reflection on Pinnock's work is required, his chapter on "Spirit and Universality" wherein he presents a position somewhere between universalism and restricitivism, but clearly falling sympathetically on the Universalist side of the divide.[26] He writes, "Jesus is the criterion of salvation even for those who never knew him or his message. Participation in salvation is not impossible for people outside

---

19. Ibid.
20. Ibid., 79–111, and 149–83.
21. Ibid., 149.
22. Ibid., 150.
23. Ibid.
24. Ibid., 150–51.
25. Ibid., 97.
26. Ibid., 185–214.

the church. The factors are behavioural as well as cognitive."[27] This is the most controversial of Pinnock's claims and while it is developed by others it is not essential to a Third Article Theology or a Spirit Christology. On the basis of the biblical survey conducted in chapter 5 and the theological implications pointed out in chapter 6, I argue against all attempts at Universalism.[28] We shall return to this theme below when we consider the contribution of Amos Yong.

Pinnock's *Flame of Love* is the only such work I know of to consciously start with the Spirit and revisit every major *loci* of systematic theology in search of enriching the tradition. At times I believe Pinnock acts as prophet, other times as false prophet. But perhaps such a new and constructive work such as his requires a healthy dose of tentative assessment from the theological community.[29]

While Pinnock alone has attempted a Third Article systematic theology there are others who are developing a similar approach in more specific areas. Here we may think of Jürgen Moltmann who, in his various "explorations in theology" has, over a long period, been putting the Spirit in a more central place and teasing out the implications this has for various doctrines—this is especially evident in his works—*The Church in the Power of the Spirit*; *The Trinity and the Kingdom*; *God in Creation*; *The Way of Jesus Christ*; *The Spirit of Life*; and *The Source of Life*.[30] Moltmann's work has also come in for intense scrutiny; however, hardly any of this seems to have focused on his attempt to move in the direction of a Third Article Theology. For this reason David Beck's, *The Holy Spirit and the Renewal of All Things: Pneumatology in Paul and Jurgen Moltmann* is all the more important.[31]

Yet another major contemporary thinker who has attempted to start with the Spirit is the late Stanley Grenz. We see this in his systematics textbook *Theology for the Community of God*—with its "community"

---

27. Ibid., 211.

28. See Print and Habets, "Critical Review Essay on Amos Yong, *Beyond the Impasse*," 53–60.

29. In this regard, see the helpful essay by Studebaker, "Integrating Pneumatology and Christology," 5–20.

30. Moltmann, *Church in the Power of the Spirit*; *Trinity and the Kingdom*; *God in Creation*; *Way of Jesus Christ*; *Spirit of Life*; *Source of Life*.

31. Beck, *Holy Spirit and the Renewal of All Things*. Both Pinnock and Dabney provide glowing endorsements of the work which further testifies to Beck's place within this discussion.

leitmotif, and more recently, with *The Matrix of Christian Theology—The Social God and the Relational Self* and *The Named God and the Question of Being*.[32] Other projected volumes would have included Christology, pneumatology, ecclesiology, and eschatology. *The Social God and the Relational Self* is a work of theological anthropology viewed in light of the doctrine of the Trinity. Because God is a "social God", a social unity made up of three persons in one being, the image of God in humans is inherently social as well. This leads Grenz to re-examine views of human sexuality; male and female, views of ecclesiology; the body of Christ, and views of community more generally; the social-cultural identity of beings, individuals, souls, and the self. Grenz provides a comprehensive survey of what the Christian tradition has meant by the *imago Dei*, but then goes further by examining the significance of the incarnation for an understanding of true humanity. The fundamental contention of the work is that the image of God is ultimately an eschatological concept, it is what the human person is to *become* rather than simply what they currently are. In *The Named God and the Question of Being* Grenz addresses an area left unexamined in the earlier volume; replacing a substance ontology of God with a relational ontology, something both Moltmann and Pannenberg are sympathetic too in their respective works. At the end of this work Grenz narrates the intent of the triune God to incorporate humankind and all creation into the dynamic of his eternal self-naming. Throughout each of these volumes Grenz constructs a Trinitarian theology which seeks to make space for the Holy Spirit in significant ways. It is a tragedy he did not live long enough to complete the series and provide the all important volume on pneumatology.

In our survey of contemporary theologians working towards what Dabney has characterized as a Third Article Theology two more theologians deserve mention: Amos Yong and Veli-Matti Kärkkäinen. Yong and Kärkkäinen are friends and collaborators on a number of works. Yong's interests lie in a theology of religions. In several works and many articles he is developing a Pentecostal-Charismatic contribution to a theology of religions. In his 2003 work, *Beyond the Impasse: Toward a Pneumatological Theology of Religions* we have a clear expression of his thought.[33]

---

32. Grenz, *Theology for the Community of God*; *Social God and the Relational Self*; and *Named God and the Question of Being*.

33. Yong, *Beyond the Impasse*. Yong has developed these in several other publica-

Yong builds on Paul Tillich's definition of religion as "ultimate concern"[34] to define a theology of religions as "the attempt to understand the human ultimate concern within a theistic framework."[35] Yong believes that the categories of "exclusivism," "inclusivism," and "pluralism" are laden with Christian assumptions that are too bound up with Christological and soteriological claims which result in an "impasse" between Christian theology and a theology of religions. As such, Christian theology takes a defensive stance against other religious claims to truth. Yong therefore promotes a pneumatological approach to a theology of religions, believing this approach can move Christian theology "beyond the impasse."

Yong's thesis is founded upon three axioms: first, that God is universally present and active in the Holy Spirit; second, the Holy Spirit is the life breath of the *imago Dei* in every human being; and third, and more controversially, that religions of the world, like everything else that exists, are providentially sustained by the Spirit of God for divine purposes. While acknowledging a need at some stage to confront the Christological questions, Yong's suggested methodology is to explore the role of the Holy Spirit for as long as possible because the Holy Spirit is "the meeting point between Christian and non-Christian, and between both and God."[36] If Christology is seen as the divisive issue for a theology of religions then pneumatology is considered the unitive bond. It is this thesis which Yong goes on to develop.

As with Pinnock's work on Universalism, Yong's work is stimulating and enlightening but at the same time challenging and disturbing. His appeal to the category of pneumatology as a way beyond the impasse created by absolute Christian truth claims is engaging but problematic. Several criticisms immediately come to the fore. Yong's focus on pneumatology to the relative neglect of Christology tends to create a religion of the Spirit. Although Yong claims that his pneumatology is theistic, even Trinitarian, he is in danger of an implicit tri-theism. Timothy Tennent observes this predominance of pneumatology over Christology in Yong's

---

tions including *Discerning the Spirit(s)*; "Spirit Bears Witness," 14–38; and *Hospitality and the Other*.

34. Tillich, *Christianity and the Encounter of World Religions*, 3. See Yong, *Beyond the Impasse*, 16.

35. Yong, *Beyond the Impasse*, 17.

36. Ibid., 100.

work and notes that that from the council of Nicaea "Christology provides the only truly objective basis for evaluating truth claims."[37] While a more Trinitarian basis for truth claims may be more appropriate Tennent's criticism of Yong's approach is welcome.[38]

As Yong's friend Kärkkäinen states: "It is too early to give a definite assessment of Yong's very recent approach. Nevertheless, his attempt to construct a viable pneumatological theology of religions should be understood as an opener, a way to ask the right questions."[39] While Yong may not provide the final answer on this issue he certainly raises many useful ideas which deserve further consideration. As such his proposals fit within a Third Article Theology, even if it does not represent the necessary direction in which such a theology may want to progress.

Veli-Matti Kärkkäinen of Fuller Theological Seminary has recently published a volume of essays entitled *Toward a Pneumatological Theology: Pentecostal and Ecumenical Perspectives on Ecclesiology, Soteriology, and Theology of Mission* in which he too is seeking to construct a Third Article Theology, although again, he does not use this terminology. This work has been followed up by his *One With God: Salvation as Deification and Justification*.[40] It comes as no surprise to learn that Kärkkäinen's *Doktorvator* is Professor Emeritus Tuomo Mannermaa of the University of Helsinki, the leading scholar of the Lutheran revisionist movement which claims to identify the theme of deification at the heart of Luther's soteriology. Throughout *One With God* Kärkkäinen advocates an adoption of *theosis* alongside that of justification as a biblical model of salvation that should be incorporated more into western soteriologies.

It is at this point that my own proposal fits. The Spirit Christology I am advocating in this work fits within the broader paradigm of a Third Article Theology.

---

37. Tennent, "Book Review: *Beyond the Impasse: Toward a Pneumatological Theology of Religions*," 180–181.

38. For a fuller account of Yong's theology see, Macchia, Del Colle, and Irvin, "Christ and Spirit: Dogma, Discernment and Dialogical Theology in a Religiously Plural World," 15-83; and *Hospitality and the Other*.

39. Kärkkäinen, *Toward a Pneumatological Theology*, 237.

40. Kärkkäinen, *One With God*.

Suggestions Towards a Third Article Theology

While Spirit Christology is the most appropriate Christology for a Third Article Theology, what of the other *loci* of dogmatics? How may a Third Article Theology be conceived in these areas? The following is indicative of such an approach.

A Third Article Theological Prolegomena

In theological prolegomena the Trinity as the ground and grammar of theology has led me to adopt the epistemology of critical realism, after the work of Thomas Torrance, Alister McGrath, and Tom Wright, to name a few. In such an account the role of the Spirit is constitutive for the apprehension of truth. By way of summary, Scripture contains truth statements but not the Truth, which is exclusively the being and act of God himself. Theological concepts, including Scripture, point beyond the statements themselves to the Truth and do so through levels of cognition: the level of experience, the theological level, and the meta-scientific level.[41] These levels are coordinated together in such a way that each is open to the other and is "translogically" related to it at certain boundary points in which the higher level is capable of explaining more fully the lower level. Torrance applies these levels of cognition to the analogical nature of Scripture:

> It is, I believe, within this open hierarchical structure of levels of thought, that we are able to cope with the problem of analogy and truth-reference, in a way that our predecessors were not able to do. The main point to remember is that there is no one-to-one or point-for-point correspondence between the concepts on one level and their counterparts on another level, but they are analogically related through the translogical relation between the different levels to which they belong and by which they are defined.[42]

In theological prolegomena the epistemological role of the Holy Spirit is the unique contribution a Third Article Theology may make. A key function of the Spirit is to mediate knowledge of God to human

---

41. See Torrance, *Theological Science*; "Stratification of Truth," in *Reality and Scientific Theology*, 131–59; Myers, "Stratification of Knowledge in the Thought of T. F. Torrance," 1–15; McGrath, *Scientific Theology*; and Wright, *New Testament and the People of God*, 32–37.

42. Torrance, "Truth and Authority," 234.

creatures through the incarnate Word. In so doing Christ and the Spirit mutually mediate one another. This held true throughout the Incarnation as it does post-Pentecost through the Church, especially through the sacraments and the Scriptures. As Elmer Colyer explains:

> Through the Spirit, we come to share in the incarnate Son's knowledge of God the Father realized in Christ's vicarious humanity. In the incarnation God adapts knowledge of God to our creaturely structures of knowledge and adapts those structures to knowledge of God. In the Holy Spirit God utilizes those creaturely structures as the means by which we apprehend God and know God in God's divine reality as Triune . . . Thus doctrine and the nature of doctrine are conditioned by the way in which they are related to Christ through the Apostolic foundation of the Church and the Scriptures *in* the Spirit.[43]

Because of the dynamic nature of revelation the Holy Spirit becomes central to understanding the dynamics of a doctrine of Scripture. The relation between God's self-revelation and the Scriptures is dynamic and ontological in origin but also in its ongoing relation, for it is one which God sustains through the mediation of the Holy Spirit as God's sovereign freedom to be present in the creaturely structures of the Word written through the mutual mediation of the Word and the Spirit.[44]

It is the divine presence of both Word *and* Spirit which renders Scripture an abiding and authoritative Word of God to humanity and it is this dynamic presence which constitutes the true content of a dynamic concept of verbal inspiration.[45] "All Scripture given by divine inspiration," writes Torrance, "is and becomes what it really is through the presence and advocacy of the Holy Spirit. The Spirit of God is God in his freedom to be present to what he has brought into being through his Word and to realise its true end in himself through a relation of himself to himself."[46] It is not that the active presence of the Spirit changes Scripture in any way in the dynamic of revelation and reconciliation. Rather, "through the Spirit God makes himself present to man and thereby acts from within him to make him subjectively open and ready and capable for

---

43. Colyer, *Nature of Doctrine in T. F. Torrance's Theology*, 152. See Torrance, *Reality and Scientific Theology*, 185–86, 192.

44. See Colyer's excellent treatment of these themes in *Nature of Doctrine*, 154–55.

45. See Webster, *Holy Scripture*, 30–39.

46. Torrance, *Karl Barth*, 91–92.

God, and thus to realise his revelation in him."[47] Based upon the transcendent freedom of God in his Spirit to be present with us, Barth's notion of the "contingent contemporaneity" of the Word and act of God[48] is understandable. The important point of this dynamism is that God is the only proper revealer of himself. Following Barth, this is a fully Trinitarian concept of revelation: "Hence it may be said that the Bible is what it is as the written Word of God precisely through the divinely ordained bond between its creaturely form and God's self-revelation,"[49] states Torrance. While Barth and Torrance were not attempting a Third Article Theology, their insights are certainly instructive for the construction of such a theology.

A Third Article Theological Anthropology

A Third Article Theology when applied to theological anthropology yields similarly creative insights. In Chapter Eight I shall tease out some of the anthropological insights further but we may preempt that discussion with the outline offered here. Definitions of the *imago Dei* have traditionally been developed as something substantive; usually identified with the *nous* or mind, or relational; the capacity to enter into genuine relationships with others, or functional; the working out of the mandate to steward the earth as God's vice-regent. A Third Article Theology notes the usefulness of each of these theological constructions but finally rejects them in favor of a teleological/eschatological definition of the *imago Dei* whereby Jesus Christ is considered the *arche* and *telos* of human being.[50] Alongside such a teleological anthropology there is the need to develop a teleological or developmental view of the *ruach/pneuma* of God in humanity.[51]

When we start with the Spirit in our anthropology we inquire as to the identity and mission of the Holy Spirit in human existence. Prelapsarian humanity was created with a transcendental determination

---

47. Ibid., 92.
48. Ibid. See Karl Barth, *CD* I/1, 145.
49. Torrance, *Karl Barth*, 93.
50. For a review of the various definitions of the *imago Dei* and an argument for a teleological view, see Grenz, *Social God and the Relational Self*, 141–77. Also see Wong, *Wolfhart Pannenberg on Human Destiny*.
51. This last point was helpfully suggested to me by one of my students, Stuart Print. See Print, "Teleology as the Key to Pneumatological Anthropology."

for God. By means of the indwelling Holy Spirit men and women have a divinely implanted religious inclination which ultimately finds its end in the triune God. Various writers have made suggestions in this direction, the most fruitful of which is the Augustinian-Pascal axiom that God created men and women for himself and "they are restless until they find their end in him."[52] Wolfhart Pannenberg's suggestion of a human exocentrism also finds a place here.[53] Building on an eschatological approach to anthropology, Pannenberg suggests that intrinsic to human nature is a dynamic that points human beings toward an ultimate destiny bound up with Christ in the eschaton. The problem, of course, is the fall which entails a movement away from God to self. Thus the transcendental determination of the human is turned from God to self; a theocentricity is replaced with an egocentricity. The egocentricity is still in place, but the goal of meeting with God is replaced with self-determination. In solving the problem of the fall and in bringing humanity to its intended *telos* in the triune God, Christ lives the life of the "perfect penitent," to use C. S. Lewis's words,[54] and turns humanity back to God, thus redeeming humanity from its self-determination to a re-created union with the incarnate Son, finally to reach fulfillment in Trinitarian communion in the eschaton. This approach requires a reconsideration of original sin and a rejection of Greek philosophical dualism between the body and the soul/spirit.[55]

A Third Article Ecclesiology

A Third Article ecclesiology is perhaps the most easily envisaged *loci* of a new dogmatics. Stanley Grenz has already made significant strides in this direction with his creative integrative motif of community. Little needs to be said here given the familiarity most readers will have with the insights of Grenz, Zizioulas, LaCugna, Boff, Gunton, and others in ecclesiology. A Third Article ecclesiology would build on many of these insights, with critical corrections, and would entail a greater articula-

---

52. See Augustine *Confessions* I, 1, 1; Blaise Pascal, *Pensees*, 10.148, 45. This is not without clear biblical precedent; see Job 28:1–28; Ps 42; Matt 5:6; and John 7:37, 38.

53. See Pannenberg, *Anthropology in Theological Perspective*; *Systematic Theology*, vol. 2, 230; and Shults, "Constitutive Relationality in Anthropology and Trinity," 304–22. Moltmann follows a similar line in *God in Creation*, 225–27.

54. Lewis, *Mere Christianity*, chapter 4.

55. On the latter see Habets, "Naked but Not Disembodied," 33–50.

tion of clergy-laity distinctions, an emphasis on the Royal Priesthood of Christ over a Protestantized version of the priesthood of all believers, reconsideration of the means of grace and real presence of Christ in the sacraments, the function of spiritual gifts, the nature of the fruit of the Spirit, and ecumenicity. Throughout the present work I have made comments in regards to many of these issues, however, more formal articulation of each theme must await further publications.

With this brief and selective survey of what a Third Article Theology is and what it may look like when applied to various *loci* of dogmatics I turn attention to the issue of the Spirit in *salvation* to further illustrate this new paradigm for theology. What may a Third Article soteriology contribute? The following are some reflections on directions and themes which a Third Article soteriology seeks to explore.

TOWARDS A THIRD ARTICLE SOTERIOLOGY

As we considered in chapter 2, the person and work of Christ cannot be separated. In Congar's considered opinion, "Christology should not be separated from soteriology . . . It is in fact almost true to say that Christology must be situated *within* soteriology, which embraces it."[56] When a Third Article Theology is applied to soteriology doctrinal enrichment is evident in themes of union with Christ, *theosis*, and a *pneumatologia crucis*. I affirm that there is nothing that cannot be said of Jesus in a Spirit Christology that one would want to say of him in a Logos Christology. However, Spirit Christology brings into relief those themes either ignored or left undeveloped in a traditionally conceived Logos Christology. In a Spirit Christology, that which is most evident and stressed has been termed a "pioneer soteriology,"[57] whereby Jesus is the second Adam who goes ahead of us and shows the way (Rom 5:14;

---

56. Congar, *I Believe in the Holy Spirit*, vol. 3, 165.

57. Haight, *Jesus Symbol of God*, 456. By using this term I do not intend all that Haight does. For Haight Jesus is only "savior because he symbolically mediates and makes God present to the world in a 'visible' and 'tangible way.' In this symbolic mediation, Jesus is a revealer of God; salvation consists in a revelation of God. Jesus is also a revealer of what it is to be human; salvation consists in Jesus being an exemplar of the *humanum*," Haight, "Case for Spirit Christology," 265–66. See further his views on salvation in which he follows Abelard in "Jesus and Salvation," 225–51. For a full critique of Haight's faulty soteriology and a renewed emphasis on the Paschal mystery see Imbelli, "New Adam and Life-giving Spirit," 233–52.

1 Cor 15:22, 45). It is an "example model" as well as a "saving model."[58] According to this model, believers can identify with Jesus and follow him; just as he was inspired, empowered, so believers in an analogous sense, are inspired, empowered, and born of the Spirit. Here the Eastern Orthodox notion of *theosis* is critically utilized.[59]

Because the cross and the resurrection are a single event, we are able to view the resurrection as an aspect of our justification. Dabney has entertained this idea and developed it to some usefulness.[60] What would a soteriology developed from the perspective of the Holy Spirit look like?[61] Dabney considers it to entail at least three core elements: "first, that it would help us to speak of God's redemption of creation as having to do with the entire life, death, and resurrection of Jesus Christ; second, that it would at the same time help us to express that God's redemption has to do with the entirety of human life and death; and finally, that God's redemption, therefore, from the very beginning, has to do with the mate-

---

58. As has repeatedly been stressed, the active and passive obedience of Christ act in unison, it is not a case of either/or; the one without the other is an insufficient basis for salvation. That is why a Spirit Christology pays special attention not only to the active obedience but also the Paschal mystery. See Imbelli, "New Adam and Life-giving Spirit."

59. Theologians pursuing *theosis* as a meaningful concept include Torrance, *Theology in Reconstruction*, 243; Pinnock, *Flame of Love*, 149–83; Allchin, *Participation in God*; Clendenin, "Partakers of Divinity," 365–79; "Deification of Humanity"; Rakestaw, "Becoming Like God," 257–69; Hughes, "Deification of Man in Christ," chap. 24; and Habets, "Reforming Theosis," 146–67; and *Theosis in the Theology of Thomas Torrance*.

60. Dabney, "Justification of the Spirit."

61. John Calvin asked this same question and in his treatment of justification incorporated the work of the Spirit at every point. See his *Institutes*, 3.11.10ff. Out of this scheme Calvin produced his famous treatment on the *triplex munus* and the "wonderful exchange." A worthy study would be to survey his fascinating insights on pneumatic-Christology as outlined in Book 2 of his *Institutes*. Here he gives the well known but then novel treatment of Christ as Prophet, Priest, and King. However, many fail to notice that energizing all three offices (in both the Old Testament and in Christ himself) is the anointing presence of the Holy Spirit (*Institutes* 2.15). See Webber, *Foundations of Dogmatics*, vol. 2, 243–57. When we consider the fact that Calvin viewed Christ as our representative, following the scholastic notion of the *gratia capitis*, the grace of the Head, we see the wonderful implications of being incorporated into the headship of Christ—full of grace. We too partake of his Spirit—of his grace. For an insightful survey of Calvin's theology, especially in relation to the Spirit, see Partee, *Theology of John Calvin*. Partee rightfully sees union with Christ as central to Calvin's theology and thus he recognizes the place of the Holy Spirit throughout Calvin's theology.

rial, the embodied, and the social."⁶² Throughout the New Testament the writers are unified in their soteriological presentations: believers have died with Christ and have been raised with Christ, all in the power of the Spirit. Paul in particular, uses the language of being baptized into Christ by the Holy Spirit (Rom 6:3f.). Paul understands the event of becoming a Christian as one in which we receive the Spirit of God in reconciliation and justification (Rom 8:1f.; Gal 3:2; 1 Cor 12:13). Hence, Christ and Spirit coinhere in themselves and in their work; Christ is of the Spirit and it is the Spirit of Christ (Rom 8:9).

Union With Christ

In Scripture the Spirit and salvation are mentioned in terms of adoption, sealing, down payment, first-fruits, Abba intimacy, conviction, confession, conversion, and sanctification, to name the most obvious. In theology we tend to speak of the Spirit's role at conversion, and sanctification, and glorification. But what else? As Dabney, Pinnock, Grenz, and Kärkkäinen have all observed, the biblical themes of union with Christ following the Pauline language of being "in Christ" are emphasized. The biblical notions on communion with God and participation are also brought to the fore. In addition, the role of the Spirit to conform us to Christ—both legally and in reality—is also highlighted.

Recent theologians have returned to a doctrine of union with Christ in order to penetrate more deeply into the mystery of salvation. The incarnation is the way in which union with Christ is achieved. Union with Christ is the soteriological correlate to the Christological notion of the hypostatic union. This makes the hypostatic union commensurate with *unio mystica*, while distinct but inseparable. The object of our *unio mystica* is the Mediator, Jesus Christ.⁶³

Only by means of the incarnation does God join us to his Son in order for men and women to enjoy the benefits of salvation in Christ. The sole access to the Father is through Christ the Son, made possible by faith which is the operation of the Spirit. John Calvin's theology of *unio mystica* ("mystical union") is instructive. Calvin viewed mystical union as a product of the Priestly activity of the incarnate Son, an activity that does not cease to exist into eternity. Calvin cuts out any extrinsecist

---

62. Dabney, "Justification of the Spirit," 68.

63. I have written more on union with Christ in Habets, *Theosis in the Theology of Thomas Torrance*, chap. 3.

notions of justification or reconciliation by positing justification as a benefit of union with Christ. In our participation in Christ we receive all the benefits of salvation including Christ's righteousness, a righteousness which equates to the filial life. Calvin insists on the forensic nature of justification but insists we are justified based upon our union with Christ. This is affirmed when he writes, "You see that our righteousness is not in us but in Christ, that we possess it only because we are partakers in Christ; indeed, with him we possess all its riches."[64]

Integral to an understanding of Calvin's doctrine of the *unio mystica* is the role of the Trinity. Calvin follows Augustine's Trinitarian axiom closely here, *opera trinitatis ad extra indivisa sunt* (the external works of the Trinity are always done as one), but nevertheless correctly posits legitimate "distinctions" or "appropriations" between the three persons. According to Calvin the *unio mystica* is a personal union as men and women participate in a real way in Christ. Christ is thus the *mediating* bond of union. This union is not without the Spirit, however, and so the Spirit functions as the *unitive* bond of union with Christ. Calvin appropriates the Augustinian notion of the Spirit as the "bond of love" (*vinculum caritatis*) between Father and Son and equally applies it to the bond of union between Christ and the believer. This enables Calvin to state that "the Holy Spirit is the bond by which Christ effectually unites us to himself."[65] Tan summarizes Calvin's position well when he writes:

> Through the unitive operation of the Holy Spirit, Christ and the elect are brought into reciprocal relationship. The one is the humanward trajectory—Christ's participation in us—where "he had to become ours and to dwell within us"; the other is the Christward movement—our participation in Christ—where we are said to be "engrafted into him" [Rom 11:17], and "to put on Christ" [*Institutes* 3.1.1.].[66]

A final feature of Calvin's *unio mystica* is the organic union it creates not only between Christ and the believer but between believers in the Body of Christ.

When Calvin speaks more directly of how the Spirit unites us to Christ at the start of Book Three of the *Institutes* he asks, "How do we receive those benefits which the Father bestowed on his only-begotten

64. Calvin, *Institutes*, 3.11.23.
65. Ibid., 3.1.1.
66. Tan, "Calvin's Doctrine of Our Union with Christ."

Son—not for Christ's own private use, but that he might enrich poor and needy men?"[67] Calvin replies, "We also, in turn, are said to be "engrafted into him" [Rom 11:17], and to "put on Christ" [Gal 3:27]; for, as I have said, all that he possesses is nothing to us until we grow into one body with him. It is true that we obtain this by faith." This is the fundamental basis of *unio mystica* for Calvin, to "put on Christ" and to be "engrafted into him."[68]

According to Tan's reading, the "putting on Christ" metaphor works within Calvin's theology to represent the imputed righteousness received by the believer in justification. The "engrafting" metaphor stands for the imparted holiness of Christ received by the believer in sanctification. While both are distinct concepts they are not separate and they are both the benefits received in faith through the *unio mystica*. "Thus, the distinction between the once-for-all "alien" righteousness of Christ freely imputed on [sic] a sinner (justification) and the progressive holiness imparted through the indwelling Spirit in the regenerated person (sanctification) is obtained without separation, since they are simultaneous realities within *unio mystica*."[69]

An external transaction between Christ and the Father applied to the believer as imputed righteousness is not wrong *per se* but it is insufficient if it is made to represent the entire doctrine of salvation. When this happens exclusively juridical categories of atonement are adopted and salvation becomes something less than evangelical. This would be a theology of the Second Article. Rather than reject the Reformation doctrine of imputation we must relocate it into the context of participation. Imputation can only rightly be understood, in Torrance's words, "not just in terms of imputed righteousness but in terms of a participation in the righteousness of Christ which is transferred to us through union with him."[70]

Starting with the Spirit in this way does not dislocate Christ from the center as some detractors imagine. When we see salvation as *unio mystica*, or as a personal participation in Christ, then we see that *all* the benefits he won for us are actually imputed and imparted to us simply because we are *in Christ* and *in the Spirit*. What a doctrine of *unio mystica*

67. Calvin, *Institutes*, 3.1.1.
68. See ibid., 3.11.10.
69. Tan, "Calvin's Doctrine of Our Union with Christ."
70. Torrance, "Distinctive Character of the Reformed Tradition," 6–7.

achieves is a more dynamic understanding of salvation whereby Christ becomes ours and we become Christ's through an organic, vital, spiritual, eternal, and mystical union in which justification and sanctification are no longer separated, since they are simultaneous realities of the *unio mystica*. Once more pneumatology and Christology are held together more rigorously than has often been the case previously.

The final goal of salvation is not only to be united to Christ by the Spirit but also to commune with the Father through the incarnate Son in or by the Holy Spirit. Union with Christ is thus understood to be participation in the divine life. Calvin is not implying that our participation in the divine nature is exactly like the hypostatic union. There is only one hypostatic union and that is found within the God-man Jesus Christ. We participate through *his* humanity and so our *unio mystica* is formulated within an asymmetrical relationship to Christ's *unio* with the Father by the Holy Spirit. Such an outline asks what difference it makes when we start theology with pneumatology. However, union with Christ is but a step in the overall dynamic of salvation.

Theosis

What a study of union with Christ highlighted is the way in which a model of salvation should be constructed, one which incorporates both legal and relational metaphors; a soteriology in which both Christ and the Spirit are active in reconciliation. Recent attempts to construct such a biblically rounded soteriology have returned to an ancient model of salvation known as *theosis*. Arguably, this is the direction a soteriology of the Third Article should progress. What follows is a summary of what this may look like.

Within the Eastern Orthodox tradition, salvation resides in the incarnation in which the Son assumes our humanity and grants us his divinity (*theosis*). In the West, the atonement has been of central significance by which we understand the wrath of God to have been propitiated by the perfect obedience and sacrifice of the Son on the cross. If we were to adopt Spirit Christology and apply it to soteriology we can see how the incarnation and the atonement *both* give significance to soteriology. Viewed from this perspective, salvation is new life in Christ in the Spirit; salvation not only involves justification by Christ but also justification by the Spirit (1 Tim 3:16; Rom 4:25; 8:11). Soteriology now takes on its full significance as God mediating to creatures the full life, death, and resurrection of the Son, and eventually, full glorification. But what is of significance is that glorification, as in the life of the Son, starts now. The eschatological *telos* is already working its way into our mundane existence; presently we are able to utter those eschatological words "Abba, Father"; already we are able to partake of the Spirit of life, the Spirit of Christ, and the Spirit of God.

Normally where the theme of *unio mystica* is emphasized a doctrine of *theosis* is also present. This should come as no surprise as the two themes are interrelated. A Third Article Theology, arguably, accepts both themes and develops them in coherent ways. In recommending a doctrine of *theosis* some context is required which I briefly outline below in relation to certain western theologians that prove useful for this purpose.

If we continue to draw upon the work of Calvin we note that in one of his rare uses of the word "deification" he writes, in reference to 2 Pet 1:4, "We should notice that it is the purpose of the Gospel to make us sooner or later like God; indeed it is, so to speak, a kind of deification."[71] Seeking to echo the same thought as Eastern Orthodox thinkers, Calvin, when writing about the thought of us partaking of the divine "nature" makes it plain that this does not mean we partake of the divine essence but what he calls *kind*. "The apostles," writes Calvin "were simply concerned to say that when we have put off all the vices of the flesh we shall be partakers of divine immortality and the glory of blessedness, and thus we shall be in a way with God so far as our capacity allows."[72]

For Calvin the doctrine of *theosis* or partaking of the divine nature was *initiated* in our election for salvation, is *effected* in our union with Christ, and is *made possible* in two interrelated ways. First, by the incarnation of the Son thus divinizing humanity through the humanizing of divinity. In his *Institutes* Calvin speaks of partaking of the divine nature in terms of the *mirifica commutatio*—or "wonderful exchange" whereby:

> Having become with us the Son of Man, he has made us with himself sons of God. By his own descent to the earth he has prepared our ascent to heaven. Having received our mortality, he has bestowed on us his immortality. Having undertaken our weakness, he has made us strong in his strength. Having submitted

71. Calvin, *Calvin's New Testament Commentaries*, vol. 12, 330.
72. Ibid.

to our poverty, he has transferred to us his riches. Having taken upon himself the burden of unrighteousness with which we were oppressed, he has clothed us with his righteousness. (4.17.2)[73]

Second, through the work of the Holy Spirit. This partaking of the divine nature, or more specifically of Christ, is experienced and further developed through the sacraments and the life of piety lived out in the Spirit's power. This emphasis upon the work of the Holy Spirit is what makes Calvin's theology especially useful in this context.

Behind Calvin's treatment of *theosis* the doctrine of the Trinity provides a control and a context into which we can understand the deification of humans. Like the classical formulations of the doctrine, Calvin's doctrine of *theosis* is built around the hypostatic union. *Theosis* is only possible because human nature has been deified in the one person of the Mediator. As men and women are united to Christ his divinization deifies them. Our divinization is only made possible by the unique work of the incarnate Son who unites us to himself so that through the Holy Spirit we may know and worship the Father.

Moving beyond Calvin we can trace a continued usage of the doctrine of *theosis* within western theology. One important theologian to adopt the language of *theosis* is Jonathan Edwards. From his reflections on the Trinity, Edwards presents a brief articulation of *theosis* as the human participation in the Triune God of Love. According to Edwards, God created humans to participate in the Triune communion which could only be achieved through union with Christ. "The saints are 'exalted to glorious dignity' and 'to fellowship' and even 'union' with God Himself, but 'care is taken' . . . that this is not their own glory, but that it comes to them as they are 'in a person that is God.'"[74] By means of an analogy Edwards shows his express commitment to the doctrine of *theosis*: the biblical analogy of marriage. According to Edwards:

> The end of the creation of God was to provide a spouse for his Son Jesus Christ that might enjoy him and on whom he might pour fourth his love, & the end of all things in providence are to make way for the exceeding expressions of Christ's love to his spouse & for her exceeding close & intimate union with & high & glorious enjoyment of him.[75]

73. Calvin, *Institutes*, 4.17.2.
74. Holmes, *God of Grace and God of Glory*, 43.
75. Edwards, *Miscellanies* 710, cited in ibid., 58.

This leads Stephen Holmes to state that "In common with Eastern Orthodox thought, Edwards was prepared to see salvation as *theosis*, being made one with God."[76] Holmes summarizes this in the simplest terms possible, "God regards the believer as one with Christ and so, ontologically, the believer is one with Christ. Under the metaphysical positions with which Edwards was working, it really is that simple."[77] Holmes is not alone in seeing *theosis* clearly articulated in Edwards's work.

Recent scholarship recognizes that "there is a wide area of overlap between Edwards's teaching on salvation and the Orthodox doctrine of divinization." McClymont goes even further than this when he contends "that Edwards and Palamas share a common Platonic or Neoplatonic philosophical heritage that they modified in analogous ways under the impact of their understanding of God's grace and the Christian experience of communion with God."[78] Edwards's theology suggests that saints participate in intra-divine relationships within the Godhead in multiple ways, identified by McClymont as knowledge of God, vision of God, communion through the Spirit and in Christ the Son with the Father, and finally through a kind of expanding family relationship. As McClymont concludes:

> Edwards taught a doctrine of divinization. The only thing missing is the word itself, although, as shown above, Edwards employed a rich vocabulary of terms and phrases such as "communion," "emanation," "participation," "partaking," and "uniting" to describe the divine-human communion from either God's side or the creature's.[79]

Viewed from the perspective of a Spirit Christology, soteriology has a dynamic message of hope and transformation for human life in the present. While we await the *Parousia*, the transformation of our bodies into resurrected bodies like that of Jesus Christ, we also have to reckon with the fact that salvation begins in the present. A soteriology that starts with the Spirit has as its concern from the very beginning the transformation of the material, the embodied, and the social.[80] Believers are raised to new life and baptized in the Spirit through the risen Christ and

---

76. Ibid.
77. Ibid., 149, and see 184, 242.
78. McClymont, "Salvation as Divinization," 141.
79. Ibid., 153.
80. Ibid., 77.

as such their new lives are to imitate that of Christ. As Jesus was obedient not to the spirit of the age but to the Father through the Holy Spirit, so we too are obedient to Christ in the self-same Spirit. We are called to follow him; to confront the demonic powers of our day in humble dependence on Christ in the Spirit. We are to stand up and counter social injustice in all its manifest forms; we are to be light, salt, and fishers of men in a world that values the shadows and the transitory. Christ our Savior has come for the re-creation of all creation through the mediation of the Spirit and he calls us to share in this work. Only then does his work become our work. "He is thus the One who *both* breaks the demonic power of sin and death *and* breaks the bread to feed the hungry, who both sheds his blood for the sins of the world *and* clothes the naked, who *both* proclaims the coming of the Kingdom *and* summons the little children to come unto him. All of that, all that we have torn apart as the 'spiritual' verses the 'material,' is part and parcel of God's baptizing of creation with the Holy Spirit."[81] As we wait for the resurrection of the body and the fulfillment of all things (*ta panta*), we are active as we pray and experience the *Veni Creator Spiritus*. Soteriology is not only concerned with forensic justification but with *all things* (Col 1:20; Rom 8:19–23). Thus, the uniqueness and supremacy of Christ is maintained. Against the position of Roger Haight and others—there is no place for a plurality of Saviors in a biblical Spirit Christology. Jesus is the one and only author and perfecter of our faith (Heb 12:2).

I have given significantly more space to the soteriological contours of the incarnation than has been the case in classical theology, which has the effect of bridging the theological wedge between Christology and soteriology. The two are intimately related and we now know why. Without the active obedience of Christ, the passive obedience would have been in vain. This has direct applications for the believer. Christianity is not about the allocation of the idiomatic "ticket to heaven," rather, it is about a lifestyle epitomized by Jesus's invitation to "follow me" (Matt 4:19; 8:22; 9:9; 10:38; 16:24; 19:21; par.). Jesus's life was both a propitiation for sin and a model to follow. Other human lives can never propitiation for sin. Believers cannot redeem themselves. There is only one Jesus, one Messiah, and one beloved Son. Believers are called to follow Christ in the way of the cross (Luke 9:23) and the power of the Spirit. Believers are invited to join the Divine dance that is a participation in the life

---

81. Ibid., 79 (italics in original).

of the intratrinitarian relations. In the colloquial language of Christian discipleship, we are to be "Christ-like" as we seek to live a "cruciform" lifestyle all in the power of the Spirit of Christ.[82]

Pneumatologia crucis

The final element I wish to comment on in the construction of a Third Article soteriology is a consideration of Dabney's whereby he wishes to begin considering a *theologia crucis* but this time starting with the Spirit and thus develop a *pneumatological crucis*. This involves a consideration of *kenosis*—not just of the Son but of the Spirit as well. This has already been introduced in Chapter Five so what follows is a brief elaboration on that discussion.

According to Dabney, the Spirit can best be personally identified in relation to the cross of Christ and all that it stands for. He writes, "the Holy Spirit can best be named by returning to the historical point of departure for Protestant theology's talk of God, the cross of Jesus Christ, and reclaiming that *theologia crucis* for a theology of the Spirit, a *pneumatologia crucis*."[83] The cross is the outcome of Jesus's humanity—as the Son obedient to the Father's will, and as representative human led by the Spirit, and as human priest. For this reason the life of Christ, empowered by the Holy Spirit, provides the context for a *pneumatologia crucis*. Such a theology does not end with the death of the eternal Son on the cross, however, but also extends to his resurrection.

The Spirit of God is the eschatological *Spiritus Vivificans* active on both sides of the cross and it is precisely here that we come face to face with the *pneumatologia crucis* that so informs a *theologia crucis*. "The Holy Spirit is the self-sacrifice and resurrection of Jesus Christ made manifest in the Trinitarian kenosis of God on the cross . . ."[84] Dabney describes this *kenosis* as the sacrifice of the Father, the forsakeness of the Son, and the "abnegation" of the Spirit. A *theologia crucis* is now able to inform a *pneumatologia crucis* in such a way that the Triune equality and economic *taxis* of the Godhead is able to be faithfully expounded and applied. In short, we return to the cross of Christ in order to construct a soteriology of the Third Article.

---

82. See Gorman, *Inhabiting the Cruciform God*.
83. Dabney, "Naming the Spirit," 30. See further *Die Kenosis des Geistes*.
84. Ibid., 58 (italics in original).

But in what does the *kenosis* (self emptying) of the Spirit in the *kenosis* of God on the cross consist? In reply we must first say that there is no independent work of the Spirit or the Son. They are, as Irenaeus said, the two hands of God in the world. There is no understanding the *kenosis* of the Spirit apart from the *kenosis* of the Son. The descent of the Spirit is seen in the consent of the Son to take upon himself creation's plight, to take up the proclamation of the coming kingdom, to submit to temptation in the wilderness, to enter into conflict with Satan, and to offer up his life on Golgotha. If Jesus gives himself up then so does the Spirit of God, the two are inextricably bound together. The *via crucis* of the Son is at the same time the *via crucis* of the Spirit; the passion of one is the passion of the other, albeit it in their own respective ways. This is what gives meaning to the blasphemy against the Holy Spirit charge (Mark 3:22–30. pars). It is, then, this *kenosis* of the Spirit and the Son which reaches its proper end on Golgotha.

It is this theme which Moltmann has developed in his powerful interpretation of the death of Jesus on the cross as nothing less than a "God-event" involving not just the Son but the Father and the Spirit as well, a history making event in which "the history of history" is played out for all to see. He maintains that for the Father the Son's cry: "My God, my God, why have you forsaken me?" represents the experience of the loss of the Son and for the Son it signifies an experience of abandonment by the Father. But what of the Holy Spirit?

The key to understanding the significance of the cross for the Spirit is found in the word which Jesus begins his cry: "My God, my God." This is the only place in the Gospel tradition in which Jesus addresses his prayer not to his "Father" but to his "God." On the cross Jesus dies a human death, a lonely, abandoned death. While it is true to say that it was the death of the abandoned Son of God this is not true enough to the situation. At his death Jesus speaks not of intimate sonship but of loss, of estrangement, and of desolation. The incarnate Son of God dies the sinner's death and experienced the bitterness of desolation. Jesus dies, therefore, not simply as "the abandoned Son of God" but as the one who in his abandonment *experienced* the utter negation of himself as the beloved Son of God. This is the profundity of the *kenosis* of the Son.

But what of the *kenosis* of the Spirit? At one and the same time this text reveals the profundity of the *kenosis* of the Spirit. The sonship of Jesus is rooted in his relationship to the Spirit. In the New Testament witness sonship and Spirit stand together. The Spirit of God is, as Paul expressed it, not just "the Spirit of the Son" (Gal 4:6) but rather the "Spirit of sonship" itself (Rom 8:15). With this in mind let us ask again our central question: What can it mean for this "Spirit of sonship" that the death of Jesus on the cross means the undoing, the coming to grief, the negating not only of "the Son" but of "sonship" itself? This is how Dabney seeks to answer this question:

> It can only represent the profoundest frustration and nullification of the work of the Spirit. For in that "fatherless" cry of Jesus, all the life and mission and work of the Spirit of God is set at nought—even as it comes to fulfillment. In that cry, all the "grief" (Isa 63:10; Eph 4:30) and "outrage" (Heb 10:29) ever experienced by the Spirit at the hands of the creature comes to a climax in which every "word of blasphemy" spoken against the Spirit (Mk 3:29) and every "quenching" of the Spirit's work (1 Thess 5:19) comes to expression. The Spirit who plumbs "everything, even the depths of God" (1 Cor 2:10), has plumbed even the depths of death in God, and in that death all the life and work of God's Spirit comes to grief. On the cross, *the negation of the Son* means the *ab-negation of the Spirit*.[85]

The death of Christ on the cross was a God event in the fullest sense of the term. Only the Incarnate Son was crucified, died, and was raised to new life, but the Father and the Spirit were no less present, albeit in distinctive ways. The death of Christ on the cross represents something other for the Spirit than for the Father or the Son. For the Father and the Son the cross means absence: the Father's experienced loss of his beloved Son, the Son's experience of abandonment by the one whom he had addressed as "Abba, Father." But the Spirit suffers neither such "loss" nor such "abandonment," Dabney reminds us. Rather, the Spirit experiences not absence but presence. For the Spirit of the Cross is the presence of God with the Son in the absence of the Father and the presence of the Spirit with the Father in the absence of the Son.[86]

Dabney does not develop both sides of this absence; however, I want to argue that both sides of the "presence in absence" get to the heart of the *kenosis* of the Spirit. Hence I would also want to make space for a *Patrologia Crucis* whereby we would finally have a complete *theologia*

---

85. Ibid., 56 (italics in original).
86. Ibid.

crucis faithful to the work of God at the cross, something which Dabney wishes us to hold when he writes:

> In the divine kenosis on the cross of Jesus Christ we see displayed, then, what can truly be termed a "God-event": the sacrifice of the Father, the forsakenness of the Son and the abnegation of the Spirit. And in this triune condescension, the three-fold love of the trinitarian God is made manifest: *the love of the Father* who will sacrifice his only begotten Son on the cross and suffer the loss of the one he had hailed as "the beloved": *the love of the Son* who will go the way of the cross into the far country of estrangement from the Father and suffer forsakenness by the one whose will he had come to perform; *and the love of the Spirit* who will lead, accompany and follow after the Son to and into and beyond the horror of death on the cross and thus suffer his own utter frustration and abnegation in the one who had prayed "Abba Father" at his testing in the garden but who can only desperately cry "my God, my God" in the desolation of the cross.[87]

Dabney's insights into a *pneumatologia crucis* are profound and helpful and I an indebted to him for these ideas. This is not to say that the concept of a *kenosis* of the Spirit will be acceptable to all in the guild or that Dabney's articulation of the concept is the last word. As long as the idea is understood economically and experientially I find it fruitful and consistent with the Great Tradition. If it is raised to the level of ontology as it is in Moltmann's work then it suffers from the charge of patripassianism.[88] However, like most elements of a Spirit Christology we have already examined, this aspect of a Third Article Theology can be utilized in more than one way thus requiring exponents to clarify what they intend to affirm by such terms.

CONCLUSION

Arguably, the three themes I have highlighted correspond to the three constituent features required of a Third Article soteriology: First, union with Christ fulfils the criteria that a Third Article Theology starts with the Spirit. Second, a doctrine of *theosis* fulfils the criteria that a Third Article Theology unfolds the Trinitarian mission of God in the world. And finally, a *pneumatologia crucis* fulfils the criteria that a Third Article

---

87. Ibid., 57 (italics in original).
88. See Habets, "Putting the 'Extra' Back into Calvinism."

Theology has as its focus the centre of God's mission—the life of Christ. In the final chapter I consider the wider implications of the model of Spirit Christology I have articulated and point to ways in which this theology may be applied in Christian ministry and mission.

8

Receiving the Promise

Spirit Christology for Ministry and Mission

Above all, the distinctive essence of Christian experience lies in the relation between Jesus and the Spirit

—James D. G. Dunn

Jesus Christ is Lord! Not only in the sense that we are committed to Him, and seek to serve Him, but because the Holy Spirit is also His Spirit, and this Spirit is now freshly moving in our midst.

—J. Rodman Williams

THROUGHOUT THIS STUDY, MY argument has been that the dominant Logos Christology inherited from the Great Tradition needs to be complemented by the equally biblical and historically sound theology known as Spirit Christology. I have sought to highlight what this recovered model is in its methodological, historical, biblical, and theological dimensions. Methodologically it is an Christological approach from below; one that seeks to give adequate space to the real humanity of Jesus Christ without doing violence to his divinity. In this way Chalcedonian orthodoxy is maintained. By focusing on the humanity of Christ, his active obedience takes on a much richer significance than it has commonly been given, especially in Western theology. Jesus' life becomes a true model for believers to follow, the paradigm of obedient sonship. Historically, the Patristic theologians were familiar with both Logos and Spirit Christology and utilized insights from both within their dogmatic formulations and worship. However, due to historical considerations the Logos concept dominated and hence Logos Christology squeezed Spirit Christology to the margins. But importantly, Ignatius, Athanasius, and the Cappadocians were still able to incorporate the Holy Spirit meaningfully into their Christological and Trinitarian formulations and it is largely from their contributions that contemporary Spirit Christologists look for a recovery. This takes on added impetus given the ecumenical endeavors of both East and West to find common ground and unity.

Biblically and theologically we have seen that Spirit Christology offers a fecundity of images, ideas, and constructions as to the identity and mission of Jesus Christ, and of the Holy Spirit. In moving from the biblical material and the economic Trinity to the theological constructions and the immanent Trinity I outlined a tentative model of the Trinity that is in harmony with Scripture and the Great Tradition. It builds upon eastern and western theologies, and it is large enough to encompass the insights of Logos Christology without succumbing to the spirit of the age or confining itself to the *ipsissima verba* of the tradition. As such a Spirit Christology has the potential to significantly contribute to the theological task today.

What I have not commented on so far is the significance of Spirit Christology for Christian life and ministry. In this final chapter I move from retrospect to prospect and consider some of the areas of significance that Spirit Christology may have for ministry and mission today.

THE FUTURE OF SPIRIT CHRISTOLOGY

Immanuel Kant once argued "from the doctrine of the Trinity, taken literally, nothing whatsoever can be gained for practical purposes, even if one believed that one comprehended it and less still if one is conscious that it surpasses all our concepts."[1] While it would be a naïve theologian who said they fully understood any doctrine, let alone this mystery of all mysteries, it is quite incorrect to assume the doctrine of the Trinity is of no practical purpose. Quite the opposite! It is one of the defining marks of contemporary theology that the doctrine of the Trinity is fruitfully informing and furthering theological investigation across the various loci.[2] So much so in fact that Christoph Schwöbel could write:

> . . . the doctrine of the Trinity matters. It is not a topic reserved for austere theological speculation or the language and practice

---

1. Kant, *Der Streit der Fakoltaten*, 252, quoted in Moltmann, *Trinity and the Kingdom*, 6.

2. See for instance, British Council of Churches, *Forgotten Trinity*, vol. 1.

of worship. The conceptual form in which the doctrine of the Trinity is expressed will affect not only the content and emphases of the doctrinal scheme of theology but also the forms of community organization in the church and its life of worship.³

This is no truer than in the area of Spirit Christology. In this chapter I will draw the threads of this study together and offer a vision of how a Spirit Christology may be worked out in the future in four main areas: Christology proper, anthropology, discipleship, and its ecumenical contingency.⁴

Spirit Christology can not be viewed as simply one more option amidst a pluralistic smorgasbord of contemporary alternatives.⁵ For Spirit Christology is much more than merely *a* Christology. It is an attempt at an interdisciplinary approach to the identity of Jesus the Christ especially through its reciprocal doctrine of pneumatology. As we have seen, this paradigm is intensely Trinitarian as well as contributing new insights into the field of hermeneutics. But what of the other *loci* of dogmatics? As systematic theology is an organic enterprise each doctrine affects every other. Hence, to tamper with a doctrine in one area will have ramifications on the other *loci* of theology. This is no truer than in the area of Christology, as Christology is central to the theological task. Having already presented a paradigm for Christology in terms of a pneumatological approach and accounted for some of the Trinitarian implications this model requires I propose to explore its productivity in advancing the theological grasp of several major issues on the agenda of contemporary theology. Since our interest is in a particular Christological model and how it works, I will not focus on an analysis of the issues themselves but on the dogmatic structure of the Christological model in relation to them.

Christology

The reciprocity of Christ and Spirit, evidenced throughout Scripture and within recent theology, argues strongly that there can be no conception of Christ that does not encompass an understanding of the Christ event,

---

3. Schwöbel, *Trinitarian Theology Today*, 1.

4. Del Colle, *Christ and the Spirit*, 196, looks at 1) contextual issues of culture and human experience, 2) emancipatory concerns of social praxis and a just society, and 3) religious pluralism and the quest for dialogue.

5. Despite Roger Haight's best intentions in *Jesus Symbol of God*.

as thoroughly pneumatological in itself. There can be no study of the identity or mission of Christ in abstraction from the mission and identity of the Holy Spirit. In the economy, the Spirit is prior to the Son hence the rationale for starting with the Spirit,[6] but the Son is always pre-eminent. Where the Spirit is today there is also knowledge of the Son; where the Son is, there the power of the Spirit is present also.

"Christology is in crisis" is a common theme heard today.[7] Schwöbel traces this crisis back to the days of Reimarus and Lessing and the separation of the historical Jesus from the Christ of faith.[8] He ultimately states that the fundamental problem or crisis facing contemporary Christology is the lack of the Trinitarian logic of the Christian understanding of God and its implications for the Christian understanding of what it means to be human.[9] Schwöbel proposes that the solution is not to be found in a compromise between the Docetic understanding of the divinity of Christ and the Ebionite understanding of his humanity. We have already seen how the Chalcedonian Definition succeeded in stating the necessary theological conditions for a Christology, by asserting the unity of the person of Christ in the language of two natures without confusion, without change, without division, and without separation. But while this is very good theology, the Definition merely rules out those conceptions of Christ that are inadequate without actually providing a constructive Christological conception of the one person. In practice, the community of faith still oscillates between a unification Christology (Eutychianism) or a disjunction Christology (Nestorianism). Into this situation Spirit Christology has its greatest potential for practical applicability. Christology is not primarily the study of the two natures of Jesus the Christ, but should be seen in terms of his relationship to the Father mediated through the Spirit. This brings a radically new perspective to Christology and indeed anthropology; Jesus is not only divine because of the possession of a divine nature but because God relates to him as Son through the eternal Spirit. Here function is alloyed to ontology but neither one in and of itself provides a sufficient basis for the unity of

---

6. Dabney, "Starting with the Spirit," 3–27.

7. Consider the articulate essay by Braaten, "Significance of New Testament Christology for Systematic Theology," 216–27.

8. Schwöbel, "Christology and Trinitarian Thought," 113ff.

9. Ibid., 120.

Jesus Christ. Christ is divine in relating to the Father through the eternal Spirit as the only begotten Son.

By bringing the humanity of Jesus Christ to the fore in Christology we open up new possibilities for witness in the world. It is humanity that all cultures share and humanity that all cultures share with Jesus. "We cannot seriously regard Logos Christology as capable of providing the basis needed for theological renewal," writes Badcock.

> The ideal of *logos*, or rationality, especially in its patristic-hellenistic adaptation, is no longer easily sustainable even in Western culture and is quite alien to much of the rest of the world. If, then, Jesus Christ is indeed the Word of God, it is *Jesus Christ*, in short, who is that Word—Jesus Christ who shared human frailty, who stood with the "poor" in the biblical sense, Jesus Christ whose human life is the perfect image of God. Whatever we say of his status as the Word from eternity to eternity cannot be allowed to detract from that.[10]

Jesus understood his mission in terms of drawing all people to himself (John 12:32). Subsequently, Christological constructions can be understood as the attempt to explicate the identity of Jesus and the content of this drawing. As such, our theological constructs are ultimately designed to point to the truth of Jesus Christ and hence to become an aid in his drawing of humanity to himself. This essentially entails that all theology should not only be biblically based but also existentially viable. Unfortunately it is not always possible to make explicit the practical links to which our theological constructs point, yet it is imperative that those links can be made. While we have examined in some detail a new paradigm for systematic theology we have yet to highlight its existential viability. I wish to briefly attend to that task.

When the paradigm of Spirit Christology presented herein is utilized, we are confronted with the person of Jesus the Messiah. Like the Samaritan women at the well (John 4) or the fledgling disciples, or Zacchaeus up a tree (Luke 19), this confrontation is with a human being—a man with a very real human history. As time is spent with Jesus of Nazareth, an unmistakable conclusion is drawn—he is the Messiah, the Coming One, the Lord, he is God. A dawning realization works its way into our consciousness and is then fleshed out in subsequent reflection. The individual moves from observation of Jesus through to recognition,

---

10. Badcock, *Light of Truth & Fire of Love*, 268.

praise, worship, and service. Finally and ultimately, total understanding catches up with existential commitment (*credo ut intelligum*).

This perspective is quite different from the philosophical approach sponsored by certain readings of Chalcedon throughout the western tradition. Under this approach Jesus is a philosophical aberration that one must comprehend in order to follow. *Ousia*, *substantia*, and *persona* roll off the tongue with ease at the level of theological precision. But practically, the centuries' old danger of Eutychianism and Nestorianism are constantly waging battle for supremacy. Influenced by this Christology, it is often hard to adequately conceive of the person or unity of Jesus Christ. A review of the literature on the doctrine of Christ's peccability and temptability is a case in point. While it is universally agreed within orthodox Christianity that Christ did not sin, the question remains: Could he have sinned? I suggest that the way one answers this question is a fair indication of the practical viability of ones Christology. To answer: "No, Jesus could not have sinned because he has a divine nature," may be theologically correct, but it is not the way the New Testament invites us to respond. It is also not anthropologically accurate either. Nowhere can we turn and find this form of logic coming from the biblical authors. Rather we read that, "we do not have a great high priest who cannot sympathize with our weaknesses, but One who has been tempted in all things as we are, yet without sin" (Heb 4:13). Peter teaches that Jesus "committed no sin; no guile was found on his lips" (1 Pet 2:22), and John said "in him there is no sin" (1 John 3:5).[11] How did they come to this conclusion? The answer, only through observing Jesus' life. John writes that on one occasion Jesus asked for a public accusation if one could be found, none was (John 8:46). On another occasion we are told that Jesus always did what was pleasing to God (John 8:29). He taught his disciples to confess their sins and yet there is no record of Jesus modeling this himself. On other occasions we are given additional testimony to the blamelessness of this man (Matt 27:4, 19; Luke 23:41).

When we step back to ask how it was that Jesus did not sin we reveal the basis of our Christology. For many, Jesus did not sin because he could not; he could not sin because he was divine.[12] This is the standard (and correct) answer from the perspective of Logos Christology.

---

11. We could add to this list Heb 7:26; 9:14; John 6:69, and 2 Cor 5:21.

12. This form of the answer has become a standard retort amongst western theologians. See Shedd, *Dogmatic Theology*, vol. 2, 334, and Macleod, *Person of Christ*, 229-30.

Without denying the validity of this theological argument we must ask, however, if this is the first thing or the most appropriate way to respond to the question in the first instance. What does this response say about the humanity of Jesus? It threatens to make Jesus' humanity different from the rest of creation, exactly the opposite of the biblical account. From the perspective of Spirit Christology, a more accurate and existentially viable answer to the question: "How it is that Jesus did not sin?" is to say that Jesus did not sin due to his total commitment to the will of the Father, lived out in his dependence upon the Holy Spirit.[13] Because of the purity of his commitment and because of his total submission to the will of the Father through the agency of the Holy Spirit, temptation could find no lodging in his being. What are required to answer these sorts of Christological questions is not simply a Logos Christology nor simply a Spirit Christology, but a complementary Christology of Logos and Spirit.

The point now crystallizes; if Jesus is indeed genuinely human, *homoousios* with other human beings, then the way that he deals with sin and temptation is the supreme model for other humans to follow. This is the point of his active obedience, his identity as the last Adam, the firstborn over all creation. This gives coherence to his sending another Comforter to sanctify believers in Christ's name. Christ was also *homoousios* with the Father, we are not. If Jesus resisted sin and temptation only in his divine nature then he is no longer a sympathetic high priest and Christology is dislocated from soteriology. When Jesus is recognized as fully human *and* fully God through the mediating work of the Holy Spirit then he truly becomes Savior, Lord, and last Adam who offers real hope for fallen creatures. Therefore, in answer to the question of Jesus' sinlessness we must start by saying that he was sinless due to the perfection of his obedience, enabled by his empowering by the Spirit. Only then can we also add that it would be impossible for the incarnate Word to sin because God can never be against himself.

With this Christology firmly in place we can then see how Jesus becomes our *finis hominum*, the goal of human existence. We strive in the Spirit to be Christlike and we are conformed to his image daily through the sanctifying work of the Spirit so that ultimately we become transformed from being *posse non peccare* in the power of the Spirit, to

---

13. We have already looked at specific instances of this in chapter 5, especially in the temptation narratives, along with the suggestion of a *pneumatologia crucis*.

being *non posse peccare* through physical resurrection, in order to be like Christ. While I shall consider several anthropological implications shortly, at this stage it may be pointed out that our humanity is not the standard by which we are to measure the humanity of Jesus. His humanity is the only true, full, and complete humanity that has ever existed and one day believers shall also be like him. However, until then, believers must remain content to be transformed into his likeness on an ever progressive ascendancy (sanctification, Christification, and *theosis*).

Another related question that puzzles many who work within the traditional Logos Christology is the intense prayer life of Jesus. We read many times of his going off to pray (Mark 6:46; Matt 26:36). On at least one occasion, and possibly on many more, Jesus spent an entire night in prayerful communion with his Father (Luke 6:12). For many this poses a mystery more than a problem. The logic of a Logos Christology goes along these syllogistic lines:

1. God knows everything
2. Jesus is God
3. Jesus knows everything
4. Jesus does not need to pray to God

Behind this reasoning is the deeper mistaken theological assumption that it is the second person of the Trinity who works directly on the human nature of Jesus which must follow that Jesus is not a real model to follow as his example is merely a hollow symbolism with no actuality.

When working from within a Spirit Christology, however, the situation is quite different. *Because* of the Trinitarian relations evident through the economy of redemption, we know that the Son is located during his time on earth in the person of Jesus; that is, the Son, the second person of the Trinity is Jesus of Nazareth.[14] Because the Son is incarnated *as* a man not merely *in* a man, the divine Son does not work directly on the humanity of Jesus of Nazareth, but rather, consciousness of divinity is mediated to Jesus Christ through the Holy Spirit just as the Father relates

---

14. This is not to deny the quite correct formula *finitum non capax infiniti* ("the finite is incapable of the infinite") but only to assert that the person of the Son is the person of Jesus Christ. That is, God did not possess a man—Jesus, but rather, God became man—Jesus the Christ, the Logos incarnate—without ceasing to be God. See Habets, "Putting the 'Extra' Back into Calvinism." Cf. Rochelle, "What Price Finitum Capax Infiniti," 110–21; Macchia, "Finitum Capax Infiniti" 185–87; and Pederson, "Christmas and the Reality of Incarnation," 381–89.

to the Son, and the Son relates to the Father through the Holy Spirit *in se*. Here we are following the formula, "the economic is the immanent Trinity." Hence, the prayer life of Jesus as evident in the New Testament is completely in accord with what we would expect from a tri-personal God. In fact, if we did not see this form of personal *perichoretic* devotion of love, then we would have grounds to be suspect of the identity of Jesus of Nazareth. From eternity past the Son has communed with the Father in the Spirit and the Father to the Son in the Spirit. This was discussed in chapter Six. If Jesus did not spend vast amounts of time in communion with his Father through the Spirit, during the incarnation, then one would have to doubt the identity of Jesus as the Messiah, the "beloved Son." Again this presents the believer with a model to follow.

In addition, the prayer life or communion of Jesus with the Father in the Spirit provides an assurance for the believer. In John 17:21 Jesus prayed for his disciples that they "may all be one; even as you, Father, are in me and I in you, that they also may be in us, so that the world may believe that you sent me." Clearly, Jesus was not asking this in an ontological, but rather a personal sense. He was praying for that *perichoretic* union between God and man that was most fully evident in the life of Jesus the Messiah to be applied, in a human and limited way, to the body of Christ, the church. This is supported by v. 23 where Jesus prays that they may be "perfect in unity, so that the world may know that You sent me, and loved them, even as you have loved me." The believer also is to relate to God through the Son in or by the Holy Spirit. Only then is it possible to utter those sacred and intimate words "Abba, Father" (Gal 4:4–7). Prayer and intimate communion with God now become possible for the community of faith. Our status as persons is lifted into the intratrinitarian relations themselves, not making us divine, but enabling us to participate in the life of God, as the Eastern Orthodox idea of *theosis* maintains.[15] As Pinnock has rightly reminded us, "We enter the dance of the Trinity not as equals but as adopted partners."[16] There is no higher privilege or greater salvation we could ever wish to attain! Having considered implications of a Spirit Christology on soteriology in

---

15. For a critical analysis of *theosis* and its compatibility with the western Reformed tradition, see Habets, *Theosis in the Theology of Thomas Torrance*; and "Reforming Theosis."

16. Pinnock, *Flame of Love*, 154.

the previous chapter I now move on to note other areas affected by Spirit Christology especially as they apply to Christian ministry and mission.

Theological Anthropology

The word "Christology" is a comprehensive term for the statement concerning the identity and significance of Jesus. In a developed Christology, this identity and significance is expressed in relation to God (the *theo*logical correlation proper), the created order (the *cosmo*logical correlation), and humanity (the *anthropo*logical correlation); each of which impinges on the others whether or not this is made explicit.[17] Because Spirit Christology highlights or gives more space to the Trinitarian relations and the real humanity of Jesus, theological anthropology has received the most significant treatment in contemporary literature.[18] In fact, we are amidst somewhat of a renaissance of studies in theological anthropology.[19]

The anthropological correlative is concerned first and foremost with soteriology as it is the soteriological question that occasions the identity

---

17. Keck, developed this insight in his article "Toward the Renewal of New Testament Christology," 362–77.

18. Due largely to the seminal work of Moltmann and Welker, the cosmological function of both Christology and especially pneumatology, is also being taken seriously, and the results are contributing towards a rich theology. Also, over the past decade and continuing into the present, the theological correlation is also being explored with most interesting results. My current work is born out of the theological correlation. It is true that Trinitarian studies in general have occasioned a complete rethinking of all three correlatives. This opinion is at least shared by James B. Torrance, "Doctrine of the Trinity in Our Contemporary Situation," 3.

19. This is in large part a parallel development and consequence of the renaissance of Trinitarian study, especially the renaissance of some form of "social" Trinitarian construct. The basic formula is that if God is one Being in three persons, then his essential identity is bound up with being a person-in-relation. On the anthropological level, to be created in the *imago Dei* means to also be a person-in-relation. Thus, the entire theme of community has also been seized upon in theological discussion. For an introduction to the literature see the seminal essay of Zizioulas, "Human Capacity and Human Incapacity," 401–48; and his agenda setting monograph, *Being as Communion*, followed up by his *Communion and Otherness*. Also see LaCugna, *God With Us*, 288–305; Boff, *Trinity and Society*; *Persons, Divine and Human*; and Torrance, *Persons in Communion*.

Perhaps the most consistent integration of the themes of persons-in-communion with the Trinitarian community motif within a systematic theology is the *magnum opus* of Grenz, *Theology for the Community of God*. Grenz subsequently reworked these ideas in his series The Matrix of Theology: *Social God and the Relational Self*, and *Named God and the Question of Being*.

of Jesus Christ. Christology and anthropology always correlate because Jesus the Savior is a true human being. But anthropology is not the constant and Christology the variable; actually, the opposite is the case. Our definition of "person" is derived from *the* one true Person—Jesus the Christ the true *eikon* of the Father. "According to Christian theology it is not we, but Jesus Christ, who is the measure of true humanity. To measure Jesus by our humanity, then, is to get it backwards."[20] Hence, a changed Christology also entails a changed anthropology. The Second Vatican Council stated, "only in the mystery of the incarnate Word does the mystery of man take on light."[21] From Del Colle's perspective:

> . . . Spirit-Christology proposes that the work of God in Jesus Christ proceeds out of the Spirit and is enacted in the Holy Spirit such that the Holy Spirit becomes gift to humanity in divinizing and missionizing power. Trinitarian Spirit-Christology proposes that the person of Jesus Christ is constituted as the enfleshment of divine Word and Wisdom in filial relation to God. It is essentially communicative through humanity because this enfleshment is enacted within the overflow of the trinitarian life of God in which the Holy Spirit as ecstatic giftedness and love conducts the life of the Father toward the Son. The Son through the same Spirit returns that life to the Father in superlative fashion, that is, eschatological glory inclusive of redeemed creation.[22]

One of the many crisis points faced by Christology today is the conception of the unity of the person of Christ without a disjunction between the "historical Jesus" and the "Christ of faith."[23] What my paradigm of Spirit Christology does is to implement a new synthesis by joining together what has been rent asunder. When the Trinitarian logic of the Christian understanding of God is made explicit, the implications for the Christian understanding of what it means to be human stand out in bold relief. To be human is to be like Jesus. Jesus is who he is because of his relationship to the Father through the Spirit and the Father's relationship to him also through the Spirit. This means that the *imago Dei*

---

20. McCready, "'He Came Down From Heaven,'" 431.

21. "Pastoral Constitution on the Church in the Modern World: *Gaudium et Spares*," 22.

22. Del Colle, "Spirit-Christology," 106.

23. This constitutes the challenge of Christology as presented by Wright, *Challenge of Jesus*.

has been concretized by the incarnation and so we now understand true humanity as the transformation into the *imago Christi*.

If the final test of the propriety of a Christian doctrine is its preachability (existential viability),[24] then the Spirit Christology presented in this study is eminently proper. When the New Testament is read from a pneuma-sarx perspective, the resulting picture is, among other things, that of a true and real person—the *man* Jesus who is also the Messiah. In the language of Niceaea and Chalcedon we are confronted with the single person who is at once *homoousios* with humanity and *homoousios* with divinity. He is the beloved Son of God, he is the royal King in David's line, he is the true spiritual father of the nations even superseding Abraham (Matt 1, 2 par.). When we ask how this is so, the evangelists insist it is because of the role of the Holy Spirit in conceiving Jesus, in baptizing him, empowering, raising, and then serving him. In like fashion believers too are born of the Spirit, however, it is by adoption not filial ontology; believers too are empowered and eventually raised by the self-same Spirit of Jesus Christ. In a paradigmatic fashion the spiritual lives of believers united to Christ by the Spirit echo that of Jesus. Jesus is indeed the "Last Adam" and the "first-born." We are raised to new life "in Christ" and "in the Spirit."

From the synoptic Gospels in particular, Jesus reveals the essence of true humanity when he defines what it really means to be human. While this representation has many varied aspects we can identify a few dominant traits. Jesus' entire life is supremely characterized in relational terms—he is the beloved Son, hence, God is his Abba, Father. In response to this filial relationship a radical obedience is both possible and desirable. This disposition of humanity toward God formed the motivation for all that Jesus did. In contradistinction to the Pharisees' outward obedience, Jesus modeled an inward compulsion (Matt 6:1; 5:20). Thus, Jesus not only revealed what true humanity is but he also opened up a way to view the relationship between God and humanity in a new and profound way. Christ revealed the paternal aspect of God in intimate terms that were unparalleled. God is our heavenly Father who loves his children with a *passion*. He lavishes good gifts upon them out of his love (Luke 11:11–13), he initiates relationships (Matt 6:30), and he seeks the lost as a shepherd seeks the lost sheep he loves (Luke 19:10). It is significant that the last reference embodies Jesus in both the true sonship and

24. Pinnock, *Flame of Love*, 243.

also in the "aggressive seeking of the Father."[25] The anthropology of Jesus is in fact integral to his view of God as Father.

Also integral to the humanity of Jesus was his call for faith. Faith is not only belief or mental assent but personal trust in all areas of life and being. Again we see the uniqueness of Christ in his call to faith in both God the Father and in himself. Both the Father and the Son act in response to faith (Matt 9:22; Mark 10:52; Luke 7:20; etc.). Faith is the most fundamental human activity in relation to God; subjecting oneself wholly to God (Father, Son, and Spirit) is the most truly human act possible. And it is so because faith is one of the most basic activities of the incarnate Son. Thus, the faith of believers is not their own but the vicarious faith of the incarnate Son for them.[26] Autonomy from God has always been the original sin, the dehumanizing force in creation. The incarnation revealed both the why and the how of human fulfillment which are bound up with living in dependence (faith) on God. This is behind one of the dominant themes on the lips of Jesus, as for instance when he said, "He who finds his life will lose it, and he who loses his life for my sake will find it" (Matt 10:39). This perspective gives coherence to the paschal mystery; rather than being the tragic end to a human life it was the portal through which all humanity can realize true life.

Starting from the exaltation of Jesus and retroactively working from that fulcra point, we can view the Spirit's activity extending backwards into the very beginning of the cosmos when God opened himself up to the possibility of loving and redeeming a world, extrinsic to himself. From the center of the paschal mystery, that is, a *theologia crucis* informed by a *pneumatologia crucis,* we see the work of the Spirit of God opening God up to the cosmos and drawing it into the sweep of his redeeming activity (Rom 8:19–22). All creation now has the opportunity of encountering the same Spirit who gave life to Jesus, establishing him as the Head of all things. "Thus the eschatological dimension of Spirit Christology completes and complements all that the Spirit has done since the beginning of time to realize God's love-intention in history."[27] Not only the history of humanity, but the entire cosmos is now caught

---

25. Wilterdink, "Christology and the Paradoxical Nature of Human Existence," 129.

26. No one has thought through the nature of the vicarious faith of Christ more than Torrance. See Torrance, *Preaching Christ Today*; "Justification: Its Radical Nature and Place in Reformed Doctrine and Life," 150–68; and *Mediation of Christ*.

27. Rosato, "Spirit Christology," 446.

up in the redemptive sweep of the paschal mystery. Indeed the three correlations mentioned above, the *theo*logical, *cosmo*logical, and *anthropo*logical, actually coinhere. They are distinct but not separate realities centered in the eschatological goal of Christ to reconcile "all things" to himself.

Significant also is the fact that the orthodox belief in the incarnation affirms a permanent incarnation—albeit in an ascended sense.[28] The incarnation was not limited to Jesus' earthly life, it extends to Jesus Christ as he continues to exist because his humanity was resurrected and he is now the great High Priest who eternally intercedes for us.[29] One day we too shall be resurrected as he was, indeed, Christ is our first fruits! So as *archē* (or *prōtotokos* of Col 1:15) original human, and now as *telos*, ultimate human, Jesus Christ is our model, our exemplar, even our template.[30] And what we shall become is inherently related to what we are becoming already. Thus, it is permissible to speak of an extension of the incarnation, not in the sense that the church is the extension of the incarnation (as in Roman Catholicism), but that all members of the church are related mystically to its Head, who alone is the incarnate One. This is achieved or actualized through the power of the Holy Spirit. It is through the Holy Spirit that believers participate in the one incarnation (but they do not replicate the incarnation). Believers are indwelt by the Spirit of Christ (but they do not become the Christ). Believers are adopted sons and daughters of the Father in the Son by the Holy Spirit. Believers are branches that bear fruit only because they are related to the True Vine (John 15) and because the Spirit is the cultivator of the fruit (Gal 5:22–23). And so an understanding of the humanity of Christ is essential not only for Christology proper, but also for anthropology and as an extension of those two, ecclesiology.[31]

---

28. The intention of this phrase is not to collapse the incarnation into the ascension but to affirm the permanent relationship established through the incarnation between God and man. See Farrow, *Ascension and Ecclesia*; and Dawson, *Jesus Ascended*.

29. For more on Christ's High Priesthood see Torrance, *Royal Priesthood*.

30. Wilterdink, "Christology and the Paradoxical Nature of Human Existence," 1, prefers "paradigm" as Jesus is more than a model or example—he is the epitome of all that God is to us and all that we may be to God.

31. Ibid., 124–32, where Wilterdink brings out many of the important points of Jesus true humanity. He does so building upon the Chalcedonian theology of true humanity and true divinity coalescing in the one person of Jesus Christ. Wilterdink calls this a "paradox" while I would prefer dialectic.

Christian Discipleship

The insights above lead the contemplative reader to ask how it is possible to "follow" the Messiah. It is one thing to affirm the ontological reality of becoming like Christ through a recognition of Jesus Christ as Lord and Messiah, it is quite another to bring this down into functional terms. What is actually required? Surely he is inimitable. If the incarnate Christ were only divine, that is, if we were Docetists, then we would be forced to agree with this notion. If, as classical Christology has tended to do in practice, we have a docetic view of Christ, then his life becomes a mere theo-drama acted out on the stage of world history. Under those conditions, our only response is to become spectators and watch God perform his *magnum opus*—incarnation. Sadly, this has largely been the Christian response throughout history. For too many believers, Jesus is so remote and transcendent, despite the incarnation, that he is unapproachable and hence the very purpose of the incarnation has a tendency to be subverted. Instead of drawing all people to himself, a theology of the cross has often resulted in drawing a crowd of onlookers, many sympathetic but all somewhat remote. This is what a Logos Christology seemingly, even unwittingly, promotes.

The paradigm of a Spirit Christology enables us to add life to this picture. That Life is the vivifying Breath of the Holy Spirit. Through the Spirit the Son was empowered to live in and endure the fallen realm of humanity. Through the Spirit the Son was kept by the power of God from sin, temptation, and disobedience. Through the Spirit the Son was in filial relationship to the Father. And when Jesus calls his disciples to follow him that is what he means; following him into filial relationship with the Father in the Holy Spirit. Now instead of watching a theo-drama we find ourselves as thespians on the stage, not just as extras in an all star cast, but as characters integral to the entire plot.[32] Jesus' life gives other human lives significance; his death and resurrection gives life eternal. The result of this paradigm is that Jesus is absolutely definitive. Weinandy reminds us that, "Because of who he is as the Son of God incarnate and because of what he has done as man, he is pre-eminent in every way. The primacy belongs to him alone, for there obviously 'is salvation in no

---

32. See Habets, "'Dogma is the Drama,'" 2–5.

one else, for there is no other name under heaven given among men by which we must be saved' (Acts 4:12)."[33] As Haight observed:

> A Spirit Christology empowers Christian life on the basis of the continuity between Jesus and us; he is a human being like us in all things except sin. This axiom from the New Testament is taken literally by Spirit Christology. Because of this continuity between Jesus and disciples, one can be inspired by an imitate Jesus. There is no gap between him and us. One can project upon him all the weaknesses of human existence in order to retrieve from him the inspiration of the power of his earthly life. Spirit Christology gives a solid grounding for a spirituality of following Christ.[34]

By focusing on the complete and very real humanity of Jesus, the incarnation "captures a fresh authenticity."[35] The Son of God knows us intimately for he is in every sense of the word "Immanuel," God with us. Therefore, he can identify tenderly with our frailty, adversity, and affliction; he too has felt the disgusting power of sin. And so in response, the Christian reaches out in worship to God Almighty, the blessed Trinity. Christology and indeed the doctrine of the Trinity arose out of the early churches's experience in worship. This was and is natural for "the Bible is supremely a manual of worship" as James B. Torrance forcefully reminds us.[36] What a Spirit Christology is able to achieve, is to highlight the significance in worship of the true humanity (*homoousia*) of the Son with human beings, along with the true divinity (*homoousia*) of the Son with the Father and the Spirit. James Torrance correctly defines worship as "the gift of participating through the Spirit in the incarnate Son's communion with the Father."[37] And so when we come together in worship I affirm, along with the BCC Study Commission, that "we are most truly human—most truly personal—when at the Eucharist we participate, through the Spirit, in the communion that is Christ's relation

---

33. Weinandy, *In the Likeness of Sinful Flesh*, 152.

34. Haight, *Jesus Symbol of God*, 465. By "imitate Christ" I am not, unlike Haight, intending to depreciate the atoning significance of Jesus Christ as the one and only Savior. I acknowledge and endorse the critique of Haight's Spirit Christology by Imbelli, "New Adam and Life-giving Spirit," 233–52.

35. Weinandy, *In the Likeness of Sinful Flesh*, 150.

36. Torrance, *Worship, Community and the Triune God of Grace*, 9. In a beautiful phrase he captures the heart of theology when he writes "True theology is theology that sings" (ibid., 10).

37. Ibid., 20.

to the Father."[38] Thus, we are re-enacting the life of the Son during his incarnation, not in the sense of an external *imitatio Christi*, but in the more profound and mystical sense of living out of our incorporation and participation in the life of the resurrected Son of God in the power of his pentecostal Spirit. In Thomas Torrance's words:

> Worship of the Father in spirit and in truth is the life of the Son in us that ascends to the Father in such worship. That is to say, Christian worship is properly a form of the life of Jesus Christ ascending to the Father in the life of those who are so intimately related to him through the Spirit, that when they pray to the Father through Christ, it is Christ the Incarnate Son who honours, worships and glorifies the Father in them.[39]

In relation to the enduring humanity of the Son, the role of his High Priesthood deserves some consideration.[40] Spirit Christology emphasizes the humanity of the Son of God in both the incarnation, and importantly, now during his "session." As human being, Hebrews 2:17 declares that "Therefore he had to become like his brothers and sisters in every respect, so that he might be a merciful and faithful high priest in the service of God, to make a sacrifice of atonement for the sins of the people." However, his priesthood did not expire on the cross with his death. As Christ was raised to eternal life so his office of priesthood was raised with him to be exercised perpetually (Heb 7:3). Christ is currently exalted at the right hand of the Father and interceding on behalf of his people (Heb 4:14, 15). This emphasis on the enduring Priesthood of Jesus Christ has profound implications on the shape and character of the Christian communities' prayer life and spirituality. It is here that Spirit Christology has a deep practical application.[41] To acknowledge Jesus as our High Priest, like us in every way and yet without sin, passed through the cross of atonement and now interceding on our behalf, invites those who love him to seek him in prayer. It entices his faith community to continually seek his counsel,

---

38. BCC, *Forgotten Trinity*, vol 1, 44.

39. Torrance, *Theology in Reconciliation*, 139.

40. The priesthood of Christ has been dealt with in the context of worship by Torrance, *Worship, Community and the Triune God of Grace*, 19–41, where he distinguishes between Unitarian and Trinitarian forms of worship.

41. In two works Anderson applies the paradigm of a Spirit Christology to the task of ministry today. Anderson, *Soul of Ministry*, and *Ministry on the Fire Line*.

comfort, and leading. It opens the way for a more dynamic and living relationship with our Lord and our God Jesus Christ and through the Son to the Father in the empowering of the Holy Spirit.

Out of an understanding of the humanity of Christ lived out in the power of the Spirit, access is gained into what it means to be like Jesus and to follow him in Christian discipleship, which is to worship him in Trinitarian terms. Worship does not consist only of verbal praise, it also involves a lived out reality; believers worship and glorify God when they *follow* him. In Pauline terms this is expressed in terms of presenting "our bodies as a living sacrifice, acceptable to God, which is your spiritual service of worship" (Rom 12:1). And so worship involves all of life, just as the incarnation involved the complete life of Jesus Christ. When we pray, we do so with confidence that the Spirit will intercede on our behalf (Rom 8:26), and that Jesus will represent us to the Father (Heb 7:25; Eph 2:18; 1 John 1:13). Because the Father, Son, and Holy Spirit are all *homoousios* with each other then it is not just correct, but also appropriate, to pray to all three members of the Godhead. The BCC Study Commission came to three conclusions in their discussion of Trinitarian prayer.[42] They consider Christian worship through prayer to be Trinitarian in three main ways: firstly, the standard and most pervasive understanding is to pray to the Father, through the Son, in the Spirit, secondly, we pray to each of the three persons - either to the Father, to the Son, or to the Holy Spirit. While we are only actually praying to one God, we have biblical and historical warrant to pray to each of the three persons.[43] Thirdly, we may pray to the one Trinitarian God in his unity, as when we sing the doxology at the end of the Psalms.[44] Because of the Trinitarian life revealed in the incarnation, and because of our incorporation into this very Trinitarian life by the exaltation of Christ and the sending of the Spirit, we can participate in Trinitarian prayer. We pray to a High Priest who knows us and we pray through his Holy Spirit. We can pray with confidence that we have two intercessors in heaven (John 14–16) on our behalf. Apart from Christ, none of us would know how to pray (Luke

42. BCC, *Forgotten Trinity*, vol. 1, 3ff.

43. See the BCC report for details along with Torrance, *Worship, Community and the Triune God of Grace*, 36.

44. Other advocates of Trinitarian worship in this sense include Bloesch, *God The Almighty*, 191ff.; Packer, *Keep in Step with the Spirit*, 261ff.; Sproul, *Mystery of the Spirit*, 18; Jungmann, *Place of Christ in Liturgical Prayer*; O'Donnell, *Mystery of the Triune God*, along with copious examples within the Nicene Fathers, especially in the Eucharistic liturgies contained within the writings of the Cappadocians.

11:1). But as we bring ourselves before God in humble obedience we find that Jesus takes what is ours and makes it his, as he, in turn, gives what is his and makes it ours. This is, as the Great Tradition says, the *mirifica commutatio* ("wonderful exchange")[45] by which Christ presents us to the Father in the Spirit through whom we cry "Abba, Father."

In response to the Son's call to "follow me," many Christians throughout the centuries have asked, "how?" The question is a valid and crucial one. For our purposes, the initial answer is to follow Christ as Christ followed his Father—in the power of the Holy Spirit. Through Christ the Spirit provides us, as he did Christ, with all the resources necessary for Christian discipleship. He produces fruit within our lives (Gal 5:22, 23) to conform our characters to Christ, he equips the church with gifts (Rom 12:6; 1 Cor 12–14), he fills and indwells, and leads and guides, and intercedes, and works in manifest ways in the lives of believers, through the church, in the world. In dependence on Christ and in the Christ Spirit, believers too can expect to take up their cross daily and follow the Lord. As such they will be asked to follow Christ into wilderness temptations, into confrontation with the powers of oppression, and into opportunities to witness to and live out their faith in God Almighty. This is the power and dynamism behind Paul's bold but true claim in Philippians 4:13, "I can do all things through Christ who strengthens me" (see Eph 3:16; 6:10; Col 1:11). Paul's prayer is shared by all believers in Christ for they each have the Spirit of the Father and the Son indwelling them. As Jesus promised, "I tell you the truth, anyone who has faith in me will do what I have been doing. He will do even greater things than these, because I am going to the Father" (John 14:12).

Ecumenism

Among the various advocates of Spirit Christology, most, if not all are adamant that this paradigm offers promising opportunities for inter-Christian, inter-faith, and international dialogue. We have seen already within this study something of a convergence of thought between Roman Catholic, Protestants, Pentecostal, and Eastern Orthodox traditions. As has been pointed out by others, Roman Catholicism is too concerned with a theology of the first article, patrology, following Rahner, while Protestants are too concerned with a theology of the second article,

---

45. See for instance, Calvin, *Institutes*, 4.17.2, and further in Torrance, *Trinitarian Faith*, 180.

Christology, following Barth, meanwhile Pentecostals are too concerned with the third article, pneumatology, in exclusion or separated from the first and second articles of the creed. Philip Rosato, a Roman Catholic, believes that Spirit Christology might offer a fruitful starting point for dialogue in the West as both traditions concentrate on a theology of the third article, in that it links the Spirit inseparably to the person of the glorified Jesus along with an opening of the way back to the Father.[46]

One of the defining marks of ecumenism during the 1990s was its focus on the Holy Spirit. The Seventh Assembly of the World Council of Churches, held in Canberra in 1991, had as its theme, "Come Holy Spirit, Renew the Whole Creation."[47] The Fifth World Conference on Faith and Order held in 1993 at Santiago de Compostela, stressed repeatedly the link between the *koinonia* of the Trinity and the *koinonia* of witness in the life of the church. Since the 1990s the emphasis has moved to the doctrine of the Trinity. However, behind this strong emphasis on the Trinity was a deep concern for the Holy Spirit. The BCC Study Commission shares similar aspirations when it wrote: "We believe that the doctrine of the Trinity has much to contribute to the process in which the divided churches of Christendom are drawing near to one another. The unity of Christians will be achieved as we gather in worship in the communion of the Holy Spirit."[48] Similarly in his pneumatology, Pinnock believes a Spirit-oriented model of development, what I have termed a retroactive hermeneutic, is the way to sensing the mind of the church and the *sensus fidelium*. The chief obstacle to theological unity, in his opinion, is the papacy in the present definition. It is his belief that "given the spirit expressed in '*Ut Unum Sint*,' a breakthrough could happen at any time. May God so grant this.[49] In an unpublished discussion paper, Gerard Kelly commented along the same lines that;

> The twentieth century is often referred to as the ecumenical century since it has been characterised by a flurry of ecumenical activity. Not only have there been ground-breaking dialogues but

---

46. Rosato, "Spirit Christology," 448. Dabney, a Wesleyan, chronicles a similar taxonomy in "Starting with the Spirit," although he does not explicitly argue for a Spirit Christology, despite this being a logical extension of his work, as we saw in chapter 7.

47. *Signs of the Spirit: Official Report of the Seventh Assembly*, 172–74.

48. BCC, *Forgotten Trinity*, vol. 1, 43.

49. Pinnock, *Flame of Love*, 241. For suggestive comments on the future of Roman Catholicism and Pentecostalism, see Habets, "*Veni Cinderella Spiritus*," 65–80.

some of these have resulted in church unions. The twentieth century has also been the century of the Holy Spirit. Not only can it be claimed that the Holy Spirit has brought the churches as close as they currently are, but it is evident that the biblical, liturgical and patristic movements of this century have combined with the ecumenical movement to foster a rediscovery of the Holy Spirit through serious theological reflection. The result has been a more complete and comprehensive theology. It is as though many of the theologies that were characteristic of the various churches have been laid out like the pieces of a jigsaw puzzle so that we gradually get a glimpse of the whole. As we approach another five hundred year mark we may be more than a little confident that as a result of "tracking the Spirit" the churches are growing together as a true sacrament of communion.[50]

The ecumenical endeavor is basic to a Spirit Christology. Spirit Christology unites Word and Spirit, East and West. It is this insight that can provide a basis for renewed discussion of the contentious *filioque* addition and move the church beyond the current ecclesiological stalemate.[51] While I cannot enter into the *filioque* debate fully, it is possible to briefly comment on what contribution a Spirit Christology may make to the discussion. The incarnation clearly highlights the *taxis* that exists within the economic Trinity. The Father sends the Son and the Son obeys the will of the Father. But we have also witnessed an alteration in the relationship between Christ and Spirit. During the incarnation Jesus was in submission to the Spirit, but, upon exaltation, Jesus became Lord of the Spirit who now pours the Spirit out on "all flesh." We have

---

50. Kelly, "Spirit, Church and the Ecumenical Endeavour," 14.

51. While the *filioque* clause is not a central concern here I note the anxiety over it that historically exists, as expressed in Needham's article "The Filioque Clause," 142–62. The Eastern tradition "pointed out that it conflicted with traditional Trinitarian theology, as wrought out in the fourth century by Athanasius and the Cappadocian fathers." For a modern restatement on this controversy see Needham who supports the Eastern view of rejecting *filioquism*, and Dabney, *Lectures in Systematic Theology*, 198–99. The Western consensus is in favor of the *filioque* clause. See Grudem, *Systematic Theology*, 246–47; Ryrie, *Holy Spirit*, 25–27; Walvoord, *Holy Spirit*, 13–17; Ferguson, *Holy Spirit*, 72–78. Unfortunately too many of these theologians gloss over the real issues involved and make too premature a judgment in favor of the addition. As long as the *monarchia* of the Godhead is clearly defined then the Eastern view of the procession or spiration of the Holy Spirit from the Father alone is no less biblically and theologically sound than a correct understanding of the Western common procession. See Haroutunian's objections to the procession in "Spirit, Holy Spirit, Spiritism," in *Dictionary of Christian Theology*, 322–23, and Heron's "Augustinian" perspective in *Holy Spirit*, 176–78, and "Who Proceedeth from the Father and the Son," 149–66.

also considered an ontological Trinitarian model that is much more dynamic than that of the Western or Eastern view, but still maintains this revealed *taxis* that is right and proper. And so within a Trinitarian Spirit Christology we can understand and concur either with the inclusion of the *filioque* with the West or the removal of the *filioque* with the East. Both positions can be seen to be right. While this may appear to sidestep the issue it really is not. It is to see the strengths of both positions and be able to maintain biblical truth and coherence, regardless of the addition or not. The Spirit is the Spirit of Sonship by which the Father is the Father of the Son and the Son is Son of the Father. This means the Spirit may proceed in one instance from the Father alone (*monarchia*) or from the Father and the Son (*filioque*).[52] Both are correct albeit different aspects of the one *simultaneous* action of the Godhead. It is only when we adopt a chronological or temporal priority to the *monarchia* of the Father, or the *spiration* of the Spirit, or the *begetting* of the Son, that genuine theological differences emerge. When they are seen as one *simultaneous* act, however, the difficulties subside.[53] The *monarchia* resides in the Godhead (Father, Son, and Spirit) along with the person of the Father. The Spirit is the Spirit of the Father as well as the Son, as we understand that without the Spirit there is no Father or Son, just as a Father requires a Son to be Father and a Son requires (in this sense) a Father to be Son.[54] Given these arguments it is my conclusion that in the interest of unity, the *filioque* clause should be dropped from the creed.[55]

The Spirit creates unity and maintains that unity. He is the one who is forming the one body of Christ on earth. As such he works for a united community; united in both Word and Spirit. As the Church moves forward in this new century may it be characterized by a movement on

52. For my own "solution" to the filioque problem, see Habets, "Filioque? Nein."

53. All Western subordinationist tendencies are removed and all Eastern *monarchian* tendencies are removed. We also remove the necessity to speak, as the East does, of the distinctions between the *theologia*, *energeia*, and *oikonomia*.

54. This formulation advances beyond the rather impersonal tendencies in Augustine's model of the Spirit as the *vinculum caritatis*. It gives the Spirit a distinct personality that has been missing in much Western theology.

55. The BCC, *Forgotten Trinity*, vol. 1, 30–34, 43, comes to the same conclusions. I am sympathetic to the outstanding historic agreement achieved on the March 13, 1991 between the World Alliance of Reformed Churches and the Eastern Orthodox churches, "Agreed Statement on the Holy Trinity," in *Theological Dialogue between Orthodox and Reformed Churches*, vol. 2, 219–26. See further in *Theological Dialogue between Orthodox and Reformed Churches*, vol. 1; and Torrance, *Trinitarian Perspectives*, 110–43.

the part of the great traditions of Christendom towards each other. My prayer is that these new proposals that build upon the old, result in open dialogue, genuine love, and a unity of purpose in calling all people to a saving relationship to the Father through the Son in the Holy Spirit.

CONCLUSION

Throughout the composition of this book two concerns have been uppermost in my mind. First, the arguments submitted here are biblical, thus honoring to God, and are in basic accord with the Great Tradition of the church of both East and West. While the book is in many ways seminal, I am convinced that its basic proposition is true and in the best sense of the term, traditional. Second, particulars of what I have written may need revision, rewriting, and even correcting at points, but the basis of what I have submitted conforms with, and further advances, traditional Christology and indeed, potentially wider areas of theology.

My aim in writing has been twofold also, the first being to present to the academic community a revision of our existing Christology and a proposal for a way forward; one that is at the same time biblical, orthodox, and culturally viable. My second aim is, that as the academy exists to serve the wider Christian community, that the Spirit Christology presented in this book will enable sincere believers to identify more with the Messiah who has become our Savior, with the Holy Spirit who conceives, equips, and sustains Christ and promises to do the same for us through recreation in the Son, and finally, with our heavenly Father who "today" receives the Son as his beloved and then, in Christ and in the Spirit, makes room in his family for each one of us.

The labor of this study has brought me peace and joy and should there be any errors, I will eagerly abandon them in light of further clarification. The desire of my heart and of this work is that it may bring glory to the Godhead—Father, Son, and Holy Spirit.

DSE

Bibliography

Abbott, W. M., editor. *The Documents of Vatican II*. New York: American, 1966.
Allchin, Arthur M. *Participation in God: A Forgotten Strand in the Anglican Tradition*. Wilton, CT: Morehouse-Barlow, 1988.
Anderson, Ray S. *Dancing with Wolves While Feeding the Sheep: The Musings of a Maverick Theologian*. Eugene, OR: Wipf & Stock, 2001.
———. *Ministry on the Fire Line: A Practical Theology for an Empowered Church*. Downers Grove, IL: IVP, 1993.
———. *The Soul of Ministry*. Kentucky: Westminster John Knox, 1997.
The Apostolic Fathers. 2nd ed. Translated by J. B. Lightfoot and J. R. Harmer. Leicester: Apollos, 1989.
Athanasius. *The Letters of Saint Athanasius Concerning the Holy Spirit*. Translated by C. R. B. Shapland, with Introduction and notes. London: Epworth, 1951.
Augustine. *The Treatise De Trinitate*. In *The Nicene and Post Nicene Fathers of the Christian Church*, first series, vol. 3. Translated by A. W. Haddan and W. G. T. Shedd.
Badcock, Gary. D. "Karl Rahner, the Trinity, and Religious Pluralism." In *The Trinity in a Pluralistic Age: Theological Essays on Culture and Religion*, edited by K. J. Vanhoozer, 143–54. Grand Rapids: Eerdmans, 1997.
———. *Light of Truth & Fire of Love: A Theology of the Holy Spirit*. Grand Rapids: Eerdmans, 1997.
Baillie, Donald M. *God Was in Christ*. 2nd ed. New York: Scribner's, 1948.
Bajis, Jordan. *Common Ground: An Introduction to Eastern Christianity for the American Christian*. Minneapolis: Light & Life, 1991.
Balz, Horst, and Gerhard Schneider, editors. *Exegetical Dictionary of the New Testament*. 3 vols. Grand Rapids: Eerdmans, 1993.
Barnett, Paul W. *Is the New Testament History?* Ann Arbor: Servant, 1986.
———. *Jesus and the Logic of History*. Leicester: Apollos, 1997.
Barr, James. *The Semantics of Biblical Language*. New York: Oxford University Press, 1961.
Barrett, C. Kingsley. "The Holy Spirit and the Gospel Tradition." *Expository Times* 67 (1956) 142–45.
———. *The Holy Spirit and the Gospel Tradition*. 2nd ed. London: SPCK, 1966.
Barth, Karl. *Church Dogmatics*. 4 vols. Edited by G. W. Bromiley and T. F Torrance. Translated by G. W. Bromiley. Edinburgh: T. & T. Clark, 1956–1975.
———. "Concluding Unscientific Postscript on Schleiermacher." In *The Theology of Schleiermacher*, edited by D. Ritschl, 261–79. Translated by G. W. Bromiley. Grand Rapids: Eerdmans, 1982.
———. *The Holy Ghost and the Christian Life*. Translated by R. B. Hoyle. London: Muller, 1938.

———. "Rudolf Bultmann: An Attempt to Understand Him." In *Kerygma and Myth*, vol. 2, edited by H. W. Bartsch, 83–132. London: SPCK, 1972.

Basil the Great. *The Treatise De Spiritu Sancto*. In *The Nicene and Post Nicene Fathers of the Christian Church*, vol 8. Translated by B. Jackson.

Battles, Ford L. *Analysis of the Institutes of the Christian Religion of John Calvin*. Grand Rapids: Baker, 1980.

Bauckham, Richard J. "The Future of Jesus Christ." *Scottish Bulletin of Evangelical Theology* 16 (1998) 97–110.

———. *God Crucified: Monotheism and Christology in the New Testament*, Carlisle: Paternoster, 1998.

———. "Jürgen Moltmann's *The Trinity and the Kingdom of God* and the Question of Pluralism." In *The Trinity in a Pluralistic Age: Theological Essays on Culture and Religion*, edited by K. J. Vanhoozer, 155–64. Grand Rapids: Eerdmans, 1997.

———. "The Worship of Jesus in Apocalyptic Christianity." *New Testament Studies* 27 (1980/81) 322–41.

———. "The Worship of Jesus in Philippians 2:9–11." In *Where Christology Began: Essays on Philippians 2*, edited by R. P. Martin and B. Dodd, 128–39. Louisville: Westminster, 1998.

———. *Jesus and the God of Israel: God Crucified and Other Studies on the New Testament's Christology of Divine Identity*. Grand Rapids: Eerdmans, 2008.

Beck, T. David. *The Holy Spirit and the Renewal of All Things: Pneumatology in Paul and Jurgen Moltmann*. Princeton Theological Monograph Series. Eugene, OR: Pickwick, 2007.

Berkhof, Hendrikus. *Christian Faith: An Introduction to the Study of the Faith*. Grand Rapids: Eerdmans, 1979.

———. *The Doctrine of the Holy Spirit*. London: Epworth, 1965.

Berkhof, Louis. *Systematic Theology*. Edinburgh: Banner of Truth, 1939.

Berkouwer, Gerrit C. *The Person of Christ*. Grand Rapids: Eerdmans, 1954.

Betz, Hans D. "Jesus as Divine Man." In *Jesus and the Historian: Written in Honor of Ernest Cadman Colwell*, edited by F. T. Trotter, 114–33. Philadelphia: Westminster, 1978.

Bettenson, Henry. *The Early Christian Fathers*. Oxford: Oxford University Press, 1969.

———. *The Later Christian Fathers*. Oxford: Oxford University Press, 1972.

Bilezikian, Gilbert. "Hermeneutical Bungee-Jumping: Subordination in the Godhead." *Journal of the Evangelical Theological Society* 40 (1997) 57–68.

Bindley, T. Herbert, editor. *The Oecumenical Documents of the Faith*. 4th ed. London: Methuen, 1950.

Black, Matthew. "The Christological Use of the Old Testament in the New Testament." *New Testament Studies* 18 (1971–1972) 1–14.

Blaising, Craig A. "Chalcedon and Christology: A 1530th Anniversary." *Bibliotheca Sacra* 138 (1981) 326–37.

Blocher, Henri. "Immanence and Transcendence in Trinitarian Theology." In *The Trinity in a Pluralistic Age: Theological Essays on Culture and Religion*, edited by K. J. Vanhoozer, 104–23. Grand Rapids: Eerdmans, 1997.

Block, Darrell I. "The Prophet of the Spirit: The Use of *RWH* in The Book of Ezekiel." *Journal of the Evangelical Theological Society* 32 (1989) 27–49.

Bibliography

Bloesch, Donald G. "A Christological Hermeneutic: Crisis and Conflict in Hermeneutics." In *The Use of the Bible in Theology: Evangelical Options*, edited by R. K. Johnston, 78–102. Atlanta: John Knox, 1985.

———. *A Theology of Word & Spirit: Authority and Method in Theology*. Christian Foundations 1. Downers Grove, IL: IVP, 1992.

———. *Holy Scripture: Revelation, Inspiration, and Interpretation*. Christian Foundations 2. Downers Grove, IL: InterVarsity, 1994.

———. *God The Almighty*. Christian Foundations 3. Downers Grove, IL: InterVarsity, 1995.

———. *Jesus Christ: Savior and Lord*. Christian Foundations 4. Downers Grove, IL: InterVarsity, 1997.

———. *The Holy Spirit: Works and Gifts*. Christian Foundations 5. Downers Grove, IL: InterVarsity, 2000.

———. *The Church: Sacraments, Worship, Ministry, Mission*. Christian Foundations 6. Downers Grove, IL: InterVarsity, 2002.

———. *The Last Things: Resurrection, Judgment, Glory*. Christian Foundations 7. Downers Grove, IL: InterVarsity, 2004.

Blomberg, Craig L. *The Historical Reliability of the Gospels*. Downers Grove, IL: InterVarsity, 1987.

———. *Jesus and the Gospels*. Leicester: Apollos, 1997.

Bobrinskoy, Boris. "The Holy Spirit in the Bible and the Church." *Ecumenical Review* 41 (1989) 357–62.

———. "The Indwelling of the Spirit in Christ: 'Pneumatic Christology' in the Cappadocian Fathers." *St Vladimir's Theological Quarterly* 28 (1984) 49–65.

Bock, Darrell L. *Luke*. IVPNTCS. Downers Grove, IL: InterVarsity, 1994.

Bockmuehl, Markus. *This Jesus: Martyr, Lord, Messiah*. Edinburgh: T. & T. Clark, 1994.

———. "'To Be Or Not To Be': The Possible Futures of New Testament Scholarship." *Scottish Journal of Theology* 51 (1998) 271–306.

Boersma, Hans. "The Chalcedonian Definition." *Westminster Theological Journal* 94 (1992) 47–63.

Boff, Leonardo. *The Trinity and Society*. New York: Orbis, 1988.

Bonnington, Mark. "The Obedient Son: Jesus in Gethsemane." *Anvil* 16. Online: www.anvil-journal.co.uk, 1–7.

Borgen, Peder. "Jesus Christ, the Reception of the Spirit, and a Cross-National Community." *Jesus of Nazareth: Lord and Christ. Essays on the Historical Jesus and New Testament Christology*, edited by J. B. Green and M. M. B. Turner, 220–35. Grand Rapids: Eerdmans, 1994.

Bousset, Wilhelm. *Kyrios Christos: A History of the Belief in Christ from the Beginning of Christianity to Irenaeus*. Nashville: Abingdon, 1913, reprinted 1970.

Bouyer, Louis. "Christology from Above and Christology from Below." *Word and Spirit: A Monastic Review* 5 [Christology] (1983) 20–23.

Boyd, Gregory A. *Cynic Sage or Son of God? Recovering the Real Jesus in an Age of Revisionist Replies*. Wheaton, IL: Bridgepoint, 1995.

———. *Jesus Under Siege*. Wheaton, IL: Victor, 1995.

Braaten, Carl E. "The Significance of New Testament Christology for Systematic Theology." In *Who Do You Say That I Am? Essays on Christology*, edited by M. A. Powell and D. R. Bauer, 216–27. Louisville: Westminster, 1999.

———. "The Trinity Today." *Dialog* 26 (1987) 245–75.

Branick, Vincent P. "The Sinful Flesh of the Son of God (Rom 8:3): A Key Image of Pauline Theology." *Catholic Biblical Quarterly* 47 (1985) 246–62.

Bray, Gerald. "Can We Dispense With Chalcedon?" *Themelios* NS 3 (1978) 2–9.

———. *The Doctrine of God*. Contours of Christian Theology. Leicester: InterVarsity, 1993.

Breck, John. "The Lord is the Spirit: An Essay in Christological Pneumatology." *Ecumenical Review* 42 (1990) 114–21.

———. "The Relevance of Nicene Christology." *St Vladimir's Theological Quarterly* 31 (1987) 41–64.

British Council of Churches. *The Forgotten Trinity*, vol. 1, *The Report of the BCC Study Commission on Trinitarian Doctrine Today*. London: BCC, 1989.

———. *The Forgotten Trinity*, vol. 2, *A Study Guide on Issues Contained in the Report of the BCC Study Commission on Trinitarian Doctrine Today*. London: BCC, 1989.

———. *The Forgotten Trinity*, vol. 3, *A Selection of Papers presented to the The BCC Study Commission on Trinitarian Doctrine Today*, edited by A. I. C. Heron. London: BCC, 1991.

Brown, Colin. "Christology and the Quest of the Historical Jesus." In *Doing Theology for the People of God: Studies in Honour of J. I. Packer*, edited by D. Lewis and A. McGrath, 67–86. Leicester: Apollos, 1996.

———. "Ernst Lohmeyer's *Kyrios Jesus*." In *Where Christology Began: Essays on Philippians 2*, edited by R. P. Martin and B. Dodd, 6–42. Louisville: Westminster, 1998.

———. "Historical Jesus, Quest of." In *Dictionary of Jesus and the Gospels*, edited by J. B. Green and S. McKnight, 326–41. Downers Grove, IL: InterVarsity, 1992.

———. *Jesus in European Protestant Thought: 1778–1860*. Grand Rapids: Baker, 1985.

———. *Miracles and the Critical Mind*. Grand Rapids: Eerdmans, 1984.

———, editor. *The New International Dictionary of New Testament Theology*. 4 vols. Grand Rapids: Regency, 1971.

———. "Person of Christ." In *The International Standard Bible Encyclopedia*, vol. 3. Edited by G. W. Bromiley, 781–801. Grand Rapids: Eerdmans, 1981.

———. "Spirit: other words used in connection with." *The New International Dictionary of New Testament Theology*, vol. 3 (Grand Rapid: Zondervan, 1975–1978) 707–9.

———. "Synoptic Miracle Stories: A Jewish Religious and Social Setting." *Foundations and Facets Forum* 2 (1986) 55–76.

———. "Trinity and Incarnation: In Search of Contemporary Orthodoxy." *Ex Auditu* 7 (1991) 83–100.

Brown, Harold O. J. *The Image of Christ in the Mirror of Heresy and Orthodoxy from the Apostles to the Present*. Garden City, NY: Doubleday, 1984.

Brown, Raymond E. *The Birth of the Messiah: A Commentary on the Infancy Narratives in Matthew and Luke*. Garden City, NY: Doubleday, 1977.

———. *Jesus God and Man: Modern Biblical Reflections*. London: Chapman, 1968.

———. *The Gospel According to John*. London: Chapman, 1971.

———. *An Introduction to New Testament Christology*. New York: Paulist, 1994.

———. "The Paraclete in the Fourth Gospel." *New Testament Studies* 13 (1967) 113–32.

———. *The Virginal Conception and Bodily Resurrection of Jesus*. London: Chapman, 1973.

Brown, Robert F. "On God's Ontic and Noetic Absoluteness: A Critique of Barth." *Scottish Journal of Theology* 33 (1980) 533–49.

Bruce, Alexander B. *The Humiliation of Christ in its Physical, Ethical and Official Aspects.* 2nd ed. New York: Hodder & Stoughton, nd.

Bruce, Frederick F. *Jesus: Lord and Savior.* Downers Grove, IL: InterVarsity, 1986.

———. *The New Testament Documents: Are They Reliable?* Grand Rapids: Eerdmans, 1960.

Brunner, Emil. *The Christian Doctrine of Creation and Redemption.* Translated by O. Wyon and D. Cairns. London: Lutterworth, 1952.

———. *The Christian Doctrine of God.* Translated by O. Wyon. Philadelphia: Westminster, 1974.

———. *The Mediator.* London: Lutterworth, 1934.

Bultmann, Rudolf. *Theology of the New Testament.* London: SCM, 1952.

Burge, Gary H. *The Anointed Community: The Holy Spirit in the Johannine Tradition.* Grand Rapids: Eerdmans, 1987.

Burgess, Stanley M., and Gary B. McGee, editors. *Dictionary of Pentecostal and Charismatic Movements.* Grand Rapids: Zondervan, 1988.

———. *The Spirit and the Church: Antiquity.* Peabody, Hendrickson, 1984.

Burkhardt, Helmut. *The Biblical Doctrine of Regeneration.* Translated by O. R. Johnston. Downers Grove, IL: InterVarsity, 1978.

Burleigh, John H. S. "The Doctrine of the Holy Spirit in the Latin Fathers." *Scottish Journal of Theology* 7 (1954) 113–32.

Burns, J. Patout, and Gerald M. Fagin. *The Holy Spirit: Message of the Fathers of the Church.* Wilmington, DE: Glazier, 1984.

Buswell, J. Oliver. *A Systematic Theology of the Christian Religion.* 2 vols. Grand Rapids: Zondervan, 1962.

Caird, George B. "The Development of the Doctrine of Christ in the New Testament." In *Christ for Us Today,* edited by N. Pittenger, 66–80. London: SPCK, 1968.

———. *New Testament Theology,* edited by L. D. Hurst. Oxford: Clarendon, 1994.

Calvert, David G. A. *From Christology to God: A Study of Some Trends, Problems and Possibilities in Contemporary Christology.* London: Epworth, 1983.

Calvin, John. *Calvin's New Testament Commentaries, vol. 12: Hebrews and 1 and 2 Peter.* Translated by W. B. Johnston. Edited by D. W. and T. F. Torrance. Grand Rapids: Eerdmans, 1963.

———. *Institutes of the Christian Religion.* 1559 Edition. 2 vols. Translated by H. Beveridge. London: Clark, 1953.

Campbell, Theodore C. "The Doctrine of the Holy Spirit in Athanasius." *Scottish Journal of Theology* 27 (1974) 408–40.

Carey, George. *God Incarnate: Meeting the Contemporary Challenges to Classic Christian Doctrine.* Downers Grove, IL: InterVarsity, 1978.

Carr, Wesley. "Towards a Contemporary Doctrine of the Holy Spirit." *Scottish Journal of Theology* 28 (1975) 501–16.

Carson, Donald A. "The Function of the Paraclete in John 16:7–11." *Journal of Biblical Theology* 98 (1979) 547–66.

———. "When is Spirituality Spiritual? Reflections on Some Problems of Definition." *Journal of the Evangelical Theological Society* 37 (1994) 381–94.

Casey, M. *From Jewish Prophet to Gentile God: The Origins and Development of New Testament Christology.* Cambridge: Clarke, 1991.

Chadwick, Henry. "Eucharist and Christology in the Nestorian Controversy." *Journal of Theological Studies* 2 (1951) 145–64.

———. *Early Christian Thought and the Classical Tradition*. Oxford: Oxford University Press, 1966.

Charlesworth, J. H., editor. *The Messiah: Developments in Earliest Judaism and Christianity*. Minneapolis: Fortress, 1992.

Chesterton, Gilbert K. *Orthodoxy*. Great Britain: Hodder & Stoughton, 1996.

Chestnut, Roberta C. *The Monophysite Christologies: Severus of Antioch, Philoxenus of Mabbug, and Jacob of Sarug*. Oxford: Oxford University Press, 1976.

Chitescu, Nicolas. "Position of Some Orthodox and Roman Catholic Theologians on the Wills of the Person of Jesus Christ and the Problem of Relations with the Non-Chalcedonians." *Greek Orthodox Theologcial Review* 13 (1968) 288–308.

Clark, Norman S. "Spirit Christology in the Light of Eucharistic Theology." *Heythrop Journal* 23 (1982) 270–84.

Clements, Keith, editor. *Friedrich Schleiermacher: Pioneer of Modern Theology*. Edinburgh: T. & T. Clark, 1987.

Clendenin, Daniel B. "Partakers of Divinity: The Orthodox Doctrine of Theosis." *Journal of the Evangelical Theological Society* 37 (1994) 365–79.

Clendenin, Daniel B. "The Deification of Humanity: Theosis." In *Eastern Orthodox Christianity: A Western Perspective*. Grand Rapids: Baker Book House (1994) 117–37.

Clifford, Alan C. *Atonement and Justification: English Evangelical Theology 1640–1790—An Evaluation*. Oxford: Clarendon, 1990.

Clines, David J. "The Image of God in Man." *Tyndale Bulletin* 19 (1968) 53–103.

Coffey, David M. "The Gift of the Holy Spirit." *Irish Theological Quarterly* 38 (1971) 202–33.

———. *Grace: The Gift of the Holy Spirit*. Sydney: Catholic Institute of Sydney, 1979.

Coffey, David M. *"Did You Receive the Holy Spirit When You Believed?" Some Basic Questions for Pneumatology*. Milwaukee: Marquette University Press, 2005.

———. "The Holy Spirit as the Mutual Love of the Father and the Son." *Theological Studies* 51 (1990) 193–229.

———. "The 'Incarnation' of the Holy Spirit in Christ." *Theological Studies* 45 (1984) 466–80.

———. "A Proper Mission of the Holy Spirit." *Theological Studies* 47 (1986) 227–50.

———. "Spirit Christology and the Trinity." In *Advents of the Spirit: An Introduction to the Current Study of Pneumatology*, edited by B. E. Hinze and D. L. Dabney, 315–38. Milwaukee: Marquette University Press, 2001.

———. "The Theandric Nature of Christ." *Theological Studies* 60 (1999) 405–431.

———. *Deus Trinitas: The Doctrine of the Triune God*. New York: Oxford University Press, 1999.

Colyer, Elmer M. *The Nature of Doctrine in T. F. Torrance's Theology*. Eugene, OR: Wipf & Stock, 2001.

"Come Holy Spirit—Renew the Whole Creation." In *Signs of the Spirit: Official Report of the Seventh Assembly of the WCC, Canberra, 1991*. Edited by Michael Kinnamon. Geneva: WCC, 1991.

Congar, Yves M. J. *I Believe in the Holy Spirit*. 3 vols. Translated by D. Smith. New York: Seabury, 1983.

———. "Pour Une Christologie Pneumatologique." *Revue Des Sciences Philosophiques Et Theologiques* 63 (1979) 435–42.

———. *The Revelation of God.* Translated by A. Manson and L. C. Sheppard. New York: Herder & Herder, 1968.
———. *The Word and the Spirit.* Translated by D. Smith. London: Geoffrey Chapman, 1986.
Corney, Tim. "Seeking Hope in the Ruins of Modernity." *Zadok Perspectives* 49 (1995). Online: http://www.gospel-culture.org.uk/2000.htm.
Cowdell, Scott. *Is Jesus Unique: A Study of Recent Christology.* New York: Paulist, 1996.
Craig, William L. *Assessing the New Testament Evidence for the Historicity of the Resurrection of Jesus.* Lampeter: Mellen, 1989.
———. *Reasonable Faith.* Illinois: Crossway, 1994.
Cranfield, Charles E. B. "Some Reflections on the Subject of the Virgin Birth." *Scottish Journal of Theology* 41 (1988) 177–89.
Crawford, R. G. "The Relation of the Divinity and the Humanity in Christ." *Evangelical Quarterly* 53 (1981) 237–40.
Crisp, Oliver D. "Did Christ Have a Fallen Human Nature?" *International Journal of Systematic Theology* 6 (2004) 270–88.
———. "Was Christ Sinless or Impeccable?" *Irish Theological Quarterly* 72 (2007) 168–86.
Cross, Terry L. "Toward a Theology of the Word and the Spirit: A Review of J. Rodman Williams's *Renewal Theology*." *Journal of Pentecostal Theology* 3 (1993) 113–35.
Crossan, John D. *The Historical Jesus: The Life of a Mediterranean Peasant.* San Francisco: Harper, 1992.
Cullmann, Oscar. *The Christology of the New Testament.* London: SCM, 1959.
———. "The Reply of Professor Cullmann to Roman Catholic Critics." *Scottish Journal of Theology* 15 (1962) 36–43.
Cunliffe-Jones, Hubert, and Benjamin Drewery, editors. *A History of Christian Doctrine.* Edinburgh: T. & T. Clark, 1978.
Cunningham, David S. *These Three Are One: The Practice of Trinitarian Theology.* Oxford: Blackwell, 1998.
Dabney, D. Lyle. "The Advent of the Spirit: The Turn to Pneumatology in the Theology of Jürgen Moltmann." *Asbury Theological Journal* 48 (1993) 81–107.
———. *Die Kenosis des Geists: Kontinuität zwischen Schöpfung und Erlösung im Werk des Heiligen Geistes.* Neukirchen-Vluyn: Neukirchener, 1997.
———. "Jürgen Moltmann and John Wesley's Third Article Theology." *Wesleyan Theological Journal* 29 (1994) 140–48.
———. "The Justification of the Spirit: Soteriological Reflections on the Resurrection;" In *Starting with the Spirit: Task of Theology II*, edited by G. Preece and S. Pickard, 59–82. Hindmarsh, SA: Australian Theological Forum, 2001.
———. "Naming the Spirit: Toward a Pneumatology of the Cross;" In *Starting with the Spirit: Task of Theology II*, edited by G. Preece and S. Pickard, 28–58. Hindmarsh, SA: Australian Theological Forum, 2001.
———. "The Nature of the Spirit: Creation as a Premonition of God," In *Starting with the Spirit: Task of Theology II*, edited by G. Preece and S. Pickard, 83–110. Hindmarsh, SA: Australian Theological Forum, 2001.
———. "Otherwise Engaged in the Spirit: A First Theology for a Twenty-first Century." In *The Future of Theology: Essays in Honor of Jürgen Moltmann*, edited by M. Volf et al, 154–63. Grand Rapids: Eerdmans, 1996.

———. "Starting with the Spirit: Why the Last Should be First." In *Starting with the Spirit: Task of Theology II*, edited by G. Preece and S. Pickard, 3–27. Hindmarsh, SA: Australian Theological Forum, 2001.

Dabney, Robert L. *Lectures in Systematic Theology*. Edinburgh: Banner of Truth, 1972.

Dahl, Nils A. *Jesus the Christ: The Historical Origins of Christological Doctrine*. Minneapolis: Fortress, 1991.

Daniélou, Jean. *A History of Early Christian Doctrine Before the Council of Nicaea. Vol. 1: The History of Jewish Christianity*. Translated J. A. Baker. London: Darton, Longman & Todd, 1971.

Davidson, Ivor J. "Pondering the Sinlessness of Jesus Christ: Moral Christologies and the Witness of Scripture." *International Journal of Systematic Theology* 10 (2008) 372–98.

———. "Reappropriating Patristic Christology: One Doctrine, Two Styles." *Irish Theological Quarterly* 67 (2002) 225–39.

———. "Theologizing the Human Jesus: An Ancient (and Modern) Approach to Christology Reassessed." *International Journal of Systematic Theology* 3 (2001) 129–53.

Davies, W. D., and Dale C. Allison. *A Critical and Exegetical Commentary on the Gospel according to Saint Matthew*. International Critical Commentary. Edinburgh: Clark, 1988.

Dawe, Donald G. "The Divinity of the Holy Spirit." *Interpretation* 33 (1979) 19–31.

Dawson, Gerrit S. *Jesus Ascended: The Meaning of Christ's Continuing Incarnation*. New York: T. & T. Clark, 2004.

De Jonge, Marinus. *Christology in Context: The Earliest Christian Response to Jesus*. Philadelphia: Westminster, 1988.

———. "The Earliest Christian Use of *Christos*: Some Suggestions." *New Testament Studies* 32 (1986) 321–43.

———. *Early Christianity and Jesus' Own View of His Mission*. Grand Rapids: Eerdmans, 1998.

———. "Jewish Expectations About the 'Messiah' According to the Fourth Gospel." *New Testament Studies* 19 (1973) 246–70.

———. "The Use of *ho christos* in the Passion Narratives." In *Jesus aux origines de la christlogie*, edited by J. Dupont, 169–92. Leuven: Leuven University, 1975.

———. "The Use of the Word 'Anointed' in the Time of Jesus." *Novum Testamentum* 8 (1966) 132–48.

De Margerei, Bertrand. *The Christian Trinity in History*. Massachusetts: St. Bede's Publications, 1982.

Deiter, Melvin E. "The Wesleyan/Holiness and Pentecostal Movements: Commonalities, Confrontation, and Dialogue." *Pneuma* 12 (1990) 4–13.

Del Colle, Ralph. *Christ and the Spirit: Spirit Christology in Trinitarian Perspective*. New York: Oxford University Press, 1994.

———. "Oneness and Trinity: A Preliminary Proposal for Dialogue with Oneness Pentecostalism." *Journal of Pentecostal Theology* 10 (1997) 85–110.

———. "A Response to Jürgen Moltmann and David Coffey." In *Advents of the Spirit: An Introduction to the Current Study of Pneumatology*, edited by B. E. Hinze and D. L. Dabney, 339–46. Milwaukee: Marquette University Press, 2001.

———. "Spirit-Christology: Dogmatic Foundations for Pentecostal-Charismatic Spirituality." *Journal of Pentecostal Theology* 3 (1993) 91–112.

———. "Trinity and Temporality: A Pentecostal/Charismatic Perspective." *Journal of Pentecostal Theology* 8 (1996) 99–113.
Demarest, Bruce A. "Christendom's Creeds: Their Relevance in the Modern World." *Journal of the Evangelical Theological Society* 21 (1978) 345–56.
Denney, James. "The Holy Spirit." In *A Dictionary of Christ and the Gospels*, edited by J. Hastings, 731–44. Edinburgh: T. & T. Clark, 1906.
Dix, Gregory. *Jew and Greek: A Study in the Primitive Church*. Westminster: Dacre, 1953.
Dobbin, Edmund J. "Towards a Theology of the Holy Spirit. I." *Heythrop Journal* 17 (1976) 5–19.
———. "Towards a Theology of the Holy Spirit. II." *Heythrop Journal* 17 (1976) 129–49.
Dominian, Jack. *One Like Us: A Psychological Interpretation of Jesus*. London: Darton, Longman & Todd, 1998.
Doriani, Daniel. "The Deity of Christ in the Synoptic Gospels." *Journal of the Evangelical Theological Society* 37 (1994) 333–50.
Dumbrell, William J. "Grace and Truth: The Progress of the Argument of the Prologue of John's Gospel." In *Doing Theology for the People of God: Studies in Honour of J. I. Packer*, edited by D. Lewis and A. McGrath, 105–22. Leicester: Apollos, 1996.
Duncan, George S. *Jesus, Son of Man*. New York: Macmillan, 1949.
Duncan, John. *Colloquia Peripatetica*. 3rd ed. Edinburgh: n.p. 1871.
Dunn, James D. G. "1 Corinthians 15.45—Last Adam, Life-giving Spirit." In *Christ and Spirit in the New Testament*, edited by B. Lindars and S. S. Smalley, 127–42. Cambridge: Cambridge University Press, 1973.
———. "2 Corinthians 3.17—'The Lord is Spirit.'" *Journal of Theological Studies* 21 (1970) 309–20.
———. *Baptism in the Holy Spirit: A Re-examination of the New Testament Teaching on the Gift of the Spirit in Relation to Pentecostalism Today*. London: SCM, 1970.
———. "Baptism in the Spirit: A Response to Pentecostal Scholarship on Luke-Acts." *Journal of Pentecostal Theology* 3 (1993) 3–27.
———. "Christ, Adam, and Preexistence." In *Where Christology Began: Essays on Philippians 2*, edited by R. P. Martin and B. Dodd, 74–83. Louisville: Westminster, 1998.
———. *The Christ and the Spirit*, (Collected Essays) vol. 1. *Christology*. Grand Rapids: Eerdmans, 1998.
———. *The Christ and the Spirit*, (Collected Essays) vol. 2. *Pneumatology*. Grand Rapids: Eerdmans, 1998.
———. "Christology as an Aspect of Theology." In *The Future of Christology: Essays in Honor of Leander E. Keck*, edited by A. J. Malherbe and W. A. Meeks, 202–12. Minneapolis: Fortress, 1993.
———. *Christology in the Making*. Philadelphia: Westminster, 1980.
———. "Jesus—Flesh and Spirit: An Exposition of Romans 1:3–4." *Journal of Theological Studies* 24 (1973) 40–68.
———. *Jesus and the Spirit: A Study of the Religious and Charismatic Experience of Jesus and the First Christians as Reflected in the New Testament*. Philadelphia: Westminster, 1975.

———. "The Making of Christology—Evolution or Unfolding?" *Jesus of Nazareth: Lord and Christ. Essays on the Historical Jesus and New Testament Christology*, edited by J. B. Green and M. M. B. Turner, 437–52. Grand Rapids: Eerdmans, 1994.

———. "Messianic Ideas and Their Influence on the Jesus of History." In *The Messiah: Developments in Earliest Judaism and Christianity*, edited by J. H. Charlesworth, 365–81. Minneapolis: Fortress, 1992.

———. "The Messianic Secret in Mark." In *The Messianic Secret*, edited by C. Tuckett, 116–31. Philadelphia: Fortress, 1988.

———. *The Partings of the Ways: Between Christianity and Judaism and Their Significance for the Character of Christianity*. London: SCM, 1991.

———. "Rediscovering the Spirit." *Expository Times* 84 (1972–1973) 7–12.

———. "Rediscovering the Spirit (2)." *Expository Times* 94 (1982–1983) 9–18.

———. "Spirit: In the New Testament." In *New International Dictionary of New Testament Theology*, vol. 3, 693–707.

———. *The Theology of Paul the Apostle*. Grand Rapids: Eerdmans, 1998.

———. *Unity and Diversity in the New Testament: An Inquiry into the Character of Earliest Christianity*. London: SCM, 1977.

Dunn, James D.G., and James P. Mackey. *New Testament Theology in Dialogue*. Great Britain: SPCK, 1987).

Dupuis, Jacques. *Toward a Christian Theology of Religious Pluralism*. Maryknoll, NY: Orbis, 1997.

Durrwell, Francois-Xavier. *Holy Spirit of God: An Essay in Biblical Theology*. Translated by B. Davies. London: Geoffrey Chapman, 1986.

Easley, Kendall H. "The Pauline usage of *Pneumati* as a Reference to the Spirit of God." *Journal of the Evangelical Theological Society* 27 (1984) 299–313.

Edwards, James R. "The Baptism of Jesus According to the Gospel of Mark." *Journal of the Evangelical Theological Society* 34 (1991) 43–57.

Egan, John P. "Toward Trinitarian Perichoresis: Saint Gregory the Theologian (Oration) 31.14." *Greek Orthodox Theological Review* 39 (1994) 83–93.

Eichrodt, Walter. *Theology of the Old Testament*. 2 vols. Translated by J. A. Baker. London: SCM, 1967.

Ellingworth, Paul. "Christology: Synchronic or Diachronic." *Jesus of Nazareth: Lord and Christ. Essays on the Historical Jesus and New Testament Christology*, edited by J. B. Green and M. M. B. Turner, 489–500. Grand Rapids: Eerdmans, 1994.

Ellis, Earl E. "Christ and Spirit in 1 Corinthians." In *Christ and Spirit in the New Testament: Studies in Honour of Charles Francis Digby Moule*, edited by B. Lindars and S. S. Smalley, 269–77. Cambridge: Cambridge University Press, 1973.

———. *Pauline Theology: Ministry and Society*. Grand Rapids: Eerdmans, 1989.

Elmore, Floyd S. "An Evangelical Analysis of Process Pneumatology." *Bibliotheca Sacra* 145 (1988) 15–29.

Elwell, Walter, editor. *Evangelical Dictionary of Theology*. Grand Rapids: Baker, 1984.

Enns, Paul. *The Moody Handbook of Theology*. Chicago: Moody, 1989.

Enns, Peter. *Inspiration and Incarnation*. Grand Rapids: Baker, 2005.

Erickson, Millard J. *Christian Theology*. Grand Rapids: Baker, 1983.

———. "Christology from Above and Christology from Below: A Study of Contrasting Methodologies." In *Perspectives on Evangelical Theology*, edited by K. S. Kantzer and S. N. Gundry, 43–55. Grand Rapids: Baker, 1979.

———. *God in Three Persons: A Contemporary Interpretation of the Trinity*. Grand Rapids: Baker, 1995.

———. *The Word Became Flesh*. Grand Rapids: Baker, 1991.

Evans, Craig A. *Jesus*. Grand Rapids: Baker, 1992.

———. *Life of Jesus Research: An Annotated Bibliography*. Leiden: Brill, 1989.

Ewert, David. *The Holy Spirit in the New Testament*. Scottdale, PA: Herald, 1979.

Fackre, Gabriel. "Jesus Christ in Bloesch's Theology." In *Evangelical Theology in Transition: Theologians in Dialogue with Donald Bloesch*, edited by E. M. Colyer, 98–118. Downers Grove, IL: InterVarsity, 1999.

Farrow, Douglas. *Ascension and Ecclesia: On the Significance of the Doctrine of the Ascension and for Ecclesiology and Christian Cosmology*. Edinburgh: T. & T. Clark, 1999.

Fatula, Mary A. *The Triune God of Christian Faith*. Collegeville: Liturgical Press, 1990.

Fee, Gordon D. "Christology and Pneumatology in Romans 8.9–11—and Elsewhere: Some Reflections on Paul as a Trinitarian." In *Jesus of Nazareth: Lord and Christ. Essays on the Historical Jesus and New Testament Christology*, edited by J. B. Green and M. M. B. Turner, 312–31. Grand Rapids: Eerdmans, 1994.

———. *Gods Empowering Presence: The Holy Spirit in the Letters of Paul*. Peabody: Hendrickson, 1994.

———. "God's Empowering Presence: A Response to Eduard Schweitzer." *Journal of Pentecostal Theology* 8 (1996) 23–30.

———. *Gospel and Spirit: Issues in New Testament Hermeneutics*. Peabody: Hendrickson, 1990.

———. *Listening to the Spirit in the Text*. Grand Rapids: Eerdmans, 2000.

———. *Paul, the Spirit, and the People of God*. Peabody: Hendrickson, 1996.

———. *Pauline Christology: An Exegetical-Theological Study*. Peabody: Hendrickson, 2007.

Feenstra, Ronald J., and Cornelius Plantinga, editors. *Trinity, Incarnation, and Atonement: Philosophical and Theological Essays*. Notre Dame: University of Notre Dame, 1989.

Ferguson, Sinclair B. *The Holy Spirit*. Contours of Christian Theology. London: InterVarsity, 1996.

Fichte, Johann G. *The Way Towards the Blessed Life*. London: Chapman, 1849.

Fiddes, Paul. *The Creative Suffering of God*. Oxford: Clarendon, 1988.

Fitzmeyer, Joseph A. "The Ascension of Christ and Pentecost." *Theological Studies* 45 (1984) 409–40.

Forbes, Christopher. *Prophecy and Inspired Speech in Early Christianity and its Hellenistic Environment*. Peabody: Hendrickson, 1997.

Forde, Gerald O. *On Being a Theologian of the Cross: Reflections on Luther's Heidelberg Disputation, 1518*. Grand Rapids: Eerdmans, 1997.

Fowl, Stephen E. *Engaging Scripture: A Model for Theological Interpretation*. Malden, MA: Blackwell, 1998.

France, Richard T. *The Evidence for Jesus*. Downers Grove, IL: InterVarsity, 1986.

———. "The Worship of Jesus: A Neglected Factor in Christological Debate?" In *Christ the Lord: Studies in Christology Presented to Donald Guthrie*, edited by H. H. Rowden, 50–70. Downers Grove, IL: InterVarsity, 1982.

Francis, D. Pitt. "The Holy Spirit A Statistical Inquiry." *Expository Times* 96 (1985) 136–37.

Frei, Hans. *The Identity of Jesus Christ*. Philadelphia: Fortress, 1975.
Frend, William H. C. *The Rise of the Monophysite Movement: Chapters in the History of the Church in the Fifth and Sixth Centuries*. Cambridge: Cambridge University Press, 1972.
Fuller, Daniel P. *Easter Faith and History*. London: Tyndale, 1965.
———. "A New German Theological Movement." *Scottish Journal of Theology* 19 (1996) 160–75.
Fuller, Reginald H. *Christ and Christianity: Studies in the Formation of Christology*. Valley Forge, PA: Trinity, 1994.
———. *The Foundations of New Testament Christology*. New York: Scribner's, 1965.
Fuller, Reginald H., and Pheme Perkins. *Who is This Christ? Gospel Christology and Contemporary Faith*. Philadelphia: Fortress, 1983.
Funk, Robert W. et al., and the Jesus Seminar, editors. *The Five Gospels: The Search for the Authentic Words of Jesus, New Translation and Commentary*. New York: Macmillan, 1993.
Gaffin, Richard B. *Perspectives on Pentecost*. Phillipsburg: Presbyterian and Reformed, 1979.
Garlington, Don B. "Jesus, the Unique Son of God: Tested and Faithful." *Bibliotheca Sacra* 151 (1994) 284–308.
Galot, Jean. *The Person of Christ*. Chicago: Franciscan Herald, 1983.
Gaventa, Beverly R., and Richard B. Hays editors. *Seeking the Identity of Jesus: A Pilgrimage*. Grand Rapids: Eerdmans, 2008.
Gaybba, Brian. *The Spirit of Love*. London: Geoffrey Chapman, 1987.
Geisler, Norman L. *Thomas Aquinas: An Evangelical Appraisal*. Grand Rapids: Baker, 1991.
Gleason, Randall. "B. B. Warfield and Lewis S. Chafer on Sanctification." *Journal of the Evangelical Theological Society* 40 (1997) 241–56.
Gonzalez, Justo L. *A History of Christian Thought*. 3 vols. Nashville: Abingdon, 1975.
———. *The Story of Christianity*. 2 vols. San Francisco: Harper, 1985.
Gorman, Michael J. *Inhabiting the Cruciform God: Kenosis, Justification, and Theosis in Paul's Narrative Soteriology*. Grand Rapids: Eerdmans, 2009.
Grant, Frederick C. *An Introduction to New Testament Thought*. New York: Abingdon, 1950.
Grant, Robert M. *Jesus after the Gospels: The Christ of the Second Century*. London: SCM, 1990.
Green, F.W. "The Later Development of the Doctrine of the Trinity." In *Essays on the Trinity and the Incarnation*, edited by A. E. J. Rawlinson, 239–300. New York: Longmans, 1928.
Green, Joel B. *The Death of Jesus: Tradition and Interpretation in the Passion Narrative*. Tubingen: Mohr/Siebeck, 1988.
Green, Joel B., and Scott McKnight, editors. *Dictionary of Jesus and the Gospels*. Downers Grove, IL: InterVarsity, 1992.
Green, Joel B., and Max M. B. Turner, editors. *Jesus of Nazareth: Lord and Christ. Essays on the Historical Jesus and New Testament Christology*. Grand Rapids: Eerdmans, 1994.
Green, M. *I Believe in the Holy Spirit* London: Hodder & Stoughton, 1975.
Greenwood, D. "The Lord is the Spirit: Some Considerations of 2 Corinthians 3:17." *Catholic Biblical Quarterly* 34 (1972) 467–72.

Bibliography

Greg, Robert C., and Dennis E. Groh. *Early Arianism*. London: SCM, 1981.
Gregory Nazianzus. *Theological Orations: Fifth Theological Oration on the Holy Spirit*. Translated by C. G. Browne. In *The Nicene and Post Nicene Fathers of the Christian Church*, vol. 7. Second Series.
Gregory of Nyssa. *Treatise on Not Three God's*. Translated by H. A. Wilson. *The Nicene and Post Nicene Fathers of the Christian Church*, vol. 5. Second Series.
———. *Treatise on the Holy Spirit Against the Macedonians*. Translated by H. A. Wilson in *The Nicene and Post Nicene Fathers of the Christian Church*, vol 5. Second Series.
———. *Treatise on the Holy Trinity*. Translated by H. A. Wilson. *The Nicene and Post Nicene Fathers of the Christian Church*, vol 5. Second Series.
Grenz, Stanley J. *The Named God and the Question of Being: A Trinitarian Theo-Ontology*. Matrix of Christian Theology, vol. 2. Louisville: WJK, 2005.
———. *Rediscovering the Triune God: The Trinity in Contemporary Theology*. Minneapolis: Fortress, 2004.
———. *The Social God and the Relational Self: A Trinitarian Theology of the Imago Dei*. Matrix of Christian Theology vol. 1. Louisville: WJK, 2001.
———. *Theology for the Community of God*. Carlisle: Paternoster, 1994.
Grillmeier, Alloys. *Christ in Christian Tradition: From the Apostolic Age to Chalcedon (451)*. Vol. 1. 2nd ed. Translated by J. Bowden. London: Mowbrays, 1975.
———. *Christ in Christian Tradition: From the Apostolic Age to Chalcedon (451)*. 2nd ed. Translated by J. Bowden. Atlanta: Knox, 1975.
Grogan, Geoffrey W. "New Testament Christology—Or New Testament Christologies?" *Themelios* 25 (1999) 60–73.
———. "The Significance of Pentecost in the History of Salvation." *Scottish Bulletin of Evangelical Theology* 4 (1986) 97–107.
Gros, Jeffrey. "Toward a Dialogue of Conversion: The Pentecostal, Evangelical, and Conciliar Movements." *Pneuma* 17 (1995) 189–201.
Grudem, W. *Systematic Theology: An Introduction to Biblical Doctrine* Grand Rapids: Zondervan, 1994.
Gruenler, R. G. *New Approaches to Jesus and the Gospels: A Phenomenological Study of Synoptic Christology*. Grand Rapids: Baker, 1982.
Guelich, Robert A. "The Gospels: Portraits of Jesus and His Ministry." in *Journal of the Evangelical Theological Society* 24 (1981) 117–25.
Gunton, Colin E. "Barth, the Trinity, and Human Freedom." *Theology Today* 43 (1986) 316–30.
———. *Christ and Creation*. Grand Rapids: Eerdmans, 1992.
———. *The One the Three and the Many*. Cambridge: CUP, 1993.
———. *The Promise of Trinitarian Theology*. 2nd ed. Edinburgh: T. & T. Clark, 1997.
———. *Theology through the Theologians: Selected Essays 1972–1995*. Edinburgh: T. & T. Clark, 1996.
———. "Two Dogmas Revisited: Edward Irving's Christology." *Scottish Journal of Theology* 41 (1988) 359–76.
———. *Yesterday and Today: A Study of Continuities in Christology*. London: Dartman, Longman & Todd, 1983.
Habets, Myk. "*Veni Cinderella Spiritus*." *Journal of Pentecostal Theology* 10 (2001) 65–80.
———. "Spirit Christology: Seeing in Stereo." *Journal of Pentecostal Theology* 11 (2003) 199–235.

———. "Reforming Theosis." In *Theosis: Deification in Christian Theology*, edited by S. Finlan and V. Kharlamov, 146–67. Eugene, OR: Pickwick, 2006.

Habets, Myk (with Stuart Print) "A Critical Review Essay on Amos Yong, Beyond the Impasse: Toward a Pneumatological Theology of Religions." *Pacific Journal of Baptist Research* 3 (2007) 53–60.

———. "Developing a Retroactive Hermeneutic: Johannine Theology and Doctrinal Development." *American Theological Inquiry* 1 (2008) 77–89.

———. "'The Dogma is the Drama': Dramatic Developments in Biblical Theology." *Stimulus* 16 (2008) 2–5.

———. "Filioque? Nein. A Proposal for Coherent Coinherence." In *Trinitarian Theology After Barth*. Princeton Theological Monograph Series. Edited by Myk Habets and Phillip Tolliday. Eugene, OR: Pickwick, forthcoming.

———. "Naked but Not Disembodied: A Case for Anthropological Duality." *Pacific Journal of Baptist Research* 4 (2008) 33–50.

———. "Putting the 'Extra' Back into Calvinism." *Scottish Journal of Theology* 62 (2009), 441–56.

———. *Theosis in the Theology of Thomas Torrance*. New Critical Thinking in Religion, Theology and Biblical Studies. Surrey: Ashgate, 2009.

Hagner, Donald A. *The Jewish Reclamation of Jesus: An Analysis and Critique of Modern Jewish Study of Jesus*. Grand Rapids: Zondervan, 1984.

Hahn, Ferdinand. *The Titles of Jesus in Christology*. Cleveland: Word, 1969.

Haight, Roger. "The Case for Spirit Christology." *Theological Studies* 53 (1992) 257–87.

———. "Jesus and Salvation: An Essay in Interpretation." *Theological Studies* 55 (1994) 225–51.

———. *Jesus Symbol of God*. New York: Orbis, 1999.

———. "The Point of Trinitarian Theology." *Toronto Journal of Theology* 4 (1988) 191–204.

Hansen, Olaf. "Spirit Christology: A Way Out of Our Dilemma?" In *The Holy Spirit in the Life of the Church: From Biblical Times to the Present*, edited by P. D. Opsahl, 172–203. Minneapolis: Augsburg, 1978.

Hanson, R. P. C. *The Search for the Christian Doctrine of God: The Arian Controversy 318–381*. Edinburgh: T. & T. Clark, 1988.

Hardy, Edward R., editor. *Christology of the Later Fathers*. Library of Christian Classics, vol. 3. Philadelphia: Westminster, 1954.

Harnack, Adolf. *History of Dogma*. New York: Dover, 1961.

———. *What is Christianity?* New York: Harper, 1900, reprinted 1957.

Harris, Murray J. *Jesus as God: The New Testament Use of Theos in Reference to Jesus*. Grand Rapids: Baker, 1992.

Hart, Trevor. "Karl Barth, the Trinity, and Pluralism." In *The Trinity in a Pluralistic Age: Theological Essays on Culture and Religion*, edited by K. J. Vanhoozer, 124–42. Grand Rapids: Eerdmans, 1997.

Hartman, Lars. "Early Baptism—Early Christology." In *The Future of Christology: Essays in Honor of Leander E. Keck*, edited by A. J. Malherbe and W. A. Meeks, 191–201. Minneapolis: Fortress, 1993.

Hastings, James, editor. *A Dictionary of Christ and the Gospels*. Edinburgh: T. & T. Clark, 1906.

Hauerwas, Stanley, "The Moral Authority of Scripture: The Politics and Ethics of Remembering," *Interpretation* (1980) 356–70.

———. *Unleashing Scripture: Freeing the Bible from Captivity to America*. Nashville: Abingdon, 1993.
Havrilak, Gregory. "Karl Rahner and the Greek Trinity." *St Vladimir's Theological Quarterly* 34 (1990) 61–77.
Hawthorn, Gerald F. et al, editors. *Dictionary of Paul and His Letters*. Downers Grove, IL: InterVarsity, 1993.
———. "Holy Spirit." In *Dictionary of the Later New Testament and its Developments*, edited by R. Martin and P. H. Davids, 489–99. Downers Grove, IL: InterVarsity, 1997.
———. "In the Form of God and Equal with God (Philippians 2:6)." In *Where Christology Began: Essays on Philippians 2*, edited by R. P. Martin and B. Dodd, 96–110. Louisville: Westminster, 1998.
———. *The Presence and the Power: The Significance of the Holy Spirit in the Life and Ministry of Jesus*. Dallas: Word, 1991.
Haya-Prats, Gonzalo J. *L'Esprit Force de L'Eglise*. Paris: Cerf, 1975.
Hays, Richard B. *Echoes of Scripture in the Letters of Paul*. New Haven: Yale University Press, 1989.
Hebblethwaite, Brian. *The Incarnation: Collected Essays in Christology*. Cambridge: CUP, 1980.
———. "The Propriety of the Doctrine of the Incarnation as a Way of Interpreting Christ." *Scottish Journal of Theology* 33 (1980) 201–22.
Helland, Roger. "The Hypostatic Union: How did Jesus Function." In *Evangelical Quarterly* 65 (1993) 311–27.
Hendry, George S. "Christology." In *A Dictionary of Christian Theology*, edited by A. Richardson, 51–64. Philadelphia: Westminster, 1969.
Hengel, Martin. *The Son of God: The Origin of Christology and the History of Jewish-Hellenistic Religion*. London: SCM, 1976.
Hengel, Martin. *The Charismatic Leader and his Followers*. Translated by J. Greig. New York: Crossroad, 1981.
———. "Christological Titles in Early Christianity." In *The Messiah: Developments in Earliest Judaism and Christianity*, edited by J. H. Charlesworth, 425–48. Minneapolis: Fortress, 1992.
———. *Studies in Early Christology*. Edinburgh: T. & T. Clark, 1995.
Heron, Alasdair I. C. *The Holy Spirit: The Holy Spirit in the Bible, the History of Christian Thought and Recent Theology*. Philadelphia: Westminster, 1983.
———. "'Who Proceedeth From The Father And The Son': The Problem of the Filioque." *Scottish Journal of Theology* 24 (1971) 149–66.
Hick, John *The Metaphor of God Incarnate: Christology in a Pluralistic Age*. Louisville: John Knox, 1995.
———, editor. *The Myth of God Incarnate*. London: SCM, 1977.
Hildebrandt, Wilf. *An Old Testament Theology of the Spirit of God*. Peabody: Hendrickson, 1995.
Hiebert, D. Edmond. "Presentation and Transformation: An Exposition of Romans 12:1–2." *Bibliotheca Sacra* 151 (1994) 309–24.
Hill, William J. "The Historicity of God." *Theological Studies* 45 (1984) 320–33.
Hinze, Bradford, E. and Dabney, D. Lyle. Eds. *Advents of the Spirit: An Introduction to the Current Study of Pneumatology*. Milwaukee: Marquette University Press, 2001.

Hobbs, Herschel H. "Word Studies in John's Gospel." *Southwestern Journal of Theology* 8 (1965) 67–79.

Hocken, Peter D. "A Catholic Response to the German Report." *Pneuma* 18 (1996) 217–24.

———. "Charismatic Movement." In *Dictionary of Pentecostal and Charismatic Movements*, edited by S. M. Burgess and G. B. McGee, 130–60. Grand Rapids: Zondervan, 1988.

Hodge, Charles. *Systematic Theology*. Grand Rapids: Eerdmans, 1997.

Hodgson, Peter C. *Jesus—Word and Presence*. Philadelphia: Fortress, 1971.

Hollenweger, Walter J. "Common Witness Between Catholics and Pentecostals." *Pneuma* 18 (1996) 185–216.

Holm, Bernard. "The Work of the Spirit: The Reformation to the Present." In *The Holy Spirit in the Life of the Church: From Biblical Times to the Present*, edited by P. D. Opsahl, 99–135. Minneapolis: Augsburg, 1978.

Holmes, Stephen R. *God of Grace and God of Glory: An Account of the Theology of Jonathan Edwards*. Grand Rapids: Eerdmans, 2000.

Hook, Norman. "A Spirit Christology." *Theology* 75 (May 1972) 226–32.

Hooker, Morna D. "Chalcedon and the New Testament." In *The Making and Remaking of Christian Doctrine: Essays in Honour of Maurice Wiles*, edited by S. Coakley and D. A. Palin, 73–93. New York: Clarendon, 1993.

———. *Jesus and the Servant*. London: SPCK, 1959.

———. *The Signs of a Prophet: The Prophetic Actions of Jesus*. London: SCM, 1997.

Horton, Stanley M. *What the Bible Says About the Holy Spirit*. Springfield: Gospel, 1976.

Hoskyns, Edwyn, and Davey, Noël. *The Riddle of the New Testament*. London: Faber & Faber, 1958.

Hughes, Philip E. *The True Image: The Origin and Destiny of Man in Christ*. Grand Rapids: Eerdmans, 1989.

Hull, J. H. E. *The Holy Spirit in the Acts of the Apostles*. London: Lutterworth, 1967.

Hunsinger, George. "Karl Barth's Christology: Its Basic Chalcedonian Character." In *The Cambridge Companion to Karl Barth*, edited by J. Webster, 127–42. Cambridge: Cambridge University Press, 2000.

Hunt, W. Boyd. "John's Doctrine of the Spirit." *Southwestern Journal of Theology* 8 (1965) 45–65.

Hunter, Harold. "Spirit Christology: Dilemma and Promise (1)." *Heythrop Journal* 24 (1983) 127–40.

———. "Spirit Christology: Dilemma and Promise (2)." *Heythrop Journal* 24 (1983) 266–77.

Hunter, Harold. "The Resurgence of Spirit Christology." *EPTA Bulletin* (1992) no numbers.

Hurd, John C. *The Origin of 1 Corinthians*. London: SPCK, 1965.

Hurst, Lincoln D. "Christ, Adam, and Preexistence Revisited." In *Where Christology Began: Essays on Philippians 2*, edited by R. P. Martin and B. Dodd, 84–95. Louisville: Westminster, 1998.

———. "Re-Enter the Pre-Existent Christ in Philippians 2:5–11?" *New Testament Studies* 32 (1986) 449–57.

Hurst, Lincoln D., and Nicholas Wright, editors. *The Glory of Christ in the New Testament: Studies in Christology in Memory of George Bradford Caird*. Oxford: Oxford University Press, 1987.

Hurtado, Larry W. *How on Earth did Jesus Become a God? Historical Questions about Earliest Devotion to Jesus.* Grand Rapids: Eerdmans, 2005.

———. *Lord Jesus Christ: Devotion to Jesus in Earliest Christianity.* Grand Rapids: Eerdmans, 2003.

———. *One God, One Lord: Early Christian Devotion and Ancient Jewish Monotheism.* London: SCM, 1988.

———. "The Origins of the Worship of Christ." *Themelios* 19 (1994) 4–8.

Imbelli, Robert P. "The New Adam and Life-giving Spirit: The Paschal Pattern of Spirit Christology." *Communio* 25 (1998) 233–52.

Inch, Morris A. *Saga of the Spirit: A Biblical, Systematic, and Historical Theology of the Holy Spirit.* Grand Rapids: Baker, 1985.

Irenaeus. *Against Heresies. The Ante Nicene Fathers.* Vol 1.

Irving, Edward. *The Collected Writings of Edward Irving.* Edited by G. Carlyle. London: Alexander Strachan, 1865.

Isaacs, Marie E. *The Concept of Spirit.* London: Heythrop Monographs, 1976.

Jansen, John F. *The Resurrection of Jesus Christ in New Testament Theology.* Philadelphia: Westminster, 1980.

Jenson, Robert W. "Jesus, Father, Spirit: The Logic of the Doctrine of the Trinity." *Dialog* 26 (1987) 245–49.

Jeremias, Joachim. *New Testament Theology: The Proclamation of Jesus.* New York: Scribner's, 1971.

Jüngel, Eberhard. *God as the Mystery of the World.* Translated by D. L. Guder. Edinburgh: T. & T. Clark, 1983.

Jungmann, Josef. *The Place of Christ in Liturgical Prayer.* London: Chapman, 1965.

Kähler, Martin. *The So-Called Historical Jesus and the Historic, Biblical Christ.* Philadelphia: Fortress, 1964.

Kaiser, Christopher B. "The Discernment of Triunity." *Scottish Journal of Theology* 28 (1975) 449–60.

Kaiser, Walter C. Jr. *Toward an Old Testament Theology.* Grand Rapids: Zondervan, 1978.

Kamlah, Eberhard. "Spirit: In the Old Testament." In *New International Dictionary of New Testament Theology,* vol. 3, 689–93.

Kangas, Ron. "The Pneumatic Person in the Gospel of John." *Affirmation and Critique* 2 (1997) 14–29.

Kärkkäinen, Veli-Matti. *One With God: Salvation ad Deification and Justification.* Collegeville, MN: Liturgical, 2004.

———. *Toward a Pneumatological Theology: Pentecostal and Ecumenical Perspectives on Ecclesiology, Soteriology, and Theology of Mission.* Edited by A. Yong. New York: University Press of America, 2002.

Kapic, Kelly M. "The Son's Assumption of a Human Nature: A Call for Clarity." *International Journal of Systematic Theology* 3 (2001) 154–66.

Käsemann, Ernst. *Commentary on Romans.* Translated and edited by G. W. Bromiley. Grand Rapids: Eerdmans, 1980.

———. "The Problem of the Historical Jesus." In *Essays on New Testament Themes.* London: SCM, 1964, 15–47.

Kasper, Walter. "Christologie von unten?" In *Grundfragen der Christology heute.* Edited by L. Scheffczyk. Herder (1975) 141–70.

———. *The God of Jesus Christ*. Translated by M. J. O'Connell. New York: Crossroad, 1983.

———. *Jesus the Christ*. New York: Paulist, 1976.

Käufmann, Gordon D. *Systematic Theology: A Historicist Perspective*. New York: Charles Scribner, 1968.

Keck, Leander E. "Toward the Renewal of New Testament Christology." *New Testament Studies* 32 (1986) 362–77.

Kee, Howard C. *Miracle and the Early Christian World: A Study in Socio-historical Method*. New Haven: Yale University Press, 1983.

Keener, Craig S. *The Spirit in the Gospels and Acts: Divine Purity and Power*. Peabody: Hendrickson, 1997.

Keller, Catherine. "Pneumatic Nudges: The Theology of Moltmann, Feminism, and the Future." In *The Future of Theology: Essays in Honor of Jürgen Moltmann*, edited by M. Volf et al, 142–53. Grand Rapids: Eerdmans, 1996.

Kelly, Gerard. "Spirit, Church and the Ecumenical Endeavour." In *Starting with the Spirit: Task of Theology II*, edited by G. Preece and S. Pickard, 153–76. Hindmarsh, SA: Australian Theological Forum, 2001.

Kelly, J. N. D. *Early Christian Doctrines*. 5th ed. London: A. & C. Black, 1977.

Kettler, Christian D., and Todd Speidell, editors. *Incarnational Ministry : The Presence of Christ in Church, Society, and Family: Essays in Honor of Ray S. Anderson*. Colorado Springs: Helmers & Howard, 1990.

Kierkegaard, Søren. *Concluding Unscientific Postscript*. Translated by D. F. Swenson. Princeton: Princeton University Press, 1944.

———. *Fear and Trembling*. Translated by R. Payne. New York: Oxford University Press, 1939.

———. *Philosophical Fragments*. Translated by D. F. Swenson. Princeton, NJ: Princeton University Press, 1962.

Killian, Sabbas J. "The Holy Spirit in Christ and Christians." *American Benedictine Review* 20 (1969) 99–121.

Kilmartin, Edward J. "The Active Role of Christ and the Holy Spirit in the Sanctification of the Eucharistic Elements." *Theological Studies* 45 (1984) 225–53.

Kimball, Charles A. *Jesus' Exposition of the Old Testament in Luke's Gospel*. Sheffield: JSOT, 1994.

Kingsbury, Jack D. "Jesus as the 'Prophetic Messiah' in Luke's Gospel." In *The Future of Christology: Essays in Honor of Leander E. Keck*, edited by A. J. Malherbe and W. A. Meeks, 29–42. Minneapolis: Fortress, 1993.

Klooster, Fred H. "Uppsala on The Holy Spirit and the Catholicity of the Church." *Calvin Theological Journal* 4 (1969) 51–98.

Knox, John. *The Humanity and Divinity of Christ: A Study of Pattern in Christology*. Cambridge: Cambridge University Press, 1967.

Konidares, Gerasimos I. "Christological Decisions of Chalcedon, Their History Down to the 6th Ecumenical Synod (451-680-1)." *Greek Orthodox Theologcial Review* 1 (1971) 63–78.

Kostenberger, Andreas J. "What Does it Mean to be Filled with the Spirit? A Biblical Investigation." *Journal of the Evangelical Theological Society* 40 (1997) 229–40.

Krasevac, Edward L. "Christology from Above and Christology from Below." *The Thomist* (1987) 299–306.

Kreitzer, Larry J. "'When He at Last is First!:' Philippians 2:9–11 and the Exaltation of the Lord." In *Where Christology Began: Essays on Philippians 2*, edited by R. P. Martin and B. Dodd, 111–27. Louisville: Westminster, 1998.

Krodel, Gerhard. "The Functions of the Spirit in the Old Testament, the Synoptic Tradition, and the Book of Acts." In *The Holy Spirit in the Life of the Church: From Biblical Times to the Present*, edited by P. D. Opsahl, 10–21. Minneapolis: Augsburg, 1978.

Küng, Hans. *Menshwerding Gottes: Ein Einfuhrung in Hegels Theologishches Denken als Prologomena zu einer kunftiger Christologie*. Frieburg-im-Briesgou: Herder, 1970.

———. *On Being a Christian*. New York: Doubleday, 1976.

Küng, Hans, and Jürgen Moltmann, editors. *Conflicts About the Holy Spirit*. New York: Seabury, 1979.

Kuyper, A. *The Work of the Holy Spirit*. Translated by H. De Vries. Grand Rapids: Eerdmans, 1941.

Kyle, Richard. "Nestorius: The Partial Rehabilitation of a Heretic." *Journal of the Evangelical Theological Society* 32 (1989) 73–83.

LaCugna, Catherine M., and Killian McDonnell. *God With Us*. San Francisco: Harper, 1991.

———. "Returning from 'The Far Country': Theses for a Contemporary Trinitarian Theology." *Scottish Journal of Theology* 41 (1988) 191–215.

Ladd, George E. "The Holy Spirit in Galatians." In *Current Issues in Biblical and Patristic Interpretation*, edited by G. F. Hawthorne, 211–16. Grand Rapids: Eerdmans, 1975.

———. *A Theology of the New Testament*. Grand Rapids: Eerdmans 1974.

Lampe, Geoffrey W. H. *God as Spirit*. Oxford: Clarendon, 1977.

———. "The Holy Spirit and the Person of Christ." In *Christ, Faith and History*, edited by S. W. Sykes and J. P. Clayton, 111–30. Cambridge: Cambridge University Press, 1972.

———. *The Seal of the Spirit*. 2nd ed. London: SPCK, 1967.

Lane, Anthony N. S. "Christology Beyond Chalcedon." In *Christ the Lord: Studies in Christology Presented to Donald Guthrie*, edited by H. H. Rowden, 257–81. Leicester: InterVarsity, 1982.

Lane, William L. *Commentary on the Gospel of Mark*. Grand Rapids: Eerdmans, 1974.

Lash, Nicholas. "Up and Down in Christology." In *New Studies in Theology I*, edited by S. Sykes and D. Holmes, 31–46. London: Duckworth, 1980.

Laube, Robert. *Pentecostal Spirituality: The Lasallian Theology of Apostolic Life*. New York: Desclee Company, 1970.

Leigh, Ron W. "Jesus: the One-Natured God-man." *Christian Scholar's Review* 11 (1982) 124–37.

Leivestad, Ragnar. *Jesus in His own Perspective*. Minneapolis: Augsburg, 1987.

Lemopoulos, Georges. "Come Holy Spirit." *Ecumenical Review* 41 (1986) 461–67.

Letham, Robert. *The Work of Christ*. Leicester: InterVarsity, 1993.

Lewis, Clive S. *Mere Christianity*. London: Fount, 1952.

Lewis, Donald, and Alister McGrath, editors. *Doing Theology for the People of God: Studies in Honour of J. I. Packer*. Leicester: Apollos, 1996.

Lewis, Gordon, and Demarest, Bruce A. *Integrative Theology: Historical, Biblical, Systematic, Apologetic, Practical*: 3 vols. in 1. Grand Rapids: Zondervan, 1996.

Liddon, Henry P. *The Divinity of our Lord and Saviour Jesus Christ*. London: Longmans, Green, 1892.

Lindars, Barnabas, and Stephen S. Smalley, editors. *Christ and the Spirit in the New Testament: Studies in Honour of Charles Francis Digby Moule.* Cambridge: Cambridge University Press, 1973.

Lindsey, F. Duane. "Isaiah's Songs of the Servant. Part 1: The Call of the Servant in Isaiah 42: 1–9." *Bibliotheca Sacra* 139 (1982) 12–31.

———. "Isaiah's Songs of the Servant. Part 2: The Commission of the Servant in Isaiah 49:1–13." *Bibliotheca Sacra* 139 (1982) 129–45.

———. "Isaiah's Songs of the Servant. Part 3: The Commitment of the Servant in Isaiah 50:4–11." *Bibliotheca Sacra* 139 (1982) 216–29.

———. "Isaiah's Songs of the Servant. Part 4: The Career of the Servant in Isaiah 52:13—53:12." *Bibliotheca Sacra* 139 (1982) 312–29.

———. "Isaiah's Songs of the Servant. Part 5: The Career of the Servant in Isaiah 52:13—53:12." *Bibliotheca Sacra* 140 (1983) 21–39.

Lockhart, Peter. "The Spirit, Christ, and Worship." *Australian Theological Forum* (2000) 1–21, http://www.atf.org.au/papers/essays/spirit.asp.

Lockyer, Herbert. *All About the Holy Spirit: A Full Inquiry In to the Attributes of the Holy Spirit.* Peabody: Hendrickson, 1995 [Formerly *The Breath of God,* 1949].

Lodahl, Michael E. *Shekinah/Spirit: Divine Presence in Jewish and Christian Religion.* New York: Paulist, 1992.

Longenecker, Richard N. *The Christology of Early Jewish Christianity.* Grand Rapids: Baker, 1981.

———. "The Foundational Conviction of New Testament Christology: The Obedience/Faithfulness/Sonship of Christ." In *Jesus of Nazareth: Lord and Christ. Essays on the Historical Jesus and New Testament Christology,* edited by J. B. Green and M. M. B. Turner, 473–88. Grand Rapids: Eerdmans, 1994.

———. "On the Concept of Development in Pauline Thought." In *Perspectives on Evangelical Theology,* edited by K. S. Kantzer and S. N. Gundry, 195–207. Grand Rapids: Baker, 1979.

Lopes, Augustus N. "Calvin, Theologian of the Holy Spirit: The Holy Spirit and the Word of God." *Scottish Bulletin of Evangelical Theology* 15 (1997) 38–49.

Lossky, Vladimir. *The Mystical Theology of the Eastern Church.* London: James Clarke, 1957, reprint 1973.

———. "The Procession of the Holy Spirit in the Orthodox Triadology." *Eastern Churches Quarterly* 7 (1948) 31–52.

Loughlin, Gerard. "Writing the Trinity." *Theology* (1994) 82–89.

Ludlow, Morwenna. *Gregory of Nyssa: Ancient and Postmodern.* Oxford: OUP, 2007.

Luther, Martin. *Luther's Works.* Edited by J. Pelikan and H. T. Lehmann. 55 vols. Philadelphia: Fortress, 1955.

Macchia, Frank D. "Discerning the Spirit in Life: A Review of *God the Spirit* by Michael Welker." *Journal of Pentecostal Theology* 10 (1997) 3–28.

Macchia, Frank D., Ralph Del Colle, and Dale T. Irvin. "Christ and Spirit: Dogma, Discernment and Dialogical Theology in a Religiously Plural World." *Journal of Pentecostal Theology* 12 (2003) 15–83.

———. "Finitum Capax Infiniti: A Pentecostal Distinctive?" *Pneuma* 29 (2007) 185–87.

McCartney, Dan and Clayton, Charles. *Let the Reader Understand: A Guide to Interpreting and Applying the Bible.* Wheaton: Victor, 1994.

McClendon, James W. *Ethics: Systematic Theology.* Vol. 1. Nashville: Abingdon, 1986.

Bibliography

McClymont, Michael J. "Salvation as Divinization: Jonathan Edwards, Gregory Palamas and the Theological Uses of Neoplatonism." In *Jonathan Edwards: Philosophical Theologian*, edited by P. Helm and O. D. Crisp, 139–60. Aldershot: Ashgate, 2003.

McCready, Douglas. "The Disintegration of John Hick's Christology." *Journal of the Evangelical Theological Society* 39 (1996) 257–70.

———. "'He Came Down From Heaven': The Preexistence of Christ Revisited." *Journal of the Evangelical Theological Society* 40 (1997) 419–32.

McDermott, Brian O. *Word Became Flesh: Dimensions of Christology*. New Testament Studies 9. Minnesota: Glazier, 1993.

McDonnell, Killian. "The Determinative Doctrine of the Holy Spirit." *Theology Today* 39 (1982) 142–61.

———. "A Trinitarian Doctrine of the Holy Spirit." *Theological Studies* 46 (1985) 191–227.

———. "Can Classical Pentecostals and Roman Catholics Engage in Common Witness?" *Journal of Pentecostal Theology* 7 (1995) 97–106.

McFadyen, Alistair I. "The Trinity and Human Individuality: The Conditions for Relevance." *Theology* 95 (1992) 10–18.

McFarlane, Graham W. P. "Strange News from Another Star: An Anthropological Insight from Edward Irving." In *Persons, Divine and Human*, edited by C. Schwöbel, and C. E. Gunton, 98–119. Edinburgh: T. & T. Clark, 1991.

———. "The Strange Tongue of a Long Lost Christianity: The Spirit and the Trinity." *Vox Evangelica* 22 (1992) 63–70.

———. *Christ and the Spirit: The Doctrine of the Incarnation According to Edward Irving*. Carlisle: Paternoster, 1996.

———. *Why Do You Believe What You Believe About the Holy Spirit?* Carlisle, UK: Paternoster, 1998.

———. *Why Do You Believe What You believe About Jesus?* Carlisle, UK: Paternoster, 2000.

McGrath, Alister E. *Christian Theology: An Introduction*. Oxford: Blackwell, 1994.

———. *Luther's Theology of the Cross*. Grand Rapids: Baker, 1985.

———. *The Making of Modern German Christology: 1750–1990*. 2nd ed. Grand Rapids: Academie, 1994.

———. *A Scientific Theology: 3 vols., Reality, Nature, Theory*. Grand Rapids: Eerdmans, 2001, 2002, 2003.

McGuckin, Paul. "Spirit Christology: Lactantius and His Sources." *Heythrop Journal* 24 (1983) 141–48.

McIntyre, John. "The Holy Spirit in Greek Patristic Thought." *Scottish Journal of Theology* 7 (1954) 353–75.

———. *The Shape of Pneumatology: Studies in the Doctrine of the Holy Spirit*. Edinburgh: T. & T. Clark, 1997.

———. *The Shape of Soteriology: Studies in the Doctrine of the Death of Christ*. Edinburgh: T. & T. Clark, 1992.

Mack, Burton L. *The Lost Gospel: The Book Q and Christian Origins*. New York: Harper Collins, 1994.

———. *A Myth of Innocence: Mark and Christian Origins*. Philadelphia: Fortress, 1988.

Mackey, James P. *The Christian Experience of God as Trinity*. London: SCM, 1983.

MacKinnon, Donald M. "Prolegomena to Christology." *Journal of Theological Studies* 33 (1982) 146–60.

Macleod, Donald. *The Person of Christ*. Downers Grove, IL: InterVarsity, 1998.

McLelland, Joseph. "The Mundane Work of the Spirit." *Theology Today* 22 (1965) 205–17.

Macquarrie, John. "Foundational Documents of the Faith: III. The Chalcedonian Definition." *Expository Times*, 91 (1979) 68–71.

———. *Jesus Christ in Modern Thought*. Philadelphia: Trinity, 1990.

Malamat, Abraham. "Charismatic Leadership in the book of Judges." In *Magnalia Dei: The Mighty Acts of God: Essays on the Bible and Archaeology in Memory of G. Ernest Wright*, edited by F. M. Cross et al, 152–68. Garden City: Doubleday, 1976.

Malherbe, Abraham J., and Wayne A. Meeks, editors. *The Future of Christology: Essays in Honor of Leander E. Keck*. Minneapolis: Fortress, 1993.

Mansfield, M. Robert. *Spirit and Gospel in Mark*. Peabody: Hendrickson, 1987.

Manson, T. William. *Jesus the Messiah: The Synoptic Tradition of the Revelation of God in Christ: with Special Reference to Form-Criticism*. Philadelphia: Westminster, 1946.

———. *The Servant-Messiah: A Study of the Public Ministry of Jesus*. Cambridge: University Press, 1953.

Marks, Ed. "The Indwelling, Pneumatic Christ as Revealed in the Epistles of Paul." *Affirmation and Critique* 2 (1997) 30–38.

Markus, Robert A. "Trinitarian Theology and the Economy." *Journal of Theological Studies* 9 (1958) 89–102.

Marsh, F. E. *Emblems of the Holy Spirit*. Grand Rapids: Kregel, 1976.

Marshall, I. Howard. *I Believe in the Historical Jesus*. London: Hodder & Stoughton, 1977.

———. "Incarnational Christology in the New Testament." In *Christ the Lord: Studies in Christology Presented to Donald Guthrie*, edited by H. H. Rowden, 1–16. Downers Grove, IL: InterVarsity, 1982.

———. *The Origins of New Testament Christology*. Downers Grove, IL: InterVarsity, 1976.

Martin, Ralph P. *Carmen Christi: Philippians 2:5–11 in Recent Interpretation and in the Setting of Early Christian Worship*. Grand Rapids: Eerdmans, 1983.

———. "Carmen Christi Revisited." In *Where Christology Began: Essays on Philippians 2*, edited by R. P. Martin and B. Dodd, 1–5. Louisville: Westminster, 1998.

Martin, Ralph P., and Peter H. Davids, editors. *Dictionary of the Later New Testament and its Developments*. Downers Grove, IL: InterVarsity, 1997.

Martin, Ralph P., and Brian J. Dodd, editors. *Where Christology Began: Essays on Philippians 2*. Louisville: Westminster, 1998.

Matera, Frank J. *New Testament Christology*. Louisville: Westminster, 1999.

Matsoukas, Nikolaos. "The Economy of the Holy Spirit: The Standpoint of Orthodox Theology." *Ecumenical Review* 41 (1989) 398–405.

Matthews, Shailer. *The Gospel and the Modern Man*. New York: Macmillan, 1910.

Meadowcroft, Tim. "Between Authorial Intent and Indeterminacy: The Incarnation as an Invitation to Human-Divine Discourse." *Scottish Journal of Theology* 58 (2005) 199–218.

———. "Relevance as Mediating Category in the Reading of Biblical Texts: Venturing Beyond the Hermeneutical Circle." *Journal of the Evangelical Theological Society* 45 (2002) 611–27.

Menzies, Robert P. *The Development of Early Christian Pneumatology: With Special Reference to Luke-Acts*. JSNTS 54. Sheffield: Sheffield, 1991.

———. "The Distinctive Character of Luke's Pneumatology." *Paraclete* 25 (1991) 17–30.
———. *Empowered for Witness: The Spirit in Luke-Acts*. JPTS 6. Sheffield: Sheffield, 1994.
Metzger, Paul L. Ed. *Trinitarian Soundings in Systematic Theology*. London: T. & T. Clark, 2005.
Meyer, Ben F. *The Aims of Jesus*. London: SCM, 1979.
———. *Critical Realism and the New Testament*. Allison Park, PA: Pickwick, 1989.
Meyer, Paul W. "The Holy Spirit in the Pauline Letters: A Contextual Exploration." *Interpretation* 33 (1979) 3–18.
Migliore, Daniel L. *Faith Seeking Understanding: An Introduction to Christian Theology*. Grand Rapids: Eerdmans, 1991.
Miller, Ed L. "The Johannine Origins of the Johannine Logos." *Journal of Biblical Theology* 112 (1993) 445–57.
———. "The Logos was God." *Evangelical Quarterly* 53 (1981) 65–77.
Milne, Bruce. *Know The Truth: A Handbook of Christian Belief*. Leicester: IVP, 1982.
Min, Anselm K. "The Trinity and the Incarnation: Hegel and Classical Approaches." *The Journal of Religion* 66 (1986) 173–93.
Minns, Denis. *Irenaeus*. London: Geoffrey Chapman, 1994.
Moltmann, Jürgen. *The Church in the Power of the Spirit: A Contribution to Messianic Ecclesiology*. Translated by M. Kohl. New York: Harper & Row, 1977.
———. *The Coming of God: Christian Eschatology*. Translated by M. Kohl. Minneapolis: Fortress, 1996.
———. *The Crucified God: The Cross of Christ as the Foundation and Criticism of Christian Theology*. Translated by R. A. Wilson and J. Bowden. New York: Harper & Row, 1974.
———. *Experiences in Theology: Ways and Forms of Christian Theology*. Translated by M. Kohl. Minneapolis: Fortress, 2000.
———. *God for a Secular Society: The Public Relevance of Theology*. Minneapolis: Fortress, 1999.
———. *God in Creation: A New Theology of Creation and the Spirit of God*. Translated by M. Kohl. San Francisco: Harper & Row, 1985.
———. *History and the Triune God: Contributions to Trinitarian Theology*. London: SCM, 1991.
———. *History and the Triune God: Contributions to Trinitarian Theology*. Translated by J. Bowden. New York: Crossroad, 1992.
———. "Jürgen Moltmann." In *How I have Changed: Reflections on Thirty Years of Theology*, edited by J. Moltmann. Translated by J. Bowden. Harrisburg, PA: Trinity, 1997.
———. *Theology of Hope: On the Ground and the Implications of a Christian Eschatology*. Translated by J. W. Leitch. New York: Harper & Row, 1967.
———. *Theology and Joy*. Translated by R. Ulrich. London: SCM, 1973.
———. *The Trinity and the Kingdom: The Doctrine of God*. Translated by M. Kohl. San Francisco: Harper & Row, 1981.
———. *On Human Dignity: Political Theology and Ethics*. Translated by M. D. Meeks. Philadelphia: Fortress, 1984.
———. *Science and Wisdom*. Translated by M. Kohl. Minneapolis: Fortress, 2003.

———. *The Source of Life: The Holy Spirit and the Theology of Life.* Translated by M. Kohl. London: SCM, 1997.

———. *The Spirit of Life: A Universal Affirmation.* Translated by M. Kohl. Minneapolis: Fortress, 1992.

———. "The Trinitarian Personhood of the Holy Spirit." In *Advents of the Spirit: An Introduction to the Current Study of Pneumatology*, edited by B. E. Hinze and D. L. Dabney, 302–14. Milwaukee: Marquette University Press, 2001.

———. *The Way of Jesus Christ: Christology in Messianic Dimensions.* Translated by M. Kohl. San Francisco: HarperSanFrancisco, 1990.

Molnar, Paul D. *Divine Freedom and the Doctrine of the Immanent Trinity.* London: T. & T. Clark, 2002.

Montague, George T. *The Holy Spirit: Growth of a Biblical Tradition, A Commentary on the Principal Texts of the Old and New Testaments.* New York: Paulist, 1976.

Montefiore, Hugh W. "Towards a Christology for Today." In *Soundings: Essays Concerning Christian Understandin*, edited by A. R. Vidler, 158. Cambridge: Cambridge University Press, 1964.

Morris, Leon. *The Lord from Heaven: A Study of the New Testament Teaching on the Deity and Humanity of Jesus.* Grand Rapids: InterVarsity, 1958.

Motyer, Stephen. "The Rending of the Veil: A Markan Pentecost?" *New Testament Studies* 33 (1987) 155–57.

Moule, Charles F. D. *The Origin of Christology.* Cambridge: Cambridge University Press, 1977.

Moule, Handley C. G. *Veni Creator: Thoughts on the Person and Work of the Holy Spirit of Promise.* London: Hodder & Stoughton, 1902.

Mueller, John T. "Part II: Luther's Doctrine of the Application of Salvation." *Bibliotheca Sacra* 113 (1956) 227–38.

———. "A Survey of Luther's Theology: Part I." *Bibliotheca Sacra* 113 (1956) 153–61.

Mühlen, Heribert. *Der heilige Geist als Person.* Munster, 1966.

———. *Una mystica persona: Die Kirche als das Mysterium der Identitat des Heiligen Geistes in Christus und den Christen: Eine Person in vielen Personen.* Munich: Schoningh, 1967.

Muller, Richard A. *Dictionary of Latin and Greek Theological Terms.* Grand Rapids: Baker, 1985.

———. "Incarnation, Immutability, and the Case for Classical Theism." *Westminster Theological Journal* 45 (1985) 22–40.

Myers, Benjamin B. "The Stratification of Knowledge in the Thought of T. F. Torrance." *Scottish Journal of Theology* 61 (2008) 1–15.

Nassif, Bradley, editor. *New Perspectives on Historical Theology: Essays in Memory of John Meyendorff.* Grand Rapids: Eerdmans, 1996.

Need, Stephen W. *Truly Divine and Truly Human: The Story of Christ and the Seven Ecumenical Councils.* Peabody: Hendrickson, 2008.

Needham, Nick. "The *Filioque* Clause: East or West?" *Scottish Bulletin of Evangelical Theology* 15 (1997) 142–62.

Newbigin, Leslie. "Come Holy Spirit Renew the Whole Creation." *Selly Oak Colleges Occasional Papers.* Birmingham: Selly Oak Colleges (1990) 1–10.

———. *The Gospel in a Pluralist Society.* Grand Rapids: Eerdmans, 1989.

———. "Truth and Authority in Modernity." In *Faith and Modernity*, edited by P. Sampson, V. Samuel, and C. Sugden, 60–115. Oxford: Regnum, 1994.

Newman, John H. *Essay on the Development of Christian Doctrine.* London: Penguin, 1845 reprinted 1974.
Newman, Paul W. "Humanity with Spirit." *Scottish Journal of Theology* 34 (1981) 415–26.
———. *A Spirit Christology: Recovering the Biblical Paradigm of Christian Faith.* Lanham: University Press of America, 1987.
Neyrey, Jerome H. *Christ is Community: The Christologies of the New Testament.* Wilmington, DW: Glazier, 1985.
Nicholls, David. "Trinity and Conflict." *Theology* (1993) 19–27.
Niesel, Wilhelm. *The Theology of Calvin.* Translated by H. Knight. Philadelphia: Westminster, 1956.
Nolland, John. *Luke 1—9:20.* Dallas: Word, 1989.
Norris, Richard A., editor and translator. *The Christological Controversy: Sources of Early Christian Thought.* Philadelphia: Fortress, 1980.
Nuttall, Geoffrey F. *The Holy Spirit in Puritan Faith and Experience.* Oxford: Blackwell, 1947.
O'Carroll, Michael. *Veni Creator Spiritus: A Theological Encyclopaedia of the Holy Spirit.* Collegeville, MN: Liturgical, 1990.
O'Collins, Gerald. *What Are They Saying About Jesus?* New York; Paulist, 1977.
———. *Christology: A Biblical, Historical, and Systematic Study of Jesus Christ.* Oxford: Oxford University Press, 1995.
O'Donnell, John J. "In Him and Over Him: The Holy Spirit in the Life of Jesus." *Gregorianum* 70 (1989) 25–45.
———. *The Mystery of the Triune God.* New York: Paulist, 1989.
Olsen, Roger E. "Trinity and Eschatology: The Historical Being of God in Jürgen Moltmann and Wolfhart Pannenberg." *Scottish Journal of Theology* 36 (1983) 213–27.
———. "Wolfhart Pannenberg's Doctrine of the Trinity." *Scottish Journal of Theology* 43 (1990) 175–206.
———. "The Future of Evangelical Theology." *Christianity Today* (February 9, 1998) 40–50.
O'Malley, John W. "Developments, Reforms, and Two Great Reformations: Towards a Historical Assessment of Vatican II." *Theological Studies* 44 (1983) 373–406.
O'Neill, John C. "On the Resurrection as an Historical Question." In *Christ, Faith, and History*, edited by S. W. Sykes and J. P. Clayton, 205–19. Cambridge: Cambridge University Press, 1972.
Opsahl, Paul D., editor. *The Holy Spirit in the Life of the Church: From Biblical Times to the Present.* Minneapolis: Augsburg, 1978.
Ormerod, Neil. "What is the Goal of Systematic Theology?" *Irish Theological Quarterly* 74 (2009) 38–52.
Osbourne, Eric. *The Emergence of Christian Theology.* Cambridge: Cambridge University Press, 1993.
Ott, Ludwig. *Fundamentals of Catholic Dogma*, 4th ed. Translated by P. Lynch. Edited by J. C. Bastible. St. Louis, MO: Herder, 1954.
Ottley, Robert L. *The Doctrine of the Incarnation.* 2 vols. London: Methuen, 1896.
Otto, Randall E. *The God of Hope: The Trinitarian Vision of Jürgen Moltmann.* New York: University Press of America, 1991.

Otto, Rudolf. *The Kingdom of God and the Son of Man*. Grand Rapids: Zondervan, 1938–1939.

Owen, John. *A Discourse on the Holy Spirit: The Works of John Owen*. Vol 3. Edinburgh: Banner of Truth, 1850–1853, reprinted 1966.

Pache, Rene. *The Holy Spirit*. Translated by J. D. Emerson. Chicago: Moody, 1954.

Packer, James I. *Celebrating the Saving Work of God*. Collected Shorter Writings of J. I. Packer: Vol. 1. Carlisle: Paternoster, 1998.

———. *Keep in Step with the Spirit*. Leicester: InterVarsity, 1984.

———. *Knowing God*. London: Hodder & Stoughton, 1973.

Packer, James I., and Allan M. Stibbs. *The Spirit Within You: The Church's Neglected Possession*. Grand Rapids: Baker, 1979.

Padgett, Alan G. "Methodist Theology Today: A Review Essay of Thomas C. Oden, *Systematic Theology*." *Evangelical Quarterly* 64 (1992) 245–50.

Paige, Terence. "Holy Spirit." In *Dictionary of Paul and His Letters*, edited by G. F. Hawthorne et al, 404–13. Downers Grove, IL: InterVarsity, 1993.

Palmer, Edwin H. *The Person and Work of the Holy Spirit: The Traditional Calvinistic Perspective*. Grand Rapids: Baker, 1974.

Palmer, Parker J. *The Active Life: A Spirituality of Work, Creativity, and Caring*. San Francisco: Jossey-Bass, 1999.

Pannenberg, Wolfhart. "Dogmatic Theses on the Doctrine of Revelation." In *Revelation as History*, edited by W. Pannenberg, 125–58. New York: Macmillan, 1968.

———. "Father, Son, Spirit: Problems of a Trinitarian Doctrine of God." *Dialog* 26 (1987) 250–57.

———. *An Introduction to Systematic Theology*. Edinburgh: T. & T. Clark, 1991.

———. *Jesus—God and Man*. Translated by L. L. Wilkins and D. A. Priebe. London: SCM, 1968.

———. *Systematic Theology*. 3 vols. Translated by G. W. Bromley. Grand Rapids: Eerdmans, 1988–1998.

Parker, D. "Jesus Christ: Model Man of Faith, or Saving Son of God?" *Evangelical Quarterly* 67 (1995) 245–64.

Parratt, John K. "The Witness of the Holy Spirit: Calvin, the Puritans, and St. Paul." *Evangelical Quarterly* 41 (1969) 161–68.

Partee, Charles. *The Theology of John Calvin*. Louisville: Westminster John Knox, 2008.

Pascal, Blaise. *Pensees*. Translated by A. J. Krailsheimer. London: Penguin, 1993.

Payne, Leanne. *Real Presence: The Holy Spirit in the Works of C. S. Lewis*. Monarch, n.p. 1988.

Payne, Robert A. "The Role of the Holy Spirit in Conversion." *Bibliotheca Sacra* 150 (1993) 203–18.

Pederson, Ann. "Christmas and the Reality of Incarnation: Finitum capax infiniti." *Word & World* 27 (2007) 381–89.

Pelikan, Jaroslav. *The Christian Tradition: A History of the Development of Doctrine. Vol 1: The Emergence of the Catholic Tradition 100–600*. Chicago: University of Chicago, 1971.

———. *Development of Christian Doctrine*. New Haven, Christianity Today: Yale University Press, 1969.

———. *Historical Theology: Continuity and Change in Christian Doctrine*. London: Hutchinson, 1971.

———. *Jesus Through the Centuries: His Place in the History of Culture.* New Haven: Yale University Press, 1985.
Pickard, Stephen, and Gordon Preece, editors. *Starting with the Spirit.* Hindmarsh: Australian Theological Forum, 2001.
Pinnock, Clark H. *Flame of Love: A Theology of the Holy Spirit.* Downers Grove, IL: InterVarsity, 1996.
———. *Most Moved Mover: A Theology of God's Openness.* Grand Rapids: Baker, 2001.
———. "The Role of the Spirit in Interpretation." *Journal of the Evangelical Theological Society* 36 (1993) 491–97.
———. *A Wideness in God's Mercy: The Finality of Jesus Christ in a World of Religions.* Grand Rapids: Zondervan, 1992.
———. "The Work of the Holy Spirit in Hermeneutics." *Journal of Pentecostal Theology* 2 (1993) 3–23.
Pinnock, Clark H., Randal Rice, John Sanders, William Hasker, and David Basinger, editors. *The Openness of God: A Challenge to the Traditional Understanding of God.* Downers Grove, IL: InterVarsity, 1995.
Piper, John. "Signs and Wonders: Then and Now." http://www.desiringgod.org/ResourceLibrary/Articles/ByDate/1991/1498_Signs_and_Wonders_Then_and_Now/.
Piper, Otto A. "The Power of the Christian Life." *Theology Today* 11 (1955) 494–507.
———. "The Virgin Birth: The Meaning of the Gospel Accounts." *Interpretation* 18 (1964) 131–48.
Pittenger, W. Norman. *The Holy Spirit.* Philadelphia: United Church Press, 1974.
———. *The Word Incarnate: A Study of the Doctrine of the Person of Christ.* Digswell: Nisbet, 1959.
Pokorny, Petr. *The Genesis of Christology: Foundations for a Theology of the New Testament.* Edinburgh: T. & T. Clark, 1987.
Polanyi, Michael. *Belief in Science and in Christian Life: The Relevance of Michael Polanyi's Thought for Christian Faith and Life.* Edited by T. F. Torrance. Edinburgh: Handsel, 1980.
———. *Personal Knowledge: Towards a Post-Critical Philosophy.* New York: Harper & Row, 1964.
Popkin, Richard H., editor. *The Pimlico History of Western Philosophy.* London: Pimlico, 1999.
Portalie, Eugene. *Guide to the Thought of St. Augustine.* Westport, CT: Greenwood, 1975.
Porter, Lawrence B. "On Keeping 'Persons' in the Trinity: A Linguistic Approach to Trinitarian Thought." *Theological Studies* 41 (1980) 530–48.
Powell, Mark A., and David R. Bauer. *Who Do You Say That I Am? Essays on Christology.* Louisville, KY: Westminster, 1999.
Poythress, Vern S. *Symphonic Theology: The Validity of Multiple Perspectives in Theology.* Grand Rapids: Academie, 1987.
Pratz, Gunther. "The Relationship between Incarnation and Atonement in the Theology of Thomas F. Torrance." *Journal for Christian Theological Research* 3 (1998) http://apu.edu/~CTRF/articles/1998_articles/pratz.html, (accessed 1998).
Prestige, George L. *Fathers and Heretics.* London: SPCK, 1968.
———. *God in Patristic Thought.* London: SPCK, 1964.
———. "[Perichoreo] and [Perichoresis] in the Fathers." *Journal of Theological Studies* 29 (1928) 242–52.

Print, Stuart, "Teleology as the Key to Pneumatological Anthropology." In *The Spirit of Truth: Reading Scripture and Constructing Theology with the Holy Spirit*. Pentecostals, Peacemaking, and Social Justice Series. Edited by Myk Habets. Eugene, OR: Pickwick, forthcoming.

Rahner, Karl. *Theological Investigations. Volume 4: More Recent Writings*. Trans. K. Smyth. London: Darton, Longman & Todd, 1974.

———. *Theological Investigations. Volume 13: Theology, Anthropology, Christology*. Trans. D. Bourke. London: Darton, Longman & Todd, 1975.

———. *Theological Investigations. Volume 17: Jesus, Man and the Church*. Trans. M. Kohl. London: Darton, Longman & Todd, 1981.

———. *The Trinity*. Translated by J. Donceel. New York: Herder & Herder, 1970.

Rahner, Karl, and Wilhelm A. Thusing. *A New Christology*. New York: Seabury, 1980.

Rakestaw, Robert V. "Becoming Like God: An Evangelical Doctrine of Theosis." *Journal of the Evangelical Theological Society* 40 (1997) 257–69.

Rawlinson, Alfred E. J. *Essays on Trinity and Incarnation*. New York: Longmans, Green, 1928.

Reed, David A. "Oneness Pentecostalism." In *Dictionary of Pentecostal and Charismatic Movements*, edited by S. M. Burgess and G. B. McGee, 644–51. Grand Rapids: Zondervan, 1988.

———. "Oneness Pentecostalism: Problems and Possibilities for Pentecostal Theology." *Journal of Pentecostal Theology* 11 (1997) 73–93.

Reike, Bo. "The Risen Lord and his Church: The Theology of Acts." *Interpretation* 13 (1959) 157–69.

Reymond, Robert L. *Jesus: Divine Messiah*. Phillipsburg, NJ: Presbyterian & Reformed, 1990.

Rhodes, J. Stephen. "Christ and the Spirit: Filioque Reconsidered." *Biblical Theological Bulletin* 18 (1988) 91–95.

Rhodes, Ron. *The Life and Times of the Preincarnate Christ*. Grand Rapids: Baker, 1992.

Richard of St. Victor. *Richard of St. Victor: The Twelve Patriarchs, The Mystical Ark, Book Three of the Trinity*. London: SPCK, 1979.

Richard, Earl. *Jesus: One and Many. The Christological Concept of New Testament Authors*. Wilmington, DW: Glazier, 1988.

Richter, Philip. "Charismatic Mysticism: A Sociological Analysis of the 'Toronto Blessing.'" In *The Nature of Religious Language: A Colloquium*, edited by Stanley E. Porter, 100–30. London: Sheffield, 1996.

Ritschl, Albrecht. *The Christian Doctrine of Justification and Reconciliation*. Edinburgh: T. & T. Clark, 1900.

Robeck, Cecil M. "Specks and Logs, Catholics and Pentecostals." *Pneuma* 12 (1990) 77–83.

Roberts, Alexander, and James Donaldson, editors. *The Ante Nicene Fathers of the Christian Church*. Grand Rapids: Eerdmans, reprinted American edition 1988.

Robichaux, Kerry S. "Christ, the Spirit, and Glory." *Affirmation and Critique* 2.1 (1997) 5–14.

———. "The Pneumatic Person of Christ." *Affirmation and Critique* 2.4 (1997) 3–13.

Robichaux, Kerry S., and John Pester. "Reconceiving the Importance of the Economical Trinity: A Review of *The Father's Spirit of Sonship* by T. G. Weinandy." *Affirmation and Critique* 1 (1996) 53–58.

Robinson, James M. *A New Quest of the Historical Jesus and Other Essays*. Philadelphia: Fortress, 1983.
Robinson, John A. T. *The Human Face of God*. Philadelphia: Westminster, 1973.
Rochelle, Jay C. "What Price Finitum Capax Infiniti." *Academy* 38 (1982) 110–21.
Rosato, Philip J. *The Spirit as Lord: The Pneumatology of Karl Barth*. Edinburgh: T. & T. Clark, 1981.
———. "Spirit Christology: Ambiguity and Promise." *Theological Studies* 38 (1977) 423–49.
———. "Spirit Christology as Access to Trinitarian Theology." In *God's Life in Trinity*, edited by M. Volf and M. Welker, 166–76. Minneapolis: Fortress, 2006.
Runia, Klaas. "Karl Barth's Christology." In *Christ the Lord: Studies in Christology Presented to Donald Guthrie*, edited by H. H. Rowden, 299–310. Downers Grove, IL: InterVarsity, 1982.
Rowden, Harold H., editor. *Christ the Lord: Studies in Christology Presented to Donald Guthrie*. Downers Grove, IL: InterVarsity, 1982.
Runia, Klaas. *The Present-Day Christological Debate*. Downers Grove, IL: InterVarsity, 1984.
Ryrie, Charles C. *Basic Theology*. Wheaton, IL: Victor, 1986.
———. *The Holy Spirit*. Revised and expanded. Chicago: Moody, 1997.
Sabatier, Paul. *The Apostle Paul: A Sketch of the Development of His Doctrine*. Translated by A. M. Hellier. London: Hodder & Stoughton, 1896.
Sample, Robert L. "The Christology of the Council of Antioch (268, CE) Reconsider(ed.)." *Christian History* 48 (1979) 18–26.
Samuel, V. C. "Brief History of Efforts to Reunite the Chalcedonian and Non-Chalcedonian Sides." *Greek Orthodox Theologcial Review* 16 (1971) 44–62.
Sanders, Ed P. *Jesus and Judaism*. Philadelphia: Fortress, 1985.
Sanders, John A. "From Isaiah 61 to Luke 4." In *Christianity, Judaism and Other Greco-Roman Cults*, edited by Jacob Neusner, 75–106. Leiden: Brill, 1975.
Sanders, J. Oswald. *The Holy Spirit and His Gifts*. Grand Rapids: Zondervan, 1940.
Scaer, David P. *Christology*. In *Confessional Lutheran Dogmatics* 6. Edited by R. D. Preus. Fort Wayne: International Foundation for Lutheran Confessional Research, 1989.
———. "The Spirit Understood Christologically." *Concordia Theological Quarterly* 61 (1997) 93–112.
Schaff, Philip, editor. *The Creeds of Christendom*. 3 vols. Grand Rapids: Baker, 1990, 1931 edition.
———, editor. *History of the Christian Church*. 8 vols. Grand Rapids: Eerdmans, 1910.
———, editor. *Nicene and Post Nicene Fathers of the Christian Church*. First series. Michigan: Eerdmans, 1954; reprinted American Edition 1980.
———, editor. *Nicene and Post Nicene Fathers of the Christian Church*. Second series. Michigan: Eerdmans, 1954; reprinted American Edition 1983.
Schillebeeckx, Edward. *Christ: the Experience of Jesus as Lord*. Translated by J. Bowden. New York: Crossroad, 1981.
———. *Jesus: An Experiment in Christology*. London: Collins, 1978.
Schleiermacher, Friedrich D. E. *The Christian Faith*. Translated by J. S. Stewart. Edited by H. R. Mackintosh. Edinburgh: T. & T. Clark, 1928.
Schoonenberg, Piet J. A. M. "Chalcedon and Divine Immutability." *Theology Digest* 29 (1981) 103–7.

———. *The Christ: A Study of the God-Man Relationship in The Whole of Creation and in Jesus Christ*. Translated by D. Couling. London: Sheed & Ward, 1972.
———. "Christ and the Spirit: As Essay in Spirit Christology." *Schola: A Pastoral Review of Sacred Heart School of Theology* 1 (1978) 29–49.
———. "De Christus van booven en de christologie van beneden: nadere overdenkingen rond de God van mensen, Bolsward, Het Witte boekhuis." *Tijdschrift voor theologie* 31 (1991) 3–27.
———. "From Transcendence to Immanence." In *Wisdom and Knowledge: Essays in Honour of Joseph Papin. The Papin Festschrift*, edited by J. Armenti, 273–82. Villanova, PA: Villanova, 1976.
———. "God as Relating and Becoming: A Meta-Thomistic Consideration." *Listening* 14 (1979) 265–78.
———. "The Kenosis or Self-Emptying of Christ." *Concilium* 2 (1966) 27–36.
———. "Spirit Christology and Logos Christology." *Bijdragen* 38 (1977) 350–75.
———. "Trinity—The Consummated Covenant: Theses on the Doctrine of the Trinitarian God." *Studies in Religion* 5 (1975–1976) 273–82.
Schreck, Christopher J. "The Nazareth Pericope: Luke 4:16–30 in Recent Study." In *L'Evangile, L'Evangile selon Luc—The Gospel of Luke*, edited by F. Neirynck, 399–471. Leuven: Leuven University Press, 1989.
Schroten, Egbert. "What Makes a Person?" *Theology* (1994) 98–105.
Shults, F. LeRon. "Constitutive Relationality in Anthropology and Trinity: The Shaping of the Imago Dei Doctrine in Barth and Pannenberg." *Neue Zeitschrift für systematische Theologie und Religionsphilosophie* 39 (1997) 304–22.
Schutter, William. "A Continuing Crisis for Incarnational Doctrine." *Reformed Review* 32 (1979) 76–91.
Schwarz, Hans. *Christology*. Grand Rapids: Eerdmans, 1998.
Schweitzer, Albert. *The Quest for the Historical Jesus: A Critical Study of its Progress from Reimarus to Wrede*. London: A. & C. Black, 1954.
Schweizer, Eduard. *Jesus Christ: The Man from Nazareth and the Exalted Lord*. London: SCM, 1989.
———. "A Very Helpful Challenge: Gordon Fee's *God's Empowering Presence*." *Journal of Pentecostal Theology* 8 (1996) 7–21.
Schwöbel, Christoph. "Christology and Trinitarian Thought." In *Trinitarian Theology Today: Essays on Divine Being and Act*, edited by C. Schwöbel, 113–46. Edinburgh: T. & T. Clark, 1995.
———, editor. *Trinitarian Theology Today: Essays on Divine Being and Act*. Edinburgh: T. & T. Clark, 1995.
Schwöbel, Christoph, and Colin E. Gunton, editors. *Persons, Divine and Human*. Edinburgh: T. & T. Clark, 1991.
Scroggs, R. "Paul: SOFOS AND PNEUMATIKOS." *New Testament Studies* 14 (1967) 33–55.
Sellers, Robert V. *The Council of Chalcedon: A Historical and Doctrinal Survey*. London: SPCK, 1953.
Shedd, William G. T. *Dogmatic Theology*. Edinburgh: T. & T. Clark, 1889.
Sheerin, Daniel J. *The Eucharist: Messages of the Fathers*, vol. 7, Wilmington: Michael Glazier, 1986.

Shelton, James B. "'Filled with the Holy Spirit' and 'Full of the Holy Spirit:' Lucan Redactional Phrases." In *Faces of Renewal: Studies in Honour of Stanley H. Horton*, edited by P. Elbert, 81–107. Peabody: Hendrickson, 1988.

———. *Mighty in Word and Deed: The Role of the Holy Spirit in Luke-Acts*. Peabody: Hendrickson, 1991.

Shoemaker, W.R. "The Use of Ruach in the Old Testament and of *pneuma* in the New Testament." *Journal of Biblical Theology* 23 (1904) 13–67.

Sklba, Richard J. "Until the Spirit from on High is Poured out on us: Reflections on the Role of the Spirit in the Exile." *Catholic Biblical Quarterly* 46 (1984) 1–17.

Smail, Tom A. "The Doctrine of the Holy Spirit." In *Theology Beyond Christendom: Essays on the Centenary of the Birth of Karl Barth, May 10, 1886*, edited by John Thompson, 87–110. Allison Park, PA: Pickwick, 1986.

———. *The Giving Gift: The Holy Spirit in Person*. London: Hodder & Stoughton, 1988.

———. *Reflected Glory: The Spirit in Christ and Christians*. London: Hodder and Stoughton, 1975.

Smail, Tom A., Andrew Walker, and Nigel Wright, editors. *Charismatic Renewal: The Search for a Theology*. Great Britain: SPCK, 1995.

Smalley, Stephen S. "The Christology of Acts." *Expository Times* 73 (1962) 358–62.

———. "The Christology of Acts Again." In *Christ and the Spirit in the New Testament*, edited by B. Lindars and S. S. Smalley, 79–84. Cambridge: Cambridge University Press, 1973.

———. *John: Evangelist and Interpreter*. London: Paternoster, 1978.

Smeaton, George. *The Doctrine of the Holy Spirit*. Edinburgh: T. & T. Clark, 1889.

Snell, Jeffrey T. "Beyond the Individual and Into the World: A Call to Participation in the Larger Purposes of the Spirit on the Basis of Pentecostal Theology." *Pneuma* 14 (1992) 43–57.

Song, Choan-Seng. *Jesus in the Power of the Spirit*. Minneapolis: Fortress, 1994.

Spence, Alan. "Christ's Humanity and Ours: John Owen." In *Persons, Divine and Human*, edited by C. Schwöbel and C. E. Gunton, 74–97. Edinburgh: T. & T. Clark, 1991.

———. "John Owen and Trinitarian Agency." *Scottish Journal of Theology* 43 (1990) 157–73.

Spencer, William D. "The Power in Paul's Teaching (1 Corinthians 4:9–20)." *Journal of the Evangelical Theological Society* 32 (1989) 51–61.

Spittler, Russell P., editor. *Perspectives on the New Pentecostalism*. Grand Rapids: Baker, 1976.

Sproul, R. C. *The Mystery of the Spirit*. Wheaton: Tyndale House, 1990.

Spurgeon, Charles H. *Holy Spirit Power: Six Sermons on the Holy Spirit*. New Kensington, PA: Whitaker, 1996.

Stagg, Frank. "The Holy Spirit in the New Testament." *RevEx* 63 (1966) 135–47.

Stead, G. Christopher. *Philosophy in Christian Antiquity*. Cambridge: Cambridge University Press, 1994.

———. "The Scriptures and the Soul of Christ in Athanasius." *Vigiliae Christianae* 36 (1982) 233–50.

Stibbe, Mark W. G. "The Theology of Renewal and the Renewal of Theology." *Journal of Pentecostal Theology* 3 (1993) 71–90.

Stonstadt, Roger. *The Charismatic Theology of St. Luke*. Peabody, MA: Hendrickson, 1988.

Stott, John R.W. *Baptism and Fullness: The Work of the Holy Spirit Today*. Downers Grove, IL: InterVarsity, 1976.

Strachan, C. Gordon. *The Pentecostal Theology of Edward Irving*. London: Darton, Longman & Todd, 1973.

Strauss, David F. *The Life of Jesus*. Philadelphia: Fortress, 1972.

Strong, Augustus H. *Systematic Theology*. Philadelphia: Judson, 1907.

Studebaker, Steven M., editor. *Defining Issues in Pentecostalism: Classical and Emergent*. Eugene, OR: Pickwick, 2008.

———. "Integrating Pneumatology and Christology: A Trinitarian Modification of Clark H. Pinnock's Spirit Christology." *Pneuma* 28 (2006) 5–20.

Studer, Basil. *Trinity and Incarnation: The Faith of the Early Church*. Translated by M. Westerhoff. Collegeville, MN: Liturgical, 1993.

Stuhlmacher, Peter. *Jesus of Nazareth—Christ of Faith*. Translated by S. Schatzmann. Peabody: Hendrickson, 1988.

———. *Vom Verstehen des Neuen Testaments: Eine Hermeneutik*. NTD Suppl. 6. 2nd ed. Göttingen: Vandenhoeck & Ruprecht, 1979.

Styler, G. M. "Stages in Christology." *New Testament Studies* 10 (1963–1964) 398–409.

Sullivan, Francis A. "Catholic-Charismatic Renewal." In *Dictionary of Pentecostal and Charismatic Movements*, edited by S. M. Burgess and G. B. McGee, 110–26. Grand Rapids: Zondervan, 1988.

———. *The Christology of Theodore of Mopsuestia*. Rome: Universitatis Gregorianae, 1956.

Swete, Henry B. *The Early History of the Doctrine of the Holy Spirit*. Philadelphia: Judson, 1907.

———. *The Holy Spirit in the Ancient Church: A Study of Christian Teaching in the Age of the Fathers*. London: MacMillan, 1912.

———. *The Holy Spirit in the New Testament*. Grand Rapids: Baker, 1910, reprint 1964.

Talbert, Charles H. "'And the Word Became Flesh': When?" In *The Future of Christology: Essays in Honor of Leander E. Keck*, edited by A. J. Malherbe and W. A. Meeks, 43–52. Minneapolis: Fortress, 1993.

Tatum, W. Barnes. *In Quest of Jesus: A Guidebook*. Atlanta: Knox, 1982.

Taylor, John V. *The Go-Between God*. London: SCM, 1972.

Tennent, Timothy C. "Book Review: Beyond the Impasse: Toward a Pneumatological Theology of Religions." *International Bulletin of Missionary Research* 27 (2003) 180–81.

Thatcher, Adrian. *Truly a Person, Truly God: A Post-Mythical View of Jesus*. London: SPCK, 1990.

Thiselton, Anthony C. "Christology in Luke, Speech-Act Theory, and the Problem of Dualism in Christology after Kant." In *Jesus of Nazareth: Lord and Christ. Essays on the Historical Jesus and New Testament Christology*, edited by J. B. Green and M. M. B. Turner, 453–72. Grand Rapids: Eerdmans, 1994.

———. *The Two Horizons: New Testament Hermeneutics and Philosophical Description*. Grand Rapids: Eerdmans, 1980.

Thom, Gideon. "A New Road to Chalcedon?" *Journal of Theology for Southern Africa* 39 (1982) 23–32.

Thomas, John C. "Max Turner's *The Holy Spirit and Spiritual Gifts: Then and Now*: An Appreciation and Critique." *Journal of Pentecostal Theology* 12 (1998) 3–21.

Thomas, W. H. Griffith. *The Holy Spirit*. Grand Rapids: Kregel, 1986; reprint 1913.

Thompson, G. H. P. "Called-Proved-Obedient: A Study in the Baptism and Temptation Narratives of Matthew and Luke." *Journal of Theological Studies* 11 (1960) 1–12.

Thompson, John. *Modern Trinitarian Perspectives*. New York: Oxford University Press, 1994.

Thompson, Marianne M. *The Humanity of Jesus in the Fourth Gospel*. Philadelphia: Fortress, 1988.

Thompson, Ross K. A. "Christian Initiation as a Trinitarian Process." *Theology* (March 1994), 90–98.

Thurmer, John A. "The Analogy of the Trinity." *Scottish Journal of Theology* 34 (1981) 509–15.

Tillich, Paul. *Christianity and the Encounter of World Religions*. 1963; reprint, Minneapolis: Fortress, 1994.

———. *Systematic Theology*. 3 vols. Chicago: University of Chicago Press, 1957–1963.

Toon, Peter. *The Development of Doctrine in the Church*. Grand Rapids: Eerdmans, 1979.

———. "Historical Perspectives on the Doctrine of Christ's Ascension. Part 1: Resurrected and Ascended: The Exalted Jesus." *Bibliotheca Sacra* 140 (1983) 195–205.

———. "Historical Perspectives on the Doctrine of Christ's Ascension. Part 2: The Meaning of the Ascension of Christ." *Bibliotheca Sacra* 140 (1983) 291–300.

———. "Historical Perspectives on the Doctrine of Christ's Ascension. Part 3: The Significance of the Ascension for Believers." *Bibliotheca Sacra* 141 (1984) 16–26.

———. "Historical Perspectives on the Doctrine of Christ's Ascension. Part 4: The Exalted Jesus and God's Revelation." *Bibliotheca Sacra* 141 (1984) 28–119.

———. *Justification and Sanctification*. London: Morgan & Scott, 1983.

Torrance, Alan J. *Persons in Communion: Trinitarian Descriptions and Human Participation*. Edinburgh: T. & T. Clark, 1996.

Torrance, James B. "The Vicarious Humanity of Christ." In *The Incarnation: Ecumenical Studies in the Nicene-Constantinoplitan Creed: A.D. 381*, edited by T. F. Torrance, 127–47. Edinburgh: Handsel, 1981.

———. *Worship, Community and the Triune God of Grace*. Downers Grove, IL: InterVarsity, 1996.

Torrance, Thomas F. *The Christian Doctrine of God, One Being—Three Persons*. Edinburgh: T. & T. Clark, 1996.

———. "The Distinctive Character of the Reformed Tradition." In *Incarnational Ministry: The Presence of Christ in Church, Society, and Family: Essays in Honor of Ray S. Anderson*. Edited by Christian D. Kettler and Todd Speidell. Colorado Springs: Helmers & Howard, 1990.

———, editor. *The Incarnation: Ecumenical Studies in the Nicene-Constantinopolitan Creed: A.D. 381*. Edinburgh: Handsel, 1981.

———. *The Mediation of Christ*. Edinburgh: T. & T. Clark, 1992.

———. *Preaching Christ Today*. Grand Rapids: Eerdmans, 1994.

———. *Royal Priesthood*. Scottish Journal of Theology: Occasional Papers no.3. Edinburgh: Oliver and Boyd, 1955.

———. *Space, Time and Resurrection*. London: Oxford University Press, 1969.

———, editor. *Theological Dialogue between Orthodox and Reformed Churches*, vol. 1. Edinburgh: Scottish Academic, 1985.

———, editor. *Theological Dialogue between Orthodox and Reformed Churches*, vol. 2. Edinburgh: Scottish Academic, 1993.

———. *Theology in Reconstruction*. London: SCM, 1965.

———. *Theology in Reconciliation: Essays Towards Evangelical and Catholic Unity in East and West*. London: Geoffrey Chapman, 1975.

———. *The Trinitarian Faith: The Evangelical Theology of the Ancient Catholic Church*. Edinburgh: T. & T. Clark, 1988.

———. *Trinitarian Perspective's: Toward Doctrinal Agreement*. Edinburgh: T. & T. Clark, 1994.

Torrey, Reuben A. *The Person and Work of the Holy Spirit*. Grand Rapids: Zondervan, 1910.

Towns, Elmer L. "Martin Luther on Sanctification." *Bibliotheca Sacra* 126 (1969) 115–22.

Tracy, David. *The Analogical Imagination: Christian Theology and the Culture of Pluralism*. New York: Crossroad, 1981.

Turner, H. E. W. *The Pattern of Christian Truth: A Study in the Relations Between Orthodoxy and Heresy in the Early Church*. London: Mowbray, 1954.

———. *Jesus the Christ*. London: Mowbrays, 1976.

Turner, Max M. B. "Atonement and the Death of Jesus in John—Some Questions to Bultmann and Forestell." *Evangelical Quarterly* 62 (1990) 99–122.

———. "The Concept of Receiving the Spirit in John's Gospel." *Vox Evangelica* 10 (1977) 24–42.

———. "'Empowerment of Mission?' The Pneumatology of Luke-Acts: An Appreciation and Critique of James B. Shelton's *Mighty in Word and Deed*." *Vox Evangelica* 24 (1994) 103–22.

———. "Holy Spirit." In *Dictionary of Jesus and the Gospels*, edited by J. B. Green and S. McKnight, 341–51. Downers Grove, IL: InterVarsity, 1992.

———. *The Holy Spirit and Spiritual Gifts: Then and Now*. Carlisle: Paternoster, 1996.

———. "Jesus and the Spirit in Lucan Perspective." *Tyndale Bulletin* 32 (1981) 3–42.

———. *Lord of the Spirit: Monotheism, Christology, and Trinitarian Worship in the New Testament*. Milton Keynes: Paternoster, 2008.

———. "The Lord of the Spirit: Monotheism, Christology, and Trinity in the New Testament." Unpublished research presentation paper, London Bible College, 1999, 1–13.

———. *Power from on High: The Spirit in Israel's Restoration and Witness in Luke-Acts*. JPTSS 9. London: Sheffield, 1996.

———. "Readings and Paradigms: A Response to John Christopher Thomas." *Journal of Pentecostal Theology* 12 (1998) 23–38.

———. "The Significance of Receiving the Spirit in Luke-Acts: A Review of Modern Scholarship." *Trinity Journal* 2 (1981) 131–58.

———. "The Significance of Spirit Endowment for Paul." *Vox Evangelica* 9 (1975) 56–69.

———. "The Spirit and the Power of Jesus' Miracles in the Lukan Conception." *Novum Testamentum* 33 (1991) 124–52.

———. "Spirit Endowment in Luke-Acts: Some Linguistic Considerations." *Vox Evangelica* 12 (1981) 45–63.

———. "The Spirit in Luke-Acts: A Support or a Challenge to Classical Pentecostal Paradigms?" *Vox Evangelica* 27 (1997) 75–101.

———. "The Spirit of Christ and Christology." In *Christ the Lord: Studies in Christology Presented to Donald Guthrie*, edited by H. H. Rowden, 168–90. Downers Grove, IL: InterVarsity, 1982.

———. "The Spirit of Christ and 'Divine' Christology." In *Jesus of Nazareth: Lord and Christ. Essays on the Historical Jesus and New Testament Christology*, edited by J. B. Green and M. M. B. Turner, 413–36. Grand Rapids: Eerdmans, 1994.

———. "The Spirit of Prophecy and the Power of Authoritative Preaching in Luke-Acts: A Question of Origins." *New Testament Studies* 38 (1992) 66–88.

———. "The Spirit of Prophecy and the Religious/Ethical Life of the Christian Community." In *Spirit and Renewal: Essays in Honour of J. Rodman Williams*, edited by M. W. Wilson, 166–90. JPTS 5. London: Sheffield, 1994.

Turner, Max M. B., and Gary M. Burge. "*The Anointed Community*: A Review and Response." *Evangelical Quarterly* 62 (1990) 253–68.

Twelftree, Graham H. *Jesus the Miracle Worker: A Historical and Theological Study.* Downers Grove, IL: InterVarsity, 1999.

———. *In the Name of Jesus: Exorcism Among Early Christians.* Grand Rapids: Baker, 2007.

Various. "The Rise of Pentecostalism." *Christian History* 58, vol. 17 (1998) 1–45.

Van Gemeren, Willem A., editor. *New International Dictionary of Old Testament Theology and Exegesis.* 5 vols. Grand Rapids: Zondervan, 1997.

———. "The Spirit of Restoration." *Westminster Theological Journal* 50 (1988) 81–102.

Vanhoozer, Kevin J. "Does the Trinity Belong in a Theology of Religions? On Angling in The Rubicon and the 'Identity' of God." In *The Trinity in a Pluralistic Age: Theological Essays on Culture and Religion*, edited by K. J. Vanhoozer, 41–71. Grand Rapids: Eerdmans, 1997.

———, editor. *The Trinity in a Pluralistic Age: Theological Essays on Culture and Religion.* Grand Rapids: Eerdmans, 1997.

Is There a Meaning in this Text? Leicester: Apollos, 1998.

Van Til, Cornelius, *A Christian Theory of Knowledge.* Philadelphia: Presbyterian & Reformed, 1969.

Verghese, Paul. "Monothelite Controversy: A Historical Survey (with Discussion)." *Greek Orthodox Theologcial Review* 13 (1968) 196–211.

Vermes, Geza, *Jesus the Jew: A Historian's Reading of the Gospels.* London: Collins, 1973.

von Balthasar, Hans Urs. *Theodramatik.* Einsieden: Johannes Verlag, 1978.

———. *Theologik.* Einsiedeln: Johannes, 1987.

Von Baer, Heinrich. *Der Heilige Geist in den Lukasschriften.* Stuttgard: Kohlammer, 1926.

Von Campenhausen, Hans. *Ecclesiastical Authority and Spiritual Power in the Church of the First Three Centuries.* London: A. & C. Black, 1969.

Wainwright, Geoffrey. *Doxology: The Praise of God in Worship, Doctrine, and Life.* New York: Oxford University Press, 1980.

Walvoord, John F. "Contemporary Issues in the Doctrine of the Holy Spirit. Part 1: The Holy Spirit in Divine Revelation." *Bibliotheca Sacra* 130 (1973) 12–23.

———. "Contemporary Issues in the Doctrine of the Holy Spirit. Part 2: Spiritual Renewal." *Bibliotheca Sacra* 130 (1973) 117–25.

———. "Contemporary Issues in the Doctrine of the Holy Spirit. Part 3: New Morality." *Bibliotheca Sacra* 130 (1973) 213–22.

———. "Contemporary Issues in the Doctrine of the Holy Spirit. Part 4: Spiritual Gifts Today." *Bibliotheca Sacra* 130 (1973) 315–28.

———. "Contemporary Issues in the Doctrine of the Holy Spirit. Part 5: Spiritual Power Today." *Bibliotheca Sacra* 131 (1974) 34–40.

———. *The Holy Spirit: A Comprehensive Study of the Person and Work of the Holy Spirit*. Grand Rapids: Zondervan, 1954.

———. *Jesus Christ our Lord*. Chicago: Moody, 1969,

———. "The Present Work of Christ. Part 8: On Earth." *Bibliotheca Sacra* 122 (1965) 291–301.

Wand, John W. C. *The Four Great Heresies*. London: Mowbrays, 1955.

Warfield, Benjamin B., editor. "The Biblical Doctrine of the Trinity." In *Biblical Doctrines*, 133–72. Great Britain: Banner of Truth, 1929.

———, editor. "The Spirit of God in the Old Testament." In *Biblical Doctrines*, 101–29. Great Britain: Banner of Truth, 1929.

Watson, Duncan S. "Why Chalcedon?" *Journal of Theology for Southern Africa* 36 (1981) 3–21.

Watson, Francis. *Text, Church and World*. Edinburgh: T. & T. Clark, 1994.

Webb, Barry G., editor. *Spirit of the Living God*. Part One. Explorations 5. Australia: Lancer, 1991.

———, editor. *Spirit of the Living God*. Part Two. Explorations 6. Australia: Lancer, 1992.

Webb, Charles. *The Person and Work of the Holy Spirit: A Wesleyan Perspective*. Grand Rapids: Baker, 1974.

Weber, Otto. *Foundations of Dogmatics*. 2 vols. Translated by D. L. Guder. Grand Rapids: Eerdmans, 1983, German edition 1962.

Webster, John. *Holy Scripture: A Dogmatic Sketch*. Cambridge: Cambridge University Press, 2003.

———. "Introduction: Systematic Theology." In *The Oxford Handbook of Systematic Theology*, edited by John Webster, Kathryn Tanner, Iain Torrance, 1–15. Oxford: Oxford University Press, 2007.

Weinandy, Thomas G. *Does God Change? The Word's becoming in the Incarnation*. Petersham, MA: St. Bede, 1985.

———. "The Immanent and Economic Trinity." *The Thomist* 57 (1993) 655–66.

Weinandy, Thomas G. "The Case for Spirit Christology: Some Reflections." *The Thomist* 59 (1995) 173–88.

———. *Does God Suffer? A Christian Theology of God & Suffering*. Edinburgh: T. & T. Clark, 2000.

———. *The Father's Spirit of Sonship: Reconceiving the Trinity*. Edinburgh: T. & T. Clark, 1995.

———. *In the Likeness of Sinful Flesh: An Essay on the Humanity of Christ*. Edinburgh: T. & T. Clark, 1993.

Welch, Claud. "The Holy Spirit and the Trinity." *Theology Today* 8 (1951) 29–40.

Welker, Michael. *God the Spirit*. Translated by J. F. Hoffmeyer. Minneapolis: Fortress, 1994.

———. "The Holy Spirit." *Theology Today* 46 (1989) 5–20.

———. "Spirit Topics: Trinity, Personhood, Mystery and Tongues." *Journal of Pentecostal Theology* 10 (1997) 29–34.

Wells, David F. *The Person of Christ: A Biblical and Historical Analysis of the Incarnation*. Westchester, IL: Crossway, 1984.

Wells, Harold. "The Holy Spirit and Theology of the Cross: Significance for Dialogue." *Theological Studies* 53 (1992) 476–92.

Wenham, David. "The Christian Life: A Life of Tension? A Consideration of the Nature of Christian Experience in Paul." In *Pauline Studies: Essays Presented to F. F. Bruce*, edited by D. A. Hagner and M. J. Harris, 80–94. England: Eerdmans, 1980.

———. "Unity and Diversity in the New Testament." In G. E. Ladd, *A Theology of the New Testament*, edited by D. A. Hagner, Revised ed., 684–719. Grand Rapids: Eerdmans, 1993.

Wheeler-Robinson, Henry. *The Christian Experience of the Holy Spirit*. London: Nisbet, 1928.

Wiles, Maurice F. "Can We Still Do Christology?" In *The Future of Christology: Essays in Honor of Leander E. Keck*, edited by A. J. Malherbe and W. A. Meeks, 229–38. Minneapolis: Fortress, 1993.

———. "The Nature of the Early Debate about Christ's Human Soul." *Journal of Ecclesiastical History* 16 (1965) 139–51.

———. *The Remaking of Christian Doctrine*. London: SCM, 1974.

Wilks, John G. F. "The Trinitarian Ontology of John Zizioulas." *Vox Evangelica* 25 (1995) 63–88.

Williams, John. *The Holy Spirit Lord and Life-Giver*. Neptune, NJ: Loizeaux, 1982.

Williams, J. Rodman. "Baptism in the Holy Spirit." In *Dictionary of Pentecostal and Charismatic Movements*, edited by S. M. Burgess and G. B. McGee, 40–48. Grand Rapids: Zondervan, 1988.

———. *The Era of the Spirit*. Plainfield, NJ: Logos, 1971.

———. *Renewal Theology: Systematic Theology from a Charismatic Perspective*. 3 vols. Grand Rapids: Academie, 1990.

Williams, Stephen. "The Trinity and 'Other Religions.'" In *The Trinity in a Pluralistic Age: Theological Essays on Culture and Religion*, edited by K. J. Vanhoozer, 26–40. Grand Rapids: Eerdmans, 1997.

Wilterdink, Garret A. "Christology and the Paradoxical Nature of Human Existence." *Reformed Review* 24 (1971) 124–32.

Witherington, Ben. *The Christology of Jesus*. Minneapolis: Fortress, 1990.

———. *The Jesus Quest: The Third Search for the Jew of Nazareth*. Downers Grove, IL: IVP, 1995.

———. *Jesus the Sage*. Minneapolis: Fortress, 1994.

———. *The Many Faces of the Christ: The Christologies of the New Testament and Beyond*. New York: Crossroad, 1998.

Winn, A. C. "The Holy Spirit and the Christian Life." *Interpretation* 33 (1979) 47–57.

Wojtyla, Karol (Pope John Paul II). *The Acting Person*. London: Reidel, 1979.

Wolfson, Harry A. *The Philosophy of the Church Fathers: Faith, Trinity, Incarnation*. 3rd ed. Massachusetts: Harvard University, 1976.

Wong, Joseph H. P. "The Holy Spirit in the Life of Jesus and of the Christian." *Gregorium* 73 (1992) 57–95.

———. *Logos–Symbol in the Christology of Karl Rahner*. Rome: Las, 1984.

Wong, Kam M. *Wolfhart Pannenberg on Human Destiny*. Aldershot: Ashgate, 2008.

Wood, Leon J. *The Holy Spirit in the Old Testament*. Grand Rapids: Zondervan, 1976.

Wrede, William. *Paul*. Translated by E. Lummis. London: Green, 1907.

Wrede, Wilhelm. *The Messianic Secret*. Greenwood, SC: Attic, 1971.

Wright, John H. "Roger Haight's Spirit Christology." *Theological Studies* 53 (1992) 729–35.

Wright, Nicholas T. *The Challenge of Jesus*. London: SPCK, 2000.

———. *Jesus and the Victory of God*. Minneapolis: Fortress, 1996.
———. *The New Testament and the People of God*. Minneapolis: Fortress, 1992.
———. *The Resurrection of the Son of God*. Minneapolis: Fortress, 2003.
Wright, Walter. "The Source of Paul's Concept of *Pneuma*." *Covenant Quarterly* 41 (1983) 17–26.
Yarnold, Edward. *The Awe-inspiring Rites*. Collegeville, MN: Liturgical, 1994.
Yates, John E. *The Spirit and the Kingdom*. London: SPCK, 1963.
Yong, Amos. *Beyond the Impasse: Toward a Pneumatological Theology of Religions*. Grand Rapids: Baker, 2003.
———. *Discerning the Spirit(s): A Pentecostal-Charismatic Contribution to Christian Theology of Religions*. Journal of Pentecostal Theology Supplement Series 20. Sheffield, UK: Sheffield, 2000.
———. *Hospitality and the Other: Pentecost, Christian Practices, and the Neighbor*. Maryknoll: Orbis, 2008.
———. "The Spirit Bears Witness: Pneumatology, Truth and the Religions." *Scottish Journal of Theology* 57 (2004) 14–38.
Young, Francis M. "A Reconsideration of Alexandrian Christology." *Journal of Ecclesiastical History* 22 (1971) 103–14.
Zizioulas, John D. *Being as Communion: Studies in Personhood and the Church*. London: Dartman, Longman & Todd, 1985.
———. "Human Capacity and Human Incapacity: A Theological Exploration of Personhood." *Scottish Journal of Theology* 28 (1975) 401–48.
———. *Communion and Otherness: Further Studies in Personhood and the Church*. Edited by P. McPartlan. London: T. & T. Clark, 2006.
———. *Credo in Spiritum Sanctum*. Vatican, 1982.
Zoba, Wendy M. "Father, Son, and . . ." *Christianity Today* 40 (1996) 18–24.
Zuck, Roy B. "The Role of the Holy Spirit in Hermeneutics." *Bibliotheca Sacra* 141 (1984) 120–29.

Scripture Index

Genesis
3	181
12:3	184

Exodus
1:22	157
4:22–23	142

Leviticus
25:9–13	150

Deuteronomy
6:13	142
6:16	142
8:3	142
15:2	150
18:15	133
18:18	157

2 Samuel
7:12	125
7:14	125

2 Kings
2:9–10	121

Psalms
2:7	136
2:8	182
7:8–9	150
8	179
16:10	176
22	166, 167
82:1–2	150
89:26–27	136
110	183
110:1	165, 180
110:4	133
115	179

Daniel
7:13	165
7:13–14	165

Nehemiah
8	111
8:5	109
9:2–3	110
9:34	109

Isaiah
7:14	125
9:2–7	131
11:1–3	210
11:1–4	131
11:1	132
11:2	142
26:19	157
29:18	149, 157
35:5	149, 157
40:3	138
40:28	179
42	135, 146
42:1	132, 135, 136, 147
42:1–4	147
42:6	125
42:7	157
42:18	157
44:3	144
49	184
49:6	125
52:7	150
52:15	182
53:12	182
55:11	112
61	133, 145, 146, 147, 148, 149, 157
61:1	148, 149, 157, 158
61:1–2	148, 150
63:10	142, 255
63:14	142

Jeremiah

31:34	105

Ezekiel

36:27	182

Joel

2:28	139
2:28–32	144, 184

Zechariah

6:1–8	144

Matthew

1—2	123, 124
1:1–17	123
1:18	157
1:20	157
2:16–18	157
2:24	152
3:2	132
3:11	131
3:16	135, 142
3:17	131, 136
4:1	142
4:1–11	140
4:17	132
4:19	252
5—7	157
5:3–6	146, 148
5:20	269
6:1	269
6:30	269
8:22	252
9:9	252
9:22	270
9:36—10:42	157
10:38	252
10:39	270
11:2–6	146, 148, 149, 157
11:2–19	146
11:3	132
11:4	158
11:4–6	148
11:10	147
11:11–12	124
11:14	132
11:19	132, 156
11:27	101
12:15–17	147
12:15	158
12:18	157
12:24	151
12:25–29	158
12:27–28	152
12:29	152, 153
12:31	152
12:31–32	153
12:32b	152
12:41	156
13:1–52	157
13:16	156
16:16	49
16:21	176
16:24	252
17:11–13	124
17:22—18:35	157
19:21	252
20:19	176
21:11	156
21:46	156
23—25	157
23:31–36	158
23:37	158
23:37–39	158
26:32	176
26:36	265
26:64	165, 179
27:4	263
27:50	169

Mark

1:2–28	150
1:3	138, 156
1:8	102, 131
1:9–11	131
1:10	135, 142
1:11	136
1:12	141
1:12–13	140
1:24	150
1:38	156
2:5	158
2:8	158
2:17	156

Mark (cont.)

3:4	158
3:11	150
3:15	150
3:16	135
3:22–30	254
3:22	151
3:22–26	152
3:22–30	254
3:23–27	158
3:27	152, 153
3:28–29	153
3:28–30	152
3:28	152
3:29	255
5:17	156
5:36	158
5:39	158
6:4	158
6:15	156
6:46	265
6:47–53	152
8:22–26	157
8:28	156
8:28–30	49
8:31	158
9:1	158
9:7	133
9:9	179
9:30	164
9:33	158
10:1	164
10:3	164
10:21	158
10:23	164
10:34	156
10:39	158
10:45	156
10:46	164
10:46–52	157
10:52	270
11:1–11	164
12:15	158
12:24	152
12:43	158
13:2	158
13:32	101
14:8	158
14:18	158
14:22	158
14:25	158
14:26	165
14:27	158
14:28	176
14:30	158
14:33	166
14:36	101, 163, 164
14:39	164
14:41–42	164
14:61	136, 165
14:61–62	164
14:62	165, 179
14:65	156
15:2	164, 165
15:5	164
15:23	164
15:30–32	164
15:34	166
15:37	166, 169
15:39	166
16:7	172
16:18	178

Luke

1–2	123, 128
1:1–4	124
1:5–25	124
1:15	124
1:26–28	124
1:26–38	124
1:32	125
1:32–33	184
1:35	157
1:39–56	125
1:46–55	157
1:68–79	157
2:1–52	125
2:11	125
2:29–32	125
2:40	210
2:52	210
3:16	131
3:21–22	133, 139
3:22	126, 131, 135, 136
3:23	125
3:23–28	126

Luke (cont.)

3:38	136
4:1	141, 142
4:1–3	140
4:3	126
4:14	141, 142, 157
4:14–15	147
4:16–19	148
4.16–30	181
4:18–19	148, 181
4:18	133, 142, 146, 147, 155, 157
4:19	150
4:16–44	147
4:31–44	147
4:40–41	150
6:12	265
6:20	148, 151
7:16	156, 157
7:18–23	146, 148, 149
7:18–28	146
7:19	49
7:20	132, 270
7:22	158
7:20–22	24
7:34	156
7:39	156
9:23	252
9:31	157
10:18	153
10:21	157
10:22	101
10:23	156
11:1	276
11:11–13	269
11:15	151
11:15–18	152
11:17	158
11:17–22	158
11:19–20	152
11:21–22	152, 153
11:47–51	158
13:33	157, 158
13:34	158
19	262
19:10	269
19:15	158
22:35–38	158
22:67	165
23:41	263
23:46	169
24:19	156, 157
24:34	172
24:44–52	178
24:47–49	183
24:50	182

John

1:1–18	126
1:6–8	127
1:9–14	128
1:12	130
1:12–13	129
1:14	54, 60, 73, 116, 127, 134, 167
1:15	127
1:18	127
1:19–23	132
1:21	156
1:32	135, 138
1:32–33	134, 135
1:33	134
1:34	134, 136
1:47	158
2:19–21	171
2:19	176
2:24	158
3:14	176
3:16	167
3:34	135, 148, 208
3:34–35	131
4	262
4:17	158
4:34	14
6:14	104, 133, 156
6:69	263
7:38–39	161
7:39	182
7:40	133, 156
7:52	157
8:28	176
8:29	263
8:46	263
10:17–18	171
12:32	176, 262
12:47	157
14–16	180, 275
14–17	169

John (cont.)

14:10	157
14:12	105, 276
14:16	174
14:18	158, 197
14:26	174
15	271
15:26	174
16:4	115
16:7	47, 173
16:12	104
16:13	104
16:14	104
16:15	104
17:18	180
17:19	181
17:21	266
18:37	157
19:30	169
20:18	172
20:22	173, 180, 182
20:30	117
20:31	117, 154
21:25	117

Acts

1–3	184
1:1–8	183
1:2	178
1:8–11	178
1:8	147, 181, 186
1:9–11	182
1:22	178
2	109
2:1	182
2:2	181
2:3	181
2:4	181
2:16–21	181
2:17	139
2:21	183
2:23	170
2:24–36	184
2:32	161, 186
2:33	131, 182
2:33–36	179
2:36	175, 177, 183
2:37	183
2:42–47	184
3:15	170
3:22–23	133
4:2	186
4:8	186
4:12	273
4:27	177
4:31	186
4:33	186
6:10	186
7:37	133
10–15	106, 109
10:38	133, 135, 139, 177, 252
10:40	186
13:30	186
13:31	172
13:33	136, 161
15:28	106, 107
16:6	186
16:7	183
16:30	183
17:18	186
18:25	186

Romans

1:3	161, 178
1:3–4	131
1:4	121, 172, 176
3:24–26	121
4:25	171, 248
5:10	162
6:3	245
8	165
8:1	121, 245
8:2	172
8:9	119, 120, 173, 245
8:10	120
8:9–10	120
8:11	172
8:15	101, 163, 255
8:16	47
8:19–22	270
8:19–23	252
8:23	104, 172
8:26	275
8:29	129, 173
8:32	167
8:34	133

Romans (cont.)

10:9	161
12:1	275
12:6	276
14:9	171

1 Corinthians

2:2	121
2:4	186
2:1–16	121
2:10	255
6:9	172
10:11	181
12	185
12–14	276
12:3	121, 179
12:13	163, 245
14:24	158, 186
15:3–8	172, 186
15:3	177
15:11	186
15:14	172, 175
15:15	170
15:20	172
15:22	244
15:23	172
15:24	174
15:25	179
15:27–28	181
15:28	176
15:44	172
15:45	120, 171, 180, 244

2 Corinthians

1:22	104, 172
3:12–4:15	121
3:17	120, 180
3:17–18	180
4:13	173
5:16	121
5:19	14, 168
5:21	121, 167, 263
8:9	101
13:4	171
13:13	120
13:14	197

Galatians

2:20	167
3:2	245
3:13–14	184
3:13	167
3:14	182
3:27	163, 247
4:4–6	131
4:4–7	266
4:6	101, 119, 163, 173, 255
5:22–23	271

Ephesians

1:10	181
1:14	172
1:21–23	181
1:22	179, 181
2:18	275
3:16	276
4:5	163
4:8	178, 179
4:8–10	183
4:10	181
4:11	186
4:30	255
5:25	167
6:10	276

Philippians

1:19	119, 121
2:5–8	152
2:5–11	101
2:8	161
2:9	179, 180
4:13	276

Colossians

1:11	276
1:15–20	101
1:15	167, 271
1:18	20, 161, 173
1:20	181, 252
2:9	20
2:12	163

1 Thessalonians

1:5	111, 186
2:13	111
5:19	255

2 Timothy

2:8	189

Hebrews

1:1–5	184
1:2	181
1:3	20
1:3–5	161
1:4	180
1:5	136
2:7	167
2:8	181
2:9	179
2:17	167, 274
4:13	263
4:14	178, 274
4:15	274
5:5	136
5:7	166, 210
5:10	133
6:5	153
7:3	274
7:16	170
7:25	275
7:26	263
9:14	140, 166, 170, 171, 263
10:29	255
12:2	252

1 Peter

1:12	104
2:22	263
3:18	172
3:22	178, 179

2 Peter

1:4	249
1:17	136
3:18	172

1 John

1:13	275

2:1	133
2:27	104, 105
3:5	263
4:2–6	105
5:6–7	105
5:9–10	105
5:6–12	105

Rev

1:10	105
1:19	105
2:7	105
20:2	153
22:17	197

EXTRA BIBLICAL REFERENCES

1 Enoch

49:2–3	131
62:1–2	131

Psalms of Solomon

17:37	131
18:7	131

Wisdom of Solomon

2:18	136

Dead Sea Scrolls

4Q521	148, 149
11QMelchizedek	150
I QS 9.11	156

Moses

10:1	153

Tosefta Sotah

13:2	155

Subject Index

Abba, 101, 129, 146, 159, 163, 166, 167, 168, 208, 226, 227, 245, 249, 255, 256, 266, 269, 276
Active Obedience, 13, 140, 161, 244, 252, 258, 264
Adoptionism (Ebionites/Ebionite), 5, 17, 20, 32, 32, 57, 58, 62, 64, 67, 77, 79, 80, 82, 87, 99, 203, 213, 221, 261
Agere sequiter esse, 22
Alexandria/Alexandrian, 31, 32, 78, 79
Anangelei, 104
Anhypostatsia, 211
Anthropology, 28, 52, 130, 213, 218, 236, 241–42, 260, 261, 267–71
Antioch/Antiochene, 32, 33, 66, 67, 74, 76, 78, 79
Apollinarianism, 38, 39, 71, 73, 79, 211
Apollinaris of Laodicea, 73, 73–74, 79
Apologists, 31, 32, 57, 58, 59–69, 79, 84, 85, 86
Apostolic Fathers, 56–58, 60, 75
Apostles Creed, 61
Arius/Arian/Arianism, 18, 33, 64, 68, 70, 71, 72, 73, 76, 82, 86
Athanasius, 8, 3133, 63, 68, 69–73, 74, 75, 76, 85, 86, 210, 258, 278
Atonement, 12, 13, 14, 25, 29, 167, 168, 177, 183, 234, 247, 248, 274
Augustine/Augustinianism, 13, 31, 75, 79, 207, 223, 225, 226, 242
Autokineton, 210

Barth, Karl, 1, 2, 26, 27, 34, 35, 38, 105, 162, 208, 212, 213, 223, 229, 241, 277
Bat qol, 136, 143
Beelzebub Controversy, 145, 151–54, 156, 160
Blasphemy of/against the Holy Spirit, 152, 153, 160, 254, 255

Calvin, John, 32, 213, 223, 244, 245, 246, 247, 248, 249, 250, 276
Cappadocians, 8, 54, 68, 69, 70, 72, 76–79, 212, 230, 259, 275, 278
  Basil of Caesarea (the Great), 50, 76, 77, 78, 138
  Gregory of Nyssa, 76, 78
  Gregory of Nazianzus (Nazianzen), 53, 74, 76, 77, 78, 115, 226
Chalcedon (Chalcedonian, Chalcedonian Definition), 4, 5, 8, 12, 15, 17, 18, 19, 20, 21, 29, 33, 38, 56, 66, 67, 69, 74, 75, 76, 79–80, 81, 82, 83, 84, 85, 86, 87, 115, 192, 195, 196, 199, 200, 206, 209, 210, 215, 218, 227, 258, 261, 263, 269, 271
Christology
  Classical, 5, 6, 12, 13, 24, 30, 31, 32, 36, 37, 39, 40, 41, 45, 50, 52, 159, 162, 193, 195, 272
  Criteria for, 189–93, 200, 220
  Last-Adam, 65, 98, 167, 180, 233, 234, 264, 269
  Vicarious Humanity, 13, 14, 135, 165, 240, 270
Communicatio idiomatum, 73, 206
Constantinople (Council of), 74, 76, 115

Dabney, D Lyle, 9, 162, 164, 166, 171, 173, 217, 229, 230, 231, 232, 233, 235, 236, 244, 245, 253, 255, 256, 261, 277, 278
Disclosure Episodes/Kairoi, 8, 90, 118-187, 209
Docetism, 19, 32, 35, 38, 39, 57, 64, 71, 72, 79, 82, 84, 99, 105, 191, 212, 261, 272

Subject Index

Doctrine
    Enrichment of, 5, 8, 50, 112–17, 118,
        201, 221, 229, 233, 235, 243
    Evolutionary Development of, 92, 93,
        94–100, 101, 114
Dualism, 19, 29, 71, 84, 85, 242

Ecumenical/Ecumenics/Ecumenism, 9,
    12, 79, 114, 192, 224, 232, 243, 259,
    260, 276–80
Edwards, Jonathan, 250, 251
Enhypostatic//Enhypostasia, 138, 191,
    206, 211
Enlightenment, 40, 41, 99, 217
Eutyches/Eutychianism (Monophysitism),
    18, 38, 39, 74, 79, 82, 261, 263
Evangelical, 4, 9, 17, 26, 36, 46, 91, 98, 107,
    190, 201, 247
Existentialism, 23, 36, 49, 105

Fideism, 48, 49, 193
Fides quaerens intellectum, 49
Filioque, 170, 207, 278, 279
Fundamentalist/Fundamentalists/
    Fundamentalism, 21, 193

Geschichtlich, 34
Greek Philosophy, 15, 17, 18, 19, 20, 33, 38,
    55, 63, 79, 83, 84, 87, 242

Habets, Myk, 103, 167, 189, 222, 235, 242,
    244, 245, 256, 265, 266, 272, 277,
    279
Hellenism/Hellenistic, 15, 18, 20, 59, 62,
    63, 65, 71, 83, 84, 86, 87, 96, 99, 125,
    144, 262
Historisch, 34
Homoousios//Homoousia, 20, 61, 68, 70,
    71, 72, 73, 264, 269, 273, 275

Ignatius of Antioch, 8, 31, 57, 258
Illumination/Illuminate etc., 104, 105, 107,
    111, 112, 115, 211
Imitatio Christi, 13, 274
Indwelling, 58, 75, 76, 113, 115, 128, 130,
    139, 167, 173, 218, 242, 247, 276
Irenaeus, 62, 65–66, 69, 71, 110, 254

Irving, Edward, 140, 200, 208, 212, 213,
    214, 215, 216
Inspiration, 4, 11, 51, 54, 62, 63, 68, 75, 80,
    99, 104, 105, 120, 134, 151, 156,
    186, 196, 200, 207, 214, 217, 222,
    240, 273

Jesus Christ
    Ascension, 32, 47, 54, 123, 161, 172,
        176, 178, 179, 180, 182, 184,
        195, 271
    Baptism, 32, 58, 63, 67, 77, 81, 98, 122,
        123, 126, 130, 131–39, 140,
        141, 142, 143, 146, 150, 153,
        157, 163, 164, 177, 186, 216
    Burial, 10
    Conception/Birth/Nativity, 10, 13,
        45, 58, 65, 75, 77, 98, 116, 122,
        123–31, 137, 138, 139, 140,
        146, 153, 157, 163, 171, 179,
        186, 203, 209, 210, 211, 216,
        218
    Death/Cross/Crucifixion/Passion, 10,
        13, 26, 29, 35, 36, 37, 46, 47, 70,
        84, 98, 113, 116, 121, 122, 123,
        139, 140, 143, 144, 146, 150,
        152, 153, 154, 158, 160, 161,
        162, 163, 164, 165, 166, 167,
        168, 169, 170, 171, 173, 174,
        175, 176, 177, 179, 180, 182,
        186, 187, 203, 209, 211, 215,
        216, 219, 232, 244, 248, 252,
        253, 254, 255, 256, 272, 274
    Divinity, 4, 24, 25, 30, 38, 43, 44, 50, 51,
        52, 57, 59, 61, 63, 65, 70, 72, 73,
        74, 77, 78, 81, 82, 84, 86, 87, 88,
        94, 96, 127, 128, 188, 191, 193,
        195, 196, 199, 206, 211, 212,
        215, 216, 225, 248, 249, 258,
        261, 265, 269, 271, 273
    Enthronement, 50, 125, 126, 176, 178
    Exaltation, 10, 47, 48, 116, 123, 130,
        153, 161, 162, 165, 168, 169,
        175, 176, 178, 179, 182, 183,
        186, 187, 203, 270, 275, 278
    Humanity, 2, 13, 17, 24, 25, 30, 31, 32,
        33, 35, 36, 38, 39, 52, 58, 59, 61,
        65, 66, 71, 72, 73, 74, 75, 77, 79,

Subject Index

Jesus Christ, Humanity (cont.),
81, 82, 85, 86, 88, 89, 96, 105,
127, 138, 139, 140, 159, 162,
171, 188, 191, 199, 206, 209,
210, 211, 212, 215, 216, 219,
240, 248, 249, 253, 258, 261,
262, 264, 265, 267, 268, 269,
270, 271, 273, 274, 275
Identity (Person), 4, 5, 6, 7, 8, 10, 11,
12, 14, 15, 16, 17, 18, 20, 21, 22,
24–29, 30, 31, 32, 36, 37, 38,
39, 40, 41, 44, 46, 47, 53, 54, 59,
60, 63, 67, 71, 72, 73, 74, 75, 80,
81, 82, 83, 84, 85, 87, 89, 90,
92, 93, 95, 96, 101, 102, 116,
117, 118, 119, 121, 122, 123,
127, 128, 129, 130, 131, 132,
134, 135, 136, 138, 140, 144,
145, 146, 147, 149, 151, 152,
154, 155, 156, 158, 159, 160,
162, 165, 168, 170, 172, 176,
177, 179, 181, 183, 186, 187,
191, 192, 193, 196, 197, 199,
200, 202, 203, 206, 207, 208,
211, 213, 218, 220, 227, 243,
250, 259, 260, 261, 262, 263,
264, 265, 266, 267, 268, 269,
271, 277
Infancy, 123, 124
Life (ministry), 8, 10, 13, 28, 29, 32, 33,
36, 39, 40, 46, 50, 51, 70, 77, 87,
89, 90, 92, 98, 103, 105, 115,
116, 117, 118, 119, 120, 122,
123, 129, 130, 131, 144–60,
161, 162, 164, 168, 176, 177,
178, 179, 202, 203, 209, 216,
232, 242, 244, 252, 257, 258,
263, 266, 269, 271, 274
Messiah/Messianic/Christos, 8, 15,
28, 45, 116, 117, 118, 121,
123, 124, 125, 126, 128, 130,
131, 132, 133, 134, 135, 136,
137, 138, 139, 141, 142, 143,
144–60, 163, 164, 165, 166,
172, 175, 176, 177, 178, 180,
182, 183, 184, 186, 196, 203,
211, 252, 262, 266, 269, 272,
280

Miracles, 2, 13, 46, 53, 77, 89, 102, 125,
129, 142, 145, 147, 148, 152,
154–60, 211
Preexistence, 4, 22, 33, 45, 46, 50, 57,
58, 60, 61, 82, 86, 95, 97, 98,
99, 101, 126, 127, 129, 195,
196, 199
Prophet, 67, 75, 121, 128, 132, 133,
134, 135, 137, 138, 139, 140,
144, 145, 146, 147, 149,
155–60, 167, 177, 186, 210,
211, 244
Resurrection, 10, 29, 35, 36, 44, 45, 46,
47, 50, 58, 75, 77, 87, 90, 91,
96, 98, 115, 116, 120, 121, 122,
123, 126, 139, 140, 153, 154,
157, 161, 162, 165, 168, 169,
170–76, 177, 178, 179, 180,
182, 183, 185, 186, 195, 199,
203, 209, 211, 216, 232, 244,
249, 251, 252, 253, 265, 271,
272, 274
Son of God, 10, 16, 33, 35, 45, 47, 51,
58, 69, 78, 86, 88, 96, 98, 117,
121, 125, 126, 127, 133, 134,
136, 137, 139, 141, 142, 143,
150, 152, 157, 163, 166, 176,
177, 206, 209, 211, 218, 254,
269, 272, 273, 274
Son of Man, 28, 45, 88, 98, 132, 153,
159, 165, 249
Soul/Mind, 69, 71, 73, 74, 79, 151, 166,
210, 214
Temptation/s, 13, 37, 53, 77, 85,
122, 123, 126, 131, 137, 138,
139–44, 163, 214, 254, 263,
264, 272, 276
Jesus Seminar, 92
John (the) Baptist, 49, 116, 123, 124, 125,
127, 130, 131, 132, 133, 134, 138,
145, 146, 148, 149, 150, 156, 157,
158, 159
Kairoi, see Disclosure Episodes
Kenosis
Of Christ, 140, 144, 167, 173, 200, 253,
254, 256
Of the Spirit, 136, 144, 165, 168, 173,
253, 254, 255, 256
Of the Father, 168, 173, 253

Subject Index

Kerygma/Kerygmatic, 34, 40, 43, 47, 48, 49, 50, 91, 93, 94, 95, 96, 105, 115, 177
Kingdom/Kingdom of God, 47, 124, 126, 132, 135, 146, 148, 150, 151, 153, 158, 159, 160, 161, 178, 184, 216, 252, 254
Lactantius, 57, 66–67
Logical Positivism, 23
Logos Christology, 2, 4, 5, 6, 7, 12, 30–40, 44, 45, 51, 54, 55, 56, 59, 60, 61, 62, 63, 64, 65, 66, 67, 69, 70, 71, 72, 73, 74, 76, 79, 80, 81, 82, 85, 86, 87, 89, 95, 102, 189, 191, 192, 193, 194, 195, 196, 197, 200, 201, 202, 203, 204, 205, 213, 218, 219, 224, 243, 258, 259, 262, 263, 264, 265, 272
Logos-sarx, 4, 71, 73
Martyr, Justin, 60–61
Messianic Secret, 149, 164
Monarchia, 57, 223, 224, 225, 226, 278, 279
Monarchian/Monarchianism, 16, 32, 57, 279
    Patripassian/Patripassianism, 63, 168, 256
Monophysitism, *see* Eutyches
Moses, 67, 132, 133, 135, 143, 156, 157, 158, 172, 186
Nestorius/Nestorian/Nestorianism, 18, 75–76, 77, 78, 261, 263
Nicaea/Nicene (Creed), 5, 12, 20, 21, 33, 36, 61, 66, 68, 69, 71, 74, 76, 79, 87, 115, 159, 192, 206, 209, 238, 275
Ontic, 20, 21, 24, 175
Ontology/Ontological, 7, 11, 12–24, 29, 33, 38, 48, 51, 52, 59, 63, 69, 72, 75, 80, 82, 83, 89, 120, 121, 126, 153, 167, 178, 180, 187, 190, 191, 196, 198, 199, 203, 206, 211, 221, 222, 223, 224, 236, 240, 251, 256, 261, 266, 269, 272, 279
Origen, 31, 33, 67–69, 70
Owen, John, 208–12, 214, 215
Passive Obedience, 13, 140, 166, 177, 244, 252,
Patrologia crucis, 255
Paul of Samosata, 66–67, 74
Pentecost, 41, 47, 50, 77, 109, 115, 118, 123, 126, 136, 157, 161, 175, 176, 178, 179, 180, 181, 182, 183, 184, 185, 186, 187, 240
Perichoresis/Divine Dance, 3, 115, 170, 173, 218, 219, 223, 224, 252, 266
Plato/Platonic/Platonism/Neo-Platonic, 60, 61, 62, 64, 68, 69, 71, 79, 86, 87, 99, 190, 251
Pneuma-sarx, 2, 4, 269
Pneumatologia crucis, 162, 165, 166, 167, 168, 173, 174, 243, 253–56, 264, 270
Pray/Prayer, ix, 13, 118, 163, 164, 228, 252, 254, 256, 265–67, 274, 275, 276, 280
Proleptic, 44, 45, 113, 160, 174
Prophorikos, 62, 65
Quest for the Historical Jesus, 13, 34, 35, 41, 42, 92, 94, 210
Regula fidei, 110
Retroactive Hermeneutic, 8, 50, 90, 103–17, 118, 131, 139, 147, 160, 164, 169, 175, 177, 211, 277
Shekinah (Glory), 128, 136, 143
Sophia, 60, 62, 65
Speech-act Theory, 111
Stoic/Stoicism, 32, 57, 60, 62, 64
Subordinationism, 61, 63, 68, 70, 72, 82, 86, 87, 199, 223, 224, 226, 279
Testimonium internum Spiritus Sancti, 36, 111
The Coming One, 131, 132, 133, 144, 145–54, 156, 159, 262
Theodore of Mopsuestia, 74–75, 77
Theodotus, 16, 58
Theologia crucis, 162, 167, 168, 173, 174, 253, 270
Theology from above, 11, 24, 30–40, 41, 42, 43, 44, 45, 46, 48, 49, 50, 51, 54, 80, 87, 89, 116, 171, 205,
Theology from below, 7, 11, 13, 24, 31, 33, 34, 38, 39, 40–48, 49, 50, 51, 52, 80, 90, 116
Theophilus of Antioch, 62–65, 66, 72
Theosis/Deification/Divinization, 206, 234, 238, 243, 244, 248–53, 256, 265, 266
Third Article Theology, 7, 8, 228–57
Unction, 77, 78, 203
Union with Christ/Unio mystica, 234, 243, 244, 245–48, 249, 250, 256
Wisdom, 62, 67, 98, 99, 142, 159, 169, 196, 210, 217, 268

www.ingramcontent.com/pod-product-compliance
Lightning Source LLC
Chambersburg PA
CBHW052146300426
44115CB00011B/1537